Graphics File Formats

second edition

Graphics File Formats

second edition

David C. Kay
John R. Levine

Windcrest® / McGraw-Hill

New York San Francisco Washington, D.C. Auckland Bogotá
Caracas Lisbon London Madrid Mexico City Milan
Montreal New Delhi San Juan Singapore
Sydney Tokyo Toronto

Published by Windcrest, an imprint of McGraw-Hill, Inc.

pbk 1 2 3 4 5 6 7 8 9 10 11 FGR/FGR 9 9 8 7 6 5 4

Library of Congress Cataloging-in-Publication Data

Kay, David C., 1933-
Graphics file formats : 2nd edition / by David C. Kay, John R. Levine.
p. cm.
Includes index.
ISBN 0-07-034025-0 (p)
1. Computer graphics. I. Levine, John R. II. Title.
T385.K376 1994
006.6—dc20 94-12054
CIP

Acquisitions editor: Brad Schepp
Editorial team: Joanne Slike, Executive Editor
David M. McCandless, Supervising Editor
Michael Christopher, Book Editor
Production team: Katherine G. Brown, Director
Susan E. Hansford, Coding
Rose McFarland, Desktop Operator
Joanne Woy, Indexer
Design team: Jaclyn J. Boone, Designer
Brian Allison, Associate Designer

WK2
0340250

Contents

Acknowledgments

We would like to thank the following people, who supplied information on the graphics file formats covered in this book. We would especially like to acknowledge those who helped with the new information in this second edition: Donna Loper of Clark College, Vancouver, for her encouragement and suggestions for the tutorial chapters; Mark Podlipec of Wellfleet Communications for his insight and assistance with FLI/FLC and QuickTime; Kevin Darling of North Carolina State University and Myles Strous of Monash Gippsland, for FLI information; Les Bartlett for his QuickTime animation expertise; Larry Gritz of George Washington University and Philipp Slusallek of Universitaet Erlangen for their assistance in understanding the Renderman interface; Tom Lane for his aid with BMP; Raul Lopez-Hernandez for his help with MPEG; and Simon Goodwin of Warley, England, for his assistance in discovering errors in the first edition.

BMP
Tom Lane, Pittsburgh, Pennyslvania

DXF
Bill Adkison, Sausalito, California
Blake Freeburg, Austin, Texas
Paul D. Bourke, Auckland, New Zealand
Neele Johnston, Sausalito, California

FLI/FLC
Mark Podlipec
Kevin Darling
Myles Strous

GIF
John Harper, Columbus, Ohio

HPGL
Walt Howard, Salt Lake City, Utah
John B. Scalia, Akron, Ohio
Peter D. Smith, Cambridge, Massachusetts

PIC
Charles Frankston, Cambridge, Massachusetts

IFF/ILBM
Steven Reiz, Amsterdam, Netherlands
Ronald van Loon, Utrecht, Netherlands
Loren J. Rittle, Urbana, Illinois
Martin J. Laubach, Austria
Eric Hedman, Finland

JPEG
Tom Lane, Pittsburgh, Pennsylvania

Macpaint
Claus Riemann, Sankt Augustin, Germany
Matthias Ulrich Neeracher, Zurich, Switzerland

MPEG
Raul Lopez-Hernandez, Pittsburgh, Pennsylvania

PICT
Dwight Mayo, Sudbury, Massachusetts

QuickTime
Les Bartlett
Mark Podlipec

Renderman
Larry Gritz
Philipp Slusallek

Targa
Ian MacPhedran, Saskatoon, Saskatchewan
William J. vanRiper, Brookline, Massachusetts

Windows Metafile
Andrew A. Vereninov, St. Petersburg, Russia
Gary Hill, Southampton, United Kingdom

PCL
Andy Brewster, Tewksbury, Massachusetts

PCX
Henk de Koning, Ede, Netherlands
Mikael Sandberg, Vasteras, Sweden
Ted Turo'cy, Pasadena, California
David W. Hertweck, Cincinnati, Ohio
Bob Frankston, Newton Highlands, Massachusetts

TIFF
Jim Rouleau, Westboro, Massachusetts
Daniel Loewus, Newfield, New York

XBM and XWD
Jeffrey Horn, Madison, Wisconsin
Amy Chan, San Jose, California
David Lewis, Winchester, Massachusetts

Introduction

In recent years, the field of computer graphics has exploded as personal computers and workstations have acquired graphics facilities surpassing even those of supercomputers a few years ago. As more and more graphics applications have been created, the ability to save pictures for later manipulation or display has become increasingly important. In the absence of widely accepted standards, each application developer invented file formats to support his or her own applications. Starting in the early 1980s, official standards groups began to create common graphics subroutine libraries, and then graphics files, to encourage portability of files and code among different applications and different hardware. In the 1990s, color, animation, and desktop video applications are employing new color capabilities and better compression techniques.

The result is a graphics "Tower of Babel," with dozens of different formats in use in hundreds of different programs. This book attempts to bring a little order to the chaos by documenting the most commonly used formats. In many cases there are few technical differences between various formats (a bitmap is pretty much a bitmap, no matter how you store it), so the choice of one format over another is either entirely arbitrary or is based on non-technical criteria. We hope the discussions here will help resolve some of the remaining technical arguments.

File format specifications are expanding to better support graphics-intensive applications such as animation and multimedia. So, in this 2nd edition of *Graphics File Formats*, we have provided basic information on the most popular of these new formats.

Who this book is for

This book is a simplified reference and guide for those who use or choose among standard graphics file formats for various applications. Graphics file formats, especially in the field of video, are becoming increasingly complex; their original specifications often cover one or more volumes. Therefore, this book cannot be a complete reference for the more complex specifications, but it does provide sufficient information to allow encoding or coding of many images, especially bitmap images. For these formats, we describe at least the basic coding concepts, so you can recognize the format and work out for yourself how to decode it in detail.

Many graphics file formats are not documented in this book. However, if the file format you are particularly interested in is not covered here, you may find useful similarities in other formats that are described. In choosing which formats to represent, we tried to strike a balance between many factors: covering popular formats while not overlooking important alternatives; providing complete descriptions of a few formats vs. covering a greater variety in lesser detail; ensuring broad readability vs. using the jargon of a particular field; and finally, simply finding sufficient information.

How to read this book

Chapters 1, 2, and 3 contain tutorial information of interest to anyone who uses graphics files. We encourage you to at least skim these three chapters, because they define many terms used later in the book. The rest of the chapters are largely independent of each other, except for the occasional cross-reference where one technique or format borrows heavily from another.

Each chapter has a table at the beginning, which gives a capsule summary of the format along with its advantages and disadvantages. While such summaries are, of necessity, partly subjective, the tables should be useful if you're trying to decide which format to use for a project or application. For every format, we provide a list of references that give more details on the format. (For the CompuServe GIF format, the reference is duplicated right here in the book.) Where we have been able to identify the original developer of the format, we have also attempted to provide a current address or phone number.

Where graphics file formats are documented

Documentation for graphics file formats comes from many places. For a few formats, there are clear (or at least definitive) documents, such as the CompuServe GIF document, the Truevision Targa manual, and the ANSI/ISO CGM standard. Even when such documents exist, however, there is always "folklore" about the formats. For example, there are about a dozen subformats of Targa, only a few of which are widely used. Occasionally, the official standards disagree with reality as defined by the contents of actual files. We have tried to note the few places where this is the case.

Particularly for workstations, a large body of free software is available, in source form, that processes graphics files. This code implicitly documents the format of the files that it reads and writes; wherever possible we have validated format descriptions against working code.

Finally, there are the graphics files themselves, which in some cases we have dumped out byte by byte to find out what is actually inside. Anyone with Internet access will find files and other information through anonymous FTP sites and Usenet interest groups, the most prominent being comp.graphics and similar graphics groups.

Let us know what you think

All authors love to hear from their readers, and we're no exceptions. If you liked this book—or even if you didn't, or if you find an error—please drop us a line, c/o TAB/McGraw-Hill, Editorial, Blue Ridge Summit PA 17294-0214. Or, electronically, to gbook@iecc.com.

David Kay and John Levine
September 1994

## CHAPTER 1

Graphics representation theory

BECAUSE you, the readers of this book, may come to it with widely varying backgrounds, we offer the following chapter on graphics-representation theory. While it is by no means a comprehensive treatment of the subject, this chapter introduces fundamental topics with which the reader should be familiar to fully utilize the information in this book.

Bitmap & vector representations

There are two principal yet very different methods of representing graphics images: *bitmaps* (also called *raster* or *pixel maps*) and *vectors*. Graphics files may employ either or both of these representations.

Definitions

Bitmap representation is the far more commonly used method because it is easier to implement and, within limits, works for any image. Bitmap representation means that an image has been broken up into a grid. The light value (lightness, darkness, or color) of each piece (pixel) of the grid is recorded individually. Figure 1-1 shows one scan line of a low-resolution image as represented by a bitmap. Typically, the position of a data point in a bitmap field determines what pixel the data point represents. In other words, the data points (bits) "map" to the image; hence the name, *bitmap*.

Figure 1-1

One line of bitmap data from an image.

Vector representation means describing an image as a series of lines or shapes, perhaps with some regions filled in with a solid or graded shade or color. Strictly speaking, the word "vector" may refer only to a line, but the popular interpretation of a vector file allows the file to include shapes such as squares and circles.

Vector files often look like programs when you examine them. They may contain English-like commands and data in ASCII, and therefore may lend themselves to editing with a word processor. For example, a circle with a 100-millimeter radius, centered at x = 2.25 centimeters and y = 5 centimeters, might be embodied by the command `circle(100,2250,5000)`, recorded in ASCII.

Figure 1-2 illustrates a simple line drawing, a type of image for which vector format is highly suitable. Figure 1-3 lists the data in the vector format DXF.

Figure 1-2

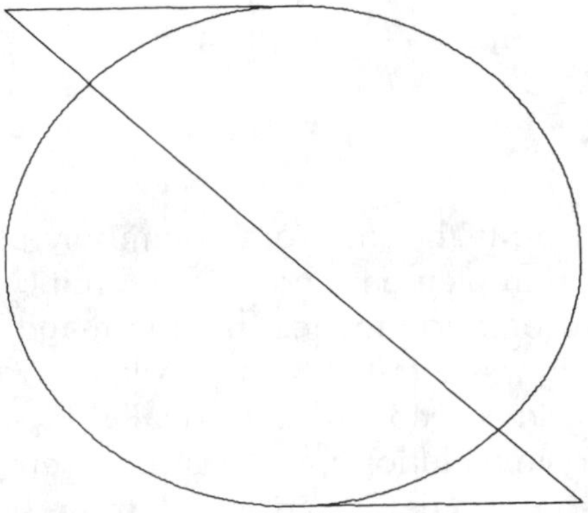

A simple line drawing, suitable for vector representation.

Figure 1-3

```
  0
SECTION
  2
HEADER
  9
$CECOLOR
 62
     0
  0
ENDSEC
  0
SECTION
  2
TABLES
  0
TABLE
  2
LAYER
  0
LAYER
  2
0
 70
     0
 62
     7
  6
CONTINUO
US
  0
LAYER
  2
obj1
 70
     0
 62
     7
  6
CONTINUO
US
  0
ENDTAB
  0
ENDSEC
  0
SECTION
  2
ENTITIES
  0
CIRCLE
  8
obj1
 62
     7
 10
9.000000
0000
 20
7.500000
0000
 30
0.000000
0000
 40
1.750000
0000
  0
POLYLINE
  8
obj1
 62
     7
 66
     1
 70
     8
  0
VERTEX
  8
obj1
 62
     7
 10
9.000000
0000
 20
9.250000
0000
 30
0.000000
0000
 70
    32
  0
VERTEX
  8
obj1
 62
     7
 10
7.250000
0000
 20
9.250000
0000
 30
0.000000
0000
 70
    32
  0
VERTEX
  8
obj1
 62
     7
 10
10.75000
00000
 20
5.750000
0000
 30
0.000000
0000
 70
    32
  0
VERTEX
  8
obj1
 62
     7
 10
9.000000
0000
 20
5.750000
0000
 30
0.000000
0000
 70
    32
  0
SEQEND
  0
ENDSEC
  0
EOF
```

Vector_Image. Vector data for Fig. 1-2, using DXF format (shown in four columns).

File formats generally implement either vectors or bitmaps, but not both. Occasionally the two methods are both used in a page-description language like Postscript, but even there the two representations are quite distinct. Each method has its own set of applications where it is best used.

For convenience, some graphics applications employ multiple representations of the same image within a graphics file. For example, a PostScript file may contain a TIFF preview. Since TIFF readers are simpler than PostScript readers, they are more common, require less memory, and offer a faster display. When a PostScript file includes a reduced-quality, TIFF-encoded copy of an image, applications can use that image for non-crucial functions, such as letting the user distinguish one image file from another.

Applications

Bitmap formats work well for images with complex variations in colors, shades, or shapes, such as photographs, paintings, and *grabbed* (digitized) video frames. Some images, such as computer screen displays, originate in bitmap format and are therefore most easily recorded in the same way.

Vector formats work well for line art, such as computer-aided design (CAD) drawings and images with simple shapes, shadings, and colorations. Charts, graphs, and certain types of freehand illustration are typically recorded as vector files. Sometimes, however, we record such images in bitmap form simply because it is easier to do so.

In certain applications, one particular type of image, known as a character font, is converted frequently between vector and bitmap form, depending on where the image is in its progression from font design to printing. While such an approach appears inelegant, it allows a good, practical tradeoff between the advantages and limitations of both methods. In vector form, for instance, fonts are easy to scale and modify for italics, boldface, and other variations. But inside the printer, which uses a television-like raster scan, it's more efficient to use the bitmap form. By contrast, a plotter, which is designed for line drawing, would require vector data.

Application programs are increasingly, but by no means universally, able to deal with both vector and bitmap images. Even word-processing programs like Microsoft Word often have the ability to integrate vector images (such as HPGL plotter files from CAD programs) and bitmap images (such as TIFF files from paint programs). Word processors, however, are not required to process images but simply link images to the document, a relatively undemanding task.

Graphics programs, because they must manipulate the image data, tend to favor the method most compatible with their purpose. Typically, they deal with the other method by file conversion, if at all. For example, CorelDraw, a PC application, uses vector representation but can *vectorize* a bitmap TIFF image by tracing the outlines of shaded areas and recording the trace lines as vectors.

An extension of the vector concept is the use of 3-D vector models and *rendering* software. Languages such as DXF can contain not only 2-D shapes, but 3-D shapes generally referred to as *models*. Using such models and rendering software, artists and others can specify a *scene* in software that includes lighting, surface attributes, reflections, transparency, and other qualities of a scene from real life. This scene is then expressed as a set of models and instructions to a rendering program, such as a Renderman interface file. The rendering program then computes the appearance of a 2-D image of the scene and generates a bitmap image.

Comparative advantages of bitmap vs. vector formats

Bitmap representation can record just about any conceivable image, since every image can be broken up into a grid as far as the human eye is concerned. As a result, program developers often resort to bitmaps to simplify programming.

However, bitmap images suffer from several problems both practical and theoretical. One practical problem is image size. A high-resolution color image file can require several megabytes of storage and even more megabytes of memory to process and display. For this reason, the ability to store images in compressed form is a very significant issue in the science of bitmap file formats.

Manipulating large volumes of data also makes heavy demands on the processor and internal data bus of the computer. For handling bitmap images, the difference in performance between a computer with a 32-bit internal bus and one with a 16-bit internal bus can be dramatic. As of this writing, manipulating large, photographic-quality color images typically requires graphics workstations or high-end personal computers to achieve any sort of tolerable response time.

Yet another problem with bitmap images is what can best be described as a lack of flexibility. This is not as much a file format issue as a processing issue, however. Part of the flexibility problem is that individual pixels have no intrinsic connection to each other. For example, in an image of a barn in a meadow, there are no pixels identified as "barn," or even "polygon #1." Consequently, if you want to do something to the barn part of the image, such as expand it or bend it, the program must do something complex, such as find all adjacent pixels that are more or less the same shade of red. Then, it might not find the gray barn roof! This problem is now being solved by using *object-oriented* bitmap techniques, where blocks of pixels obtain an identity when they are created and can therefore be identified as "barn" or "polygon #1."

Another flexibility problem for bitmap images derives from their fixed resolution. When the image is broken up into pixels, the resolution is fixed at *X* pixels across by *Y* pixels down. If you attempt to enlarge the image, the pixels get big enough to reveal their rectangular shape—an effect known as *aliasing* or *staircasing*. Smart graphics programs can compensate for this problem by interpolating a line between pixels, but again, time-consuming processing is involved. Likewise, if you shrink an image and then store it in its reduced form, resolution is often lost; if restored to its original size, the image will be fuzzy and aliased, and shaded areas may be patterned as shown in Fig. 1-4.

Vector representation has more limitations than bitmap representation in terms of what it can, in practice, represent, but it has the advantage of being far more efficient and flexible than bitmap representation for many applications. For example, a straight line can be described by its two endpoints. A curved line can be approximated by a series of linked straight lines. If different codes are used for

Figure 1-4

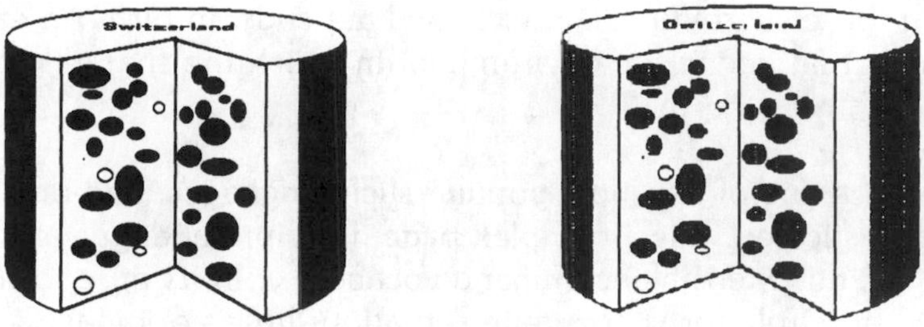

The effect of reducing then enlarging a bitmap image.

various shapes, vector representation becomes even more effective: a circle segment, for example, can be described by the code for a circle, a radius, and two endpoints.

In this scheme, our barn from the previous example might be stored as a named collection of associated polygons, with each polygon filled by a different shade or color. Because the collection has a single identity, such as "polygon #1," it could easily be moved or manipulated. It could also be scaled up or down with no effect on resolution.

Page-description languages, display lists, & metafiles

Graphics-description languages, also called *page-description languages* (PDLs), *display lists*, or *metafiles*, are sort of file formats—and sort of not. Strictly speaking, in file formats, the position of a data record carries some information; in graphics-description languages, the position of a data record is less relevant. For that reason, if you consider the earlier definitions of bitmap and vector files, it will become apparent that graphics-description languages are inherently well suited for vector representation but not for bitmap representation. Special provisions can be made for bitmaps within language files, however.

Such languages depend on sophisticated interpretation programs. For example, commands in these languages, such as the command to draw a shape, are often calls to subroutine-like modules. The manner in which these subroutines are executed depends, in turn, on earlier commands that define the environment in which the shape is to be drawn.

PostScript is one of the most popular such languages, and one of the most sophisticated. It is a complex page-description language with an extensive (and extensible) command vocabulary. In its pure form it is designed primarily for vector representation. It was originally designed for output devices: printers and computer screens. Nearly everything, even an odd shape such as a character typeface, is described using vector representation in PostScript. However, certain images, such as photographs, are poorly served by vectors. Accordingly, PostScript was designed so that its files might also include bitmaps.

Page-description languages, such as PostScript, are so complex that a complete discussion is beyond the scope of this book. And, they are also well described elsewhere. Nonetheless, certain aspects of PostScript and other graphics-description languages will be discussed when they relate to common problems in image conversion between formats.

Monochrome & color images

Electronically stored images, like photographs, may be either multicolor or black-and-white, which is also called *monochrome* since a single color may be substituted for black. Monochrome and multicolor images are supported by both vector and bitmap formats. Vector formats lend themselves to the use of *spot* color, where a uniform color is used in a defined region. Bitmap formats, in general, are suitable for anything from spot color to photographic color.

The technologies used to accurately depict the full range of monochrome and color images are so varied and complex that several volumes would be required to explore them thoroughly. However, certain fundamental concepts that are key to understanding graphics file formats are explained in the following text.

Monochrome

Monochrome images in their simplest form comprise pure "color" regions, typically black, and pure white regions. Typical images in this form are line drawings and charts. The files for these images often make no reference to color at all; they assume that the output device (e.g., a black-and-white laser printer) will use whatever color it is equipped for. These files are relatively compact for a given image size. In bitmap monochrome files, for example, a single bit can represent a pixel: 1 for black, 0 for white, or vice versa.

In some monochrome images, such as photographs and shaded illustrations, shades of gray (or of some other color) are needed. Such images are often called *grayscale* images.

Because the human eye will happily interpret a sufficiently fine pattern of black and white pixels as gray, a monochrome file format can be used for grayscale images; the data can still be black and white. The image in Fig. 1-1, for example, uses this method to achieve shading. The process of using dots of black or some single color to get continuous shades of that color is called *halftoning* or *dithering*. Halftoning is ultimately used for nearly all images printed in volume, since regular printing presses can apply only a single color of ink at a time. However, this is not to say that image files ultimately destined for printing have to be monochrome files in halftone form; the images may be converted to halftones very late in the process—preferably in the printing device.

There are disadvantages in using halftone or dithered image data in a monochrome file as a method of achieving grayscale. First, halftone data makes image editing difficult because most graphics programs will be unable to distinguish between dots used for shading and dots used for lines. Using halftone data can also introduce moire patterns when the image is displayed. Furthermore, given a fixed number of pixels in the output device, halftoning reduces the effective resolution of the image. Several pixels must be used up, some black, some white, to represent the gray value of a single point. To achieve four shades, for instance, at least three pixels must be used—four, to keep a rectangular pixel outline. But where the output device is capable of only two values, such as black and white on a laser printer, there is no alternative for the final output file; it must contain halftone data. At stages prior to printing, however, there is a better alternative: true grayscale representation.

True grayscale monochrome

Grayscale images can also be recorded as true shades of gray, rather than as stored data in halftoned or dithered format. True grayscale is the preferred representation for most electronic image applications because it simplifies editing. (Editing an image in halftone or dithered form generally causes problems. The editing process disrupts the very delicate arrangement of black and white pixels, causing visible defects such as rough edges, or the sort of patterns shown in Fig. 1-4.)

Where true shades of gray (brightness) are used, an image is said to be a certain number of bits *deep*. A bitmap monochrome image is described in terms of three dimensions: the number of pixel columns (width), the number of pixel rows (height), and the number of bits used to represent pixel brightness (depth), also called *grayscale resolution*. A bitmap image of 500 columns, by 500 rows, by 16 shades of gray, for instance, is 500 × 500 × 4. These dimensions are useful figures because they give a rough idea of the image's file size, without compression. In this example, that file size is 500 × 500 × (½ byte), or 125,000 bytes. The human eye can easily discern about 64 shades of gray in a given image, so for realistic images, a depth of 6 bits is necessary ($2^6 = 64$).

It is also common to combine grayscale and dithering to get the effect of a deeper display than you really have. Nextstep on the NeXT machine's 2-bit-deep display does this quite effectively. This is also true for color displays. For example, Silicon Graphics' Indigo system, which uses 24-bit color data, uses 8-bit dithered-color video. The tradeoff, of course, is resolution.

Ensuring grayscale accuracy

Accurate representation of shades of gray can become a problem when images are converted between electronic and physical media. The problem arises, for instance, when you scan a photograph. The scanner typically responds in a roughly linear fashion to variations in light intensity: twice the brightness yields a grayscale value twice as large. Your eye, however, responds as the cube root of intensity. So, a spot that looks twice as bright as another actually has eight times greater intensity, or reflectivity.

Nearly all input and output media are limited in the range of lightness and darkness they can achieve, while still retaining a characteristic nonlinearity. In printed material, for instance, these limits are imposed by the ink, paper, and quality of halftoning used. In scanners, the sensitivity of the sensors is limited and may not be perfectly linear. In CRTs, the light output of the screen phosphor also has certain limits and nonlinearities.

Handling these problems is largely a matter of knowing the limitations and behavior of a medium and making proper adjustments of the data. Some file formats, therefore, contain information that allow grayscale adjustments to be made. This information generally characterizes the source of the image data, not its destination. The reader should note, however, that very few applications currently handle such corrections, and few file formats allow them.

For example, consider an image scanned by a nonlinear scanner. Nonlinearities in input and output devices are typically summarized by a quantity called *gamma*, used in the equation $\mathrm{OUTPUT}=(\mathrm{INPUT})^{\mathrm{gamma}}$. A scanner output file, then, may record a value for gamma for the scanner, where INPUT would be the original light intensity of a pixel, and OUTPUT would be the grayscale value created by the scanner for that pixel.

The application program, finding a value for the scanner's gamma, can then reconstruct the original grayscale information accurately. If no value for gamma were supplied, the program would be justified in assuming that the data were already adjusted for the scanner's gamma, or that some default gamma should apply.

Some devices' nonlinearities do not conform to the simple logarithmic curve expressed by gamma. To handle this situation, a graphics file may instead record a response curve in the form of a table.

Other grayscale data that may be present in a file include information about the contrast of the original image and its overall lightness or darkness. These data are typically needed when the image data has been scaled or shifted in value to fit the range of values possible in a particular representation scheme. Without this information, for example, an intentionally low-contrast image might be given an inappropriately high contrast.

Color

Until recently, the use of color in electronically stored images was restricted to certain professional applications, largely due to the cost and performance of color input, output, and processing hardware. The color revolution is now in full swing, with costs of color input and output devices dropping, printing technologies proliferating, and popular PC applications software, such as desktop publishing, making use of the higher processing power of today's PCs to support color.

Because the structures of color graphics files reflect the underlying principles and practices of color, we will begin by examining those fundamentals.

Spot color

The simplest form of color representation is what we will call *limited spot color*, where the color is typically chosen from a short list of solid colors available in the output device and is applied to some graphic element in the image. A file for a plotter equipped with various colored pens, for example, would specify which pen is to be used for drawing a specific circle. Since spot color generally applies to lines and shapes, it is most often used in applications where data are stored in vector format or a graphics-description language.

With the increasing availability of color printers capable of printing a wide range of hues, spot color can also refer to a color achieved by mixing primary colors (see "Color mixing," below).

Color mixing

When a wider range of colors is needed, it is achieved by mixing a limited number of primaries. There are two fundamental color mixing schemes, RGB and CMYK, depending upon the intended output medium.

RGB color stands for the red, green, and blue additive primaries typically used in devices that emit light, such as computer monitors. Color screens comprise triads of phosphor spots, each spot emitting red, blue, or green light. Each triad forms a pixel when seen at a distance. By adjusting the amount of red, green, and blue light, you can generate a wide range of colors. Since the resulting color comes from adding light of different pure colors, it is called *additive* color.

CMYK color stands for the cyan, magenta, and yellow subtractive primaries, plus black for contrast, typically used for printed materials. A larger value for a given primary results in larger spots of that color, applied in a fine pattern on a white page. Each of the three primary inks absorbs certain colors from the white light impinging on the printed page. Because CMYK operates by removing specific colors from white, it is called *subtractive* color. Although, in theory, three primaries (CMY) should be sufficient, in reality, the available inks simply do not subtract enough. As a result, even with a white page completely covered with C, M, and Y dots, and no white showing, the result is gray. In theory, a file format could leave this problem for the printing device to solve by applying additional black where necessary and could stick to describing color with the three primaries.

This method is simply not practical, however. As a result, CMYK is a somewhat less efficient scheme for recording color in a given precision, and often results in larger files than RGB.

Although RGB is the "native" method of mixing colors for computer and video screens (that is, the light output is made up of red, green, and blue spots), and CMYK is the native method for printing, an output device or its software driver will often be able to handle files of either type, by translating the data. Not all colors translate well, however, and this can be an issue in file conversion or interpretation. In theory, the conversion goes as follows: Given a maximum value attained by a primary, such as 255 for an 8-bit value, Cyan = 255-Red; Magenta = 255-Green; and Yellow = 255-Blue.

Another increasingly popular color specification method, HSI, can be used independently of the mixing scheme. HSI stands for Hue, Saturation, and Intensity. *Hue* is what we think of as the color such as orange, puce, or Navaho white. *Saturation* describes the amount of white. The brown color of baking chocolate, for example, is very saturated, while the color of milk chocolate is the same hue, but less saturated. *Intensity* describes the brightness and, for example, is mainly what distinguishes an orange in sunlight from an orange in shade. Also, the word *luminosity* is often substituted for intensity in which case HSI becomes HSL.

HSI is a more intuitive method of specifying color, and is now commonly available in graphics application software. Even some graphics adapters will now accept HSI data. HSI data must ultimately be converted into either RGB or CMYK, however. Computer monitors, for instance, still require red, green, and blue input signals; an HSI-compatible adapter must therefore make a translation from HSI to RGB.

In video applications, another common color scheme is *YCbCr*. The *Y* term signifies *luminosity*; the *Cb* term signifies chrominance for the *blue* primary; and the *Cr* term signifies chrominance for the *red* primary. The green primary derives from a combination of these three values. Luminosity is, roughly speaking, the brightness of a pixel; chrominance is the color. This separation of luminance from chrominance allows image-compression techniques to take advantage of the eye's lesser need for resolution of color than of brightness. This color scheme is increasingly used as applications move to support desktop video. Even some formats for still images, such as TIFF, also have the option of implementing YCbCr.

These various color schemes (and there are others, as well) are also described as color *spaces*: a volume in three or four dimensions wherein a point defines a color. Conversion between color spaces is theoretically simple but pragmatically complex. The 4-D color space CMYK is less efficient than RGB, because the black component duplicates the darkening effect of combining C, M, and Y components. Therefore, files of equivalent quality (color and spatial resolution) will generally be larger in the CMYK representation than in the RGB representation. Nor is conversion always easily reversible; an image converted from RGB to CMYK will not resume exactly its original appearance if converted back to RGB. In part, the disparity occurs because the two coordinate systems describe different shapes in true-color space, yet certain colors that exist in RGB space simply do not exist in CMYK space. The algorithm that maps the RGB value into CMYK must force-fit outlying values into the CMYK color space, thus introducing a distortion. The original location of that value in RGB space is therefore lost. As an analogy, consider how you might represent lengths approaching one meter on a yardstick, which is shorter. To record a measurement at such extreme values you might make an approximation on the yardstick, but when converting back to meters you could not reconstruct the original value. Yes, a scaled-down mapping of centimeters to "yardstick marks" can be constructed, but at some expense of resolution. A reverse mapping back to centimeters will introduce inaccuracies due to rounding errors.

Color image planes

Each pixel in a color bitmap image (or each graphic element in a color vector image) requires a set of three or four values; one for each primary color (RGB, CMYK) or independent variable (HSI), depending on the color-representation scheme used. These sets of values are typically organized in one of two ways in a graphics file.

The most common way of organizing bitmap image data is by color, into *color planes*. This approach is most easily envisioned as three or four monochrome images, one for each primary color, analogous to *color separations* in the printing industry. In an RGB scheme, for instance, all the data for red, for every pixel in the image, would be grouped together; then all the data for green, then all the data for blue.

As an alternative, the image data can be organized into a single *image plane*, in which the red, green, and blue values for each pixel are grouped together. This is the approach also used for most vector images, in which the RGB, CMYK, or HSI values are grouped together, along with the vector.

The number of colors that an input or output device supports is quantified by a total number of bits. For example, 24-bit color generally considered to be adequate for even demanding applications, refers to a device with eight bits of resolution for each of three primary colors. Thus, 24-bit color supplies 2^{24} or more than 16 million colors. The disadvantage of using such high-resolution color images is their file size. A 1024 × 1024 × 24-bit bitmap image requires three- MBytes, uncompressed.

Some computer monitor graphics adapters circumvent file size problems, and reduce cost, by adopting a *palette* or *color map* approach to color. This approach may be reflected in the graphics file format. Here, a single image can have only so many different colors, even though each color has a high resolution. For instance, the image might be made up of colors from a 16-bit palette, or 65,536 different colors. Those colors could, however, be 24-bit colors. A 1024 × 1024 resolution image using a 16-bit palette requires only about two MBytes. For practical purposes, an 8-bit palette out of a 24-bit color space is usually adequate to produce pleasing, TV-quality color. The pixel data for a palette image consists of *n*-bit pixel codes, with each of the *n* codes pointing to a trio of RGB values held in a palette table. The data file therefore must include not only the pixel data, but the table of palette data as well.

Ensuring color accuracy

As with monochrome (grayscale) images, accuracy problems can arise when color images are transported between various media. Solutions for most color problems are similar to those for grayscale problems. The usual approach is to use color-plane organization and treat each plane as a separate monochrome image, using the grayscale accuracy-correction methods discussed previously. This compensates for errors within each primary color.

Errors between the color planes must also be corrected, however. Otherwise, the image's overall hue will be shifted toward one primary or another. This correction is typically done by comparing the image's *white point* (or some other color points, such as pure red, green, and blue) against some standard, then correcting accordingly.

In electronic form, an image is *white* when the primary values are equal. But when these values are converted to an output, such as on a monitor, the resulting light might or might not be what you think of as white. Likewise, a color scanner may output a white pixel, one with equal values for R, G, and B, in response to a spot on the paper image that is not quite the same white as the white on your monitor. To fully resolve these problems, an input or output device's idea of white must be calibrated according to some standard.

Several colorimetric standards are in use. A number of organizations have created standards, including CIE (Committee Internationale de l'Eclairage), NTSC (National Television System Committee), SMPTE (Society of Motion Picture and Television Engineers), and ISO (International Standards Organization, for which ANSI, the American National Standards Institute, is the U.S. representative body). In each standard, a set of numbers is used to define an objectively measured color. Therefore, the color that an input or output device records as white can be measured by its vendor and defined by a set of numbers. The resulting number based definition is called the device's *white point*.

To accurately record a color image, therefore, the graphics file must also record values indicating the white point of the originating device, according to some standard. An image originally created on the computer monitor will use the monitor's white point. A scanned image will use the scanner's white point.

As is the case with monochrome-accuracy measures, relatively few devices and applications today are set up to maintain color-accuracy information and it is rarely accommodated by the file format. Where color accuracy is important, therefore, you are advised to be aware of the presence or absence of this information in various file formats, and whether (and how) the information is used by the applications you have chosen.

Common methods of encoding data

Regardless of variations in graphics file formats, data are encoded in certain common ways. Furthermore, graphics data are compressed to consume less storage space in a file in certain conventional ways. The details of compression vary, however, and typically are described in the file-format specification. For more information on compression, see chapter 2.

Note that there are probably more different encoding and compression schemes than pages in this book. Many of these schemes are, however, combinations and variations of the following basic concepts.

Binary & symbolic coding

Graphics data may be encoded in either symbolic or binary form, or in some mixture of both. Commands and data in a PostScript file, for example, are generally recorded in symbolic form—you can read them with a word processor. A TIFF file is recorded in binary form. To read it easily, you would need a debugger or another binary interpreter.

Symbolic coding (almost always in ASCII) is comparatively inefficient, by a factor of at least two. Many vector files and graphics-description languages are recorded in symbolic form, however, where the inefficiency of ASCII is offset by the high efficiency of vector representation.

Binary coding is generally used for bitmap data. One notable exception is PostScript, which generally uses ASCII for bitmaps. PostScript files containing bitmap data are, therefore, often much larger than just about any other bitmap file for the same data. Level 2 and Display PostScript, however, allow binary encoding for certain applications.

Bit & byte order in binary data

Symbolically encoded digits generally appear in their natural order, as printed. Binary encoded data can use different byte orders and, in the case of bitmap images, can use different bit orders as well.

In a simple one-bit-deep bitmap image, for instance, the image can be scanned left to right, top to bottom, or in any other combination of directions. Furthermore, the first pixel scanned out of *n* could be mapped to either the high bit or the low bit of an *n*-bit-long data word. You would have to know the scanning order, word length, and bitmapping order to properly decode this image.

Where there is more than one bit per pixel in a bitmap image, even more variations are possible. Each pixel's multibit value can be recorded all at once, such as a 16-bit value being recorded as two consecutive bytes. This order can be thought of as creating a single 16-bit-deep image plane. Alternatively, this image could be broken up into 16 one-bit-deep *bit planes*, in which the most-significant bits of all pixels would be recorded together to form one plane, then all the next-most-significant bits to form another plane, and so forth.

Byte order can also vary, affecting both bitmap and vector images. Byte order usually depends on the processor used in the computer. One variation is the ordering of least- and most-significant bytes for numbers in excess of one byte. Such numbers can be encoded with the most-significant byte either first or last. A 16-bit integer, such as 51210 might appear as the two bytes 00000001 00000000 (or 01 00 in hexadecimal form), or as 00000000 00000001 (00 01 hex).

The individual elements of floating-point numbers (i.e., the sign, the fraction, and the exponent) can be stored in various orders. Within the fraction and the exponent, byte order can be either least-significant byte (LSB) first or most-significant byte (MSB) first. Here again, the order of these elements generally depends on the computer's CPU.

In the memory (and generally in the files) of PCs and other Intel CPU computers, the LSB comes first; in Motorola CPU systems, such as Apple Macintosh computers, the MSB comes first. UNIX workstations from Sun, IBM, and HP usually store MSB data first; those from Intel and DEC store LSB data first. Data stored in files on these systems almost always reflects the native order of the machine—that is, the order in which data is stored in memory, reading from low to high addresses.

Because of these differences, a graphics file format must record some information about the bit and byte order if it is to be used by a variety of computers from different manufacturers. A file format developed for a particular computer will generally lack byte order information, but if the CPU of that system is known the correct order can be inferred. Bit order and word length may be controlled by the image source alone, such as a scanner, or may be regulated by the file-format specification.

## CHAPTER 2

Image compression

AS users demand greater graphic content and higher image quality in their computer applications, the amount of data required increases rapidly—more rapidly than larger storage media and greater I/O power alone can accommodate. This increased need has put the spotlight on data-compression techniques: ways to store the same amount of information using fewer bits. Multimedia applications, in which computers display video or animation, are among the most demanding users of data compression. Yet, even in "still" image work, users wish to work with higher resolution and better color quality, or simply with more images. All such enhancements require more data from the same physical system, and therefore increase the need for compression.

Compression is simply representing information more efficiently; "squeezing the air" out of data, so to speak. It takes advantage of three common qualities of graphical data; they are often redundant, predictable, or unnecessary. A scheme such as run-length encoding (RLE), which utilizes redundancy, says "Here are three identical red pixels," rather than saying, "Here's a red pixel, now a red pixel, now a red pixel." Huffman and arithmetic coding rely on a statistical model to exploit predictability, using shorter codes for more frequently occurring pixel values. The presence of unnecessary data suggests the use of a *lossy* (defined under "lossy compression," following) scheme. For instance, for casual viewing the human eye does not demand the same resolution for the color information in an image that it requires for the intensity information. The data representing high color resolution can be discarded. Decades ago, artists exploited this fact and offered "tinted" photographs, in which color had been applied with a brush (low resolution) over a black-and-white photo (a high-resolution intensity map). Today, color video compression schemes often employ the same principle.

Compression is a matter of trade-offs, however. The more efficient (and therefore the more complicated) the compression algorithm, the more processing power or time is needed to decompress the image. Time is of less concern for still images, but for video or animation it is crucial. Most personal computers in use at this time do not have sufficient CPU power to decode high-quality compressed video. Neither do they generally have the I/O power to read or write high-quality uncompressed video data, unless they are specially enhanced. Accordingly, programs trade off quality for quantity, often automatically. Frame rates, resolution, color depth, and frame size are all often minimized to permit video.

Compression is now routinely used for storing large volumes of image data, whether single images or movies. Unsurprisingly, hardware and software for compression and decompression are increasingly being made part of the computer platform. The System 7 operating system of Macintosh computers, for instance, now includes a *compression engine* offering several different flavors of compression and decompression, called *codecs* for coder/decoder. Standard coding/decoding schemes, such as JPEG for still images and MPEG for motion images, are increasingly being supported in both platforms and file formats, yet proprietary schemes are equally common.

In this chapter we will review a range of compression schemes, ranging from simple run-length encoding to predictive schemes, to complex lossy methods. In some of these schemes, the processing details are so complex as to be beyond the scope of a book such as this. In fact, some algorithms are so complex (and in some cases, are legally protected) that many developers might be well-advised to purchase code for reading and writing rather than to write the code. Further complications arise because the names of certain schemes, like JPEG, actually refer to a *family* of algorithms, each one of which could be implemented in a variety of ways, resulting in quite different file formats.

⇨ Run-length compression

One of the simplest ways to compress a file is run-length encoding. In this scheme, a series of repeated values (e.g., pixel values) is replaced by a single value and a count. For example, using letters to represent values, a series of values such as *abbbbbbbccddddeeddd* would be replaced by 1*a*7b2*c*4d2*e*3*d*. This approach is simple to implement and works well with long strings of repeated values. Images with large areas of a constant shade or hue, like those typically produced with "paint" programs, are good candidates for this kind of compression.

One popular implementation of run-length compression is PackBits, used for bitmap data on the Apple MacIntosh. Assuming 8-bit data, PackBits encodes repeated values in two bytes. The first byte contains a number, *n*, between −127 and −1, inclusive; this provides the repetition count, −*n*+1. The second byte contains the value to repeat. Non-repeated values, like the series *abcde*, are denoted by a 1-byte starting code, *m*, between 0 and 127, inclusive; this gives the length of the string, *m*+1 (*m* would be 4 in this example). Repetitive runs cannot be longer than 128 bytes and must be broken up into multiple runs. Generally, compression does not cross from one scan line to the next.

Run-length encoding is used in many of the bitmap file formats described in this book, such as MacPaint, TIFF, GEM, PCX, and FLI.

Huffman encoding

Huffman encoding (Huffman 1952) is a common scheme for compression. It works by substituting more efficient codes for data. This approach, which was created in 1952 for text files, has spawned many variations. The basic scheme is to assign a binary code to each unique value, with the codes varying in length. Shorter codes are used for the more frequently occurring values. These assignments are stored in a conversion table, which is sent to the decoding software before the codes are sent.

For instance, there are six unique values in *abbbcccddeeeeeeeeef*. The frequencies with which they appear are as follows:

a:1 *b*:3 *c*:3 *d*:2 *e*:9 *f*:1

To build a minimum code for each, a binary tree is used as shown in Fig. 2-1. The basic algorithm pairs together the least frequently occurring elements; the pair is then treated as one element and their frequencies are combined. This continues until all pairs are combined.

Figure 2-1

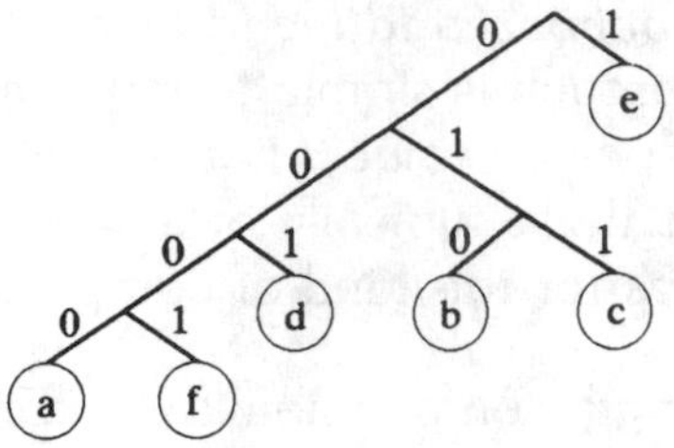

A binary tree for Huffman encoding.

The least frequently used values in this example are *a* and *f*, so they make up the first pair; *a* is assigned the 0 branch, and *f* is assigned the 1 branch. This means 0 and 1, respectively, will be the *least* significant bits of the codes for *a* and *f*. The *more* significant bits come from the tree, as it is built.

The frequencies of these first two are then combined, for a total of 2. Since 2 is now the lowest frequency, this pair is combined with *d* (which also has a frequency of 2). The original pair is assigned to the 0 branch of this tree, and *d* is assigned to the 1 branch. So the code for *a* will end in 00; *f* will end in 01; *d* will end in 1 and be one bit shorter than the codes for *a* and *f*.

The tree continues like this, so that the least frequent values are described by longer codes and the most frequent by single (or near-single) bits; yet no codes are wasted and none are any longer than they have to be.

The compression efficiency of Huffman encoding varies with the precise algorithm and the type of image. The algorithm varies with different formats, but few get any better than 8:1 compression. Huffman tends to perform less well for files containing long runs of identical pixel values, which can be better compressed using run-length or other encoding.

Huffman encoding also needs accurate statistics on how frequently each value occurs in the original file. Without accurate statistics, the final file is not much smaller, and may even turn out longer than the original. So to work properly, Huffman is usually done in two passes. In the first pass, the statistical model is created; in the second, the data is encoded. As a result, and because variable-length codes require a lot of processing to decode, Huffman compression and decompression are relatively slow processes.

A final problem with Huffman (also found in other variable-length compression schemes) is sensitivity to dropped or added bits. Since all the bits are jammed together without regard to byte boundaries, the decoder's only way of knowing when a code is finished is by reaching the end of a branch. If a bit is dropped or added, the decoder starts in the middle of a code and the rest of the data becomes nonsense.

LZW compression

LZW is a more recent compression algorithm, developed by a Sperry researcher named Welch, and building on work by Lempel and Ziv (Welch 1984). This algorithm, designed originally for hardware implementation (and for which UNISYS has been granted patent #4,558,302), also has several popular variations. (Some of those may also be patented. Interestingly, from a patent standpoint, some software implementations are often considered to be in the public domain, such as the UNIX *compress* utility.)

Unlike Huffman, LZW does not need to construct a table of codes in advance of coding. Starting with a simple table, it builds a more effective table of codes as it goes along; it is *adaptive*. Also unlike Huffman, LZW implementations do not generally use shorter codes for more frequently occurring values. The LZW scheme exploits redundancies in the patterns it finds.

LZW starts with a table with one code entry for each possible value in the data; 256 entries, for example, for 8-bit data. It then adds entries to the table for each unique pattern of values it finds. It is necessary to fix the maximum length of the table so a code length can be established. (Some implementations of LZW, such as that used in Compuserve's GIF format, allow for variable length.)

Consider the sequence *ababaaacaaaad* for instance, where each letter represents, for simplicity, 2-bit data values. The LZW encoder and decoder start with the same table, and they track as the table expands. The initial code table would be:

For *ababaaacaaaad*:

a:00 *b*:01 *c*:10 *d*:11

The LZW algorithm looks for the longest pattern it can recognize—the longest it can find in the table. It finds the first value, *a*, and recognizes it, then tries for the pattern *ab*, and doesn't recognize it. So it transmits the code for the value it recognizes (000) and makes a new table entry for the one it doesn't. The encoder table becomes:

a:000 *b*:001 *c*:010 *d*:011 *ab*:100

The encoder then takes the last value, *b*, and tries for a pattern with the next value. It comes up with *ba*, which is unrecognized, so it sends the code for *b* (001). The decoder has now received these same data and, doing basically the same thing, adds the code for *ab* to its table.

Now comes the good part. The encoder can now recognize the next instance of the sequence *ab*, and so can the decoder. So a 3-bit code can now replace two 2-bit codes; not a big win in this simple instance, but much bigger in realistic examples. Even in this example, all subsequent multiple iterations of the value *a* will be entered into the table and will therefore translate into a single 3-bit code.

LZW encoding provides typical compression ratios between 1:1 and 3:1, although highly patterned images can sometimes be compressed as much as 10:1. *Noisy* images, those with random variations in data values, are hard to compress with LZW. Randomness is the antithesis of patterning, and LZW relies on finding patterns. To solve noise problems, low-end bits can be truncated or values can be locally averaged.

LZW is used in the GIF and TIFF formats described in this book.

Arithmetic compression

Arithmetic compression, like Huffman coding, uses shorter codes for frequently occurring things and longer codes for infrequently occurring things. It is a more efficient scheme, though, which (like LZW) compresses sequences of values, not just values. Furthermore, its coding scheme does a far better job on files in which most of the data consists of the same sequence, repeated. In fact, arithmetic compression comes close to theoretical limits for compression. Some useful references for arithmetic compression theory are articles by Abrahamson (1989), Langdon (1984), Rissanen (1979), and Witten (1987), listed at the end of this chapter.

There are several algorithms for arithmetic compression, all of them far too complex to detail here, and some of them undoubtedly proprietary. Simply put, arithmetic compression involves mapping every different sequence of pixel values to a region on an imaginary number line between 0 and 1. That region is then represented as a binary fraction of variable precision (number of bits). Less common sequences require a higher precision (more bits).

Take, for example, a set of pixel values, represented by letters, as we did in the previous discussion of Huffman encoding. Assume every pixel in a 1900-pixel image had one of those six values, and that they appeared with the following frequencies:

a:100 *b*:300 *c*:300 *d*:200 *e*:900 *f*:100

Another way of stating this pattern is that pixel values appeared with the probabilities P(*a*) = .0526, P(*b*) = .1579, P(*c*) = .1579, P(*d*) = .1052, P(*e*) = .4737, P(*f*) = .0526. A series of pixels, such as *eb*, would have a probability of P(*e*) × P(*b*). We could represent a pixel value, or for that matter, a series, by its probability. The trouble is that these probabilities are not unique so we could not distinguish *b* from *c* (both 0.1579); *eb* from *ec* (both 0.4737 × 0.1579); or, for that matter, *eb* from its reverse, *be*.

However, if we interpret the probability of each value as the length of a line segment, and stack up those segments in some arbitrary order as shown at the left side of Fig. 2-2, a better way of representing a series emerges.

Figure 2-2

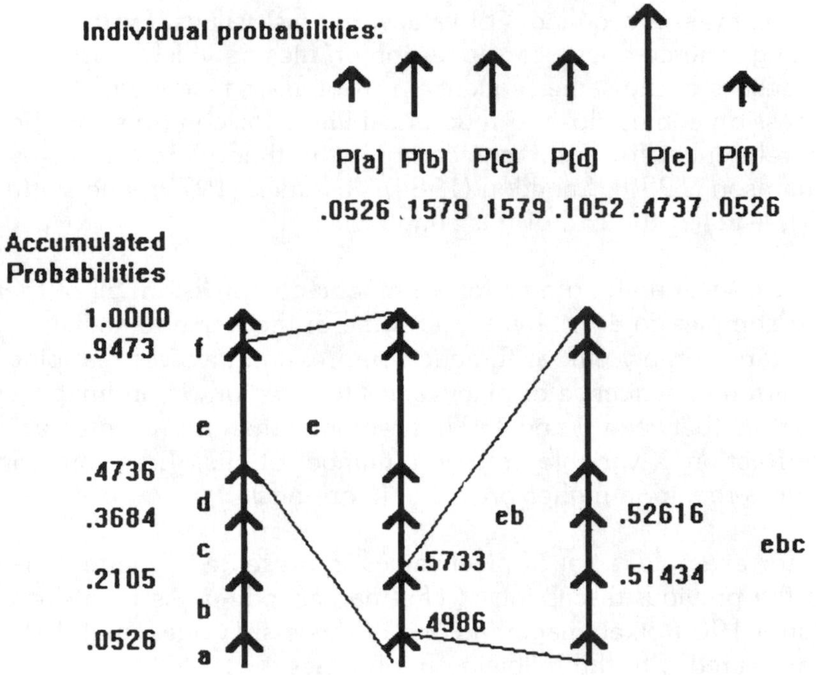

Mapping sequences into a set of ranges between 0 and 1.

Now we represent the value *b*, for example, with a line segment from 0.0526 to 0.2105; the length of that line segment is its probability, P(*b*). The value *c* has the same probability, and therefore the same length on the line, but a unique range: from 0.2105 to 0.3684. We can now represent any pixel value uniquely by a number pointing anywhere in its assigned line segment. The number 0.25, for instance, indicates the value *c*, because it falls within the range for *c*. Notice that a two-digit fraction is sufficient to represent *c*.

To represent a series of two characters, we can subdivide each of these line segments. A series starting with the value *b*, for instance, would mean subdividing the range for *b* (0.0526 to 0.2105). A series in which the second value was *a* (with probability 0.0526) would be represented by the first 5.26% of that range; the value *b* (with probability 0.1579) would be represented by the next 15.79%, and so forth. The series *ba*, then, would be represented by any number in the range from .0526 to .0554, such as .053. The series *ee* (where higher probabilities give larger segments) would be represented by any number in a wider range, 0.4737 to 0.6981, such as 0.5.

We now have a scheme for uniquely encoding any sequence of values: a pointer to some location along the number line from 0 to 1. Of course, as the sequence gets longer, we need more digits (translation: more bits) because we have to point with greater precision. Clearly, we need to call an end to a sequence and start a new one when we reach the precision limits of our software.

Interestingly, we also need greater precision (more bits) for sequences using low-probability values, such as *a* and *b*. Such sequences are represented by a tiny segment of a tiny segment. Conversely, we need fewer bits for sequences involving high-probability values like *e*. Recall that the single-digit fraction 0.5 sufficed to represent the series *ee*, but a three-digit fraction was needed for *ba*. Even though binary fractions, not decimal, are used in reality, the result is similar. The bigger the line segment, the more likely that we can find a low-precision binary fraction, such as ½, ¼, or ⅛, to represent it.

As with Huffman, then, arithmetic coding efficiently represents more frequently occurring sequences of pixel values (more-probable values) with fewer bits. The unique result of this scheme, however, is to allow, on average, something other than an integral number of bits per value communicated.

Arithmetic compression can reduce file size dramatically, depending on the source and the accuracy of the statistical model used. To expect compressions of 100:1 is not unreasonable.

Lossy compression

Lossy compression refers to techniques in which some aspect of the original data is discarded (or lost, hence, *lossy* compression), because it was deemed unnecessary to the final application. Such techniques should obviously not be used in critical applications such as medical imaging, but are just fine for commercial television and general photography.

The things which can be discarded in lossy compression include things the eye does not need for perception in a given situation, such as unnecessarily sharp edges or high spatial resolution of color. Typical U.S. color TVs, for instance, deliver fewer than 50 color changes across the screen, though your eye never notices.

Lossy compression is increasingly popular for computer video applications. The current interest in multimedia applications, which generally include video or animation, is causing computer and operating system designers to begin including lossy compression capabilities as part of the base system. Apple Computer, for example, now includes lossy compression in its System 7 operating system, in the form of its Compact Video Compressor.

The most commonly cited lossy compression scheme is the baseline algorithm of JPEG, which is described in more detail in a separate chapter in this book. A qualitative description will be given here. JPEG, the Joint Photographic Experts Group of the International Standards Organization (ISO), defines several algorithms. The algorithm most commonly referred to as JPEG is the lossy, baseline algorithm. JPEG also defines a lossless algorithm based on differential pulse-code modulation. Both actually employ multiple-compression algorithms in combination, including Huffman or arithmetic compression.

JPEG algorithms begin by separating the chroma (color) information from the luminance (brightness) information, to take advantage of the human eye's tolerance for lower color resolution. Next, the image is broken up into smaller tiles. The lossy algorithm then applies a mathematical technique to the tiles, known as *Discrete Cosine*

Transform (DCT). After this transformation, individual pixels no longer exist. They are represented by a series of patterns describing how rapidly the pixel values vary. Since individual pixel identities are lost in DCT, this form of JPEG is called lossy.

DCT is not unlike measuring traffic congestion on a highway by noting how fast traffic is moving rather than by counting cars. Given enough information about traffic speed and the highway, you can reconstruct a pretty accurate profile of traffic density along a highway, although you could never construct an exact picture of each individual car.

Another non-mathematical way of envisioning lossy JPEG is to think of breaking each tile up into a series of images of decreasing fuzziness. Imagine these as a series of images taken as a photographer brings a camera into focus. This is roughly analogous to lossy JPEG, except that in JPEG the broad area of, for example, the red that originates from a barn is apparent in fuzzier images yet disappears in later images, in favor of details such as the barn's edges. Each original tile is reconstructed by overlaying these images. Because chrominance and luminosity are treated separately, the more detailed "photos" of chrominance can be discarded. And, in fact, so may the photos of luminance detail, depending on the needs of the application or the platform's capabilities.

JPEG is supported in a variety of formats and software, although each typically has its own peculiarities. TIFF 6.0, for instance, supports JPEG encoding, but the prospective developer should obtain the detailed TIFF specification to ensure proper handing of details. Similarly, the Photo Compressor in the QuickTime portion of Apple's System 7 operating system supports the standard baseline JPEG bitstream (version 9R9).

MPEG is an emerging standard related to JPEG and is intended for the storage of moving pictures. It was developed by the Motion Pictures Experts Group. An MPEG file contains JPEG-like frames, along with information for interpolating other frames between the JPEG-like frames. The format is so complex that special hardware is generally needed to encode or decode MPEG files at a reasonable speed. An overview of MPEG is given in Chapter 30.

References

Abrahamson, D.M. "An Adaptive Dependency Source Model for Data Compression." *Communications of the ACM, vol. 32, no. 1*. January 1989.

Huffman, D.A. "A method for the construction of minimum-redundancy codes." *Proc. Inst. Electr. Radio Eng. vol. 40, no. 9*. September 1952.

Langdon, G.G. Jr. "An Introduction to Arithmetic Coding." *IBM Journal of Research and Development, vol. 28, no. 2*. March 1984.

Rissanen, J.J., and G.G. Langdon, Jr. "Arithmetic Coding." *IBM Journal of Research and Development*. December 1979.

Welch, T.A. "A Technique for High Performance Data Compression." *IEEE Computer, vol. 17, no. 6*. June 1984.

Witten, I.H., R.M. Neal, and J.G. Cleary. "Arithmetic coding for data compression." *Communications of the ACM, vol. 30, no. 6*. June 1987.

## CHAPTER 3

Choosing formats

CHOOSING a particular format for a given application generally involves several interdependent considerations, including quality; flexibility; computation, storage, or transmission efficiency; and support by existing programs. The suitability of a format for a given purpose is best determined by knowing its original purpose. The intended purpose of each format discussed in this book is given in the introductory summary of that format's chapter.

Assessing aspects of a format

Quality

To obtain high *quality* in an image requires high-resolution, high-depth (bits per pixel) calibration of color to a known reference (e.g., CIE), and correction for media characteristics. High-quality representations of real-life objects (which, for the sake of discussion, we shall call images, not graphics) are generally done with bitmap formats. Vector formats can construct realistic images, but with images obtained from life (such as scans or video frames) the original data are generally obtained as a bitmap, and are converted to vectors only at the expense of greater computing resources and additional software development.

For the highest-quality vector graphics (used for line drawings), a format must support curves and splines, plus variable line widths, solid and graduated fills, and accurate color control typically calibrated to Pantone PMS colors or other print-color standards. A vector-based application typical of this quality level is CorelDraw, found principally on PCs and UNIX workstations.

Of all the formats discussed in this book, the single format most capable of representing images or graphics with high quality is color PostScript. Color PostScript offers the ability to record high-resolution, color-calibrated graphics and images, with corrections for media characteristics (e.g., screen vs. paper). Where only bitmap images are used, TIFF might be preferable. TIFF is more compact yet capable of comparable quality, and TIFF readers are somewhat easier to implement than PostScript bitmap readers. Few other formats allow for photometric adjustment.

Flexibility

Flexibility is the ease or reliability with which a format can adapt to change, such as when crossing platforms, crossing different types of graphics display or other output media, or adjusting for different scales or aspect ratios. Here again, the winner is PostScript in terms of absolute flexibility; however, it is also a complex language that relies on a sophisticated interpretation program. TIFF is also a highly flexible format in terms of image size, resolution, and color correction. It tends to suffer from incompatible implementations, however.

Efficiency

Efficiency relates to the computing, storage or transmission resources consumed in the use of a format. At first glance, vector and language formats appear to be efficient for storage in that they use geometric abstractions like lines and arcs, yet many are implemented in ASCII, which is inefficient. Furthermore, they require additional computing power and software development to encode or decode these abstractions. A PostScript printer, for instance, requires either more time or more computing power to decode graphics than does a purely bitmap printer. Transmitting a vector image to the PostScript printer might be faster, however, than transmitting a bitmap to a bitmap printer. Likewise, image compression techniques reduce storage and transmission requirements at the expense of greater computing time and power for encoding and decoding. In general, computing power per dollar advances faster than storage or transmission capacity per dollar, and so dictates an increase in the use of data abstraction and/or compression.

The efficiency of a format is also closely linked to the type and quality of data formatted. Images, for instance, should be stored with the minimum bits-per-pixel depth necessary for the application, if efficiency is an issue. Also, vector data are more efficiently represented in binary form than in ASCII.

Support

For most systems managers and programmers, the chief issue is, "What formats do existing programs support?" The answer to this question changes far too rapidly to be documented accurately here. At best, we can give a general indication of format support as of this writing. Most programs support a rapidly increasing variety of graphics formats, either directly through menu choices in the program, or indirectly through conversion programs. It is best to contact vendors directly to see what formats are currently supported.

Note, however, that there can be wide variations in "support." Some programs support only input of a given format; some support only output. Also, certain features of a format might be ignored, capabilities might be limited, or a format might be supported only on a particular platform. Worse, some vendors abuse the customization capabilities of a format to the extent that their applications often fail to either read or write other programs' implementations!

Application considerations

The following tables provide a general indication of the support provided by various types of applications. From these tables you can infer which formats are the more popular for certain types of applications, such as graphic arts.

Do not rely on these tables for details on specific software packages. If you are interested in specific applications, contact the vendors to determine which formats are supported and to what degree. For instance, Version 1.0 of Zsoft's PC PaintBrush IV Plus supports standard TIFF 5.0 monochrome and grayscale, but only supports its own color RGB version of TIFF. This sort of information can be obtained in up-to-date form from vendors only. The individual format chapters in this book can be helpful in such discussions by pointing out the variations common within each format.

Applications that run on PCs under Microsoft Windows will generally exchange Windows bitmaps or metafiles, in addition to supporting any other formats shown below. Note: PIC refers to Lotus PIC in all tables.

Graphic arts

See Table 3-1.

Table 3-1 **Graphic arts format support**

Software	CGM	EPS	PCX	PIC	TIFF	WMF	Own	Other
Adobe Illustr. (AI)		x		x	x			DXF, PC paint
CorelDraw	x	x	x	x	x			DXF, Adobe
Island Graphics	x	x			x		TIFF	
Micrografix Designer	x			x	x	x	DRW	DXF
Zsoft(Paintbrush)			x		x		TIFF	PCL

Spreadsheets

Spreadsheet software often allows output or conversion of graphs to popular formats, as indicated by Table 3-2. Most have their own proprietary graphics output format.

Business graphics

Business graphics software generally provides only a few alternative output formats. (See Table 3-3.)

Spreadsheet graphics format support Table 3-2

Software	CGM	EPS	HPGL	PCX	PIC	TIFF	Windows	Own	Other
Microsoft Excel			x		x		x		
Lotus 1-2-3	x				x				
Lotus 1-2-3/G							x		
Quattro Pro		x			x				
Wingz							x		

Business graphics format support Table 3-3

Standard graphics formats written

Software	CGM	EPS	HPGL	PCX	PIC	TIFF	DXF	Other
Lotus Freelance Plus	x	x	x					
Harvard Graphics	x	x	x	x		x		
Lotus Graphwriter	x	x	x					

CAD

Most CAD programs use their own proprietary file formats for principal storage, and they provide translation for DXF and IGES. On UNIX workstations, the more commonly supported exchange format is IGES, although some engineers report that IGES exchange tends to be somewhat less reliable than DXF as of this writing. On Macintoshes, PICT and Mac clipboard translation is available. Levels of support for other graphics formats vary widely. Most CAD programs provide vector output, such as HPGL, PICT, or EPS, and a few provide bitmap graphics output, such as PCX, MacPaint, or PICT bitmaps. A few representative CAD programs are listed in Table 3-4.

Table 3-4 **CAD graphics format support**

Software	DXF	IGES	HPGL	EPS	Other
Autodesk	x	x	x		
IBM CAD	x	x	x	x	TIFF, PIF, IFF, GDF, PM Metafile
CV VersaCAD	x	x	x	x	PICT, X Windows BMP, Sun rasterfile
HP ME10	x	x	x		PCL

Word processing

The following table lists graphics formats that can be read by various popular word-processing software. The *Proprietary* column indicates that the word processor has a screen-capture capability with its own bitmap format. (See Table 3-5).

Table 3-5 **Word processor graphics format support**

	Graphics formats read							
Software	**CGM**	**EPS**	**HPGL**	**PCX**	**PIC**	**TIFF**	**Proprietary**	**Other**
Ami Professional			x	x	x	x		
Display Write 5	x			x	x			
Microsoft Word		x	x	x	x	x	x	
MS Word for Windows	x	x	x	x	x	x	x	
MultiMate	x			x	x	x	x	
Professional Write								First Graphics, Harvard
WordPerfect		x		x	x	x		
Wordstar							x	

Desktop publishing

Desktop publishing applications support perhaps the greatest variety of graphics file formats for input. Two of the most popular packages are shown in Table 3-6.

Desktop publishing graphics support Table 3-6

	PageMaker (PC)	Ventura
CGM	x	x
EPS	x	
Excel Chart	x	
Excel Paint	x	
HPGL	x	x
Gem		x
Lotus PIC	x	x
MS Windows BMP		x
PCX	x	
Macintosh Paint	x	
Macintosh PICT		x
Mouse Systems	x	
PC Paintbrush	x	
Tek. PLOT 10	x	
TIFF		x
Windows Draw	x	
Windows Metafile	x	x
Windows Paint	x	
Micrografix DRW	x	
Micrografix PIC	x	
Micrografix GRF	x	
Videoshow	x	x

Input & output device considerations

While input and output devices are not prime considerations in choosing file formats, the chosen format should be able to handle whatever data is available from an input device. Likewise, it should be able to provide all the data that an output device can use.

Input devices

Most input devices generate bitmaps. The principal exceptions are pointing devices, such as the digitizer tablet and the mouse, which generate vector data. Popular bitmap input devices include scanners (color or monochrome), video cameras with *capture* boards, and facsimile machines or boards.

The application program (and not the input device) actually determines the file format of the data. A paint program, for instance, uses a mouse for input but still generates a bitmap file. A scanner transmits bitmap information, but a sophisticated graphics arts program might convert it to vector form. With the exception of *paint* applications, most often the type of file format (bitmap or vector) matches the input device.

Scanners are perhaps the most popular input devices. Scanners are now available in several forms, offering a wide range of capabilities. Inexpensive scanners are typically monochrome, with between two and 256 shades of gray, and resolution varying from 60 to 400 dots per inch (dpi). In some, you can obtain grayscale information by selecting a lower resolution in dpi, in which case the software will dither the image, averaging a group of binary pixel values. Most of the monochrome scanners have a color bias, such as red-blindness or green-blindness, in that certain colors do not register when scanning a color original. Just about any bitmap, printer, or graphics metafile format will suffice for these images with the possible exception of MacPaint, which is highly limited in spatial resolution, depth, and image size.

For more money, you can get scanners with higher spatial resolution, greater depth per pixel, and color. Again, most of the bitmap, printer, or graphics metafile formats in this book will suffice for devices with up to 24-bit color. At the highest end of the scale, spatial resolution and depth increase further, and you also get colorimetric or photometric data. For these files, turn to formats like TIFF or PostScript that can carry the depth, resolution, and photometric and colorimetric data.

Facsimile is an increasingly popular means of scanning and reproducing graphics. Generally the data streams for such images are currently defined by CCITT specifications that include data compression. Certain file formats, like TIFF and PostScript, support these specifications internally and therefore make receiving fax data simpler. For fax transmission, many fax boards emulate common printers and therefore accept file formats such as Hewlett-Packard's PCL.

Video input is less commonly found, but is becoming increasingly popular for multimedia and other applications. Bitmap formats, such as Truevision's Targa, Amiga's IFF/ILBM, and CompuServe's GIF, are commonly used for today's multimedia applications. High-frame-rate multimedia applications are extremely demanding in terms of efficiency and compression. They tend to draw from the television industry for standards, and data-file or data-stream specifications are still evolving rapidly. Of the file formats discussed here, QuickTime, FLI/FLC, JPEG, and MPEG fall into this high-end category.

Output devices

Most output devices use bitmaps as well, with the notable exceptions of PostScript printers (which use both vector and bitmap data) and all plotters.

Dot-matrix printers, including laser printers, are the most common output device. These are intrinsically bitmap devices; however, if they offer built-in interpreters, such as PostScript or HPGL, as many now do, they might as well be considered intrinsically vector devices as well. Most printers have their own data format or an industry-standard format such as PCL. Printers without interpreters generally offer faster output and lower cost. Color printers run the range from simple color-ribbon dot-matrix to color ink-jet, to color laser printers and dye transfer. The high-end printers either employ their own formats, and therefore require custom drivers in the application, or they support color PostScript.

Plotters, like dot-matrix printers, generally require data in the manufacturer's own format. Many, however, have standardized on HPGL. Applications that generally output to plotters, such as CAD programs, can be expected to offer HPGL output reliably; a few might read HPGL files as well.

Platform & cross-platform considerations

Most file formats originated to work best with a particular platform. Some are explicitly intended for one platform, such as Sun rasterfiles. Some are implicitly biased, like Amiga's IFF/ILBM, but with an eye toward being a standard. Others, like TIFF, are deliberately designed for cross-platform use. Many file formats also originated for a specific application, such as MacPaint, PCX, or DXF and the platform that originally supported it.

Generally, these biases are not insurmountable by apt programmers. Nonetheless, users might end up relying on fragile schemes to surmount them. Macintosh files, for instance, might draw upon certain capabilities in the Macintosh system software, called resources. These resources are listed in the resource forks of Macintosh files. No equivalent forks are recognized under DOS on the PC, so a special header must be prefixed to the file on the PC if the resource data is to be retained. When the file returns to a Macintosh, software on the Macintosh might need to be aware of the header's existence.

The more common conversion problem is one of byte order, as discussed in chapter 1. Transmitting a file between, say, a PC and a UNIX workstation is not sufficient to "get it right," even if both support the given format. Each platform has a different natural byte order. The receiver might presume, because of the known platform bias of a format, that the bytes would be in a specific order, but it could not be certain unless the format was designed to communicate byte-order information.

Of the formats covered in this book, on PCs you will most commonly find PCX, TIFF, IFF, IMG, TGA, DXF, HPGL, PCL, PIC, CGM, FLI/FLC, and Windows formats. On Macintosh you will most commonly find MacPaint, PICT, TIFF, CGM, QuickTime RLE, and PostScript. On UNIX platforms: BMP, Sun rasterfile, XBM, XWD, Island Graphics Bitmap (TIFF), DXF, JPEG, MPEG, and UNIX Plot.

GIF, which is a data transmission format for CompuServe, is found on all platforms. TIFF is specifically designed for multiple platforms but appears more commonly in PCs and Macintoshes. HPGL and PCL output to peripheral ports is found everywhere printers and plotters are used, but the data is not always easily obtainable as a file. Because they are principally output device formats, readers for HPGL and PCL are less common than writers. PostScript is most commonly found on Macintoshes, but is increasingly supported on PCs and UNIX workstations.

## CHAPTER 4

PCX

Name	PCX
Image type	Bitmap (raster)
Intended use	Proprietary format for PC-based paint program, now quite public
Owner	Zsoft Corporation (404) 428-0008
Last version/ revision/ release date	1991
Platforms	PC
Supporting applications	Desktop publishing, graphics arts, video capture
Similarities	Somewhat like MacPaint in compression, but capable of far superior image quality
Overall assessment	Commonly supported, therefore good for exchange in the PC environment; reasonably efficient storage for paint-type images (i.e., images with large areas of constant tone); tricky to interpret because of the many possible variations.

Advantages

PCX is one of the oldest and therefore most widely supported bitmap formats for PCs. Current versions support 24-bit color, implemented either as a palette of up to 256 colors or as full, 24-bit RGB, with image sizes up to 64K × 64K pixels. Data are compressed through run-length encoding.

Disadvantages

The file format has no provisions for storing grayscale or color-correction tables; neither does it store CMYK- or HSI-model data, although some Zsoft programs allow you to adjust color values using HSI. Its run-length compression scheme can be inefficient, especially for scanned or video images. PCX files can use a variety of palette techniques due to the age and evolution of PCX; as a result, most readers cannot handle the full range of possible PCX implementations.

Variants

PCX is upgraded with new versions of Zsoft products; a code in the file header determines what version of Zsoft products the file supports. The variations, listed by header code, are given in Tables 4-1 and 4-2.

Zsoft products corresponding to PCX version numbers Table 4-1

Version number	Zsoft product and version
0	Version 2.5 of PC Paintbrush
2	Version 2.8 of PC Paintbrush with palette information
3	Version 2.8 of PC Paintbrush without palette information
4	PC Paintbrush for Windows (not the "plus" version)
5	Version 3.0 and higher of PC Paintbrush and PC Paintbrush IV Plus; also, PC Paintbrush Plus for Windows; Publisher's Paintbrush

Image characteristics corresponding to PCX version number Table 4-2

Version number	Image characteristics
0	Basic monochrome (2-color) or 4-color image
2	As above, plus 16-color images
5	As above, plus 256 colors from 24-bit palette; also full, 24-bit RGB color

These variations make more sense when you realize that, roughly speaking, they track the growth in graphics capability of the PC, from the CGA (Color Graphics Adapter) to the EGA (Enhanced Graphics Adapter) and VGA (Video Graphics Adapter), and finally, to the extended VGA and beyond.

The version number is not, however, a guide to how the image is encoded. A file with a version code of 5, for instance, might employ a palette or might not. If you are creating a PCX reader, the most reliable guideline to decoding comes from the bits-per-pixel and number-of-color-planes information in the header, as discussed later under *Keys to interpreting data*.

Overview of file structure

The PCX format comprises three parts: the file header, bitmap data, and (in later versions) a palette of up to 256 colors.

The file begins with a header of a fixed 128 bytes. It contains, in addition to the version number, resolution of the printed or scanned image (in dots per inch), dimensions (in pixels), bytes per scan line, bits per pixel, and the number of color planes. The header might also contain a palette, and a code indicating whether that palette is grayscale or color.

The heart of the file is bitmap data. Bitmap data are recorded in run-length compressed form similar to the Packbits compression scheme. The pixel values are generally one-byte pointers to locations in a palette.

If the version code is 5 and there is a single bit plane, there is a 256-color palette of RGB values, one byte for each primary (R, G, and B) at the end of the file.

Format details

The PCX format is relatively simple to write, but tricky to read unless the details of the encoded image (such as bit depth and palette) are already known. Accordingly, the following description focuses on the worst case: reading a PCX file of indeterminate characteristics and age. All numbers are in little-endian (Intel) format.

Header

The header is summarized by Table 4-3.

PCX file header Table 4-3

Start Byte	Size in Bytes	Contents	Interpretation
0	1	Zsoft flag	10 (0A hex) = Zsoft PCX file
1	1	Version no.	0 = PC Paintbrush 2.5 2 = " 2.8 with palette 3 = " 2.8 without palette 4 = " for Windows 5 = " 3.0 and up; also PC Paintbrush IV, IV Plus; Publisher's Paintbrush
2	1	Encoding	1 = PCX run-length encoding
3	1	Bits per pixel	Number of bits/pixel, each plane
4	8	Image dimensions	Image limits as: Xmin, Ymin, Xmax, Ymax in pixel units
12	2	Horiz. resolution	Dots/inch in *X*, when printed
14	2	Vert. resolution	Dots/inch in *Y*, when printed
16	48	Header palette	See palette discussion
64	1	Reserved	Reserved for Zsoft use; always 0
65	1	Planes	Number of color/grayscale planes
66	2	Bytes per line	Memory needed for one color plane of each horiz. line
68	2	Header palette interp.	1 = color or B&W 2 = grayscale
70	2	Video screen size, *X*	Number of pixels horiz. of video output −1
72	2	Video screen size, *Y*	Number of pixels vert. of video output −1
(74	54	blanks to end of header)	

- **Byte 0, Zsoft flag** Always decimal 10, hex 0A.

- **Byte 1, Version number** A somewhat unreliable guide to what the file contains; see the preceding discussion, "*Variations*."

- **Byte 2, Encoding** As of this writing, always 1. There is currently only one *encoding* (compression) method, the run-length scheme described below in "*Bitmap data*."

- **Byte 3, Bits per pixel** Actually, bits per pixel per plane. Might take the values 1, 2, 4, or 8.

- **Bytes 4–11, Image dimensions** The image dimensions are given as minimum and maximum limits, even though a single set of dimensions would suffice. Generally, the minimum limits are zero. All limits appear as 16-bit unsigned integers, in units of pixels, as noted. Image size in pixels can be computed by: XSIZE = Xmax–Xmin+1; YSIZE = Ymax–Ymin+1.

- **Bytes 12–15, Horizontal and vertical resolution in dots per inch** These two 16-bit numbers are somewhat extraneous. They play no part in defining the stored image; however, when combined with the image dimensions, they communicate the original size of a scanned image, or intended size of a printed image, in inches.

- **Bytes 16–63, Header palette** This field appears to be used only for files with a single bit plane, 16 or fewer colors, and a version code of 2 (see *Keys to interpreting data*, following). When used, the palette holds 16 "triples" of 1-byte palette values. See the following section for details.

- **Byte 65, Planes** PCX images can be a single plane or multiple color planes (see chapter 1). This header byte gives the number of planes and is critical to proper interpretation of the PCX file.

- **Byte 66, Bytes per line** Actually, bytes per line per plane—the number of bytes of memory required to store one plane of one scan line of the unpacked image; always an even number.

* **Byte 68, Header palette interpretation** 1 = color/monochrome; 2 = grayscale. Not used in Paintbrush IV or IV Plus.

* **Bytes 70–73, Video screen size, X and Y** Used only by IV and Paintbrush IV Plus; not essential, but possibly useful for communicating proper aspect ratio and thus avoiding squeeze-type distortion.

Keys to interpreting data

Because data can be recorded in several ways in a PCX file, there must be reliable indicators of those ways. As mentioned previously, the version number is not an adequate guide.

The most reliable guides are the bits per pixel (header byte 3) and the number of color planes (header byte 65). Table 4-4 shows how data should be interpreted according to these guides.

Interpretation of PCX data Table 4-4

Bits/pixel/plane	Number of planes	Interpretation
1	1	monochrome
1	2	4-color
1	3	8-color
1	4	16-color
2	1	4-color, CGA header palette*
2	4	16-color
4	1	16-color, EGA header palette*
8	1	256-color, palette at file's end
8	3	16.7M-color

*Note: In asterisked modes, the header palette is used unless the version code is 5 or greater, in which case the palette at the end of the file is used.

The number of planes tells whether a palette was used. More than one plane means "no palette." If a palette is used, a combination of version number and bits per pixel determines which of the several kinds of palettes supported by PCX is used.

Bitmap data

If no palette is used, the data are actual pixel values; otherwise, they are pointers to palette values. In the latter case, they give the offset (in 3-byte triplets; e.g., 1 = byte 3) from the start of whatever palette is used.

When data are actual pixel values, they are stored by scan line, by color plane. For instance, for three colors, red, green, and blue (RGB), the data are formatted:

(Line 0:) RRRRRR...GGGGGG...
BBBBBB... (Line 1:) RRRRRR...GGGGGG...BBBBBB...

If there are two planes, the colors are arbitrary. If there are three planes, the colors are RGB. When four color planes are used, they are usually the 1-bit planes of the IBM CGA/EGA standard: red, green, blue, and *intensity* (RGBI). The intensity bit simply gives a pixel a nominally higher brightness.

When data are pointers to a palette, they constitute a complete image plane; that is, they are not broken up into separate color planes. The data then are simply formatted as follows (where the *P* characters represent various pointer values):

(Line 0:) PPPPPPP (Line 1:) PPPPPPP...

The length of *P* depends on the pixel depth in bits/pixel/plane; for example, with a depth of four bits, *P* is half of a byte.

In all cases, there are coding breaks between scan lines. There are, however, no coding breaks between color planes within a scan line. There is also no delimiting symbol provided to mark the end of a scan line, although a scan line might or might not end with extra zeros. That is, there are no line numbers such as those shown here, and no null characters, spaces, carriage returns, linefeeds, or other characters between scan lines.

No matter what type of bitmap data is recorded, the same run-length compression scheme is used. The unpacking algorithm is as follows. (In the palette-based images, which are the kind most commonly used today, there is only one plane.)

Palettes

As indicated by Table 4-4 earlier, any PCX file that has more than one bit per pixel, yet has only one color plane, uses a palette. Unfortunately, the evolution of graphics adapters on the PC has resulted in three different palette implementations in PCX, and it requires careful examination to figure out which implementation is to be used. Files with a version code of 5 are the easiest to ascertain. If they have only one color plane, they use the 256-color "VGA" palette at the end of the file. Other palette-based files use the header palette, which has two possible implementations: EGA and CGA.

- **256-color, end-of-file "VGA" palette** The 256-color palette starts 768 bytes before the end of the file (EOF), and is preceded by a code of 12 decimal (0C hex). (768 = 256 × 1 byte for each of R, G, and B.) A pixel value of *n*, therefore, points to location EOF-768+3*n in the palette; the next three bytes contain the red, green, and blue values, respectively, for that pixel. However, because the VGA provides only 64 levels for R, G, and B, the palette values must be divided by four when reading a PCX file for VGA display.

- **16-color "EGA/VGA" header palette** The header palette, located at bytes 16–63, is organized into triples: 16 sets of three data bytes, one byte each for R, G, and B. In files created with (or for) an EGA, each primary color can take only four levels, so the 256-value range offered by each byte is broken up into four subordinate ranges. Each range corresponds to a level: 0–63 = level 0, 64–127 = level 1, 128–192 = level 2, and 193–254 = level 3.

- **"CGA" header palette** This palette is considered obsolete and is not used for files with a version code of 5 or higher. In this scheme, only the top-end bits of bytes 16 and 19 are needed (header offset 0 and 3).

- **Byte 16** The top nibble (four bits) of byte 16 provides a value between 0 and 15 called the background color. Background color is used as follows. The CGA supports two alternative "4-color" palettes. Header byte 19 determines which is used, as described in the following paragraph. The first—palette 0, or the "yellow" palette—is composed of background color plus green, red, and yellow (brown on some CGAs). The second—palette 1, or the "white" palette—is background, cyan, magenta, and white. The word background indicates that this color is variable; it can actually take on any of 16 values generated by the 4-bit IRGB code given in the top nibble of byte 16.

- **Byte 19** The top three bits of byte 19 give the variables *C*, *P*, and *I*. The *C* stands for color burst enable, where 0 = color and 1 = monochrome. The *P* stands for palette, where 0 = "yellow"' palette and 1 = "white" palette. And *I* stands for intensity, where 0 = dim and 1 = bright, a variation on the two alternative CGA palettes.

24-bit color

Some recent Zsoft products produce PCX files with full 24-bit color (no palette). These can be identified by a version code of 5 or higher, with eight bits/pixel/plane and three-bit planes.

References

Zsoft Corporation. *Technical Reference Manual*. 1991.

Rimmer, Steve. *Bit-Mapped Graphics*. 1990. Blue Ridge Summit, PA: Windcrest Books, an imprint of TAB BOOKS.

Wilton, Richard. *Programmer's Guide to PC & PS/2 Video Systems*. 1987. Redmond, WA: Microsoft Press.

## CHAPTER 5

MacPaint

Name	MacPaint (PNTG)
Image type	Binary bitmap
Intended use	Native format for Macintosh MacPaint
Owner	Apple Computer, Inc.
Last version/ revision/ release date	1989
Platforms	Macintosh, PC
Supporting applications	Most Mac-based applications, plus a number of PC applications including Pagemaker
Similarities	PackBits compressed data in PICT, TIFF
Overall assessment	A common format for Mac-based bitmap images, but very limited; reasonably compact for storage or transmission

Advantages

Widespread support on Macintosh; compact; simple to implement

Disadvantages

Limited to 1-bit black-and-white (delivers grayscale only through dithering); images come in one size only: 720 pixels high by 576 pixels across.

Variants

No variants exist. Occasionally, however, on non-Macintosh platforms, you might find it prefixed by a special header, and other extra data might be appended to the end. Known as a *MacBinary header*, this header contains Macintosh-specific data and is not specifically related to MacPaint files. It is optionally prefixed to files of any kind by *MacBinary-compatible* communications programs when the files are transmitted in binary mode. When a file is received by such a program on a Macintosh, the header is used to reconstruct a normal Mac file. On other platforms, the disposition of header data depends on the program. If the MacBinary II specification is implemented (July 87) and MacPaint Version 2.0 files are being used, there will also be extra, Macintosh-specific resource-fork data appended to the file.

Overview of file structure

On MacPaint files on the Macintosh, the data fork contains the essential bitmap data. The resource fork is empty in early MacPaint files. In Version 2.0 of MacPaint, two resources were added: PREC, the standard print record resource created by the print manager, and PREF, a preference resource describing the particular setup of MacPaint. (Macintosh files and files for certain UNIX and PC window environments have a *forked* data structure. Because this structure is familiar to programmers who use those environments and is unimportant to others, it is not discussed further in this book.)

When transferred to most other platforms, there is no fork structure, just data. As noted above, MacPaint files (sometimes abbreviated as PNTG or PNT files in literature) might begin with a 128-byte MacBinary header when found on other platforms.

MacPaint files begin with a series of patterns used by the MacPaint program for filling areas. These are not referenced by the image data, however. They are therefore of no value unless you are transferring the image to a paint program and wish to work with the same patterns while using that program.

The remainder of the file is simply run-length encoded bitmap-image data, one bit deep. The encoding algorithm is referred to as *packbits* and is employed by certain TIFF files, and (in modified form) by PCX.

Format details

MacBinary header

While not properly part of a MacPaint file, the MacBinary header, if present, is 128 bytes long and has the following structure. This header can be found on any ex-Macintosh file, including PICT (see chapter 26). Its presence is generally detected by the presence of zeros at offset locations 0 and 74 of the file. Byte 82 is also zero according to the MacBinary II specification, but can be nonzero in subsequent versions of MacBinary. Generally, bytes from offset 99 up can be ignored by readers and zeroed by writers. See Table 5-1.

MacBinary header Table 5-1

Offset	Length	Content and interpretation
00	1	"Version number," always 0.
01	1	Length of original MacPaint file name, which follows, up to 63 char.
02	63	Original file name in ASCII; valid only up to given length.
65	4	Macintosh file type code, PNTG, in ASCII.
69	4	Code denoting authoring application on Macintosh, in ASCII; MPNT if MacPaint.
73	1	8 finder flags: ignore if reading; set to 0 if writing.
74	1	Always 0.
75	4	File X,Y position in Mac window: ignore if reading; zero if writing.
79	2	Finder file window or folder ID: ignore if reading; zeros if writing.
81	1	"Protected" flag in low-order bit.
82	1	Always 0.

Table 5-1 **Continued**

Offset	Length	Content and interpretation
83	4	Length of data fork for Macintosh reconstruction of file.
87	4	Length of resource fork (zero).
91	4	Creation date in Motorola format.
95	4	Modification date in Motorola format.
		MacBinary II additions
99	2	Ignore if reading; zero if writing.
101	1	8 additional finder flags; ignore / zero.
116	4	Unpacked file length; used by some communications programs; ignore / zero.
120	2	Zero
122	1	Minimum MacBinary II version used by writing program; use 129.
123	1	Minimum MacBinary II version required of reading program.
124	2	CRC of previous 124 bytes; ignore / zero.

Note that Macintosh numbers larger than one byte are stored with the most-significant byte (MSB) first, a characteristic of the Macintosh's Motorola microprocessor. The most important such number in this format is the length of the data fork. This value must be properly set if the file is to be read by a Macintosh MacBinary-compatible program. The creation and modification dates in the header are also 4-byte numbers. They represent the number of seconds since midnight, January 1, 1904.

Version number

MacPaint data begin with a 4-byte version number. The default is 2, indicating that paint patterns follow. It is often set to 0, indicating that MacPaint's default paint patterns were used. However, because paint patterns are generally ignored, so is the version number.

Paint patterns

Paint Patterns begin at an offset of four bytes into the file. These patterns have no relation to the bitmap data, and are generally ignored or left blank. They might be useful for communicating a pattern palette if the image is being transferred between paint programs.

If you do choose to use them, they are simple to decode or encode. There are 38 patterns altogether; each one is 8 × 8 pixels (eight bytes, eight pixels each), uncompressed, with no delimiting bytes. They occupy 304 bytes, from offset 4 through offset 308. The 204 bytes between the paint patterns and the bitmap, which follows, should be filled with zeros.

Bitmap data

Bitmap data begin after the paint patterns, at an offset of 512 bytes into the file. The data are one bit deep (eight pixels per byte; 0 = white, 1 = black), and are divided up into pixel strips of varying length. The strip might consist of either a repeated, run-length encoded one-byte pattern, or a series of different 1-byte patterns. This byte-compression scheme is known as *PackBits* and is used in many other formats as well as in MacPaint. The first bit of the first byte in the encoded strip is a flag that determines which type of strip is being used.

For example, before encoding, the beginning of the bitmap might be as shown in Fig. 5-1 below:

Figure 5-1

```
Unpacked Data:     101010101010101010101010101000001111111111111111
Byte Boundaries:   |       |       |       |       |       |
                   1       2       3       4       5       6
```

Original pixel data.

Upon encoding, the first three bytes (a repeated pattern) would be the first data "*strip*," and would be run-length encoded into two bytes, as shown in Fig. 5-2.

Figure 5-2

```
Packed Data:           1111111010101010
Byte Boundaries:       |       |       |
                       1       2
Content of bytes:        Count   Pattern
```

Run-Length encoding in MacPaint.

In this example, the high-order bit of the first, or *count* byte, is set to 1. This signifies that a strip of identical 1-byte-long patterns is represented. In other words, data for this strip are run-length encoded. The 2s complement of this byte is the zero-based run-length count; that is, zero indicates a count of 1. The pattern to be repeated is given by the following *pattern* byte. Data must be repeated three or more times to be run-length encoded.

To signify the other kind of strip, a strip of different 1-byte-long patterns, the initial bit in the count byte is zero. The count byte then provides a zero-based count of how many pattern bytes follow (e.g., 0 indicates a count of 1).

In our example above, there are no further repeated 1-byte patterns—at least, none is repeated three times or more. The packed data would continue as follows:

If the ending pattern of all ones continued one more byte, PackBits would encode the data differently. There would be two additional strips, not one. The first would begin with a count byte of 00000000 and a data byte of 10100000, and the second with a count byte of 11111110 and a data byte of 11111111, run-length encoding the repeated data.

Using this scheme, a strip may not encode more than 129 bytes of bitmap data. Actually, strips never exceed 72 bytes, unpacked. (72 × 8 bits = 576 bits, the width of a single scan line in a true PNTG file.) When encoding a file using the PackBits algorithm, be sure to begin a new strip at the start of each scan line.

PICT users should note that this same basic scheme is also used for *PixData* in the Macintosh PICT format, in conjunction with the PackBitsRect and PackBitsRgn opcodes (see chapter 26). PixData, however, also includes a total count of all bytes in the bitmap, called *byteCount*.

References

"MacPaint Document Format." *Macintosh Technical Note #86*. Apple Computer Developer Technical Support.

Birse, Cameron, Guillermo Ortiz, and Jon Zap. "Things You Wanted To Know About _PackBits," *Macintosh Technical Note #171*. 1987, 1990. Apple Computer Developer Technical Support.

Apple Computer, Inc. *Inside Macintosh*. 1988. Reading, MA: Addison-Wesley Publishing Co.

CHAPTER 6

TIFF

Name	TIFF (Tag Image File Format)
Image type	Bitmap (raster)
Intended use	Data exchange for desktop publishing and related applications
Owner	Aldus Corporation. Supported by Aldus Developer's Desk, 411 First Ave. South, Seattle, WA 98104, (206) 628-6593. CompuServe: GO ALDSCV, Message Section #10. Applelink: Aldus Developer's Icon
Last version/ release date revision/	Revision 6.0, released June 3, 1992
Platforms	MacIntosh, PC, and Unix workstation platforms
Supporting applications	Desktop publishing, graphics arts
Similarities	GIF in use of tagged fields and LZW
Overall assessment	Useful for exchange between unrelated applications or platforms; enhanced by creation of "baseline" standard in revision 6.0. TIFF options offer potential for high-quality images, and for high-quality exchange between media, such as between paper and computer monitor.

Advantages

Among TIFF's chief advantages are its suitability for a wide range of applications and its independence of a computer's architecture, operating system, and graphics hardware. It is reasonably compact and handles black-and-white, grayscale, and color images well, allowing a user to adjust for the unique characteristics of a scanner, monitor, or printer. TIFF also resists obsolescence. As a result, TIFF can be one of the best choices of bitmap format for data exchange between media. TIFF allows color resolution up to 48 bits (a 16-bit field each for R, G, and B), either as full RGB color or in a 64K-color palette (see chapter 1 for a discussion of color-imaging techniques) TIFF also allows image data such as opacity or transparency, if desired. TIFF is well-documented, with much useful background about computer graphics in the specification. The specification is available through CompuServe (use GO ALDSVC) or AppleLink (use Aldus Developer's icon).

Disadvantages

The versatility of TIFF also creates some problems, in that the many varieties of "extended" TIFF make it necessary for TIFF creators and users to communicate about exactly what kind of extensions are in use, and how they are to be used.

As a data-exchange format between applications, TIFF has had one notable flaw. Vendors can register proprietary, undisclosed data-field formats with Aldus Developer's Desk. This feature has had the unfortunate effect of allowing some vendors to claim TIFF compatibility while actually maintaining a closed format. Compounding this flaw is the common failure of developers to fully or properly execute this complex file-format specification. Revision 6.0, however, specifies certain baseline capabilities for all TIFF 6.0 software, which should improve TIFF's value for inter-application exchange.

Variants

Two variants are defined in revision 6.0 of TIFF: *baseline* and *extended* TIFF. Within both of these variants are many optional capabilities. Furthermore, TIFF data vary according to photometric type and compression method.

The previous TIFF revision, 5.0, allowed four variants, defined by four photometric classes: TIFF-B for monochrome, TIFF-G for grayscale, TIFF-P for palette-based color, TIFF-R for RGB color, plus

TIFF-X for all classes. The TIFF 6.0 specification, released in June, 1992, encourages programmers to support a baseline level of capability instead, which roughly equates to TIFF-X. For practical purposes, this change mostly affects the development of TIFF readers. TIFF writers, such as driver software for a monochrome scanner, may be limited to a subset of the baseline; for example, grayscale data only.

In TIFF 6.0, capabilities beyond baseline are considered *extensions*. This is a sort of "all other" category that includes advanced color-handling features, such as CMYK and YCbCr images, and special compression schemes such as JPEG. The use of any of these features makes a TIFF reader or writer *extended*. The creator of extended TIFF software or data files should specify precisely which extensions are implemented. The number and complexity of these extensions puts discussions of all of them beyond the scope of this book. We instead provide brief summaries of the most important extensions.

Pixel data are stored in any of several compression formats. Compression formats are referred to by a code number, as follows:
(#1) No compression
(#2) CCITT Group 3 modified Huffman run-length encoding (see chapter 2)
(#3) Facsimile-compatible CCITT Group 3
(#4) Facsimile-compatible CCITT Group 4
(#5) LZW (Lempel-Ziv & Welch) compression (see chapters 2 and 6)
(#32773) Packbits compression (originally developed for MacIntoshes; see chapter 5 for a description).

Only numbers 1, 2, and 32773 must be processed by baseline TIFF readers. The other compression formats fall into the extended category.

As mentioned previously, *private* data fields are allowed under TIFF, although they must be registered with Aldus Developer's Desk. Private data values are also allowed within certain data fields; for example, private codes are allowed within the data compression field, including:
(#32766) 2-bit NeXT RLE
(#32771) Word-aligned version of type 2
(#32809) 4-bit Thunderscan delta and RLE
(#32900) Pixar "picio"' RLE
(#32901) Silicon Graphics RLE.

Note: Compression applies only to pixel data, not to other data. For a general discussion of compression schemes, refer to chapter 2.

Baseline capabilities

All TIFF 6.0 readers and writers must *handle* the baseline set of data fields. How data fields are handled differs according to whether they are required or optional. For example, there is a *required* field that specifies how the image data are compressed; all TIFF readers must respond correctly to this field if it is present in the data file, or must assume a default of 1, signifying uncompressed data, if it is not. There are also *optional* baseline fields, which the TIFF reader may ignore or process, but which must not cause the reader to terminate or malfunction. For instance, an "extra samples" field may indicate the presence of an additional pixel component, such as opacity. A baseline TIFF reader must continue to process the basic image data, even if it opts not to process the opacity information.

Overview of file structure

The TIFF format has a three-level hierarchy. From highest to lowest, the levels are:

1. A file header
2. One or more directories called IFDs, containing codes and their data, or pointers to the data
3. Data.

The highest level in the hierarchy, the file header, contains only three entries: a code indicating the byte order (least-to-most significant, "little-endian," or "big-endian"); a code number identifying the file as TIFF; and a pointer to the Image File Directory (IFD).

The IFD provides an indefinitely long series of 12-byte entries. Each begins with a numeric code, called a *tag*, that specifies what type of data follow. The IFD entry also contains either the data or, more commonly, a pointer (offset) to the data. Accordingly, in this chapter we will refer to such IFD entries as *tagged pointers*. The IFD entry also gives the type of data (e.g., 1-byte integer) and how many data values there are—the *count*. This approach allows data fields (a) to be located anywhere in the file, (b) to be of nearly any length, and (c) to contain a wide variety of information. One pointer, for instance, might point to a 768-byte field of color-palette data; another might point to a 64-byte grayscale-correction curve for a scanner. There may be several related images in a file, in which case there may be several IFDs. The last entry in an IFD points to any subsequent IFD.

Each pointer has a tag, a code number that identifies what kind of data field is being pointed to. The TIFF specification lists all the official, non-proprietary tag numbers, gives them useful names (such as SamplesPerPixel, decimal code number 277), describes what data the pointer identifies, and tells how the data are organized.

Format details

The file header

The TIFF file begins with a header that occupies the first eight bytes, and has the structure shown in Table 6-1.

Table 6-1 **TIFF file header**

Offset	Length	Description
0	2	Byte order: MM or II
2	2	"Version number": always 42
4	4	Pointer to first IFD

* **Byte order field** The first header entry is in byte counts 0 and 1. It is a two-letter ASCII record containing the codes for the letters *MM* or *II* (4D4D hex or 4949 hex, respectively). *MM* stands for Motorola architecture, signifying that bytes comprising 16- or 32-bit numbers are stored in the order of most-to-least significant. *II* denotes a file created in the Intel architecture, where bytes are stored in the opposite order. By reading this record, a Mac or UNIX workstation-based file reader can detect a file created on a PC, or vice versa, and interpret it properly.

- **Version field** The second header entry, a 2-byte number termed *Version* in the specification, actually has nothing to do with any version number or with the revision number (currently 5.0) of the specification. It is always the decimal number 42 (2A hex), chosen for its "deep philosophical significance" according to earlier TIFF specifications! (We suspect it is a reference to Douglas Adam's *The Hitchhiker's Guide to The Galaxy*, wherein the answer to "life, the universe, and everything" is found to be 42.) For practical purposes, this code identifies the file as a TIFF file.

- **First IFD offset pointer** The final header entry is a 4-byte pointer to the location of the first Image File Directory (IFD). The order of bytes here, as elsewhere, depends on the *MM* or *II* designation in the first entry. As this is the first pointer we have encountered, let us note that all TIFF pointers refer to a byte-count offset from the start of the file. For example, this pointer begins at an offset of 4, the fifth byte in the file.

Image file directories

Most likely, the next structure in the file after the header will be the first (or only) IFD, but not necessarily. From here on, everything is found by following pointers. So, to locate the first IFD, use the header's pointer.

An IFD consists of 12-byte entries, typically tagged pointers. The structure of an IFD and its entries is diagrammed in Table 6-2.

Table 6-2

TIFF IFD structure

Offset	Length	Description
0	2	Entry count
2	12	Entry 0
14	12	Entry 1
•	•	•
•	•	•
•	•	•
$n*12 + 2$	12	Entry *n*
$n*12 + 4$	4	Pointer to subsequent IFD, if any, or 0000

- **Entry count field** Since there may be any number of IFD entries, the first field in an IFD is a 2-byte count of the number of entries.
- **IFD entries** IFD entries are 12-byte fields, beginning with the tag code that specifies what type of data are present. The entries are ordered numerically within the IFD, according to the tag numbers, a feature that helps TIFF readers quickly determine what fields are and are not present.
- **Terminating field** The last entry in an IFD will be four bytes of zero, unless there is more than one IFD. (Creators of TIFF writers, take note: You must terminate your last or only IFD in this way.) Most applications will have only one IFD. There may be more if an application supports special features like multiple-image copies at different resolutions, image masks, or image planes. If there is more than one IFD, the last entry of the preceding IFD contains a 4-byte pointer to the next one.

IFD entries

Each entry in an IFD has the four-part structure diagrammed in Table 6-3.

Table 6-3 **TIFF IFD entry structure**

Offset	Length	Description
0	2	Tag
2	2	Type of data
4	4	Count field
8	4	Data pointer or data field

*Offset is within pointer

- **Tag** The first two bytes are the tag, which, if public, may be looked up in the specification. Public tags are those above 254 (FE hex); they currently end at 532 (214 hex). Private tags may be assigned to individual companies to cover proprietary program features or features of little interest to the general user. These codes are assigned by the TIFF administrator (Aldus Developer's Desk), in blocks of five.

* **Type code** The next two bytes are a code indicating what type of data are in the field being pointed to. Note that some tags allow a variety of types, so TIFF readers should always check this code. TIFF 6.0 supports a variety of data types; the codes, the data types, and their names are as follows:

1 = 1-byte integer	(type BYTE)
2 = 1-byte integer, ASCII	(type ASCII)
3 = 2-byte integer	(type SHORT)
4 = 4-byte integer	(type LONG)
5 = 8-byte fraction	(type RATIONAL) (4-byte numerator followed by 4-byte denominator)
6 = 1-byte signed integer	(type SBYTE)
7 = 1 byte of anything	(type UNDEFINED) (e.g., a pointer to a complex data structure)
8 = 2-byte signed integer	(type SSHORT)
9 = 4-byte signed long	(type SLONG)
10 = 8-byte signed fraction	(type SRATIONAL) (SLONG numerator, SLONG denominator)
11 = 4-byte floating point	(type FLOAT) (IEEE format)
12 = 8-byte floating point	(type DOUBLE) (double-precision IEEE)

It is likely that additional types will be added in the future, so TIFF readers should not treat unrecognized types as an error.

ASCII data fields must be terminated with one or more bytes of zero (null characters), unless the data are stored directly in the IFD (see *Data pointer* or *Data field*, following). The null character is counted in the count field of the pointer (see *Count field*, following). If a padding null character is used to make the field an even number of bytes in length (helpful for some computer architectures), the padding is not counted. If there are multiple strings (not recommended) they should be separated by a single null character.

* **Count field** This 4-byte field specifies the number of values in the data field, not the number of bytes. The number of bytes can be computed by multiplying the count by the number of bytes in the data type. For example, a count of 64 with a data type of LONG means there will be 256 bytes. (The count was referred to as the *length* in earlier revisions of TIFF.)

✻ **Data pointer or data field** The final four bytes are usually a pointer to the start of a data field. Sometimes, however, this field contains not a pointer, but the actual data. To determine which data the field contains, compute the data length in bytes as described immediately above. If there are four bytes of data or less, as computed by the product of *count* and the byte count indicated by *type*, then the field contains data. Otherwise, the field is a pointer (the offset in bytes from the start of the file to the start of the data field).

Baseline TIFF

The baseline specification mostly affects TIFF readers, which should:

- Process all *required* data fields for all types of images: bi-level (monochrome), grayscale, palette color, and RGB color images.
- Process data according to TIFF's byte-order field, which specifies that data are in either big-endian or little-endian byte order (see chapter 1). This allows easy transport across UNIX, PC, and Macintosh platforms.
- Ignore or implement baseline options or private fields. For example, a TIFF reader may deal with the optional grayscale correction field in any way its creator sees fit. It may also ignore the field, but it cannot fail to read the data file simply because the field is present.
- Likewise, ignore or accept new field types, above and beyond the currently specified types—short, byte, ASCII, long, and rational.
- Insert a correct default value if the TIFF writer does not provide it, where the TIFF specification defines a default value.
- Process at least the first image if multiple images are contained within a single TIFF file. Subsequent images are typically lower-resolution versions included for convenience in displaying small *thumbnail sketches*). TIFF editors, if they change the first image, must likewise change or delete the subsequent images.

TIFF writers should:

- Provide all *required* baseline data fields for the type of image: bi-level (monochrome), grayscale, palette color, and RGB color images.
- Use only data values that are defined in the specification. Undefined values, such as a zero offset, may not be used to communicate special information.
- Ensure that every block of data is referenced only once. TIFF works by means of pointers to blocks of data. If there is more than one reference, an application that updates data in a TIFF file may not be able to find and correct the second reference. Subsequently, other readers might attempt to employ the now-incorrect second reference.

Baseline fields

TIFF readers must be able to process all the fields in Table 6-4, or must assume the specified default if the field is not present, regardless of the image-type expected. TIFF writers must include all fields required for the type of image data written, except where the default value is desired.

Table 6-4

Required fields and their defaults. X indicates field must be written in TIFF file for given image type.

Field name	Default	Bi-level	Grayscale	Palette	RGB
ImageWidth	none	X	X	X	X
ImageLength	none	X	X	X	X
BitsPerSample	1		X	X	X
ColorMap	none			X	
Compression	1	X	X	X	X
PhotometricInterp.	none	X	X	X	X
StripOffsets	none	X	X	X	X
RowsPerStrip	(2**32)-1	X	X	X	X
StripByteCounts	none	X	X	X	X

Table 6-4 **Continued**

Field name	**Default**	**Bi-level**	**Grayscale**	**Palette**	**RGB**
XResolution	none	X	X	X	X
YResolution	none	X	X	X	X
ResolutionUnit	2	X	X	X	X

Any of the fields below may appear in a baseline TIFF 6.0 file. TIFF readers must not fail to read a TIFF file in which these fields are present, although they may ignore the particular data of these fields.
Artist
CellLength
CellWidth
Copyright
DateTime
ExtraSamples
FillOrder
FreeByteCounts
GrayResponseCurve
GrayResponseUnit
HostComputer
ImageDescription
Make
MaxSampleValue
MinSampleValue
Model
NewSubfileType
Orientation
PlanarConfiguration
Software
SubfileType
Thresholding

Following are descriptions of the baseline fields. Fields that baseline TIFF readers must support are marked with an asterisk (*) *after* the field name. Note that readers must handle both byte orders (*MM* and *II*) and supply defaults. Furthermore, readers must not fail if optional tag codes, multiple images, or unknown tag codes are encountered—they must read at least one image.

Each of the following descriptions of tag fields follows the structure shown in Table 6-3. Tag names are used, but remember that the names are strictly for documentation purposes; the IFD actually uses numeric codes. The codes are given in both decimal and hexadecimal form (in parentheses), followed by data type, length, and range of data value. Also remember that tags with four or fewer data bytes provide the data in the tag field itself; otherwise a pointer to the data (an offset in the TIFF file) is provided.

A special note for data fields defined as unsigned integers (types BYTE, SHORT, or LONG): The TIFF 6.0 specification allows TIFF files to use any of these data types (BYTE, SHORT, or LONG) for any unsigned integer field. For some data fields, such as BitsPerSample, this choice will affect whether the data field of an IFD entry contains the data itself (which must fit in four bytes when given in the IFD) or a pointer (offset) to the data. In the following descriptions, we presume that the specified type is used when we indicate that the data field is a pointer or actual data. The reader should be aware that this may vary under TIFF 6.0.

✳ Artist

CODE	TYPE	COUNT	DATA
315 (13B H)	ASCII	Unlimited	ASCII name or pointer to one

The *Artist* field points to a null-terminated ASCII string, designed to be used for the name of the author of the image.

✳ BitsPerSample*

CODE	TYPE	COUNT	DATA
258 (102 H)	SHORT	SamplesPerPixel	Pixel depth

This tag gives or points to pixel depth; e.g,. for grayscale, SamplesPerPixel will be 1, and there will therefore be a single SHORT value for *BitsPerSample*. In this case, the value for BitsPerSample will fit in the 4-byte tag field. For instance, for 8-bit grayscale, the tag field will contain the number 8. For 24-bit RGB color, the COUNT is 3; if the data type is SHORT, six bytes are required (more than can fit in the tag). The tag would therefore contain, not the three 2-byte values for R, G, and B themselves, but a pointer to them. Alternatively, since TIFF 6.0 allows writers to depart from the specification for data fields using unsigned integers, the TIFF writer could use a data type of BYTE, and therefore fit the data into the IFD. The default is 1.

✳ CellLength

CODE	TYPE	COUNT	DATA
265 (109 H)	SHORT	1	Number of rows in dithering grid

CellLength, together with *CellWidth*, define a dithering or halftoning grid. This grid is used when monochrome (bi-level) data is being used to represent grayscale images, a condition indicated by Thresholding =2. The grid allows devices capable of grayscale output to convert the bi-level image to true grayscale.

✳ CellWidth

CODE	TYPE	COUNT	DATA
264 (108 H)	SHORT	1	Number of columns in dithering grid

See *CellLength*.

✳ ColorMap*

CODE	TYPE	COUNT	DATA
320 (140 H)	SHORT	3*(2**BitsPerSample)	Pointer to three tables

This tag provides a pointer to three consecutively stored tables, one each for R, G, and B, together comprising a color palette. Each table has 2**BitsPerSample* entries of length SHORT (2 bytes). When a *ColorMap* is used, pixel values are indices to this palette and begin at 0; for example, a pixel value of 8 points to the ninth entry in each table.

✳ Compression*

CODE	TYPE	COUNT	DATA
259 (103 H)	SHORT	1	Integer code, 1, 2, or 32773

The *Compression* data field contains a single code number (1, 2, or 32773 in baseline TIFF) which indicates whether the pixel data are compressed, and if so, how. A code of 1 indicates no compression; 2 indicates CCITT Group 3 1-dimensional modified Huffmann run-length encoding covered under *Compression Code 2 (Huffman)* in this chapter; 32773 indicates PackBits compression (see chapter 5). Code 5, LZW compression, is part of Extended TIFF in revision 6.0. Note that pixel data may be of any length, and if stored uncompressed it is tightly packed, ignoring byte boundaries within a given scan line. Scan lines begin and end on byte boundaries, filled with zeros at the end if necessary for word- or double-word-aligned systems. Also note that CCITT Group 3 compression is for bi-level images only, where *0= white* and *1= black* (unless the tag *PhotometricInterpretation* is present with a value of 1). The Compression default is 1.

✳ Copyright

CODE	TYPE	COUNT	DATA
33432 (8298 H)	ASCII	number of characters+1	Null-terminated string

The *Copyright* tag points to a string identifying the copyright holder for the image.

✳ DateTime

CODE	TYPE	COUNT	DATA
306 (132 H)	ASCII	20	Pointer to ASCII timestamp

The *DateTime* field points to a null-terminated ASCII timestamp in the form *YYYY:MM:DD HH:MM:SS*, using 24-hour time. The length of 20 characters includes the space between fields and the terminating null character.

✳ ExtraSamples

CODE	TYPE	COUNT	DATA
338 (152H)	SHORT	# extra image planes	Plane interpretation code

When *SamplesPerPixel* exceeds the minimum necessary for the type of image (e.g., exceeds 1 for grayscale), this indicates that additional image planes exist, defining a matte, for example. *ExtraSamples* provides the interpretation of these additional data; there is one code per additional plane. A code of 0 indicates an image plane of unspecified purpose. A code of 1 indicates opacity values; if the image is RGB, the RGB data in the file are already scaled according to the opacity value for each pixel. A code of 2 indicates transparency values; if the image is RGB, the RGB data are not already scaled according to the transparency value.

✳ FillOrder

CODE	TYPE	COUNT	DATA
266 (10A H)	SHORT	1	1 or 2, indicating bit order

This tag is used when bi-level images are stored with data in *reverse* order in a byte: pixel 0 in the low order position, proceeding to pixel 7 in the low-order position. *FillOrder* should be used only when necessary, and only for bi-level data (*BitsPerSample* = 1) where Compression = 1 or 2. This tag is generally omitted, allowing the default of 1 to be assumed.

✳ GrayResponseCurve

CODE	TYPE	COUNT	DATA
291 (123 H)	SHORT	2**BitsPerSample	Pointer to table

The data for *GrayResponseCurve* are a pointer to a grayscale correction table, 2**BitsPerSample long, that records *gamma* of the image source as described in chapter 1. As with the *ColorResponseCurve* tag (see Extended TIFF, following), each pixel value is an index to the table. Because such photometric curves historically have been recorded in a fractional range, the 2-byte values in the table have implicit units, given by the tag *GrayResponseUnit*, of from 10^{-1} to 10^{-5}. *GrayResponseUnit* records the exponent, unsigned.

✳ GrayResponseUnit

CODE	TYPE	COUNT	DATA
290 (122 H)	SHORT	1	Integer, 1–5

The single integer recorded in the *GrayResponseUnit* tag is an unsigned value, used as a negative exponent of ten to yield the *GrayResponseCurve's* photometric unit; that is, 1= 0.1, 2= 0.01, 3= 0.001, 4= 0.0001, and 5= 0.00001.

✻ HostComputer

CODE	TYPE	COUNT	DATA
316 (13C H)	ASCII	unlimited	Name or pointer to one

HostComputer is a null-terminated string identifying hardware and operating system used to create the image. Not a substitute for byte 0 of header.

✻ ImageDescription

CODE	TYPE	COUNT	DATA
270 (10E H)	ASCII	unlimited	Description or pointer to one

ImageDescription is a null-terminated ASCII identifier; for example, person's name on photograph.

✻ ImageLength*

CODE	TYPE	COUNT	DATA
257 (101 H)	SHORT or LONG	1	# of scan lines

The single SHORT or LONG value contained in the *ImageLength* tag gives the vertical dimension (height) of the image in terms of scan lines.

✻ ImageWidth*

CODE	TYPE	COUNT	DATA
256 (100 H)	SHORT or LONG	1	# of pixels across

The single SHORT or LONG value contained in the *ImageWidth* tag gives the horizontal dimension (width) of the image in terms of pixels.

⁜ Make

CODE	TYPE	COUNT	DATA
271 (10F H)	ASCII	unlimited	vendor name or pointer to one

Make is a null-terminated ASCII string giving name of the vendor of the image-digitizing equipment (e.g., the scanner) used to create the data file. See also *Model* and *Software*.

⁜ MaxSampleValue

CODE	TYPE	COUNT	DATA
281	SHORT	SamplesPerPixel	Maximum pixel component value(s)

The *MaxSampleValue* tag provides the maximum value of each pixel component; for example, the three maximum values for the R, G, and B component of a color image. It is provided only as a convenient statistic; it saves the trouble of searching the data file and should not be used to change the image presentation. The default data value is 2**(*BitsPerSample*)–1.

⁜ MinSampleValue

CODE	TYPE	COUNT	DATA
280	SHORT	SamplesPerPixel	Minimum pixel component value(s)

MinSampleValue, but provides the minimum value of each pixel component. The default data value is 0.

⁜ Model

CODE	TYPE	COUNT	DATA
272 (110 H)	ASCII	Unlimited	Model name or pointer to one

Model is a null-terminated ASCII string giving model of equipment, generally the image digitizer; typically used together with *Make* and *Software*.

⁂ NewSubfileType

CODE	TYPE	COUNT	DATA
254 (FE H)	LONG	1	32 flag bits

When the *NewSubfileType* tag field appears in an IFD, it indicates that the image belonging to the IFD is somehow related to an image in another IFD. No means are provided, however, to indicate what the related IFD is. The 4-byte data field, representing (potentially) 32 flags, tells how the images are related. Only flag bits 0–2 are currently used. If bit 0 is set, this image is a lower-resolution version of another image. If bit 1 is set, the image is one page of a multi-page image set. If bit 2 is set, the image is a 1-bit deep, single-plane mask to be logically ANDed with pixels of another image. The tag *PhotometricInterpretation* must also be present and must be set to 4 for this action to take place. A resolution higher than that of the masked image is suggested for such masks.

⁂ Orientation

CODE	TYPE	COUNT	DATA
274 (112 H)	SHORT	1	Code indicating orientation of rows & columns

The *Orientation* tag provides an optional code that indicates which directions the scan lines of an image run, by telling where they start. The table below indicates which edges of the image correspond to the first row and column. For example, a code of 5 indicates that the image is stored sideways and inverted, in that the scan lines (rows) run vertically beginning at the left edge and proceed from the top to the bottom. Baseline TIFF readers need support only the default orientation code of 1.

	code value						
	1	2	3	4	5	6	7
first row	top	top	bottom	bottom	left	right	right
first column	left	right	right	left	top	top	bottom

✳ PhotometricInterpretation*

CODE	TYPE	COUNT	DATA
262 (106 H)	SHORT	1	integer code, 0–4

The integer code contained in the *PhotometricInterpretation* tag field determines whether the image is monochrome or color, and how the light levels are represented. A code of 0 or 1 indicates a monochrome or grayscale image. A code of 0 indicates a pixel value of 0= white and a value of 2***BitsPerSample*–1= black; 1 indicates the opposite. A code of 2 indicates RGB color, where 0= minimum and 2***BitsPerSample*–1= maximum. A code of 3 means a palette (*ColorMap*) is used. A code of 4 means the image is a logical mask (see *NewSubfileType*).

✳ PlanarConfiguration

CODE	TYPE	COUNT	DATA
284 (11C H)	SHORT	1	integer code, 1 or 2

The *PlanarConfiguration* tag, used only when *SamplesPerPixel* > 1, determines whether data are stored in a single image plane (code = 1) or in color planes (code = 2). The latter is not recommended and therefore not required for baseline TIFF readers. Note that TIFF pixel data are stored in strips of a user-determined length (*StripByteCounts*), pointed to by a *StripOffsets* tag field in the IFD. For RGB data in a single-image plane, values appear in the sequence RGBRGB.... in each strip. For RGB in color-plane form, each strip contains red, green, or blue values, repeating in that sequence. The strips are those listed in the table indicated by *StripOffsets*. The default is 1 (see *RowsPerStrip*, *StripByteCounts*, and *StripOffsets*).

✳ ResolutionUnit*

CODE	TYPE	COUNT	DATA
296 (128 H)	SHORT	1	integer code, 1–3

The integer code in the *ResolutionUnit* tag field denotes the unit of measurement used in conjunction with XResolution and YResolution.

A code of 1 indicates that no units apply; the reading application will scale the image as it chooses. A code of 2 indicates inches (the default), and a code of 3 indicates centimeters.

✳ RowsPerStrip*

CODE	TYPE	COUNT	DATA
278 (216 H)	SHORT or LONG	1	integer value

TIFF images are divided into strips of any given length (*StripByteCounts*); *RowsPerStrip* specifies how many rows are recorded per strip. Associated tags are *ImageLength* and tags prefixed by *Strip*, and *Tile* if the tiling extension is supported. In the absence of this tag field, the entire image is assumed to be recorded in a single strip. The latter approach is not advised, however, because of buffer problems and decompression issues. The specification advises that strips should be about 8K bytes long (see *ImageLength* and *StripByteCounts*). For maximum compatibility with older TIFF readers, use the LONG form of *RowsPerStrip*. New readers must handle both data types.

✳ SamplesPerPixel

CODE	TYPE	COUNT	DATA
277 (115H)	SHORT	1	integer value

The data value contained in the *SamplesPerPixel* tag field determines the number of color planes. for example, 1 for monochrome or grayscale images and 3 for RGB, except where *ExtraSamples* is used (see chapter 1 for a discussion of color planes and image planes). The default is 1.

✳ Software

CODE	TYPE	COUNT	DATA
305 (131 H)	ASCII	unlimited	software name or pointer to one

Software is a null-terminated ASCII string giving name and version of authoring application.

✻ StripByteCounts*

CODE	TYPE	COUNT	DATA
279 (117 H)	SHORT or LONG	(see text)	pointer to table of strip lengths

The *StripByteCounts* tag field is provided as an aid to buffering data during decompression, and is required for baseline TIFF. It provides a pointer to a table that stores the post-compression length of each individual strip in bytes. There is one entry per strip. If the *PlanarConfiguration* is 1, meaning a single image plane is used, the number of entries in the table is (*ImageLength*+*RowsPerStrip*–1)/*RowsPerStrip*, using integer calculations. If *PlanarConfiguration* is 2 (not recommended), then given *n* samples per image (given by *SamplesPerImage*) there are *n* strips, and *n* *StripByteCounts*.

✻ StripOffsets*

CODE	TYPE	COUNT	DATA
273 (111 H)	SHORT or LONG	(see text)	pointer to table of offsets

The *StripOffsets* tag field is essential to locating bitmap data. It provides a pointer to a table that stores the offset location of each individual strip. The table contains one entry per strip. The number of entries is computed the same way as for *StripByteCounts*. Use of the LONG data type is recommended for maximum compatibility with earlier TIFF readers.

✻ Thresholding

CODE	TYPE	COUNT	DATA
263 (107 H)	SHORT	1	code specifying dithering

When bi-level image files are actually dithered (i.e., halftoned) representations of grayscale images, the *Thresholding* tag may be used to allow the reading application to reconstruct a true grayscale image. A code of 1 indicates no dithering; 2 indicates an ordered dither; 3 indicates a randomized dither. The default is 1.

✳ XResolution*

CODE	TYPE	COUNT	DATA
282 (11A H)	RATIONAL	1	pixels/unit width measure

The *XResolution* tag field describes the original width resolution of the image in units given by *ResolutionUnit*. Multiplied by the *ImageWidth*, it provides the physical width of the original image.

✳ YResolution*

CODE	TYPE	COUNT	DATA
283 (11B H)	RATIONAL	1	pixels/unit length

The *YResolution* tag field describes the original length resolution of the image in units given by *ResolutionUnit*. Multiplied by the *ImageLength*, it provides the physical length of the original image.

Extended TIFF

TIFF 6.0 defines numerous extensions. These allow TIFF to offer the following general capabilities:

- Alternative compression schemes: CCITT, LZW (with and without differencing), and JPEG
- Alternative color-representation schemes: CMYK, YCbCr, and CIE L*a*b*
- Image-quality enhancements: Halftone "hinting," RGB colorimetry
- Special image effects: Alpha data (matting, masks and overlays), tiled images
- Document storage and retrieval aids: document and page names, page numbers, and position on the page.

These extensions take the form of additional tags and/or special codes for baseline tags. For instance, JPEG compression is signified by a Compression tag with a code of 6, and requires a number of additional tags.

Note: A full description of all these extensions and how they are to be used is beyond the scope of this book; you should obtain the TIFF specification in order to implement them. The TIFF specification also provides valuable background and references that you should read before attempting to employ these extensions. The descriptions that follow provide only brief introductions to the purposes and implementations of certain popular extensions.

Colorimetry

To allow color images to be reproduced accurately on a variety of media, TIFF provides extensions for colorimetric data reference to the 1931 CIE color standard (see chapter 1 and reference 3 at end of this chapter for more information on the CIE standard).

WhitePoint

CODE	TYPE	COUNT	DATA
318 (13E H)	RATIONAL	2	pointer to CIE coordinates

The *WhitePoint* tag provides the *x,y* coordinates necessary to specify a point on the CIE chromaticity diagram, in this case the white point of the image source. This point defines true (CIE) color of the image source when it is generating a data output of R=G=B. There is no default.

ReferenceBlackWhite

CODE	TYPE	COUNT	DATA
532 (214 H)	RATIONAL	6	3 pairs of black/white endpoints

The *ReferenceBlackWhite* tag implements a concept called *headroom*, used in film, print, and video. In effect, it defines the normal endpoints of the range of intensity for each color component, endpoints generally chosen to produce primary colors that match industry standards. The data pairs provide a *ReferenceBlack* (the first value) and *ReferenceWhite* (the second value), for each primary of R, G, and B, or YCbCr. The tag is not used in any other color- or monochrome-representation scheme. The defaults are 0 for *ReferenceBlack* and 2***BitsPerSample*–1 for white. For details of its implementation, see the TIFF 6.0 specification.

⁕ PrimaryChromaticities

CODE	TYPE	COUNT	DATA
319 (13F H)	RATIONAL	6	pointer to CIE coordinates

The *PrimaryChromaticities* tag points to a table of six values that define the true color of the three primaries of the image source. For each primary, the color corresponds to that primary having a value of *ReferenceWhite*, while the other two are set to *ReferenceBlack*. There are three pairs of *x,y* coordinates, one for each primary. There are no defaults under TIFF 6.0.

⁕ TransferFunction (formerly ColorResponseCurve)

CODE	TYPE	COUNT	DATA
301 (12D H)	SHORT	1* or 3*(2**BitsPerSample)	pointer to correction tables

The *TransferFunction* tag provides a pointer to either one (for grayscale) or three (for color) consecutive tables of correction factors. This is TIFF's way of recording the gamma of the image source, as discussed in chapter 1. Each table is 2***BitsPerSample* long (one correction value for each possible sample value), composed of SHORT (two-byte) data. When a *TransferFunction* tag is used, the values given by pixel RGB data are actually indices to the R, G, and B color-correction tables. If a palette is used, using the tag *ColorMap*, gamma correction may be included in the *ColorMap*. The range of values contained in the correction tables is 0–65535, where 0 is the minimum intensity and 65535 is the maximum for a 16-bit *BitsPerSample*. The range may be less if the *TransferRange* tag is used. The default content of these tables defines the NTSC standard gamma for monitors, which is 2.2. Also, see the WhitePoint and

PrimaryChromaticities tag fields. The implementation can be complex; refer to the TIFF 6.0 specification for details.

✻ TransferRange

CODE	TYPE	COUNT	DATA
342 (1156 H)	SHORT	6	3 pairs of black/white endpoints

The *TransferRange* tag allows RGB or YCbCr images (e.g., Kodak PhotoYCC) to provide high- or low-intensity components beyond the range normally allowed by the *BitsPerSample*, in conjunction with *TransferFunction*. It does so by providing three pairs of black/white endpoints, used for offsetting and re-scaling the three component output values read from the *TransferFunction* correction tables. The process is complex; refer to the TIFF 6.0 specification for details.

CMYK color representation

CMYK color representation is discussed in chapter 1. TIFF CMYK is an extension specifically for printing applications, and is not currently recommended for other applications. *SamplesPerPixel* should be 4 (unless there are *ExtraSamples*); *BitsPerSample* is recommended to be 8,8,8,8; and *PhotometricInterpretation* should be 5, indicating CMYK. Higher pixel component values specify a larger spot of that component color, and therefore a generally darker pixel.

Optional CMYK tags for this extension include the following.

- *InkSet*, code 332, a single SHORT value that defaults to 1 for CMYK and is set to 2 for any other set of inks.
- *NumberOfInks*, code 334, a single SHORT value that defaults to 4, and is otherwise set to the number of inks.
- *InkNames*, code 333, a set of null-terminated ASCII strings describing the names of the inks.
- *DotRange*, code 336, generally a single pair of BYTE or SHORT values that define component values corresponding to 0% spot coverage and 100% spot coverage.

➢ *TargetPrinter*, code 337, an ASCII string identifying a type, make, and/or model of printer for which the CMYK data are appropriate.

YCbCr color representation

TIFF 6.0 allows color image representation in the form of YCbCr. This form of color is more suitable for digital video than is RGB, in part because it is better adapted to lossy compression by *subsampling*. In YCbCr, there is one intensity value, *Y*, and two chroma values, *Cb* and *Cr*, that comprise the image data in a TIFF file. In various combinations and with certain additional coefficients, these data can be used to reconstruct the requisite pixels of red, green, and blue. Or, vice versa, they can be used to construct YCbCr from an RGB image. YCbCr requires *PhotometricInterpretation* = 6, *SamplesPerPixel* = 3, *BitsPerSample* = 8,8,8, Compression = 1, 5, or 6, and a non-default value for *ReferenceBlackWhite*. Translation between YCbCr and RGB requires three special tags, plus colorimetry tags as needed.

✳ YCbCrCoefficients

CODE	TYPE	COUNT	DATA
529 (211 H)	RATIONAL	3	pointer to three conversion coefficients

The *YCbCrCoefficients* pointed to by this tag give the proportional representation of each primary (red, green, and blue) in the intensity value, Y, and so allow RGB to be reconstructed. The coefficients, in order, are termed LumaRed, LumaGreen, and LumaBlue. The reconstruction of RGB is as follows: Red = Cr*(2-2*LumaRed)+Y; Blue = Cb*(2–2*LumaBlue)+Y; Green = (Y–LumaBlue*Blue–LumaRed*R)/LumaGreen. A scale factor may also be needed, because codes commonly exceed the ReferenceWhiteBlack limits in video; see the TIFF 6.0 specification for more details. Defaults are LumaRed = 299/1000, LumaGreen = 587/1000, and LumaBlue = 114/1000.

⁕ YCbCrSubSampling

CODE	TYPE	COUNT	DATA
530 (212 H)	SHORT	2	subsampling factors

The *YCbCrSubSampling* tag allows the use of compression by *subsampling* color; that is, by effectively reducing the resolution of the two chroma planes, Cb and Cr, that are *overlaid* upon the higher-resolution luminance plane to provide an image acceptable to the eye. "Plane" is used figuratively; *PlanarConfiguration* should still be *1*. The data field of this tag holds two factors, the first (called *SubsampleHoriz*) determining the horizontal chroma resolution, and the second (SubsampleVert) determining the vertical resolution. The factors are 1, 2, or 4, signifying equal resolution, half-resolution, or quarter-resolution (compared to luminance resolution) respectively. Both subsampling factors default to 2.

The YCbCr tag also determines the data structure of the TIFF file. Assuming *PlanarConfiguration* =1, there will be n luminance (*Y*) values preceding each pair of *Cb* and *Cr* values, where *n* is the product of *SubsampleHoriz* and *SubsampleVert*. These *n* values represent a matrix (*data unit*) of pixels *SubsampleHoriz* wide by *SubsampleVert* high. Subsequent matrices are taken in a normal left-to-right, top-to-bottom scanning pattern.

⁕ YCbCrPositioning

CODE	TYPE	COUNT	DATA
531 (213 H)	SHORT	1	positioning code

The *overlaying* of chroma planes upon the luminance plane may be done in two ways, indicated by the code in this tag. A code of 1 indicates that the chroma pixels are offset from luminance pixels horizontally by ½ *SubsampleHoriz*, less half a column, and vertically by ½ *SubsampleVert*, less half a row. A code of 2 indicates the planes are exactly aligned at the 0th row and column. In both cases, chroma samples overlay a matrix of 1, 2, 4, 8, or 16 luminance pixels, depending upon *YCbCrSubsampling*. (Note: "overlay" and "pixel" are used figuratively here, since chrominance and luminance must be combined algebraically, not simply summed, in order to form a full pixel.)

CIE L*a*b* color

TIFF 6.0 provides for use of CIE L*a*b*, a standard that permits very accurate exchange of color images between media. This CIE color space comprises three orthogonal axes: one luminance (L*), and two chrominance (a* for red-to-green and b* for yellow-to-blue). They are relative to a CIE tristimulus white point *XnYnZn* defined as "100% diffuse reflectance at all visible wavelengths." The use of L*a*b* in a TIFF file is indicated by a PhotometricInterpretation code of 8. *BitsPerSample* should also be 8; a* and b* data should be considered signed values. As with RGB and YCbCr, these data are stored as three samples per pixel, exclusive of *ExtraSamples*.

For all but very low light conditions, the following equations relate L*a*b* to CIE *XYZ* tristimulus values and RGB data as follows:

$L^* = 116(Y/Yn)^{1/3}-16$	$Y = 0.2990R + 0.5870G + 0.1140B$	$Yn = Y$ at white point
$a^* = 500[(X/Xn)^{1/3}-(Y/Yn)^{1/3}]$	$X = 0.6070R + 0.1740G + 0.2000B$	$Xn = X$ at white point Y and Yn as above
$b^* = 200[(Y/Yn)^{1/3}-(Z/Zn)^{1/3}]$	$Z = 0.0000B + 0.0660G + 1.1110B$	$Zn = Z$ at white point Y and Yn as above

The TIFF 6.0 specification provides many valuable additional notes about the use of CIE L*a*b*.

Enhanced halftoning (grayscale and color)

TIFF 6.0 provides a *HalftoneHints* extension field, designed to enhance the quality of printed continuous-tone images, especially where monochrome (e.g., laser) printing is used to preview color images. In printing, tone variations are accomplished by varying dot size. Such variations are not continuous; they occur in discrete increments. This is especially noticeable in laser printing or other dot-matrix, low-resolution technologies, and is of particular importance at the endpoints of the tonal range where the last step is to solid black (or other primary color) or solid white. Variations in pixel value that fall within these last steps will be lost.

For a fixed dot pitch (dots per inch, or dpi) of the printer, a fixed image resolution, and a given halftone pattern, there is no cure other than to either nonlinearly map intensity values to more suitable values (e.g., use *GrayResponseCurve* or *TransferFunction*), or select the visually most important range of grayscale values and linearly map it to the range between the lightest halftone value achievable, and the darkest. The *HalftoneHints* field helps TIFF readers do the latter.

✻ HalftoneHints

CODE	TYPE	COUNT	DATA
321 (141 H)	SHORT	2	lightest and darkest values

The data field of *HalftoneHints* gives two values: the lightest pixel value (maximum intensity) to be accommodated by the halftone process, and the darkest, in that order. Areas of the image with pixel values below and above these limits will be represented by the halftone shades at those limits. Variations above the limits will be lost. See the TIFF 6.0 specification for valuable background information on the use of this tag, especially with color images.

Compression summary

TIFF 6.0 defines two types of compression as Baseline, signified by compression codes 2 and 32773. All others are considered extensions. Type 2 is an RLE compression, described below. Type 32773 (PackBits) is described in chapter 5, with the discussion of the MacPaint format. The only difference between MacPaint and TIFF is that TIFF allows variable-image dimensions; uncompressed bytes per row is therefore (ImageWidth+7)/8. Implementing types 3 and 4 should be done in consultation with a CCITT document (reference 2 at the end of this chapter), and with reference to a TIFF Class F document, available from the same sources that provide TIFF specifications. Type 5, LZW, is now considered an extended field, in recognition of the need for licensing with that format. It was commonly implemented under revision 5.0 of TIFF, and is so documented here.

Type 6 is new as of revision 6.0 of TIFF, and implements one of the JPEG compression variants. See chapter 17 for a discussion of JPEG compression in general; the details of the TIFF JPEG implementation are extensive enough to preclude their discussion here.

Compression code 2: CCITT Group 3, 1-dimensional modified Huffman run-length encoding

Refer to chapter 2 for a synopsis of Huffman run-length encoding. TIFF's compression code 2 implementation is specific to 1-bit monochrome (black-and-white) images and, as such, encodes data as alternating runs of black or white pixels. TIFF uses two different families of codes for black and for white runs. When the tag *PhotometricInterpretation* has a value of 2, data encoded with white codes in this scheme should be interpreted as black, and vice versa.

TIFF's Huffman compression table is pre-established, as given in Table 6-5. The black and the white family each comprise three sets of codes:

- *Terminating codes* for run lengths from 0 to 63, in increments of 1; there are different codes for black and for white in this range.
- *Make-up codes* for run lengths from 64 to 1728, in increments of 64; there are different codes for black and for white in this range.
- *Additional make-up codes* for run lengths from 1729 to 2560, also in increments of 64; the codes for black and for white are the same in this range.

A run of any length, from 0 to 2563, can therefore be assembled from a make-up code followed by a terminating code. Runs in excess of this length use one or more of 2560 codes, followed by a make-up code and a terminating code. A single terminating code must end all runs.

All encoded scan lines begin with a white run, set to zero if the line actually begins with black. All scan lines begin on a byte boundary; fill bits are used at the end of a line, if necessary, to make this so. There is no special encoding for the end of a line; line lengths are determined by TIFF's *ImageWidth* tag field. Errors in transmission or copying can be fatal, since failure to decode exactly *ImageWidth* pixels for each line is considered an unrecoverable error.

Table 6-5 **TIFF encoding table for compression = 2**

Run Length	White Code	Black Code
0	00110101	0000110111
1	000111	010
2	0111	11
3	1000	10
4	1011	011
5	1100	0011
6	1110	0010
7	1111	00011
8	10011	000101
9	10100	000100
10	00111	0000100
11	01000	0000101
12	001000	0000111
13	000011	00000100
14	110100	00000111
15	110101	000011000
16	101010	0000010111
17	101011	0000011000
18	0100111	0000001000
19	0001100	00001100111
20	0001000	00001101000
21	0010111	00001101100
22	0000011	00000110111
23	0000100	00000101000

24	0101000	00000010111
25	0101011	00000011000
26	0010011	000011001010
27	0100100	000011001011
28	0011000	000011001100
29	00000010	000011001101
30	00000011	000001101000
31	00011010	000001101001
32	00011011	000001101010
33	00010010	000001101011
34	00010011	000011010010
35	00010100	000011010011
36	00010101	000011010100
37	00010110	000011010101
38	00010111	000011010110
39	00101000	000011010111
40	00101001	000001101100
41	00101010	000001101101
42	00101011	000011011010
43	00101100	000011011011
44	00101101	000001010100
45	00000100	000001010101
46	00000101	000001010110
47	00001010	000001010111
48	00001011	000001100100
49	01010010	000001100101
50	01010011	000001010010
51	01010100	000001010011
52	01010101	000000100100
53	00100100	000000110111
54	00100101	000000111000
55	01011000	000000100111

Table 6-5 **Continued**

Run Length	White Code	Black Code
56	01011001	000000101000
57	01011010	000001011000
58	01011011	000001011001
59	01001010	000000101011
60	01001011	000000101100
61	00110010	000001011010
62	00110011	000001100110
63	00110100	000001100111
64	11011	0000001111
128	10010	000011001000
192	010111	000011001001
256	0110111	000001011011
320	00110110	000000110011
384	00110111	000000110100
448	01100100	000000110101
512	01100101	0000001101100
576	01101000	0000001101101
640	01100111	0000001001010
704	011001100	0000001001011
768	011001101	0000001001100
832	011010010	0000001001101
896	011010011	0000001110010
960	011010100	0000001110011
1024	011010101	0000001110100
1088	011010110	0000001110101
1152	011010111	0000001110110
1216	011011000	0000001110111
1280	011011001	0000001010010
1344	011011010	0000001010011
1408	011011011	0000001010100

1472	010011000	0000001010101
1536	010011001	0000001011010
1600	010011010	0000001011011
1664	011000	0000001100100
1728	010011011	0000001100101
1792	00000001000	(black codes identical to white)
1856	00000001100	•
1920	00000001101	•
1984	000000010010	•
2048	000000010011	
2112	000000010100	
2176	000000010101	
2240	000000010110	
2304	000000010111	
2368	000000011100	
2432	000000011101	
2496	000000011110	
2560	000000011111	

Compression code 5: LZW compression

Refer to chapter 2 for a synopsis of LZW compression. Note that software patents may apply to your implementation. The LZW compression scheme used by TIFF is the same as that employed by GIF when GIF compresses 8-bit data (code size = 8 in GIF terminology). See chapter 7 for details on the GIF LZW implementation. The similarities include Clear code, End of Information code, size and structure of the code table, and code lengths.

In both TIFF and 8-bit GIF, the code table begins with entries #0–255, which simply contain the values 0–255, respectively; it skips two codes for Clear (#256) and EndOfInformation (#257), and then continues up to and including entry #4094. The Clear code resets the table to the original 256 codes. Stored codes are never shorter than nine bits nor longer than 12.

Unlike GIF, TIFF's LZW compression operates only on 8-bit data. To obtain 8-bit original data, TIFF disregards pixel boundaries; that is, two 4-bit pixels are combined, or one 16-bit pixel is split. Note also that TIFF LZW compression is applied to each strip, independently, regardless of *PlanarConfiguration*.

The basic encoding algorithm is as follows:
Clear table & write Clear code
Clear string buffer (String), test string buffer (Test), byte buffer (Byte)
For each byte in original data,

```
        {
        read value into Byte
        concatenate String+Byte into Test
        Is content of Test in table?
        If yes, append Byte to String.
        If no, write code for String, add table entry for Test,
        and make String = Byte
        }
```

Write code for String, then End Of Information code.

The basic decoding loop is:
Read new compression code (Newcode).
If Newcode = End Of Information code (EOI), quit.
If Newcode = Clear Code,

```
        {
        Initialize table.
        Read next compression code into Newcode (quit if EOI).
        Look up Newcode in table and write corresponding value.
        Copy Newcode into previous code (Prevcode).
        }
```

If Newcode is in the table (and not Clear or EOI)

```
        {
        Write value corresponding to Newcode.
        Add an entry to the table for the concatenation of
the value for Prevcode and the first byte of the value for Newcode.
        Copy Newcode into Prevcode.
        }
```

If Newcode is not in the table (and not Clear or EOI)

{
Concatenate and write: value for Prevcode + first byte of that same value.
Add an entry to the table for the above value.
Copy Newcode into Prevcode.
}

Note that both the compressor and decompressor must handle varying code length. The compressor should transmit only as many bits as required for the code, starting from a minimum of nine bits. The decompressor must automatically adjust code lengths to match. It begins by using nine-bit codes, switches to 10 bits once table entry *#511* is stored, and so forth.

✳ Predictor

CODE	TYPE	COUNT	DATA
317 (13D H)	SHORT	1	integer code, 1 or 0

Predictor may be used for LZW compression (compression code 5). A code of 1 (the default) signifies that no prediction scheme was used before coding. A value of 2 indicates use of horizontal differencing: pixel values are the difference between one pixel and the next, not absolute values. For RGB files, regardless of *PlanarConfiguration*, differences are done within a primary color, not across colors.

⇨ References

Aldus Corporation Developer's Desk. *TIFF• Revision 6.0, Final.* June 3, 1992.

International Telegraph and Telephone Consultative Committee (CCITT). *Terminal Equipment and Protocols for Telematic Services*, *Vol. VII, Fascicle VII.3*, pages 16–31 and 40–48, respectively, for Group 3 and Group 4 facsimile. 1985. Geneva.

Commission Internationale de l'Eclarage. *CIE Colorimetry: Official Recommendations of the International Commission on Illumination, Publication 15-2.* 1986.

## CHAPTER 7

GIF

Name	GIF (Graphics Interchange Format)
Image type	Bitmap (raster)
Intended use	On-line transmission of graphics data across CompuServe network
Owner	CompuServe Incorporated
Last version/ revision/ release date	GIF89a, 31 July 1990
Platforms	Most personal computers and many UNIX workstations
Supporting applications	Not a primary format for any application, but many applications can convert to or from GIF
Similarities	PCX image size and color depth; more like TIFF in structure
Overall assessment	Excellent for cross-platform exchange, good for storage, reasonably straightforward to implement although LZW compression adds complexity

Advantages

GIF provides enough information, and organizes it well enough, that widely differing input and output devices can easily exchange images. Because of the popularity of the CompuServe network, GIF is also supported on numerous platforms. CompuServe increases its popularity by distributing the format specification freely. GIF supports 24-bit color, implemented as a palette of up to 256 colors, and image sizes up to 64K × 64K pixels. GIF features include LZW compression, the sequencing or overlay of multiple images, interlaced screen painting, and text overlays.

Disadvantages

The current version of GIF can have no more than 256 24-bit colors. It has no provisions for storing grayscale or color-correction data; neither does it store CMYK- or HSI-model data.

Variants

GIF does not have a variety of distinct modes, as do some formats like TIFF or PCX. Nonetheless, GIF can vary in many ways. Some variations and options include:

- Multiple images
- Bits per pixel
- Palette size and colors
- Dimensions (in pixels) of the *logical* screen (an image plane encompassing all subsequent images)
- Aspect ratio of the logical screen
- Dimensions and position of images within the logical screen
- Existence, size, and placement of overlaying text
- Sequencing of images—delayed, user-prompted, interleaved transition, or restoration of previous image
- Application extensions—creator-assigned, unofficial codes indicating that the data are intended for a specific application.

There are also variations between the earlier GIF spec and the current one, of which there have been two: one in 1987, 87a, and one in 1989, 89a. New implementations should use the most recent one, which is described here.

Overview of file structure

To understand GIF, bear in mind that it is designed primarily as a transmission format for a data stream, rather than as a storage format for a file. In other words, it has a sequential organization unlike many other storage formats, like TIFF, which commonly use random organization. This sequential nature has little practical effect on the image, except in the special and rare case of multiple images transmitted and displayed sequentially. As you study GIF, however, it might be useful to visualize multiple color images appearing sequentially on a single screen.

GIF has five principal components that appear in a fixed order. All components are made up of one or more blocks. Each block is distinguished by an identifying code, or tag, in the first byte. The sequence of components is: the header block; the logical screen descriptor block; an optional "global" color-table block (palette); blocks of image data or special-purpose blocks; and the trailer block, a terminating code.

The contents of these components are as follows:

- The header is a single block that identifies the data stream as GIF, and indicates the earliest-version GIF decoder (87a or 89a) required to properly interpret the data that follow.
- The logical screen descriptor block defines the size, aspect ratio, and color depth of an image plane that encompasses the image or images that follow. It is analogous to the monitor screen on which the images originated. It also indicates whether a global color table follows.
- The global color table, if present, constitutes a palette of 24-bit RGB triplets, one byte per primary. This is a default palette, used if subsequent images do not come with their own *local* palettes.
- Subsequent data appear as either *graphic* or *special-purpose* blocks. Graphic blocks typically contain the bitmap image or images; they might, alternatively, contain overlaying text.

Special-purpose blocks contain either a special application code or a nonprinting comment.

When the data are for an image, as is most often the case, three component blocks appear in sequence: the image descriptor, denoting the dimensions and palette of the image and its position on the logical screen; an optional *local* color table (a palette for this image only); and LZW-compressed bitmap data. The bitmap data are divided into contiguous *sub-blocks* of up to 256 bytes. The data might include special *clear codes* used by the LZW algorithm.

For multiple images, this sequence is repeated. When special image sequencing or overlaying is to be done, images are preceded by a *graphic rendering block* that details the process. Finally, the trailer block is simply one byte containing the number 3B (hex), indicating the end of the data stream.

Note that it is possible for a GIF data stream in a file to contain no bitmap data at all. When this occurs, its purpose is generally to transmit a global color table, serving as a palette for subsequent data streams that have no palettes of their own.

Format details

The CompuServe GIF specification is sufficiently clear, so we simply reproduced it in Fig. 7-1, by permission of CompuServe Incorporated.

Figure 7-1

GRAPHICS INTERCHANGE FORMAT(sm)

Version 89a

(c)1987,1988,1989,1990

Copyright

CompuServe Incorporated

Columbus, Ohio

Figure 7-1 *Continued*

CompuServe Incorporated
Graphics Interchange Format

Document Date : 31 July 1990
Programming Reference

Cover Sheet for the GIF89a Specification

DEFERRED CLEAR CODE IN LZW COMPRESSION

There has been confusion about where clear codes can be found in the data stream. As the specification says, they may appear at anytime. There is not a requirement to send a clear code when the string table is full.

It is the encoder's decision as to when the table should be cleared. When the table is full, the encoder can chose to use the table as is, making no changes to it until the encoder chooses to clear it. The encoder during this time sends out codes that are of the maximum Code Size.

As we can see from the above, when the decoder's table is full, it must not change the table until a clear code is received. The Code Size is that of the maximum Code Size. Processing other than this is done normally.

Because of a large base of decoders that do not handle the decompression in this manner, we ask developers of GIF encoding software to NOT implement this feature until at least January 1991 and later if they see that their particular market is not ready for it. This will give developers of GIF decoding software time to implement this feature and to get it into the hands of their clients before the decoders start "breaking" on the new GIF's. It is not required that encoders change their software to take advantage of the deferred clear code, but it is for decoders.

APPLICATION EXTENSION BLOCK - APPLICATION IDENTIFIER

There will be a Courtesy Directory file located on CompuServe in the PICS forum. This directory will contain Application Identifiers for Application Extension Blocks that have been used by developers of GIF applications. This file is intended to help keep developers that wish to create Application Extension Blocks from using the same Application Identifiers. This is not an official directory; it is for voluntary participation only and does not guarantee that someone will not use the same identifier.

E-Mail can be sent to Larry Wood (forum manager of PICS) indicating the request for inclusion in this file with an identifier.

Table of Contents

1. Disclaimer.

The information provided herein is subject to change without notice. In no event will CompuServe Incorporated be liable for damages, including any loss of revenue, loss of profits or other incidental or consequential damages arising out of the use or inability to use the information; CompuServe Incorporated makes no claim as to the suitability of the information.

2 Foreword.

This document defines the Graphics Interchange Format(sm). The specification given here defines version 89a, which is an extension of version 87a.

The Graphics Interchange Format(sm) as specified here should be considered complete; any deviation from it should be considered invalid, including but not limited to, the use of reserved or undefined fields within control or data blocks, the inclusion of extraneous data within or between blocks, the use of

Figure 7-1 *Continued*

methods or algorithms not specifically listed as part of the format, etc. In general, any and all deviations, extensions or modifications not specified in this document should be considered to be in violation of the format and should be avoided.

3. Licensing.

The Graphics Interchange Format(c) is the copyright property of CompuServe Incorporated. Only CompuServe Incorporated is authorized to define, redefine, enhance, alter, modify or change in any way the definition of the format.

CompuServe Incorporated hereby grants a limited, non-exclusive, royalty-free license for the use of the Graphics Interchange Format(sm) in computer software; computer software utilizing GIF(sm) must acknowledge ownership of the Graphics Interchange Format and its Service Mark by CompuServe Incorporated, in User and Technical Documentation. Computer software utilizing GIF, which is distributed or may be distributed without User or Technical Documentation must display to the screen or printer a message acknowledging ownership of the Graphics Interchange Format and the Service Mark by CompuServe Incorporated; in this case, the acknowledgment may be displayed in an opening screen or leading banner, or a closing screen or trailing banner. A message such as the following may be used:

"The Graphics Interchange Format(c) is the Copyright property of CompuServe Incorporated. GIF(sm) is a Service Mark property of CompuServe Incorporated."

For further information, please contact :

CompuServe Incorporated
Graphics Technology Department
5000 Arlington Center Boulevard
Columbus, Ohio 43220
U. S. A.

CompuServe Incorporated maintains a mailing list with all those individuals and organizations who wish to receive copies of this document when it is corrected or revised. This service is offered free of charge; please provide us with your mailing address.

4. About the Document.

This document describes in detail the definition of the Graphics Interchange Format. This document is intended as a programming reference; it is recommended that the entire document be read carefully before programming, because of the interdependence of the various parts. There is an individual section for each of the Format blocks. Within each section, the sub-section labeled Required Version refers to the version number that an encoder will have to use if the corresponding block is used in the Data Stream. Within each section, a diagram describes the individual fields in the block; the diagrams are drawn vertically; top bytes in the diagram appear first in the Data Stream. Bits within a byte are drawn most significant on the left end. Multi-byte numeric fields are ordered Least Significant Byte first. Numeric constants are represented as Hexadecimal numbers, preceded by "0x". Bit fields within a byte are described in order from most significant bits to least significant bits.

5. General Description.

The Graphics Interchange Format(sm) defines a protocol intended for the on-line transmission and interchange of raster graphic data in a way that is independent of the hardware used in their creation or display.

The Graphics Interchange Format is defined in terms of blocks and sub-blocks which contain relevant parameters and data used in the reproduction of a graphic. A GIF Data Stream is a sequence of protocol blocks and sub-blocks representing a collection of graphics. In general, the graphics in a Data Stream are assumed to be related to some degree, and to share some control information; it is recommended that encoders attempt to group together related graphics in order to minimize hardware changes during processing and to minimize control information overhead. For the same reason, unrelated graphics or graphics which require resetting hardware parameters should be encoded separately to the extent possible.

A Data Stream may originate locally, as when read from a file, or it may originate remotely, as when transmitted over a data communications line. The Format is defined with the assumption that an error-free Transport Level Protocol is used for communications; the Format makes no provisions for error-detection and error-correction.

The GIF Data Stream must be interpreted in context, that is, the application program must rely on information external to the Data Stream to invoke the decoder process.

6. Version Numbers.

The version number in the Header of a Data Stream is intended to identify the minimum set of capabilities required of a decoder in order to fully process the Data Stream. An encoder should use the earliest possible version number that includes all the blocks used in the Data Stream. Within each block section in this document, there is an entry labeled Required Version which specifies the earliest version number that includes the corresponding block. The encoder should make every attempt to use the earliest version number covering all the blocks in the Data Stream; the unnecessary use of later version numbers will hinder processing by some decoders.

7. The Encoder.

The Encoder is the program used to create a GIF Data Stream. From raster data and other information, the encoder produces the necessary control and data blocks needed for reproducing the original graphics.

Figure 7-1 *Continued*

The encoder has the following primary responsibilities.

- Include in the Data Stream all the necessary information to reproduce the graphics.

- Insure that a Data Stream is labeled with the earliest possible Version Number that will cover the definition of all the blocks in it; this is to ensure that the largest number of decoders can process the Data Stream.

- Ensure encoding of the graphics in such a way that the decoding process is optimized. Avoid redundant information as much as possible.

- To the extent possible, avoid grouping graphics which might require resetting hardware parameters during the decoding process.

- Set to zero (off) each of the bits of each and every field designated as reserved. Note that some fields in the Logical Screen Descriptor and the Image Descriptor were reserved under Version 87a, but are used under version 89a.

8. The Decoder.

The Decoder is the program used to process a GIF Data Stream. It processes the Data Stream sequentially, parsing the various blocks and sub-blocks, using the control information to set hardware and process parameters and interpreting the data to render the graphics.

The decoder has the following primary responsibilities.

- Process each graphic in the Data Stream in sequence, without delays other than those specified in the control information.

- Set its hardware parameters to fit, as closely as possible, the control information contained in the Data Stream.

9. Compliance.

An encoder or a decoder is said to comply with a given version of the Graphics Interchange Format if and only if it fully conforms with and correctly implements the definition of the standard associated with that version. An encoder or a decoder may be compliant with a given version number and not compliant with some subsequent version.

10. About Recommendations.

Each block section in this document contains an entry labeled Recommendation; this section lists a set of recommendations intended to guide and organize the use of the particular blocks. Such recommendations are geared towards making the functions of encoders and decoders more efficient, as well as making optimal use of the communications bandwidth. It is advised that these recommendations be followed.

11. About Color Tables.

The GIF format utilizes color tables to render raster-based graphics. A color table can have one of two different scopes: global or local. A Global Color Table is used by all those graphics in the Data Stream which do not have a Local Color Table associated with them. The scope of the Global Color Table is the entire Data Stream. A Local Color Table is always associated with the graphic that immediately follows it; the scope of a Local Color Table is limited to that single graphic. A Local Color Table supersedes a Global Color Table, that is, if a Data Stream contains a Global Color Table, and an image has a Local Color Table associated with it, the decoder must save the Global Color Table, use the Local Color Table to render the image, and then restore the Global Color Table. Both types of color tables are optional, making it possible for a Data Stream to contain numerous graphics without a color table at all. For this reason, it is recommended that the decoder save the last Global Color Table used until another Global Color Table is encountered. In this way, a Data Stream which does not contain either a Global Color Table or a Local Color Table may be processed using the last Global Color Table saved. If a Global Color Table from a previous Stream is used, that table becomes the Global Color Table of the present Stream. This is intended to reduce the overhead incurred by color tables. In particular, it is recommended that an encoder use only one Global Color Table if all the images in related Data Streams can be rendered with the same table. If no color table is available at all, the decoder is free to use a system color table or a table of its own. In that case, the decoder may use a color table with as many colors as its hardware is able to support; it is recommended that such a table have black and white as its first two entries, so that monochrome images can be rendered adequately.

The Definition of the GIF Format allows for a Data Stream to contain only the Header, the Logical Screen Descriptor, a Global Color Table and the GIF Trailer. Such a Data Stream would be used to load a decoder with a Global Color Table, in preparation for subsequent Data Streams without a color table at all.

12. Blocks, Extensions and Scope.

Blocks can be classified into three groups : Control, Graphic-Rendering and Special Purpose. Control blocks, such as the Header, the Logical Screen Descriptor, the Graphic Control Extension and the Trailer, contain information used to control the process of the Data Stream or information used in setting hardware parameters. Graphic-Rendering blocks such as the Image Descriptor and the Plain Text Extension contain information and data used to render a graphic on the display device. Special Purpose blocks such as the Comment Extension and the Application Extension are neither used to control the process of the Data Stream nor do they contain information or data used to render a graphic on the display device. With the exception of the Logical Screen Descriptor and the Global Color Table, whose scope is the entire Data Stream, all other Control blocks have a limited scope, restricted to the Graphic-Rendering block that follows them. Special Purpose blocks do not delimit the scope of any Control blocks; Special Purpose blocks are transparent to the decoding process. Graphic-Rendering blocks and extensions

Figure 7-1 *Continued*

are used as scope delimiters for Control blocks and extensions. The labels used to identify labeled blocks fall into three ranges : 0x00-0x7F (0-127) are the Graphic Rendering blocks, excluding the Trailer (0x3B); 0x80-0xF9 (128-249) are the Control blocks; 0xFA-0xFF (250-255) are the Special Purpose blocks. These ranges are defined so that decoders can handle block scope by appropriately identifying block labels, even when the block itself cannot be processed.

13. Block Sizes.

The Block Size field in a block, counts the number of bytes remaining in the block, not counting the Block Size field itself, and not counting the Block Terminator, if one is to follow. Blocks other than Data Blocks are intended to be of fixed length; the Block Size field is provided in order to facilitate skipping them, not to allow their size to change in the future. Data blocks and sub-blocks are of variable length to accommodate the amount of data.

14. Using GIF as an embedded protocol.

As an embedded protocol, GIF may be part of larger application protocols, within which GIF is used to render graphics. In such a case, the application protocol could define a block within which the GIF Data Stream would be contained. The application program would then invoke a GIF decoder upon encountering a block of type GIF. This approach is recommended in favor of using Application Extensions, which become overhead for all other applications that do not process them. Because a GIF Data Stream must be processed in context, the application must rely on some means of identifying the GIF Data Stream outside of the Stream itself.

15. Data Sub-blocks.

a. Description. Data Sub-blocks are units containing data. They do not have a label, these blocks are processed in the context of control blocks, wherever data blocks are specified in the format. The first byte of the Data sub-block indicates the number of data bytes to follow. A data sub-block may contain from 0 to 255 data bytes. The size of the block does not account for the size byte itself, therefore, the empty sub-block is one whose size field contains 0x00.

b. Required Version. 87a.

c. Syntax.

```
      7 6 5 4 3 2 1 0                           Field Name      Type
     +---------------+
   0 |               |                          Block Size      Byte
     +---------------+
   1 |               |
     +-             -+
   2 |               |
     +-             -+
   3 |               |
     +-             -+
     |               |                          Data Values     Byte
```

```
     +-               -+
up   |                 |
     +-    .  .  .    -+
to   |                 |
     +-               -+
     |                 |
     +-               -+
255  |                 |
     +-----------------+
```

i) Block Size - Number of bytes in the Data Sub-block; the size must be within 0 and 255 bytes, inclusive.

ii) Data Values - Any 8-bit value. There must be exactly as many Data Values as specified by the Block Size field.

d. Extensions and Scope. This type of block always occurs as part of a larger unit. It does not have a scope of itself.

e. Recommendation. None.

16. Block Terminator.

a. Description. This zero-length Data Sub-block is used to terminate a sequence of Data Sub-blocks. It contains a single byte in the position of the Block Size field and does not contain data.

b. Required Version. 87a.

c. Syntax.

```
      7 6 5 4 3 2 1 0                       Field Name      Type
     +---------------+
  0  |               |                      Block Size      Byte
     +---------------+
```

i) Block Size - Number of bytes in the Data Sub-block; this field contains the fixed value 0x00.

ii) Data Values - This block does not contain any data.

d. Extensions and Scope. This block terminates the immediately preceding sequence of Data Sub-blocks. This block cannot be modified by any extension.

e. Recommendation. None.

17. Header.

a. Description. The Header identifies the GIF Data Stream in context. The Signature field marks the beginning of the Data Stream, and the Version field identifies the set of capabilities required of a decoder to fully process the Data Stream. This block is REQUIRED; exactly one Header must be present per Data Stream.

Figure 7-1 *Continued*

b. Required Version. Not applicable. This block is not subject to a version number. This block must appear at the beginning of every Data Stream.

c. Syntax.

```
      7 6 5 4 3 2 1 0        Field Name     Type
     +---------------+
   0 |               |       Signature      3 Bytes
     +-             -+
   1 |               |
     +-             -+
   2 |               |
     +---------------+
   3 |               |       Version        3 Bytes
     +-             -+
   4 |               |
     +-             -+
   5 |               |
     +---------------+
```

i) Signature - Identifies the GIF Data Stream. This field contains the fixed value 'GIF'.

ii) Version - Version number used to format the data stream. Identifies the minimum set of capabilities necessary to a decoder to fully process the contents of the Data Stream.

Version Numbers as of 10 July 1990 : "87a" - May 1987 "9a" - July 1989

Version numbers are ordered numerically increasing on the first two digits starting with 87 (87,88,...,99,00,...,85,86) and alphabetically increasing on the third character (a,...,z).

iii) Extensions and Scope. The scope of this block is the entire Data Stream. This block cannot be modified by any extension.

d. Recommendations.

i) Signature - This field identifies the beginning of the GIF Data Stream; it is not intended to provide a unique signature for the identification of the data. It is recommended that the GIF Data Stream be identified externally by the application. (Refer to Appendix G for on-line identification of the GIF Data Stream.)

ii) Version - ENCODER : An encoder should use the earliest possible version number that defines all the blocks used in the Data Stream. When two or more Data Streams are combined, the latest of the individual version numbers should be used for the resulting Data Stream. DECODER : A decoder should attempt to process the data stream to the best of its ability; if it encounters a version number which it is not capable of processing fully, it should nevertheless, attempt to process the data stream to the best of its ability, perhaps after warning the user that the data may be incomplete.

18. Logical Screen Descriptor.

a. Description. The Logical Screen Descriptor contains the parameters necessary to define the area of the display device within which the images will be rendered. The coordinates in this block are given with respect to the top-left corner of the virtual screen; they do not necessarily refer to absolute coordinates on the display device. This implies that they could refer to window coordinates in a window-based environment or printer coordinates when a printer is used.

This block is REQUIRED; exactly one Logical Screen Descriptor must be present per Data Stream.

b. Required Version. Not applicable. This block is not subject to a version number. This block must appear immediately after the Header.

c. Syntax.

```
      7 6 5 4 3 2 1 0        Field Name                    Type
   0 +---------------+
     |               |       Logical Screen Width          Unsigned
     +-             -+
   1 |               |
     +---------------+
   2 |               |       Logical Screen Height         Unsigned
     +-             -+
   3 |               |
     +---------------+
   4 | |     | |     |        <Packed Fields>              See below
     +---------------+
   5 |               |       Background Color Index        Byte
     +---------------+
   6 |               |       Pixel Aspect Ratio            Byte
     +---------------+

   <Packed Fields>  =   Global Color Table Flag            1 Bit
                        Color Resolution                   3 Bits
                        Sort Flag                          1 Bit
                        Size of Global Color Table         3 Bits
```

i) Logical Screen Width - Width, in pixels, of the Logical Screen where the images will be rendered in the displaying device.

ii) Logical Screen Height - Height, in pixels, of the Logical Screen where the images will be rendered in the displaying device.

iii) Global Color Table Flag - Flag indicating the presence of a Global Color Table; if the flag is set, the Global Color Table will immediately follow the Logical Screen Descriptor. This flag also selects the interpretation of the Background Color Index; if the flag is set, the value of the Background Color Index field should

Figure 7-1 *Continued*

be used as the table index of the background color. (This field is the most significant bit of the byte.)

Values :

0 - No Global Color Table follows, the Background Color Index field is meaningless.

1 - A Global Color Table will immediately follow, the Background Color Index field is meaningful.

iv) Color Resolution - Number of bits per primary color available to the original image, minus 1. This value represents the size of the entire palette from which the colors in the graphic were selected, not the number of colors actually used in the graphic. For example, if the value in this field is 3, then the palette of the original image had 4 bits per primary color available to create the image. This value should be set to indicate the richness of the original palette, even if not every color from the whole palette is available on the source machine.

v) Sort Flag - Indicates whether the Global Color Table is sorted. If the flag is set, the Global Color Table is sorted, in order of decreasing importance. Typically, the order would be decreasing frequency, with most frequent color first. This assists a decoder, with fewer available colors, in choosing the best subset of colors; the decoder may use an initial segment of the table to render the graphic.

Values :

0 - Not ordered.

1 - Ordered by decreasing importance, most important color first.

vi) Size of Global Color Table - If the Global Color Table Flag is set to 1, the value in this field is used to calculate the number of bytes contained in the Global Color Table. To determine that actual size of the color table, raise 2 to [the value of the field + 1]. Even if there is no Global Color Table specified, set this field according to the above formula so that decoders can choose the best graphics mode to display the stream in. (This field is made up of the 3 least significant bits of the byte.)

vii) Background Color Index - Index into the Global Color Table for the Background Color. The Background Color is the color used for those pixels on the screen that are not covered by an image. If the Global Color Table Flag is set to (zero), this field should be zero and should be ignored.

viii) Pixel Aspect Ratio - Factor used to compute an approximation of the aspect ratio of the pixel in the original image. If the value of the field is not 0, this approximation of the aspect ratio is computed based on the formula:

Aspect Ratio = (Pixel Aspect Ratio + 15) / 64

The Pixel Aspect Ratio is defined to be the quotient of the pixel's width over its height. The value range in this field allows specification of the widest pixel of 4:1 to the tallest pixel of 1:4 in increments of 1/64th.

Values :

0 - No aspect ratio information is given.

1..255 - Value used in the computation.

d. Extensions and Scope. The scope of this block is the entire Data Stream. This block cannot be modified by any extension.

e. Recommendations. None.

19. Global Color Table.

a Description. This block contains a color table, which is a sequence of bytes representing red-green-blue color triplets. The Global Color Table is used by images without a Local Color Table and by Plain Text Extensions. Its presence is marked by the Global Color Table Flag being set to 1 in the Logical Screen Descriptor; if present, it immediately follows the Logical Screen Descriptor and contains a number of bytes equal to 3 × 2^(Size of Global Color Table+1).

This block is OPTIONAL; at most one Global Color Table may be present per Data Stream.

b. Required Version. 87a

c. Syntax.

```
       7 6 5 4 3 2 1 0        Field Name    Type
      +===============+
    0 |               |       Red 0         Byte
      +-             -+
    1 |               |       Green 0       Byte
      +-             -+
    2 |               |       Blue 0        Byte
      +-             -+
    3 |               |       Red 1         Byte
      +-             -+
      |               |       Green 1       Byte
      +-             -+
   up |               |
      +-   . . . .   -+       . . .
   to |               |
```

Figure 7-1 *Continued*

```
       +-              -+
       |                |           Green 255       Byte
       +-              -+
   767 |                |           Blue 255        Byte
       +================+
```

d. Extensions and Scope. The scope of this block is the entire Data Stream. This block cannot be modified by any extension.

e. Recommendation. None.

20. Image Descriptor.

a. Description. Each image in the Data Stream is composed of an Image Descriptor, an optional Local Color Table, and the image data. Each image must fit within the boundaries of the Logical Screen, as defined in the Logical Screen Descriptor.

The Image Descriptor contains the parameters necessary to process a table based image. The coordinates given in this block refer to coordinates within the Logical Screen, and are given in pixels. This block is a Graphic-Rendering Block, optionally preceded by one or more Control blocks such as the Graphic Control Extension, and may be optionally followed by a Local Color Table; the Image Descriptor is always followed by the image data.

This block is REQUIRED for an image. Exactly one Image Descriptor must be present per image in the Data Stream. An unlimited number of images may be present per Data Stream.

b. Required Version. 87a.

c. Syntax.

```
      7 6 5 4 3 2 1 0        Field Name                    Type
     +---------------+
   0 |               |       Image Separator               Byte
     +---------------+
   1 |               |       Image Left Position           Unsigned
     +-             -+
   2 |               |
     +---------------+
   3 |               |       Image Top Position            Unsigned
     +-             -+
   4 |               |
     +---------------+
   5 |               |       Image Width                   Unsigned
     +-             -+
   6 |               |
     +---------------+
   7 |               |       Image Height                  Unsigned
     +-             -+
   8 |               |
     +---------------+
   9 | |  | | |   |  |       <Packed Fields>               See below
     +---------------+

   <Packed Fields>  =     Local Color Table Flag        1 Bit
                          Interlace Flag                1 Bit
```

```
Sort Flag                       1 Bit
Reserved                        2 Bits
Size of Local Color Table       3 Bits
```

i) Image Separator - Identifies the beginning of an Image Descriptor. This field contains the fixed value 0x2C.

ii) Image Left Position - Column number, in pixels, of the left edge of the image, with respect to the left edge of the Logical Screen. Leftmost column of the Logical Screen is 0.

iii) Image Top Position - Row number, in pixels, of the top edge of the image with respect to the top edge of the Logical Screen. Top row of the Logical Screen is 0.

iv) Image Width - Width of the image in pixels.

v) Image Height - Height of the image in pixels.

vi) Local Color Table Flag - Indicates the presence of a Local Color Table immediately following this Image Descriptor. (This field is the most significant bit of the byte.)

Values :

0 - Local Color Table is not present. Use Global Color Table if available.

1 - Local Color Table present, and to follow immediately after this Image Descriptor.

vii) Interlace Flag - Indicates if the image is interlaced. An image is interlaced in a four-pass interlace pattern; see Appendix E for details.

Values :

0 - Image is not interlaced.

1 - Image is interlaced.

viii) Sort Flag - Indicates whether the Local Color Table is sorted. If the flag is set, the Local Color Table is sorted, in order of decreasing importance. Typically, the order would be decreasing frequency, with most frequent color first. This assists a decoder, with fewer available colors, in choosing the best subset of colors; the decoder may use an initial segment of the table to render the graphic.

Figure 7-1 *Continued*

Values :

0 - Not ordered.

1 - Ordered by decreasing importance, most important color first.

ix) Size of Local Color Table - If the Local Color Table Flag is set to 1, the value in this field is used to calculate the number of bytes contained in the Local Color Table. To determine that actual size of the color table, raise 2 to the value of the field + 1. This value should be 0 if there is no Local Color Table specified. (This field is made up of the 3 least significant bits of the byte.)

d. Extensions and Scope. The scope of this block is the Table-based Image Data Block that follows it. This block may be modified by the Graphic Control Extension.

e. Recommendation. None.

21. Local Color Table.

a. Description. This block contains a color table, which is a sequence of bytes representing red-green-blue color triplets. The Local Color Table is used by the image that immediately follows. Its presence is marked by the Local Color Table Flag being set to 1 in the Image Descriptor; if present, the Local Color Table immediately follows the Image Descriptor and contains a number of bytes equal to 3x2^(Size of Local Color Table+1). If present, this color table temporarily becomes the active color table and the following image should be processed using it. This block is OPTIONAL; at most one Local Color Table may be present per Image Descriptor and its scope is the single image associated with the Image Descriptor that precedes it.

b. Required Version. 87a.

c. Syntax.

```
      7 6 5 4 3 2 1 0        Field Name                    Type
     +===============+
   0 |               |       Red 0                         Byte
     +-             -+
   1 |               |       Green 0                       Byte
     +-             -+
   2 |               |       Blue 0                        Byte
     +-             -+
   3 |               |       Red 1                         Byte
     +-             -+
     |               |       Green 1                       Byte
     +-             -+
  up |               |
     +-   . . .     -+       . . .
  to |               |
     +-             -+
     |               |       Green 255                     Byte
     +-             -+
 767 |               |       Blue 255                      Byte
     +===============+
```

d. Extensions and Scope. The scope of this block is the Table based Image Data Block that immediately follows it. This block cannot be modified by any extension.

e. Recommendations. None.

22. Table Based Image Data.

a. Description. The image data for a table based image consists of a sequence of sub-blocks, of size at most 255 bytes each, containing an index into the active color table, for each pixel in the image. Pixel indices are in order of left to right and from top to bottom. Each index must be within the range of the size of the active color table, starting at 0. The sequence of indices is encoded using the LZW Algorithm with variable-length code, as described in Appendix F

b. Required Version. 87a.

c. Syntax. The image data format is as follows:

```
 7 6 5 4 3 2 1 0        Field Name                 Type
+---------------+
|               |       LZW Minimum Code Size      Byte
+---------------+

+===============+
|               |
/               /       Image Data                 Data Sub-blocks
|               |
+===============+
```

i) LZW Minimum Code Size. This byte determines the initial number of bits used for LZW codes in the image data, as described in Appendix F.

d. Extensions and Scope. This block has no scope, it contains raster data. Extensions intended to modify a Table-based image must appear before the corresponding Image Descriptor.

e. Recommendations. None.

23. Graphic Control Extension.

a. Description. The Graphic Control Extension contains parameters used when processing a graphic rendering block. The scope of this extension is the first graphic rendering block to follow. The extension contains only one data sub-block.

This block is OPTIONAL; at most one Graphic Control Extension may precede a graphic rendering block. This is the only limit to the number of Graphic Control Extensions that may be contained in a Data Stream.

b. Required Version. 89a.

Figure 7-1 *Continued*

c. Syntax.

```
      7 6 5 4 3 2 1 0        Field Name                   Type
     +---------------+
   0 |               |       Extension Introducer         Byte
     +---------------+
   1 |               |       Graphic Control Label        Byte
     +---------------+

     +---------------+
   0 |               |       Block Size                   Byte
     +---------------+
   1 |   |     |   | |       <Packed Fields>              See below
     +---------------+
   2 |               |       Delay Time                   Unsigned
     +-             -+
   3 |               |
     +---------------+
   4 |               |       Transparent Color Index      Byte
     +---------------+

     +---------------+
   0 |               |       Block Terminator             Byte
     +---------------+

<Packed Fields>  =      Reserved                          3 Bits
                        Disposal Method                   3 Bits
                        User Input Flag                   1 Bit
                        Transparent Color Flag            1 Bit
```

i) Extension Introducer - Identifies the beginning of an extension block. This field contains the fixed value 0x21.

ii) Graphic Control Label - Identifies the current block as a Graphic Control Extension. This field contains the fixed value 0xF9.

iii) Block Size - Number of bytes in the block, after the Block Size field and up to but not including the Block Terminator. This field contains the fixed value 4.

iv) Disposal Method - Indicates the way in which the graphic is to be treated after being displayed.

Values : 0 - No disposal specified. The decoder is not required to take any action. 1 - Do not dispose. The graphic is to be left in place. 2 - Restore to background color. The area used by the graphic must be restored to the background color. 3 - Restore to previous. The decoder is required to restore the area overwritten by the graphic with what was there prior to rendering the graphic. 4-7 - To be defined.

v) User Input Flag - Indicates whether or not user input is expected before continuing. If the flag is set, processing will continue when user input is entered. The nature of the User input is determined by the application (Carriage Return, Mouse Button Click, etc.).

Values : 0 - User input is not expected. 1 - User input is expected.

When a Delay Time is used and the User Input Flag is set, processing will continue when user input is received or when the delay time expires, whichever occurs first.

vi) Transparency Flag - Indicates whether a transparency index is given in the Transparent Index field. (This field is the least significant bit of the byte.)

Values : 0 - Transparent Index is not given. 1 - Transparent Index is given.

vii) Delay Time - If not 0, this field specifies the number of hundredths (1/100) of a second to wait before continuing with the processing of the Data Stream. The clock starts ticking immediately after the graphic is rendered. This field may be used in conjunction with the User Input Flag field.

viii) Transparency Index - The Transparency Index is such that when encountered, the corresponding pixel of the display device is not modified and processing goes on to the next pixel. The index is present if and only if the Transparency Flag is set to 1.

ix) Block Terminator - This zero-length data block marks the end of the Graphic Control Extension.

d. Extensions and Scope. The scope of this Extension is the graphic rendering block that follows it; it is possible for other extensions to be present between this block and its target. This block can modify the Image Descriptor Block and the Plain Text Extension.

e. Recommendations.

i) Disposal Method - The mode Restore To Previous is intended to be used in small sections of the graphic; the use of this mode imposes severe demands on the decoder to store the section of the graphic that needs to be saved. For this reason, this mode should be used sparingly. This mode is not intended to save an entire graphic or large areas of a graphic; when this is the case, the encoder should make every attempt to make the sections of the graphic to be restored be separate graphics in the data stream. In the case where a decoder is not capable of saving an area of a graphic marked as Restore To Previous, it is recommended that a decoder restore to the background color.

ii) User Input Flag - When the flag is set, indicating that user input is expected, the decoder may sound the bell (0x07) to alert the user that input is being expected. In the absence of a specified Delay Time, the decoder should wait for user input indefinitely. It is recommended that the encoder not set the User Input Flag without a Delay Time specified.

Figure 7-1 *Continued*

24. Comment Extension.

a. Description. The Comment Extension contains textual information which is not part of the actual graphics in the GIF Data Stream. It is suitable for including comments about the graphics, credits, descriptions or any other type of non-control and non-graphic data. The Comment Extension may be ignored by the decoder, or it may be saved for later processing; under no circumstances should a Comment Extension disrupt or interfere with the processing of the Data Stream.

This block is OPTIONAL; any number of them may appear in the Data Stream.

b. Required Version. 89a.

c. Syntax.

```
      7 6 5 4 3 2 1 0        Field Name                    Type
     +---------------+
   0 |               |       Extension Introducer          Byte
     +---------------+
   1 |               |       Comment Label                 Byte
     +---------------+

     +===============+
     |               |
   N |               |       Comment Data                  Data Sub-blocks
     |               |
     +===============+

     +---------------+
   0 |               |       Block Terminator              Byte
     +---------------+
```

i) Extension Introducer - Identifies the beginning of an extension block. This field contains the fixed value 0x21.

ii) Comment Label - Identifies the block as a Comment Extension. This field contains the fixed value 0xFE.

iii) Comment Data - Sequence of sub-blocks, each of size at most 255 bytes and at least 1 byte, with the size in a byte preceding the data. The end of the sequence is marked by the Block Terminator.

iv) Block Terminator - This zero-length data block marks the end of the Comment Extension.

d. Extensions and Scope. This block does not have scope. This block cannot be modified by any extension.

e. Recommendations.

i) Data - This block is intended for humans. It should contain text using the 7-bit ASCII character set. This block should not be used to store control information for custom processing.

ii) Position - This block may appear at any point in the Data Stream at which a block can begin; however, it is recommended that Comment Extensions do not interfere with Control or Data blocks; they should be located at the beginning or at the end of the Data Stream to the extent possible.

25. Plain Text Extension.

a. Description. The Plain Text Extension contains textual data and the parameters necessary to render that data as a graphic, in a simple form. The textual data will be encoded with the 7-bit printable ASCII characters. Text data are rendered using a grid of character cells defined by the parameters in the block fields. Each character is rendered in an individual cell. The textual data in this block is to be rendered as mono-spaced characters, one character per cell, with a best fitting font and size. For further information, see the section on Recommendations below. The data characters are taken sequentially from the data portion of the block and rendered within a cell, starting with the upper left cell in the grid and proceeding from left to right and from top to bottom. Text data is rendered until the end of data is reached or the character grid is filled. The Character Grid contains an integral number of cells; in the case that the cell dimensions do not allow for an integral number, fractional cells must be discarded; an encoder must be careful to specify the grid dimensions accurately so that this does not happen. This block requires a Global Color Table to be available; the colors used by this block reference the Global Color Table in the Stream if there is one, or the Global Color Table from a previous Stream, if one was saved. This block is a graphic rendering block, therefore it may be modified by a Graphic Control Extension. This block is OPTIONAL; any number of them may appear in the Data Stream.

b Required Version. 89a.

c. Syntax.

```
                7 6 5 4 3 2 1 0        Field Name                    Type
               +---------------+
             0 |               |       Extension Introducer          Byte
               +---------------+
             1 |               |       Plain Text Label              Byte
               +---------------+

               +---------------+
             0 |               |       Block Size                    Byte
               +---------------+
             1 |               |       Text Grid Left Position
Unsigned
               +-             -+
             2 |               |
               +---------------+
             3 |               |       Text Grid Top Position
Unsigned
               +-             -+
             4 |               |
               +---------------+
             5 |               |       Text Grid Width
```

Figure 7-1 *Continued*

```
 Unsigned
                 +---------------+
               6 |               |
                 +---------------+
               7 |               |        Text Grid Height
Unsigned
                 +---------------+
               8 |               |
                 +---------------+
               9 |               |        Character Cell Width          Byte
                 +---------------+
              10 |               |        Character Cell Height         Byte
                 +---------------+
              11 |               |        Text Foreground Color Index   Byte
                 +---------------+
              12 |               |        Text Background Color Index   Byte
                 +---------------+

                 +===============+
                 |               |
               N |               |        Plain Text Data               Data
Sub-blocks
                 |               |
                 +===============+

                 +---------------+
               0 |               |        Block Terminator              Byte
                 +---------------+
```

i) Extension Introducer - Identifies the beginning of an extension block. This field contains the fixed value 0x21.

ii) Plain Text Label - Identifies the current block as a Plain Text Extension. This field contains the fixed value 0x01.

iii) Block Size - Number of bytes in the extension, after the Block Size field and up to but not including the beginning of the data portion. This field contains the fixed value 12.

iv) Text Grid Left Position - Column number, in pixels, of the left edge of the text grid, with respect to the left edge of the Logical Screen.

v) Text Grid Top Position - Row number, in pixels, of the top edge of the text grid, with respect to the top edge of the Logical Screen.

vi) Image Grid Width - Width of the text grid in pixels.

vii) Image Grid Height - Height of the text grid in pixels.

viii) Character Cell Width - Width, in pixels, of each cell in the grid.

ix) Character Cell Height - Height, in pixels, of each cell in the grid.

x) Text Foreground Color Index - Index into the Global Color Table to be used to render the text foreground.

xi) Text Background Color Index - Index into the Global Color

Table to be used to render the text background.

xii) Plain Text Data - Sequence of sub-blocks, each of size at most 255 bytes and at least 1 byte, with the size in a byte preceding the data. The end of the sequence is marked by the Block Terminator.

xiii) Block Terminator - This zero-length data block marks the end of the Plain Text Data Blocks.

d. Extensions and Scope. The scope of this block is the Plain Text Data Block contained in it. This block may be modified by the Graphic Control Extension.

e. Recommendations. The data in the Plain Text Extension is assumed to be preformatted. The selection of font and size is left to the discretion of the decoder. If characters less than 0x20 or greater than 0xf7 are encountered, it is recommended that the decoder display a Space character (0x20). The encoder should use grid and cell dimensions such that an integral number of cells fit in the grid both horizontally as well as vertically. For broadest compatibility, character cell dimensions should be around 8x8 or 8x16 (width x height); consider an image for unusual sized text.

26. Application Extension.

a. Description. The Application Extension contains application-specific information; it conforms with the extension block syntax, as described below, and its block label is 0xFF.

b. Required Version. 89a.

c. Syntax.

```
      7 6 5 4 3 2 1 0        Field Name                    Type
     +---------------+
   0 |               |       Extension Introducer          Byte
     +---------------+
   1 |               |       Extension Label               Byte
     +---------------+

     +---------------+
   0 |               |       Block Size                    Byte
     +---------------+
   1 |               |
     +---------------+
   2 |               |
     +---------------+
   3 |               |       Application Identifier        8 Bytes
     +---------------+
   4 |               |
     +---------------+
   5 |               |
     +---------------+
   6 |               |
     +---------------+
   7 |               |
     +---------------+
```

Figure 7-1 *Continued*

```
 8  |               |
    +---------------+
 9  |               |
    +---------------+
10  |               |        Appl. Authentication Code   3 Bytes
    +---------------+
11  |               |
    +---------------+
    +===============+
    |               |        Application Data            Data Sub-blocks
    |               |
    +===============+
    +---------------+
 0  |               |        Block Terminator            Byte
    +---------------+
```

i) Extension Introducer - Defines this block as an extension. This field contains the fixed value 0x21.

ii) Application Extension Label - Identifies the block as an Application Extension. This field contains the fixed value 0xFF.

iii) Block Size - Number of bytes in this extension block, following the Block Size field, up to but not including the beginning of the Application Data. This field contains the fixed value 11.

iv) Application Identifier - Sequence of eight printable ASCII characters used to identify the application owning the Application Extension.

v) Application Authentication Code - Sequence of three bytes used to authenticate the Application Identifier. An Application program may use an algorithm to compute a binary code that uniquely identifies it as the application owning the Application Extension.

d. Extensions and Scope. This block does not have scope. This block cannot be modified by any extension.

e. Recommendation. None.

27. Trailer.

a. Description. This block is a single-field block indicating the end of the GIF Data Stream. It contains the fixed value 0x3B.

b. Required Version. 87a.

c. Syntax.

```
     7 6 5 4 3 2 1 0        Field Name      Type
    +---------------+
 0  |               |       GIF Trailer     Byte
    +---------------+
```

d. Extensions and Scope. This block does not have scope, it terminates the GIF Data Stream. This block may not be modified by any extension.

e. Recommendations. None.

Appendix
A. Quick Reference Table.

Block Name	Required	Label	Ext.	Vers.
Application Extension	Opt. (*)	0xFF (255)	yes	89a
Comment Extension	Opt. (*)	0xFE (254)	yes	89a
Global Color Table	Opt. (1)	none	no	87a
Graphic Control Extension	Opt. (*)	0xF9 (249)	yes	89a
Header	Req. (1)	none	no	N/A
Image Descriptor	Opt. (*)	0x2C (044)	no	7a (89a)
Local Color Table	Opt. (*)	none	no	87a
Logical Screen Descriptor	Req. (1)	none	no	87a (89a)
Plain Text Extension	Opt. (*)	0x01 (001)	yes	89a
Trailer	Req. (1)	0x3B (059)	no	87a
Unlabeled Blocks				
Header	Req. (1)	none	no	N/A
Logical Screen Descriptor	Req. (1)	none	no	87a (89a)
Global Color Table	Opt. (1)	none	no	87a
Local Color Table	Opt. (*)	none	no	87a
Graphic-Rendering Blocks				
Plain Text Extension	Opt. (*)	Cx01 (001)	yes	89a
Image Descriptor	Opt. (*)	Cx2C (044)	no	87a (89a)
Control Blocks				
Graphic Control Extension	Opt. (*)	CxF9 (249)	yes	89a
Special Purpose Blocks				
Trailer	Req. (1)	Cx3B (059)	no	87a
Comment Extension	Opt. (*)	CxFE (254)	yes	89a
Application Extension	Opt. (*)	CxFF (255)	yes	89a

legend:
(1) if present, at most one occurrence
(*) zero or more occurrences
(+) one or more occurrences

Notes : The Header is not subject to Version Numbers.
(89a) The Logical Screen Descriptor and the Image Descriptor retained their syntax from version 87a to version 89a, but some fields reserved under version 87a are used under version 89a.

Appendix

B. GIF Grammar.

A Grammar is a form of notation to represent the sequence in which certain objects form larger objects. A grammar is also used to represent the number of objects that can occur at a given position. The grammar given here represents the sequence of blocks that form the GIF Data Stream. A grammar is given by listing its rules. Each rule consists of the left-hand side, followed by some form of equals sign, followed by the right-hand side. In a rule, the right-hand side

Figure 7-1 *Continued*

describes how the left-hand side is defined. The right-hand side consists of a sequence of entities, with the possible presence of special symbols. The following legend defines the symbols used in this grammar for GIF.

Legend:
<> grammar word
::= defines symbol
* zero or more occurrences
+ one or more occurrences
| alternate element
[] optional element

Example:

```
<GIF Data Stream> ::= Header <Logical Screen> <Data>* Trailer
```

This rule defines the entity <GIF Data Stream> as follows. It must begin with a Header. The Header is followed by an entity called Logical Screen, which is defined below by another rule. The Logical Screen is followed by the entity Data, which is also defined below by another rule. Finally, the entity Data is followed by the Trailer. Since there is no rule defining the Header or the Trailer, this means that these blocks are defined in the document. The entity Data has a special symbol (*) following it which means that, at this position, the entity Data may be repeated any number of times, including 0 times. For further reading on this subject, refer to a standard text on Programming Languages.

The Grammar.

```
<GIF Data Stream> ::=  Header <Logical Screen> <Data>* Trailer

<Logical Screen> ::=   Logical Screen Descriptor [Global Color Table]

<Data> ::= <Graphic Block> | <Special-Purpose Block>

<Graphic Block> ::= [Graphic Control Extension] <Graphic-Rendering Block>

<Graphic-Rendering Block> ::= <Table-Based Image> | Plain Text Extension

<Table-Based Image> ::= Image Descriptor [Local Color Table] Image Data

<Special-Purpose Block> ::= Application Extension | Comment Extension
```

NOTE : The grammar indicates that it is possible for a GIF Data Stream to contain the Header, the Logical Screen Descriptor, a Global Color Table and the GIF Trailer. This special case is used to load a GIF decoder with a Global Color Table, in preparation for subsequent Data Streams without color tables at all.

Appendix

C. Glossary.

Active Color Table - Color table used to render the next graphic. If the next graphic is an image which has a Local Color Table associated with it, the active color table becomes the Local Color Table associated with that image. If the next graphic is an image without a Local Color Table, or a Plain Text Extension, the active color table is the Global Color Table associated with the Data Stream, if there is one; if there is no Global Color Table in the Data Stream, the active color table is a color table saved from a previous Data Stream, or one supplied by the decoder.

Block - Collection of bytes forming a protocol unit. In general, the term includes labeled and unlabeled blocks, as well as Extensions.

Data Stream - The GIF Data Stream is composed of blocks and sub-blocks representing images and graphics, together with control information to render them on a display device. All control and data blocks in the Data Stream must follow the Header and must precede the Trailer.

Decoder - A program capable of processing a GIF Data Stream to render the images and graphics contained in it.

Encoder - A program capable of capturing and formatting image and graphic raster data, following the definitions of the Graphics Interchange Format.

Extension - A protocol block labeled by the Extension Introducer 0x21.

Extension Introducer - Label (0x21) defining an Extension.

Graphic - Data which can be rendered on the screen by virtue of some algorithm. The term graphic is more general than the term image; in addition to images, the term graphic also includes data such as text, which is rendered using character bit-maps.

Image - Data representing a picture or a drawing; an image is represented by an array of pixels called the raster of the image.

Raster - Array of pixel values representing an image.

Appendix

D. Conventions.

Animation - The Graphics Interchange Format is not intended as a platform for animation, even though it can be done in a limited way.

Byte Ordering - Unless otherwise stated, multi-byte numeric fields are ordered with the Least Significant Byte first.

Color Indices - Color indices always refer to the active color table, either the Global Color Table or the Local Color Table.

Color Order - Unless otherwise stated, all triple-component RGB color values are specified in Red-Green-Blue order.

Figure 7-1 *Continued*

Color Tables - Both color tables, the Global and the Local, are optional; if present, the Global Color Table is to be used with every image in the Data Stream for which a Local Color Table is not given; if present, a Local Color Table overrides the Global Color Table. However, if neither color table is present, the application program is free to use an arbitrary color table. If the graphics in several Data Streams are related and all use the same color table, an encoder could place the color table as the Global Color Table in the first Data Stream and leave subsequent Data Streams without a Global Color Table or any Local Color Tables; in this way, the overhead for the table is eliminated. It is recommended that the decoder save the previous Global Color Table to be used with the Data Stream that follows, in case it does not contain either a Global Color Table or any Local Color Tables. In general, this allows the application program to use past color tables, significantly reducing transmission overhead.

Extension Blocks - Extensions are defined using the Extension Introducer code to mark the beginning of the block, followed by a block label, identifying the type of extension. Extension Codes are numbers in the range from 0x00 to 0xFF, inclusive. Special purpose extensions are transparent to the decoder and may be omitted when transmitting the Data Stream on-line. The GIF capabilities dialogue makes the provision for the receiver to request the transmission of all blocks; the default state in this regard is no transmission of Special purpose blocks.

Reserved Fields - All Reserved Fields are expected to have each bit set to zero (off).

Appendix

E. Interlaced Images.

The rows of an Interlaced images are arranged in the following order:

```
Group 1 : Every 8th. row, starting with row 0.      (Pass 1)
Group 2 : Every 8th. row, starting with row 4.      (Pass 2)
Group 3 : Every 4th. row, starting with row 2.      (Pass 3)
Group 4 : Every 2nd. row, starting with row 1.      (Pass 4)
```

The Following example illustrates how the rows of an interlaced image are ordered.

```
          Row Number                        Interlace Pass

        0 -----------------------------------  1
        1 -----------------------------------           4
        2 -----------------------------------        3
        3 -----------------------------------           4
        4 -----------------------------------     2
        5 -----------------------------------           4
        6 -----------------------------------        3
        7 -----------------------------------           4
        8 -----------------------------------  1
```

9	---				4
10	---			3	
11	---				4
12	---		2		
13	---				4
14	---			3	
15	---				4
16	---	1			
17	---				4
18	---			3	
19	---				4

Appendix
F. Variable-Length-Code LZW Compression.

The Variable-Length-Code LZW Compression is a variation of the Lempel-Ziv Compression algorithm in which variable-length codes are used to replace patterns detected in the original data. The algorithm uses a code or translation table constructed from the patterns encountered in the original data; each new pattern is entered into the table and its index is used to replace it in the compressed stream.

The compressor takes the data from the input stream and builds a code or translation table with the patterns as it encounters them; each new pattern is entered into the code table and its index is added to the output stream; when a pattern is encountered which had been detected since the last code table refresh, its index from the code table is put on the output stream, thus achieving the data compression. The expander takes input from the compressed data stream and builds the code or translation table from it; as the compressed data stream is processed, codes are used to index into the code table and the corresponding data is put on the decompressed output stream, thus achieving data decompression. The details of the algorithm are explained below.

The Variable-Length-Code aspect of the algorithm is based on an initial code size (LZW-initial code size), which specifies the initial number of bits used for the compression codes. When the number of patterns detected by the compressor in the input stream exceeds the number of patterns encodable with the current number of bits, the number of bits per LZW code is increased by one.

The Raster Data stream that represents the actual output image can be represented as:

```
  7 6 5 4 3 2 1 0
 +---------------+
 | LZW code size |
 +---------------+

 +---------------+ ----+
 |  block size   |     |
 +---------------+     |
 |               |     +-- Repeated as many
 |  data bytes   |     |   times as necessary.
 |               |     |
```

Figure 7-1 *Continued*

```
+---------------+ ----+
 . . .      . . . ------- The code that terminates the LZW
                          compressed data must appear
                          before Block Terminator.
+---------------+
|0 0 0 0 0 0 0 0|  Block Terminator
+---------------+
```

The conversion of the image from a series of pixel values to a transmitted or stored character stream involves several steps. In brief these steps are:

1. Establish the Code Size - Define the number of bits needed to represent the actual data.

2. Compress the Data - Compress the series of image pixels to a series of compression codes.

3. Build a Series of Bytes - Take the set of compression codes and convert to a string of 8-bit bytes.

4. Package the Bytes - Package sets of bytes into blocks preceded by character counts and output.

ESTABLISH CODE SIZE

The first byte of the Compressed Data stream is a value indicating the minimum number of bits required to represent the set of actual pixel values. Normally this will be the same as the number of color bits. Because of some algorithmic constraints however, black & white images which have one color bit must be indicated as having a code size of 2. This code size value also implies that the compression codes must start out one bit longer.

COMPRESSION

The LZW algorithm converts a series of data values into a series of codes which may be raw values or a code designating a series of values. Using text characters as an analogy, the output code consists of a character or a code representing a string of characters.

The LZW algorithm used in GIF matches algorithmically with the standard LZW algorithm with the following differences:

1. A special Clear code is defined which resets all compression/decompression parameters and tables to a start-up state. The value of this code is 2**<code size>. For example if the code size indicated was 4 (image was 4 bits/pixel) the Clear code value would be 16 (10000 binary). The Clear code can appear at any point in the image data stream and therefore requires the LZW algorithm to process succeeding codes as if a new data stream was starting. Encoders should output a Clear code as the first code of each image data stream.

2. An End of Information code is defined that explicitly indicates the end of the image data stream. LZW processing terminates when this code is encountered. It must be the last code output by the encoder for an image. The value of this code is <Clear code>+1.

3. The first available compression code value is <Clear code>+2.

4. The output codes are of variable length, starting at <code size>+1 bits per code, up to 12 bits per code. This defines a maximum code value of 4095 (0xFFF). Whenever the LZW code value would exceed the current code length, the code length is increased by one. The packing/unpacking of these codes must then be altered to reflect the new code length.

BUILD 8-BIT BYTES

Because the LZW compression used for GIF creates a series of variable length codes, of between 3 and 12 bits each, these codes must be reformed into a series of 8-bit bytes that will be the characters actually stored or transmitted. This provides additional compression of the image. The codes are formed into a stream of bits as if they were packed right to left and then picked off 8 bits at a time to be output.

Assuming a character array of 8 bits per character and using 5 bit codes to be packed, an example layout would be similar to:

```
    +---------------+
0   |               |     bbbaaaaa
    +---------------+
    |               |     dcccccbb
    +---------------+
2   |               |     eeeedddd
    +---------------+
3   |               |     ggfffffe
    +---------------+
4   |               |     hhhhhggg
    +---------------+
          . . .
    +---------------+
N   |               |
    +---------------+
```

Note that the physical packing arrangement will change as the number of bits per compression code change but the concept remains the same.

PACKAGE THE BYTES

Once the bytes have been created, they are grouped into blocks for output by preceding each block of 0 to 255 bytes with a character count byte. A block with a zero byte count terminates the Raster Data stream for a given image. These blocks are what are actually output for the GIF image. This block format has the side effect of allowing a decoding program the ability to read past the actual image data if necessary by reading block counts and then skipping over the data.

Figure 7-1 *Continued*

FURTHER READING

[1] Ziv, J. and Lempel, A. : “A Universal Algorithm for Sequential Data Compression”, IEEE Transactions on Information Theory, May 1977. [2] Welch, T. : “A Technique for High-Performance Data Compression”, Computer, June 1984. [3] Nelson, M.R. : “LZW Data Compression”, Dr. Dobb’s Journal, October 1989.

Appendix

G. On-line Capabilities Dialogue.

NOTE : This section is currently (10 July 1990) under revision; the information provided here should be used as general guidelines. Code written based on this information should be designed in a flexible way to accommodate any changes resulting from the revisions.

The following sequences are defined for use in mediating control between a GIF sender and GIF receiver over an interactive communications line. These sequences do not apply to applications that involve downloading of static GIF files and are not considered part of a GIF file.

GIF CAPABILITIES ENQUIRY

The GIF Capabilities Enquiry sequence is issued from a host and requests an interactive GIF decoder to return a response message that defines the graphics parameters for the decoder. This involves returning information about available screen sizes, number of bits/color supported and the amount of color detail supported. The escape sequence for the GIF Capabilities Enquiry is defined as:

ESC[>0g   0x1B 0x5B 0x3E 0x30 0x67

GIF CAPABILITIES RESPONSE

The GIF Capabilities Response message is returned by an interactive GIF decoder and defines the decoder’s display capabilities for all graphics modes that are supported by the software. Note that this can also include graphics printers as well as a monitor screen. The general format of this message is:

#version;protocol{;dev, width, height, color-bits, color-res}...<CR>

‘#’	GIF Capabilities Response identifier character.
version	GIF format version number; initially ‘87a’.
protocol=‘0’	No end-to-end protocol supported by decoder Transfer as direct 8-bit data stream.
protocol=‘1’	Can use CIS B+ error correction protocol to transfer GIF data interactively from the host directly to the display.
dev = ‘0’	Screen parameter set follows.
dev = ‘1’	Printer parameter set follows.
width	Maximum supported display width in pixels.

height	Maximum supported display height in pixels.
color-bits	Number of bits per pixel supported. The number of supported colors is therefore 2**color-bits.
color-res	Number of bits per color component supported in the hardware color palette. If color-res is '0' then no hardware palette table is available.

Note that all values in the GIF Capabilities Response are returned as ASCII decimal numbers and the message is terminated by a Carriage Return character.

The following GIF Capabilities Response message describes three standard IBM PC Enhanced Graphics Adapter configurations with no printer; the GIF data stream can be processed within an error correcting protocol:

#87a;1;0,320,200,4,0;0,640,200,2,2;0,640,350,4,2<CR>
ENTER GIF GRAPHICS MODE

Two sequences are currently defined to invoke an interactive GIF decoder into action. The only difference between them is that different output media are selected. These sequences are:

ESC[>1g Display GIF image on screen

0x1B
0x5B 0x3E 0x31 0x67

ESC[>2g Display image directly to an attached graphics printer. The image may optionally be displayed on the screen as well.

0x1B 0x5B 0x3E 0x32 0x67

Note that the 'g' character terminating each sequence is in lowercase.

INTERACTIVE ENVIRONMENT

The assumed environment for the transmission of GIF image data from an interactive application is a full 8-bit data stream from host to micro. All 256 character codes must be transferable. The establishing of an 8-bit data path for communications will normally be taken care of by the host application programs. It is however up to the receiving communications programs supporting GIF to be able to receive and pass on all 256 8-bit codes to the GIF decoder software.

## CHAPTER 8

GEM bit image

Name	GEM IMG
Image type	Bitmap
Intended use	Image storage and transfer among GEM applications
Owner	Digital Research (now Novell)
Last version/ revision/ release date	1989
Platforms	IBM PC and Atari
Supporting applications	GEM applications such as Ventura Publisher, GEM Draw, GEM Scan, and GEM Paint. On the Atari ST where GEM is the standard operating environment, most graphical applications support this format.
Similarities	Other bitmap formats
Overall assessment	Useful in GEM applications, a widely supported format for monochrome images

Advantages

Well-supported by GEM graphical environment applications

Disadvantages

Mediocre compression, not well-documented, no provision for color map

Variants

So-called old and new versions

Overview of file structure

The Digital Research GEM environment defines a bit-image file format usually known as .IMG after the conventional filename extension. Images can be monochrome, grayscale, or color, although in practice most images are a single plane.

Format details

An .IMG file consists of a header followed by the image data. Images more than one bit deep are stored plane by plane. Color images are stored from the most-significant to the least-significant plane. Planes are stored in groups of four, representing red, green, blue, and gray planes. For example, a color image three bits deep in each color would be stored with its planes in the order R1, G1, B1, X1, R2, G2, B2, X2, R3, G3, B3, X3, with R, G, B, and X being red, green, blue, and gray planes, respectively.

Image header

The image header consists of eight or nine 16-bit words, as in Table 8-1. Each word is stored in big-endian format with the more-significant byte first.

GEM IMG file header Table 8-1

Offset	Description
0	File version number (currently always *1*)
2	Header length in words (*8* or *9*)
4	Total image depth

Table 8-1 **Continued**

Offset	Description
6	Pattern length, typically *2*
8	Original pixel width in microns
10	Original pixel height in microns
12	Image width in pixels
14	Image height in pixels
16	Optional flag word

The image depth is the total number of planes. For example, for a color image that is three bits per pixel, it would be 12. The pattern length is the number of bytes in pattern-repeat chunks, below. The image width must be a multiple of eight, because image data are stored in bytes with eight pixel bits per byte. If the high order bit is one in the optional flag word, the image is grayscale; if it is zero the image is color. In images without the flag word, there is no way to tell whether an image is supposed to be grayscale or color.

The original pixel height and width can help to rescale an image when moving it between displays with different pixel-aspect ratios.

Image data

Each image plane is stored as a sequence of scan lines. Each scan line is an optional repeat count followed by one or more image-data chunks. If the repeat count is present, it specifies the number of times the following scan line is repeated in the actual image. In data bytes, the eight bits represent eight pixels, with the high-order bit being the leftmost pixel.

A repeat-count chunk is stored as (in hex):

00 00 FF *NN*

meaning *NN* copies of the following scan line.

Three chunk types are possible in a scan line: bit strings, pattern runs, and solid runs.

- **Bit strings** The simplest and most common type simply represents a series of literal-data bytes, stored as:

  80 *NN*

  followed by the *NN* literal-data bytes.

- **Pattern runs** A repeating group of bytes is stored as:

  00 *NN*

  followed by the pattern bytes. The number of pattern bytes is set by the pattern size-word in the header, meaning that all patterns in a file are of the same length; typically two bytes. For example, assuming a pattern length of two, the chunk 00 02 12 34 would mean two repeats of the bytes 12 34.

- **Solid runs** A solid run represents one or more bytes either of all one or all zero pixels. A byte other than 00 or 80 signifies a solid run. If the high bit of the byte is set, it is a run of ones; if not, it is a run of zeros. The low seven bits of the byte are the number of bytes of ones or zeros. For example, 8F means 15 bytes of ones, while 0C means 12 bytes of zeros.

  In practice, many .IMG files use only a single bit-string chunk per line, storing the image completely uncompressed.

Scan line examples

Assume that an image is 64 bits wide, meaning eight data bytes per scan line, and the pattern size is two bytes. This file data:

00 00 FF 06 80 02 12 34 05 83 00 03 AB CD 80 01 98 01

means six scan lines each containing:

12 34 00 00 00 00 00 FF FF FF

followed by a scan line containing:

AB CD AB CD AB CD 98 00

## CHAPTER 9

IFF/ILBM

Name	ILBM
Image type	Bitmap, embedded in multimedia
Intended use	Storage and interchange
Owner	Electronic Arts
Last revision/ version/ release date	EA IFF 85, January 1985
Platforms	Ubiquitous on Amiga; also limited support on PC and Macintosh
Supporting applications	Deluxe Paint, many others,
Similarities	TIFF, a little
Overall assessment	Well-standardized bitmap interchange format

Advantages

Well-standardized, extensible

Disadvantages

Mediocre compression; extensibility means that incompatible extensions exist.

Variants

4-bit color map, 24-bit direct color, Amiga HAM and EHB modes

Overview of file structure

Electronic Arts has defined the multimedia Interchange Format Files standard to facilitate the transfer of images, text, musical scores, sound, and other data among programs on Amigas and other computers. Here we document the general structure of IFF and the details of ILBM, the IFF Interleaved Bitmap. There are other less commonly used IFF graphics subformats not documented here, including DR2D, a 2-D-structured drawing format, and several 3-D CAD formats.

Although the ILBM format allows general bitmaps to be represented, its details are designed to work efficiently with Amiga hardware. In particular, the HAM (hold-and-modify) and EHB (extra-half-bright) modes directly correspond to Amiga screen modes. Non-Amiga platforms usually support only the original modes, not the HAM and EHB variants.

Images are typically 320 or 640 pixels wide, corresponding to Amiga screen modes. Images can be up to four bits deep if 640 pixels wide, five bits deep if 320 pixels wide, and six bits in HAM or EHB mode. Although color maps can be stored with eight bits per color, Amiga hardware usually supports only four bits per color so only the high four bits for each color-map color entry are commonly used.

An ILBM file can contain considerable information about its bitmap. It contains the size of the original display page and the position of the bitmap within that page. It can contain a mask that tells which pixels are opaque and which are transparent when overlaying the image on other data. It can contain the coordinates of a hot spot if the image is a cursor.

Format details

IFF files are a sequence of self-describing *chunks*. Programs read files a chunk at a time and can usually safely ignore chunks they do not understand.

Normal ILBM images contain a set of pixel values. The Amiga HAM format is a variant which contains image-component delta values, documented at the end of this section.

Low-level data

Data in IFF files use the native big-endian formats of the 68000. Two- and 4-byte numbers are stored with the high-order byte first. Numbers can be signed or unsigned, but all values in a bitmap happen to be unsigned. When a number is interpreted as a set of bits, bit 0 is the low-order bit. All data longer than a byte, even 4-byte numbers, are aligned on a two-byte boundary, adding a padding byte when necessary. Text fields are 7-bit ASCII.

Chunks

Chunks have a consistent format as shown in Table 9-1.

Table 9-1 **IFF chunk header**

Offset	Length	Name	Description
0	4	ID	Chunk type ID
4	4	Size	Size of chunk data
8	Size	Data	Data for the chunk

Chunk IDs are four characters consisting of uppercase letters, digits, and spaces. The special chunk type named by four spaces is filler, and is always ignored. All other chunk types are file data.

Chunks can be nested. The most common nested chunk is a FORM, whose data contain a form type in the first four data bytes, followed by a set of chunks. A bitmap image is contained in a FORM of type ILBM. In principle, IFF files can contain many forms with a variety of data types, but in practice a single file will contain a single form.

Within the enclosing form, an ILBM image must contain a BMHD bitmap-header chunk, and it might also contain a CMAP color-map chunk, a GRAB hot-spot chunk, a CAMG Amiga-specific chunk, and other optional chunks. The last chunk is the BODY, which contains the actual bitmap.

BMHD: Bitmap header

The first embedded chunk in the form after the ILBM type field should be a bitmap header (see Table 9-2).

ILBM bitmap header Table 9-2

Offset	Length	Name	Description
0	4	ID	"BMHD"
4	4	Size	Chunk data size, 20 bytes
8	2	*w*	Width, in pixels
10	2	*h*	Height, in pixels
12	2	*x*	Original *x* position
14	2	*y*	Original *y* position
16	1	*n*Planes	Depth of the image
17	1	masking	Masking type, below
18	1	compression	Compression type, below
19	1	pad1	Unused, should be zero
20	2	trclr	Transparent color, below
22	1	*x*Aspect	*x* aspect ratio
23	1	*y*Aspect	*y* aspect ratio
24	2	*p*Width	Original page width
26	2	*p*Height	Original page height

The original *x*, *y*, *p*Width, page *p*Height are for documentation only and do not affect the image. (The image can be larger than the page.) The pixel-aspect ratio is *x*Aspect/*y*Aspect, corresponding to pixel width/height. In the case of square pixels, *x*Aspect and *y*Aspect are the same. It is the ratio of the aspect values, not their absolute values, that determines the aspect ratio.

Masking

The masking field determines the way the transparent and opaque pixels are identified.

- **mskNone (code 0)** Means that there is no mask, and all pixels are opaque.
- **mskHasMask (code 1)** Means that there is an explicit mask stored as an extra plane, with a row of mask bits stored after the pixel data for each row. A set mask bit means an opaque pixel; a zero mask bit means a transparent pixel.
- **mskHasTransparentColor (code 2)** Means that one pixel value is reserved to indicate a transparent pixel. Any pixel whose value is equal to transparentColor is transparent.
- **mskLasso (code 3)** A rarely used variant of transparent color. Any transparentColor pixels adjacent to the edge of the bitmap are transparent. This is analogous to the operation in some paint programs of drawing a "lasso" around an area and then filling in from the lasso.

Compression

The pixel data can be compressed. The *compression* field can contain cmpNone (code 0) for no compression, or *cmpByteRun1 (code 1) for a simple RLE compression*. RLE compression uses a version of the familiar PackBits method. A bit row is sent as a series of subrecords, each consisting of a control byte followed by one or more data bytes. If the control byte C has the value 0 through 127 (0 through 7F H,) the following *C*+1 bytes are taken as literal data; for example, the control byte 04 means to take the next five bytes as literal data. A control byte of 128 (80 H) is a no-op, and the next byte in the data stream is the next control byte. If the control byte *C* has the value 129 to 255 (81 to FF H), the following data byte is repeated 257–C times. For example, the subrecord F8 99 would mean nine occurrences of a 99 byte, because F8 is decimal 248 and 257–248 is 9.

CAMG: Commodore Amiga specific

A CAMG chunk contains a single 32-bit data word that encodes some Amiga-screen data modes as binary mode bits (see Table 9-3).

Table 9-3

ILBM CAMG chunk

Offset	Length	Name	Description
0	4	ID	"CAMG"
4	4	Size	Chunk data size, 4 bytes
8	4	mode	Amiga viewport modes

Two of the mode bits affect the encoding of the file. If the vmEXTRA_HALFBRITE (code 80 H) bit is set, the high bit of each pixel, if set, means that the pixel is displayed in half-brightness. If the vmHAM (code 800 H) is set, the image consists of color delta values for hold-and-modify mode rather than pixel values. HAM coding is described in detail below.

Some old ILBM images do not contain a CAMG chunk. If so, and the image is six bits deep, it is probably in HAM format.

CMAP: Color map

The optional CMAP section contains a color map (see Table 9-4). Almost all images contain color maps, unless they have 24-bit pixels, in which case they are direct color. The color map consists of 3-byte entries. The first entry maps pixel value 0, the second maps pixel value 1, and so on. In an entry the first byte is the red value, the second byte is the blue value, and the third byte is the green value for the pixel.

Because Amiga hardware has only four bits per color, usually only the high four bits of each byte are significant.

Table 9-4 **ILBM CMAP chunk**

Offset	Length	Name	Description
0	4	ID	"CMAP"
4	4	Size	Chunk data size, 3 times the number of entries
8	3*N	cmap	Color map entries

There is no padding within the CMAP section, although there will be a padding byte at the end of the section if there is an odd number of entries. Usually, there should be a color map entry for each pixel value. For example, if the image is four bits deep, there are 16 possible values so the color map would contain 16 entries or 48 bytes.

EXTRA_HALFBRITE

If the vmEXTRA_HALFBRITE flag is set in the CAMG chunk, the color map has entries for only half of the possible pixel values. If the high bit in a pixel is set, the pixel is half the brightness it would be otherwise. Programs that read ILBM images can either treat this as a special case when reading pixels, or else create an effective color map that includes the high bit. For example, if the CMAP color map has 32 entries, the effective color map has 64 entries. Each entry in the second half of the color map is half the brightness of the corresponding entry in the first half. For example, if entry 1 contained 5,10,15 entry 33 would contain 2,5,7.

CTBL & SHAM: Dynamic color tables

Amiga hardware makes it possible to use a different color map for each scan line, greatly increasing the number of colors in an image. The semistandard CTBL and SHAM chunks contain per-line color maps. The more common CTBL chunk in Table 9-5, was defined by Newtek.

ILBM CTBL chunk Table 9-5

Offset	Length	Name	Description
0	4	ID	"CTBL"
4	4	Size	Chunk data size, 32 times the number of rows
8	32**N*	cmap	Color map entries

Each color map contains 16 entries. Each entry is two bytes. Within each entry, the low four bits of the first byte are the red value. The high four bits of the second byte are the green value and the low four bits are the blue value.

The SHAM chunk, used by other programs, is the same as CTBL except that the ID is SHAM. There is a 2-byte version field that is currently always zero before the color map, so the length is two bytes greater than that of a corresponding CTBL chunk.

A non-HAM image with a CTBL chunk is known as *dynamic hires*. A HAM image with a CTBL chunk is known as *Dynamic HAM* or *DHAM*; one with a SHAM chunk is known as *Sliced HAM* or *SHAM*.

BODY: Image data

The BODY chunk for ILBM contains the actual image pixels. (HAM images are somewhat different; see later.) Within the body, the pixels are stored a row at a time. Within each row, the pixels are stored a plane at a time: first are all of the low-order bits of all the pixels in the row, then all the next-to-low-order bits of all of the pixels in the row, and so forth, one bit row for each plane in the image. If the image has an explicit pixel mask, the mask is sent as an extra bit row after the last bit plane.

Each bit row is sent either as literal data bytes or with packbits compression, depending on the header compression field. In the literal data bytes, the high bit in each byte belongs to the leftmost of the eight pixels represented by the byte. If the number of bytes in the bit row is odd, the row is followed by a padding byte. In a compressed row, the literal row (including the padding byte, if any) is compressed using the packbits scheme described above.

If there is a color map, each pixel is looked up in the color map to get the actual color values once all the pixels in a row have been assembled. If there is no color map and the image is 24 bits deep, it is a direct color image. The highest eight bits are the red value, the middle eight bits are the green value, and the low eight bits are the blue value. An image less than 24 bits deep with no color map would be treated as grayscale, but such images are uncommon.

HAM images

If the vmHAM bit is set in the CAMG chunk, the values in the row are treated quite differently once the planes have been assembled. The high two bits in each value are a flag, and the low *n*Planes–2 bits are used as color values, here called *C*. Invariably there are six planes in a HAM image, with 4-bit color values. The possible flag values are:

0 Look up *C* in the color map and use the high *n*Planes–2 bits of the values there as the red, green, and blue values for this pixel.

1 Use *C* as the blue value for the pixel, and copy the red and green values from the pixel to the left.

2 Use *C* as the red value for the pixel, and copy the blue and green values from the pixel to the left.

3 Use *C* as the green value for the pixel, and copy the red and blue values from the pixel to the left.

At the beginning of each line, the colors are initialized to the background value, color map entry zero. Colors do not carry over from one line to the next. In a regular HAM file there is a single CMAP color map for the whole image. In DHAM and SHAM files there is a different color map for each line in the CTBL or SHAM chunk.

HAM example

Assume that *n*Planes is six so each value in a row has two flag bits and four value bits, color map entry eight contains 2,4,6 and entry 12 (hex C) contains C,D,E. Then a row starting with the hex values:

08 19 23 35 0C 20

corresponds to the RGB values:

2,4,6 2,4,9 3,4,9 3,5,9 C,D,E 0,D,E

HAM images can be an effective way to encode digitized photographs, where colors tend to change gradually and image quality will not be greatly affected if some pixels are slightly off-color. The effect is that colors smear a little, not unlike those of a TV image.

Miscellaneous chunks

There are several other defined chunk types that describe the intended usage of the picture. In most cases, programs can safely ignore these chunks. All of them should appear before the BODY chunk.

ANNO: Annotation

The ANNO field contains a text comment, typically the name of the picture, Table 9-6.

ILBM ANNO chunk Table 9-6

Offset	Length	Name	Description
0	4	ID	"ANNO"
4	4	Size	Chunk size, string length +8
8	N	Name	Text annotation

GRAB: Hot spot

A GRAB chunk, Table 9-7, defines the hot spot if the image is used as a cursor. The hot spot coordinates are relative to the image, with (0,0) being the upper left pixel. It is not often used.

Table 9-7 **ILBM GRAB chunk**

Offset	Length	Name	Description
0	4	ID	"GRAB"
4	4	Size	Chunk data size, 4 bytes
8	2	*x*	*X* coordinate
10	2	*y*	*Y* coordinate

DEST: Destination plane mapping

The DEST chunk, Table 9-8, describes an image where some but not all of the original image's planes are stored in the file. This too is not often used.

Table 9-8 **ILBM DEST chunk**

Offset	Length	Name	Description
0	4	ID	"DEST"
4	4	Size	Chunk data size, 8 bytes
8	1	depth	Original image depth
9	1	pad1	Unused, should be zero
10	2	planePick	Map of stored planes
12	2	planeOnOff	Default values for unstored planes
14	2	planeMask	Restore mask

The three values *planePick*, *planeOnOff*, and *planeMask* are bit maps with each bit corresponding to a plane in the original image, with the low bit of each value corresponding to the low-order plane in the original image. A 1 bit in planePick means that the corresponding plane is present in the file, with the lowest 1 bit in planePick corresponding to the low-order (first stored) plane in the file. The number of 1 bits in planePick should be the same as the depth of the stored image. For planes not stored in the file, corresponding to 0 bits in planePick, planeOnOff provides the default values for those planes. A 1 bit in planeMask means that the corresponding plane should be loaded from the file, or planeOnOff, when the image is loaded; a 0 bit means to leave the plane alone.

If there is a color map, the values in the color map correspond to the original expanded pixels, not the values in the file.

DEST chunks should not appear in an ILBM image intended for interchange, because the effect of plane mapping depends greatly on the program that is reading the file.

SPRT: Sprites

The SPRT chunk, Table 9-9, identifies the image as a sprite, an image that is easily movable on the screen using hardware in the Amiga. This is not often used.

ILBM SPRT chunk Table 9-9

Offset	Length	Name	Description
0	4	ID	"SPRT"
4	4	Size	Chunk data size, 4 bytes
8	4	Precedence	Relative sprite precedence

Sprites with numerically smaller sprite-precedence values appear to be "in front of" sprites with larger values.

CRNG: Color register range

A CRNG chunk, Table 9-10, describes a color register range used by the Deluxe Paint application for a kind of poor man's animation.

There might be multiple color ranges and hence multiple CRNG chunks in a single image.

Table 9-10 **ILBM CRNG chunk**

Offset	Length	Name	Description
0	4	ID	"CRNG"
4	4	Size	Chunk data size, 8 bytes
8	2	Pad1	Reserved, should be zero
10	2	Rate	Color cycle rate
12	2	Active	Nonzero means range is active
14	1	Low	Low color value
15	1	High	High color value

The low and high values identify a range of pixel values affected. If active is nonzero, this range is active and the colors should be cycled. The cycling rate is set by active, which contains 273 times the number of steps per second. This peculiar value is set to make the common 60 cycles per second correspond to a value of 2^{14} or 16,384.

CCRT: Color-cycling range and timing

This is another color-cycling range used by the obsolescent Commodore Graphicraft program (see Table 9-11).

Table 9-11 **ILBM CCRT chunk**

Offset	Length	Name	Description
0	4	ID	"CCRT"
4	4	Size	Chunk data size, 14 bytes
8	2	Direction	Cycling direction
10	1	Start	Minimum pixel value
11	1	End	Maximum pixel value
12	4	Seconds	Step time in seconds
16	4	Microsec	Step time in microseconds
20	2	Pad	Reserved should be zero

The *direction* field contains zero to turn off cycling, one to cycle in increasing pixel value order, and negative one to cycle in decreasing pixel value order. The step time is the sum of the *seconds* and *microsec* fields.

Example

Table 9-12 is an example of a small 4 × 4 cursor, two bits deep with the pixel values:

0 1 2 3
1 2 3 0
2 3 1 0
3 0 1 2

Sample ILBM file Table 9-12

Offset	Data
0–3	"FORM" (chunk type)
4–7	88 (size of form contents)
8–11	"ILBM" (form type)
12–15	"BMHD" (subchunk, bitmap header)
16–19	20 (chunk size)
20–21	4 (width)
22–23	4 (height)
24–25	0 (original *x*)
26–27	0 (original *y*)
28	2 (depth)
29	0 (masking, none)
30	0 (compression, none)
31	0 (pad)
32–33	0 (transparent color, not used)
34	10 (*x* aspect)
35	10 (*y* aspect)
36–37	4 (page width)

Table 9-12 **Continued**

Offset	Data
38–39	4 (page height)
40–43	"CMAP" (subchunk, color map)
44–47	12 (size)
48–59	color map data, four 3-byte entries
60–63	"CAMG" (subchunk, Amiga modes)
64–67	4 (size)
68–71	0 (nothing unusual)
72–75	"BODY" (actual data)
76–79	16 (size)
80–81	hex 50 00 (first row, low bit)
82–83	hex 30 00 (first row, high bit)
84–85	hex A0 00 (second row, low bit)
86–87	hex 60 00 (second row, high bit)
88–89	hex 60 00 (third row, low bit)
90–91	hex C0 00 (third row, high bit)
92–93	hex A0 00 (fourth row, low bit)
94–95	hex 90 00 (fourth row, high bit)

Reference

Morrison, Jerry. *EA IFF 85 Standard for Interchange Format Files.* January 14, 1985. Electronic Arts.

## CHAPTER 10

Truevision Targa

Name	Targa
Image type	Bitmap
Intended use	Support Truevision image-capture hardware
Owner	Truevision, Inc., 7340 Shadeland Station, Indianapolis IN 46256-3925 (317) 841-0332
Last version/ revision/ release date	Version 2.0, 1991
Platforms	IBM PC and Macintosh
Supporting applications	Truevision TIPS, RIO, Logo Editor, Tempra, TOPAS, many image-processing and ray-tracing applications
Similarities	Other bitmap formats
Overall assessment	A widely used format in high-end image capture and processing

Advantages

A competent bitmap format, with provision for extensive annotation

Disadvantages

Many different subformats, not all supported by all applications

Variants

Original 1.0 1984 format, and 2.0 1989 format. Application developers can register private subrecord types.

Overview of file structure

Targa files were introduced by AT&T to support their Targa and ATVISTA image-capture boards, a product line since spun off to Truevision, Inc. The format has since become common both for digitized images and for high-quality images produced by ray tracers, and for other graphics applications.

Targa files store bitmap images along with some optional description information. The original file format contains a header, an optional Image ID, a color map, if appropriate, and the image data. The new format adds several new optional sections that describe both the image and the software that created it.

Files in the new format can be identified by a signature string in the new file footer at the end of the file, described later. All the new information comes after the old, so programs expecting files in the old format can read just the old fields from either kind of file.

Although the Targa format supports a variety of image formats and depths, the majority of files being produced now are 24- or 32-bit true color (image types 2 and 10). There are also a lot of 16-bit files from older models of PC image-capture boards.

Format details

Targa files start with a fixed-size header, followed by variable-sized ID, color map, and image sections. The ID area is at offset 18, immediately after the header.

Multibyte values are stored low byte first, in Intel format. There is no padding or alignment of values or sections beyond byte alignment.

Images can be color mapped. There are two kinds of color mapped images, *pseudo color* in which each pixel value in the image selects a single value from the color map, and *direct color* in which each pixel in the image contains red, green, and blue values that are separately looked up. Images in which the pixels hold the actual red, green, and blue values are called *true color*. Images in which the pixels hold grayscale values are called *black-and-white*.

Images are always stored by row, but the rows can be in top to bottom or bottom to top order, and the pixels can be stored left to right or right to left. In real images, pixels are almost always left to right. Some models of scanner scan top to bottom and others bottom to top, so there is no predominant row order.

Header & ID field

Table 10-1 lists the header fields.

Table 10-1 **Targa file header**

Offset	Length	Description
0	1	ID field length
1	1	Color-map type
2	1	Image type
Color map		
3	2	First color-map entry
5	2	Color-map length
7	1	Color-map entry size
Image data		
8	2	Image *X* origin
10	2	Image *Y* origin
12	2	Image width
14	2	Image height
16	1	Bits per pixel
17	1	Image-descriptor bits

The ID field is intended to be a string that identifies or describes the image. It can be up to 255 bytes long. If there is no ID field, as is usually the case, ID field length is set to zero. The color-map and image-data header fields are described below.

Color map

Header field *Color map type* contains 1 if the image contains a color map, and 0 if not. If there is no color map, the color-map fields in the header should all be 0. Very few Targa files contain color maps, because they were used only by an early display card that never gained wide acceptance. Most files are true color.

In a color map, it is not necessary to define every possible pixel value. The first color-map entry and color-map length define the range of pixel values contained in the file's color map.

Color-map entry size should contain 15, 16, 24, or 32. Fifteen- and sixteen-bit color-map entries are in the form (with each letter being a bit):

A RRRRR GGGGG BBBBB

Each entry is two bytes. The A bit in 16-bit entries is an application-specific attribute that can safely be left zero.

In 24-bit color-map entries, each color is a byte, which are stored in the file in the order B, G, R. In 32-bit color-map entries, each color is a byte, which are stored in the file usually in the order B, G, R, A, where A is a byte of attribute information that can be described in more detail elsewhere in the file.

Image

Image type in the header describes both the image type and the compression scheme used. Table 10-2 lists the common image type values. Other values have been used for other kinds of compression. The most common types are two and ten. In the future, new compression types are likely to be added to provide more effective compression than RLE allows.

Table 10-2

Image type codes

Code	Description
0	No image present
1	Color-mapped, uncompressed
2	True color, uncompressed
3	Black-and-white, uncompressed
9	Color-mapped, RLE compressed
10	True color, RLE compressed
11	Black-and-white, RLE compressed

The header fields *Image X origin* and *Image Y origin* contain the screen position of the lower left corner image. Screen position (0,0) is the lower left corner of the screen. *Image width* and *Image height* contain the size of the image in pixels. *Bits per pixel* is the number of bits per pixel in the image data, usually 8, 16, 24, or 32.

The *Image descriptor* byte contains several bit fields. The low four bits give the number of attribute bits per pixel. The meaning of these bits may be further defined by the *Attributes type* field, described later. The next two bits describe the order in which pixels are stored in rows and rows are stored in the file. Bit value hex 00 is left to right, bottom to top. Right to left, bottom to top is 10 H. Left to right, top to bottom is 20 H. Right to left, top to bottom is 30 H. The high two bits have been used to indicate scan-line interleaving, but this use is deprecated by Truevision. A 00 H means noninterleaved, 40 two-way even-odd interleaving, and 80 four-way interleaving.

Each pixel is stored as one to four bytes. The pixel format depends on the image type. The pixel size is given in the Bits per pixel field in the file header.

* **Color mapped images** Each pixel is looked up in the color table to find the actual color.

* **True color images** Each pixel contains the actual pixel color. Some early Targa true color files contain a color map even though the map is not used. Fifteen- and sixteen-bit pixels are in the form (with each letter being a bit):

  A RRRRR GGGGG BBBBB

  Each entry is two bytes. The A bit in 16-bit entries is an application-specific attribute that can safely be left zero.

  The Truevision specification states that each pixel appears in the file in the order B,G,R,A for 32-bit images or B,G,R for 24-bit images. There has been some confusion about pixel byte order, and some Targa images use the order R,G,B,A or A,R,G,B. Robust software should be prepared to handle any of the orders, probably based on a command argument.

  Typically, a 32-bit image is captured from an NTSC television image, and the attribute information is seven bits of alpha channel (black-and-white brightness, roughly) and one bit of overlay information. The overlay bit typically means that the pixel should be overlaid with some other image, such as a live NTSC feed. Unless the image is specifically intended for applications involving image mixing, the *A* bits should be all zero for maximum portability.

* **Black and white images** Each pixel contains an actual grayscale value.

RLE compression

Any image type can be RLE compressed. In a compressed image, each row is compressed separately. Each compressed row is a series of groups, each of which consists of a control byte and one or more pixels. The high bit of the control byte says whether the group is literal or repeated, and the low seven bits give the group length. The group length is one more than the value in the control byte, so control byte values 0 H through 7F H correspond to lengths of 1 through 128 pixels. If the high bit is one, the group is a repeating group and there is one pixel following, which is repeated some number of times. If the high bit is zero, the group is a literal group and there are as many pixels as the length indicates. For example, a control byte of 0F H is a literal group and is followed by 16 pixels. A control byte of 88 H is a repeating group and is followed by one pixel that is repeated in the image nine times.

New fields

Files in the new 2.0 format contain a *file footer*, which identifies the file as being in the new format and points to the optional new fields that follow the image data. There might be a *developer directory*, for application-specific data, and an *extension* area which contains a set of new fields that describe the image in various ways. The developer directory and some fields in the extension area point to data chunks elsewhere in the file. The relative order of the developer directory, the extension area, and the data chunks is mostly unimportant, although the conventional order is the developer data, the developer directory, the extension area, the data chunks pointer to and from the extension area, and finally the file footer.

File footer

The file footer, Table 10-3, must be the last thing in the file. If the file ends with the string "TRUEVISION-TARGA." followed by a null, the file footer is valid.

Targa file footer — Table 10-3

Offset	Length	Description
0	4	Extension area file position
4	4	Developer directory file position
8	17	ID string "TRUEVISION-TARGA."
25	1	Binary zero, string terminator.

Developer directory

Individual applications can store private information in a Targa file. Such information typically describes the image that the file contains, or something about how it was produced. A program might completely ignore all the developer information and still process the image in a Targa file. As of this writing, there are no widely used developer fields.

If the developer-directory file position in the footer is nonzero, it is the file position of the developer directory, Table 10-4. Each entry contains a two-byte tag that identifies the field type, the file position, and the size of the field. The contents of each field are up to the developer who defined the field. Truevision keeps a registry of tag types.

Table 10-4 **Developer directory**

Offset	Length	Description
0	2	Number of entries
2	2	Tag 1
4	4	Position 1
8	4	Size 1
12	2	Tag 2
14	4	Position 2
18	4	Size 2
...		

Extension area

If the extension-area pointer in the footer is nonzero, it points at the extension area (see Table 10-5). Text fields must be null-terminated. All fields are optional. Unused fields are set to zeros if numeric, or blanks or nulls if text. The most commonly used fields are the postage-stamp image and the various documentation fields; everything else is usually blank or zero.

Creation is the time that the file was created. *Job time* is elapsed time for accounting purposes. *Version number* and *Version letter* would contain 305 and *A* for program version 3.05A. *Pixel aspect* is the aspect ratio of a pixel, expressed as a fraction.

Attribute type gives the meaning of the attribute bits in color-map entries or true-color pixels. Values are 0—no alpha data; 1—undefined and can be ignored; 2—undefined and should be preserved; 3—regular alpha data; and 4—premultiplied alpha data. Code 4 means that the red, green, and blue values in color map entries or pixels have been multiplied by the alpha value.

Extension area Table 10-5

Offset	Length	Description
0	2	Extension area size, should be 495
2	41	Author's name, text
43	81	Author's comments, line 1, text
124	81	Author's comments, line 2, text
205	81	Author's comments, line 3, text
286	81	Author's comments, line 4, text
367	2	Creation month (1–12)
369	2	Creation day (1–31)
371	2	Creation year (e.g., 1991)
373	2	Creation hour (0–23)
375	2	Creation minute (0–59)
377	2	Creation second (0–59)
379	41	Job name, text
420	2	Job time hours (0 or more)
422	2	Job time minutes (0–59)
424	2	Job time seconds (0–59)
426	41	Creating program name, text
467	2	Version number times 100
469	1	Version letter
470	1	Background or transparent color Blue

Table 10-5 **Continued**

Offset	Length	Description
471	1	Background or transparent color Green
472	1	Background or transparent color Red
473	1	Background or transparent color Alpha
474	2	Pixel aspect numerator
476	2	Pixel aspect denominator
478	2	Gamma value numerator
480	2	Gamma value denominator
482	4	Color-correction table file offset
486	4	Postage-stamp image file offset
490	4	Scan-line table file offset
494	1	Attribute type

Scan-line table

The extension area can point to a scan-line table elsewhere in the file. This table is an array containing the file positions of the beginning of each row of image data. There is one entry for each row in the image.

Postage-stamp image

The extension area can point to a "*postage-stamp*" image, a miniature version of the main image. The first two bytes of the postage-stamp image are the width and height of the miniature image. Following those bytes are image data in the same format as the main image. The postage-stamp image should not be larger than 64 × 64 pixels.

Color-correction table

The color-correction table contains 256 extended pixel values that remap the values in the color map. Each entry in the table is eight bytes long, consisting of four 16-bit values, in the order alpha, red, green, blue. A white pixel is four hex FFFF values, and a black pixel is four zero values.

Reference

Truevision Targa File Format Specification Version 2.0. Technical Manual Version 2.2. January 1991. Indianapolis, IN: Truevision, Inc.

CHAPTER 11

Microsoft Windows Device Independent Bitmap

Name	BMP/DIB
Image type	Bitmap
Intended use	Display and storage under Microsoft Windows
Owner	Microsoft
Last version/ revision/ release date	Windows 3.0, 1991
Platforms	Intel 286/386/486 PCs that run Windows
Supporting applications	Windows Paint and, in principle, anything that runs under windows
Similarities	Other bitmap formats with color maps, e.g., PCX and Sun Rasterfile

Advantages

Well-supported under Microsoft Windows. Support sparse for bitmaps.

Disadvantages

Poorly supported everywhere else

Variants

Windows 3.0 can also read BMP files from OS/2 Presentation manager 1.x. The two variants are both described below.

Description

Microsoft Device Independent Bitmap files can contain images that are 1, 4, 8, or 24 bits per pixel. The 1-, 4- and 8-bit images have color maps while the 24-bit images are direct color.

Format details

Since these files are normally used on Intel '86 series computers, they use Intel conventions: low byte stored first and no word alignment. Each file contains a file header, a bitmap header, a color map (unless the image is 24-bit direct color,) and the image. Images in Windows 3 format files may be compressed using an RLE scheme.

File Header

All DIB files contain a common file header (see Table 11-1).

Table 11-1

Windows BITMAPFILEHEADER file header

Offset	Size	Name	Description
0	2	bfType	ASCII "BM"
2	4	bfSize	Size in bytes of the file
6	2	bfReserved1	Zero
8	2	bfReserved2	Zero
10	4	bfOffBits	Byte offset in files where image begins

The *bfOffBits* field contains the distance in bytes from the beginning of the file to the beginning of the image data bits, to make it easier to skip over the header.

The two different variant file formats are distinguished by the first word of the bitmap header, file offset 14. It will contain 12 for an OS/2 format file, and 40 for a Windows 3.x format file.

Windows 3 Bitmap header

Following the file header is the bitmap header and, optionally, the color map. The bitmap header structure is sometimes referred to as a BITMAPINFO, with the fields up to the color map a BITMAPINFOHEADER (see Table 11-2).

Table 11-2 **Windows BITMAPINFOHEADER image header**

Offset	Size	Name	Description
14	4	biSize	Size of this header, 40 bytes
18	4	biWidth	Image width in pixels
22	4	biHeight	Image height in pixels
26	2	biPlanes	Number of image planes, must be 1
28	2	biBitCount	Bits per pixel, 1, 4, 8, or 24
30	4	biCompression	Compression type, below
34	4	biSizeImage	Size in bytes of compressed image, or zero
38	4	biXPelsPerMeter	Horizontal resolution, in pixels/meter
42	4	biYPelsPerMeter	Vertical resolution, in pixels/meter
46	4	biClrUsed	Number of colors used, below
50	4	biClrImportant	Number of "important" colors
54	4*N	bmiColors	Color map

biSizeImage may be (and usually is) zero if the data are uncompressed.

Color map

Images using 1, 4, or 8 bits per pixel must have a color map. The color map sizes are normally 2, 16, or 256 entries, respectively, but can be smaller if the image does not need a full set of colors. If the biClrUsed field is nonzero, it contains the number of colors used, which is also the number of entries in the color map. If the field is zero, the color map is the full size. For 24-bit images there is no color map, and the image is direct RGB color. The biClrUsed field may be nonzero to make a suggested color table size.

Since the display device may not have as many colors available as the image requires, entries in the color map should have the most important colors first. The biClrImportant field, if nonzero, tells how many of the colors are important for good image reproduction.

Color map entries are four bytes each (see Table 11-3).

Windows RGBQUAD color map entry Table 11-3

Offset	Name	Description
0	rgbBlue	Blue value for color map entry.
1	rgbGreen	Green value for color map entry.
2	rgbRed	Red value for color map entry.
3	rgbReserved	Zero

Windows 3 Bitmap data

The bitmap data immediately follows the color map. The data may be uncompressed, or for 4- and 8-bit images may use an RLE compression scheme.

Bits are logically (and physically, in the absence of compression) stored a row at a time. Each row is padded to a 4-byte boundary with zero bytes. Rows are stored in order from the bottom of the image to the top.

* **Bitmap with 1 bit per pixel** Each pixel is a single bit, packed eight per byte. The high-order bit in the byte is the leftmost pixel.

* **Bitmaps with 4 bits per pixel** Uncompressed images are packed two pixels per byte, with the high nibble being the leftmost pixel and each row padded with zeros to a 4-byte boundary.

  Compressed images use an RLE encoded format, consisting of a sequence of groups. There are three kinds of groups: repeating groups, literal groups, and special groups. A repeating group is two bytes. The first byte is a pixel count and the second byte is a pair of pixels. The group represents the number of pixels in the first byte, with the two pixels in the second byte alternating. For example, the hex bytes

  05 24

  represent the pixels

  2 4 2 4 2

  A literal group is a zero byte, a byte with the pixel count, and the literal pixels. The pixel count must be at least three (one or two pixels can be encoded as a repeating group). The literal pixels are padded out with zeros to an even number of bytes. For example, the hex bytes

  00 05 12 34 50 00

  (note the even byte padding) represent the pixels

  1 2 3 4 5

  The special sequence 00 00 represents the end of a row. The special sequence 00 01 represents the end of the bitmap. The special sequence 00 02 *xx yy* is a position delta, saying to continue the image *xx* pixels to the right and *yy* pixels down.

* **Bitmaps with 8 bits per pixel** Uncompressed images are packed one pixel per byte, with each row padded to a 4-byte boundary.

Compressed images use an RLE encoded format, consisting of a sequence of groups. There are three kinds of groups: repeating groups, literal groups, and special groups. A repeating group is two bytes. The first byte is a pixel count and the second byte is a pixel value. For example, the hex bytes

05 24

represent the pixels

24 24 24 24 24

A literal group is a zero byte, a byte with the pixel count, and the literal pixels. The pixel count must be at least three. The literal pixels are padded out with zeros to an even number of bytes. For example, the hex bytes:

00 05 12 34 56 78 9A 00

(note the even byte padding) represent the pixels 12 34 56 78 9A. The special sequences are the same as in 4-bit images.

* **Bitmaps with 24 bits per pixel** Each pixel is three bytes, containing the blue, green, and red values in that order. Each row is zero-padded to a 4-byte boundary.

OS/2 1.x Bitmap header

The OS/2 bitmap format is similar to, yet simpler than, the Windows 3.0 format. The bitmap header structure is sometimes referred to as a BITMAPCOREINFO, with the fields up to the color map a BITMAPCOREHEADER (see Table 11-4).

Table 11-4

OS/2 BITMAPCOREINFO image header

Offset	Size	Name	Description
14	4	bcSize	Size of this header, 12 bytes.
18	2	bcWidth	Image width in pixels.

Table 11-4 **Continued**

Offset	Size	Name	Description
20	2	bcHeight	Image height in pixels.
22	2	bcPlanes	Number of planes, must be 1.
24	2	bcBitCount	Bits per pixel, 1, 4, 8, or 24.
26	3*N	bmciColors	Color map

Color map

Images using 1, 4, or 8 bits per pixel must have a color map. The color map sizes are 2, 16, or 256 entries, respectively. Color map entries are three bytes each (see Table 11-5).

Table 11-5 **OS/2 RGBTRIPLE color map entry**

Offset	Name	Description
0	rgbtBlue	Blue value for color map entry.
1	rgbtGreen	Green value for color map entry.
2	rgbtRed	Red value for color map entry.

OS/2 1.x Bitmap data

The bitmap data immediately follows the color map. Each row is zero-padded to a multiple of four bytes. The bit encoding is identical to the uncompressed Windows 3.0 bitmap.

Reference

Microsoft Corp. *Microsoft Windows Programmer's Reference*. 1990. Microsoft Press.

## CHAPTER 12

WordPerfect Graphics

Name	WPG
Image type	Metafile
Intended use	Store graphics for use with WordPerfect and DrawPerfect
Owner	WordPerfect (now Novell)
Last version/ revision/ release date	2.0, with WordPerfect 6
Platforms	DOS, Windows, Mac, Unix, VMS
Supporting applications	DrawPerfect, WordPerfect, most other WP applications, imported by many other applications
Similarities	Windows metafile, Lotus PIC
Overall assessment	A competent simple metafile format

Advantages

Well-supported under WordPerfect and related applications. Support sparse for bit maps.

Disadvantages

Half-hearted support everywhere else

Variants

WP 5.1 added some new record types beyond those supported by WP 5.0. Revised version 2 of the format in WP 6.x.

Overview of file structure

WordPerfect Graphics is a metafile format defined for DrawPerfect and WordPerfect 5.x. It is most commonly used to embed business graphics into WordPerfect documents, but in principle is a general purpose graphics format. A file can contain either a single bitmap or a sequence of drawing records, such as lines, boxes, and text.

Here we describe the format of WPG 1.0 files, supported by WordPerfect 5.x, which is the version most commonly encountered. WordPerfect considers the details of the 2.0 format proprietary, and makes it available only with a nondisclosure agreement.

Although WPG permits very complex image data, most WPG files are in fact quite simple, using mostly lines, polylines, and rectangles.

Format details

A WPG file consists of a header followed by a series of records. Each record has a header containing the record's type and length, which makes it possible for programs to skip unknown record types.

All multi-byte fields are in Motorola (big-endian) order. Distances are measured in Word Perfect Units (WPU), which are 1/1200 inch. In arcs and circles, angles are in degrees measured counterclockwise from the origin. *X* and *Y* positions are measured in WPU from the lower lefthand corner of the image. Color images use a palette stored in the file.

File header

See Table 12-1 for a WPG file header.

WPG file header Table 12-1

Offset	Size	Description
0	4	File ID, 0xFF, "W", "P", "G"
4	4	File offset of first record, 16 in 1.0 files
8	1	Product type, always 1
9	1	File type, always 22
10	1	Major version, always 1
11	1	Minor version, always 0
12	2	Encryption key, always 0 for non-encrypted
14	2	Reserved, contains 0

Record header

Following the header is a sequence of drawing records. Each record starts with a header containing the type and the length of the record. The length field, which gives the length of the record excluding the header, uses a variable-length encoding depending on its value. (See Tables 12-2, 12-3, and 12-4.)

Record header, byte length up to 254 bytes Table 12-2

Offset	Size	Description
0	1	Record type
1	1	Record length

Table 12-3 **Record header, short length up to 32,767 bytes**

Offset	Size	Description
0	1	Record type
1	1	Flag, contains 255 (hex FF)
2	2	Record length

Table 12-4 **Record header, long length over 32,767 bytes**

Offset	Size	Description
0	1	Record type
1	1	Flag, contains 255 (hex FF)
2	2	High 16 bits of length + hex 8000
4	2	Low 16 bits of length

If the byte length is 255, the actual length is a following short or long value. If the high bit of the subsequent short value is set, the length is a long; otherwise it's a short.

In practice, most records are small and most lengths are stored in a byte.

Record types

Table 12-5 shows the various record types.

Table 12-5 **Record types**

Code	Description
1	Fill attributes
2	Line attributes
3	Marker attributes
4	Polymarker
5	Line
6	Polyline

7	Rectangle
8	Polygon
9	Ellipse
10	Reserved
11	Bitmap type 1
12	Graphic text
13	Graphic text attributes
14	Color map
15	Start of WPG data
16	End of WPG data
17	Postscript data
18	Reserved for output attributes
19	Curved polyline
20	Bitmap type 2
21	Start figure
22	Start chart
23	PlanPerfect data
24	Graphics text type 2
25	Start of WPG data type 2
26	Graphics text: type 3 (ASCII screen text)
27	Postscript type 2 data

The first record in each file must be a type 15 (Start of WPG data), and the last record must be a type 16 (End of WPG data). Except in files that include a single bitmap, the second record is usually type 25 (Start of WPG data type 2).

Colors

Colors in pictures are specified as the first 16 colors of the palette and should be the standard IBM VGA colors, to avoid peculiar display problems. If no color-map record is included, the picture uses a default palette, Table 12-6, containing the 16 VGA colors and 16 shades of gray. (See Table 12-6.)

Table 12-6 **Standard colors**

Number	Color
0	Black
1	Blue
2	Green
3	Cyan
4	Red
5	Magenta
6	Brown
7	Light gray
8	Dark gray
9	Light blue
10	Light green
11	Light cyan
12	Pink
13	Light magenta
14	Yellow
15	White
16	Black (same as color 0)
17–30	Shades of gray
31	White (same as color 15)

Start WPG data (type 15)

First record in every WPG file. (See Table 12-7.)

Table 12-7 **Start WPG Data**

Offset	Size	Description
0	1	Version, always 1
1	1	Flags: hex 80 = Postscript data included in file
2	2	Width of image in WPU
4	2	Height of image in WPU

End WPG data (type 16)

Should be the last record in each file. This record consists only of the header.

Start of WPG data type 2 (type 25)

Usually appears at the start of each file, after the Start WPG Data record. This record consists of a sequence of subrecords, in the formats described below. Often the record contains no subrecords. (See Table 12-8.)

Start WPG Data type 2 subrecord header Table 12-8

Offset	Size	Description
0	1	Subtype, 0 to 4
1	2	Length of following subrecord
3	N	Subrecord

The subrecord types are listed in Table 12-9.

Start WPG Data type 2 subrecord types Table 12-9

Offset	Size	Description
		Subtype 0, foreground/background
0	1	Background color
1	1	Foreground color
		Subtype 1, obsolete
		Subtype 2, page information
0	1	Shade colors
1	1	Shade intensity
2	1	Top to bottom shading flag
3	2	Left margin
5	2	Right margin

Table 12-9 **Continued**

Offset	Size	Description
7	2	Top margin
9	2	Bottom margin
11	2	Border style
13	2	Effective form length in WPU
15	2	Effective form width in WPU
17	1	Effective form type (usually 1 for plain)
18	1	Effective form name length
19	41	Null-terminated form name
41	1	Form orientation (0 for portrait, 1 for landscape)
		Subtype 3, page shading
0	1	Shade colors
1	1	Shade intensity
1	1	Top to bottom shading flag
		Subtype 4, grid information
0	1	Option flags (32 for grid, 64 for snap to grid)
1	2	Grid *X* size (WPU)
3	2	Grid *Y* size (WPU)
5	1	Grid display step size

Color map (type 14)

Must precede records that use the colors. The record can give a complete color map, or a portion of the map to override some but not all of the default colors. (See Table 12-10.)

Table 12-10 **Color map**

Offset	Size	Description
0	2	Index of first color
2	2	Number of colors
4	3*N	Colors as R,G,B triples

Bitmap (types 11 & 20)

A WPG file that contains just a bitmap typically uses a type 11 bitmap. This is the only bitmap supported by WP 5.0. In files used by WP 5.1, a type 20 bitmap may be used along with other record types.

Although the format permits 1-, 2-, 4-, and 8-bit pixels, 8-bit images are rare and are poorly supported. (See Tables 12-11 & 12-12.)

WP 5.0 bitmap (type 11) Table 12-11

Offset	Size	Description
0	2	Width in pixels
2	2	Height in pixels
4	2	Bits per pixel (1, 2, 4, or 8)
6	2	*X* resolution (pixels/in)
8	2	*Y* resolution (pixels/in)
10	*N*	Bitmap data, see below

WP 5.1 bitmap (type 20) Table 12-12

Offset	Size	Description
0	2	Bitmap rotation angle (0 to 359)
2	2	*X* location in image of lower left corner (WPU)
4	2	*Y* location in image of lower left corner (WPU)
6	2	*X* location in image of upper right corner (WPU)
8	2	*Y* location in image of upper right corner (WPU)
10	2	Width in pixels
12	2	Height in pixels
14	2	Bits per pixel (1, 2, 4, or 8)
16	2	*X* resolution (pixels/in)
18	2	*Y* resolution (pixels/in)
20	*N*	Bitmap data, see below

Both formats use the same compression scheme. Single-bit images use the foreground and background colors defined; 2-, 4-, and 8-bit images use colors from the color map. The image is compressed using a PackBits-like scheme. (See Table 12-13.)

Table 12-13 **Bitmap compressed data**

Byte value N	Meaning
0	Take next byte as a count, repeat previous scan line that many times
1–127	Take following *N* bytes from file
128	Take next byte as a count, insert that many 255 (hex FF) bytes
129–255	Repeat following byte *N*–128 times

Fill attributes (type 1)

Determine how subsequent rectangles, polygons, and ellipses should be filled. The record is a single byte, encoding the fill type (Table 12-14).

Table 12-14 **Fill types**

Code	Meaning
0	Hollow
1	Solid
2	Narrow-spaced +45-degree lines
3	Medium-spaced +45-degree lines
4	Widely spaced +45-degree lines
5	Narrow-spaced +45 and –45-degree lines
6	Medium-spaced +45 and –45-degree lines
7	Widely spaced +45 and –45-degree lines
8	Narrow-spaced vertical lines (shaded)
9	Medium-spaced vertical lines
10	Widely spaced vertical lines
11–17	Dots, lowest to highest density

18	Narrow-spaced horizontal lines
19	Medium-spaced horizontal lines
20	Widely spaced horizontal lines
21	Narrow-spaced vertical & horizontal lines
22	Medium-spaced vertical & horizontal lines
23	Widely spaced vertical & horizontal lines
24	Narrow-spaced –45-degree lines
25	Medium-spaced –45-degree lines
26	Widely spaced –45-degree lines
27	Partial weave
28	Weave
29	Fine checkerboard
30	Horizontal zigzag
31	45-degree wide line
32	Wide checkerboard
33	Fine 45-degree bricks
34	Medium 45-degree bricks
35	Wide 45-degree bricks
36	Fine 45-degree bricks reversed
37	Medium 45-degree bricks reversed
38	Wide 45-degree bricks reversed
39	Horizontal brick thin
40	Horizontal brick medium
41	Vertical brick thin
42	Vertical brick medium
43	Waves
44	Wide vertical zigzag
45	Medium vertical zigzag
46	Movie pattern
47	Skewed-brick pattern
48	Interconnected dot pattern
49	Shadow squares horizontal

Table 12-14 **Continued**

Code	Meaning
50	Dot black vertical
51	Vertical slanted thick boxes
52	Vertical cursive black
53	45-degree shingle pattern
54	45-degree wide black arrows
55	Horizontal T lines
56	Black box 45-degree dots
57	Corner piece pattern
58	45-degree triangles And dot lines
59	Horizontal heartbeat-monitor pattern
60	Vertical lines/horizontal waves
61	Light and dark wave patterns
62	45-degree white umbrella pattern
63	45-degree black umbrella pattern
255	Fill with background color

Determine how subsequent lines and curves should be drawn. (See Table 12-15.)

Table 12-15 **Line types**

Offset	Size	Description
0	1	Style
		0 = Invisible
		1 = Solid
		2 = Long dash
		3 = Dotted
		4 = Dash/dot
		5 = Medium dash
		6 = Dash/dot/dot
		7 = Short dash
		8 = Dash/dot/dash

Offset	Size	Description
		9 = Longer dash
		10 = Short dots
		11 = Short, widely spaced dots
		12 = Medium, widely spaced dashes
		13 = Medium/short/medium
		14 = Long/short/long
		15 = Dash/short dot/dash
1	1	Color
2	2	Line width (WPU)

Line (type 5)

Draw a single line segment, using the current line attributes. (See Table 12-16.)

Line Table 12-16

Offset	Size	Description
0	2	Start *X* (WPU)
2	2	Start *Y* (WPU)
4	2	End *X* (WPU)
6	2	End *Y* (WPU)

Marker attributes (type 3)

Determine the marker used at line ends in polyline commands. (See Table 12-17.)

Marker types Table 12-17

Offset	Size	Description
0	1	Style, add 128 for filled rather than hollow
		0 = None
		1 = Dot

Table 12-17 **Continued**

Offset	Size	Description
		2 = Plus
		3 = Star
		4 = Circle
		5 = Square
		6 = Triangle
		7 = Upside-down triangle
		8 = Diamond
		9 = *X*
1	1	Color
2	2	Size (WPU)

Polyline (type 6), polymarker (type 4), and polygon (type 8)

For a polyline, draw a series of line segments starting at the first point in the record, using the current line attributes. For maximum portability, draw no more than 400 lines per record. For a polymarker, draw a sequence of points with the current marker type used at each point. For a polygon, draw a series of lines starting at the first point in the record, using the current line attributes, and connect the last point back to the first. (See Table 12-18.)

Table 12-18 **Polyline, polymarker, or polygon**

Offset	Size	Description
0	2	Number of points
2	2	First *X* (WPU)
4	2	First *Y* (WPU)
6	2	Second *X* (WPU)
8	2	Second *Y* (WPU)
	...	

Rectangle (type 7)

Draw a rectangle, using the current line and fill attributes. (See Table 12-19.)

Rectangle Table 12-19

Offset	Size	Description
0	2	Lower left *X* (WPU)
2	2	Lower left *Y* (WPU)
4	2	Width (WPU)
6	2	Height (WPU)

Ellipse or arc (type 9)

Draw an arc or ellipse, using the current line and, if the arc is closed, the current fill attributes. (See Table 12-20.)

Ellipse Table 12-20

Offset	Size	Description
0	2	Center *X* (WPU)
2	2	Center *Y* (WPU)
4	2	Horizontal radius (WPU)
6	2	Vertical radius (WPU)
8	2	Rotation angle from horizontal
10	2	Beginning of arc (0–359)
12	2	End of arc (0–359)
14	2	Flags, ORed together
		1 = "pie slice," connect ends to center
		2 = "chord," connect ends to each other

To draw a circle, make sure the two radii are equal; the beginning and end of the arc should be 0 and 359. Connect the ends.

Bezier curve (type 19)

Draw a Bezier curve using the current line attributes. Not supported in WP 5.0; for portability also include an approximation drawn with polylines. (See Table 12-21.)

Table 12-21 **Bezier curve**

Offset	Size	Description
0	4	Size of equivalent WP5.0 data that follows
4	2	Number of following point groups
6	2	Start *X* (WPU)
8	2	Start Y (WPU)
		Following six items repeat for each point group
10	2	Control *A X* (WPU)
12	2	Control *A Y* (WPU)
14	2	Control *B X* (WPU)
16	2	Control *B Y* (WPU)
18	2	Point *X* (WPU)
20	2	Point *A Y* (WPU)

WP 5.0 graphics text attributes (type 13)

Define the attributes for subsequent text records. (See Table 12-22.)

Table 12-22 **Graphics text attributes**

Offset	Size	Description
0	2	Character cell width (WPU), or −1 for proportional spacing
2	2	Character cell height (WPU)
4	10	Reserved

14	2	Font flags: 3408 (hex 0D50) = typewriter 4432 (hex 1150) = sans-serif 6480 (hex 1950) = serif
16	1	Reserved
17	1	Horiz alignment, 0=left, 1=center, 2=right
18	1	Vertical alignment, 0=base, 1=center, 2=cap, 3=bottom, 4=top
19	1	Color
20	2	Rotation angle (0–359)

Proportional fonts are not actually supported within this record; use type 24 instead.

WP 5.0 graphics text (type 12)

Draw text using the current attributes. (See Table 12-23.)

Graphics text Table 12-23

Offset	Size	Description
0	2	Text length
2	2	*X* position (WPU)
4	2	*Y* position (WPU)
6	N	Text to draw

WP 5.1 graphics text (type 24)

Draw text using the current attributes. Not supported in WP 5.0; for portability follow by approximate text in types 12 and 13. (See Table 12-24.)

Table 12-24 **WP 5.1 graphics text**

Offset	Size	Description
0	4	Size of equivalent WP 5.0 data that follows
4	2	Baseline angle (0-359)
6	2	Length of text in bytes
8	2	*X*1 (lower left) coordinate
10	2	*Y*1 (lower left) coordinate
12	2	*X*2 (upper right) coordinate
14	2	*Y*2 (upper right left) coordinate
16	2	*X* scale factor in percent
18	2	*Y* scale factor in percent
20	1	Text subtype, 0=window, 1=line, 2=bullet chart, 3=text chart, 4=free-format chart
21	*N*	Text, including WP formatting codes

Graphics text 3 (type 26)

DOS screen dump data. (See Table 12-25.)

Table 12-25 **Graphics text 3**

Offset	Size	Description
0	*N*	Bitmapped screen dump data

PostScript data 1 (type 17)

PostScript output data. NOTE: The bounding box in the record is in PostScript units of 1/72", not in WPU. (See Table 12-26.)

Table 12-26

Postscript data 1

Offset	Size	Description
0	2	*X* lower left
2	2	*Y* lower left
4	2	*X* upper right
6	2	*Y* upper right
8	*N*	PostScript data

PostScript data 2 (type 27)

Encapsulated PostScript output data. (See Table 12-27.)

Table 12-27

Postscript data 2

Offset	Size	Description
0	4	Length of subsequent Type 20 bitmap preview
4	2	Rotation angle (0-359)
6	2	Lower left *X* (WPU)
8	2	Lower left *Y* (WPU)
10	2	Upper right *X* (WPU)
12	2	Upper right *Y* (WPU)
14	40	Filename of EPS file
54	2	Original bounding box lower left *X*
56	2	Original bounding box lower left *Y*
58	2	Original bounding box upper right *X*
60	2	Original bounding box Upper right *Y*
62	*N*	EPS data

CHAPTER 13

Sun Rasterfiles

Name	Sun Rasterfiles
Image type	Bitmap
Intended use	Image storage
Owner	Sun Microsystems
Last version/ revision/ release date	October 1991
Platforms	Sun Workstations
Supporting applications	FrameMaker, many Sun utilities
Overall assessment	A competent raster format

Advantages

Well-supported on Suns

Disadvantages

Not widely supported on other systems

Overview of file structure

Sun Microsystems was one of the first manufacturers of workstations with bitmapped screens. They defined a simple raster format for bit images used on their systems. There are now several variant rasterfiles versions, but the two most common are the original and a slightly compressed version using run-length encoding. There are provisions for single-plane black-and-white images as well as direct-color images and images with a color map.

Although the format appears to allow arbitrarily deep images, only certain combinations are supported by most rasterfile applications. Images can be one bit deep for monochrome bitmap pictures, with or without a color map. They can be eight bits deep for grayscale or color-mapped images. They can be 24 or 32 (with the high 8 bits ignored) bits deep for either direct color or per-component color-mapped images.

Format details

In this description, the capitalized names after some constant values are the symbolic names used in C language header files that define the format. The file starts with a 32-byte header consisting of eight four-byte integers, Table 13-1.

Sun Rasterfile header Table 13-1

Offset	Name	Description
0	Magic	Magic number 59a66a95H (RAS_MAGIC)
4	Width	Image width in pixels
8	Height	Image height in pixels
12	Depth	Bits per pixel
16	Length	Size of image data in bytes, or zero
20	Type	Encoding type, below
24	Maptype	Type of colormap, below
28	Maplength	Length of colormap, below

The magic number both identifies the file as a rasterfile and identifies the file byte order. If the magic number is in the reverse byte order (i.e., 956aa659H), the file was written on a machine with the reverse byte order, and all multibyte fields in the file must be byte-swapped.

The encoding types are in Table 13-2.

Table 13-2 **Sun raster image encoding types**

Code	Description
0	(RT_OLD) for old files
1	(RT_STANDARD) for standard files
2	(RT_BYTE_ENCODED) for RLE files
3	(RT_FORMAT_RGB) XRGB or RGB instead of XBGR or BGR, below
4	(RT_FORMAT_TIFF) embedded TIFF file
5	(RT_FORMAT_IFF) embedded IFF file
65535	(RT_EXPERIMENTAL) various experimental formats

RT_OLD and RT_STANDARD files are the same except that RT_OLD files often leave the length field in the header zero. RT_OLD files are considered obsolete.

Color maps

There are three color formats, Table 13-3. Black-and-white or grayscale images do not need a color map (RMT_NONE). For color images, the color map is three byte arrays each *maplength* long, the first being the red values, the second the green values, and the third being the blue values corresponding to each pixel value (RMT_EQUAL_RGB). The color map should generally contain 2^{depth} entries. Raw color maps provide a single color map shared among all colors, and do not seem very useful except, perhaps, to remap the shades of gray in a grayscale image.

Table 13-3 **Sun raster color types**

Code	Description
0	(RMT_NONE) No color map
1	(RMT_EQUAL_RGB) 8 bits per color, single map
2	(RMT_RAW) Uninterpreted color map

Image data

After the color map, if any, are the pixels in the image. The pixels are written left to right within a row, and by row from top to bottom. Each row is padded to a multiple of 16 bits. Some documentation says that rows are padded to 32 bits, but that does not appear to be the case.

For images that are one pixel deep, the pixels are individual bits with the leftmost pixel being the high bit in a byte. If there is no color map, the image is black-and-white. The color map size can be two, in which case it maps the two colors used by the image.

For images that are eight pixels deep, each pixel is a byte. If there is no color map, the pixels are grayscale, with 0 being black and 256 being white. If there is a color map, each pixel is interpreted relative to the color map.

For images that are 24 or 32 bits deep, each pixel contains eight bits each of red, blue, and green. In 32-bit images, the high byte of each pixel is ignored and is usually zero. The order of bytes within a 24-bit pixel, or the remaining bytes after the ignored byte in a 32-bit pixel, is usually blue, then green, then red. However, when the format is RT_FORMAT_RGB the order is red, green, then blue. (Rasterfiles are not altogether consistent, and some have red and blue in the opposite positions than the format code would indicate.) If there is no color map the pixels are direct color values. If there is a color map, each pixel component is looked up individually in the appropriate color map for that color. For 24-bit pixels, if the width in pixels is odd there is an extra byte at the end of each row to pad the row to a multiple of 16 bits.

Compression

If the encoding type is RT_BYTE_ENCODED, the image is compressed using a simple RLE scheme. Within the image data, any byte except 128 (hex 80) represents itself. The byte sequence 128, 0 (80 H, 0 H) represents a single 128 byte. The byte sequence 128, *N*,

M represents a series of *N* bytes each with the value *M*. The length field in the header represents the number of bytes in the compressed image. The size of the uncompressed image can be computed from the height, width, and depth fields in the header.

References

Sun Microsystems. "Rasterfile (5)," *Sun OS 4.0 Programmer's Manual*. 1990.

McGee, Pat. "Format For Byte-Encoded Rasterfiles," *Sun-Spots Digest, Volume 6, Issue 84*.

## CHAPTER 14

PBM

Name	PBM (Portable Bitmap Utilities)
Image type	Bitmap (raster)
Intended use	Format conversion
Owner	Jef Poskanzer, author of the PBM utilities. Can be used without a fee
Last version/ revision/ release date	October 1991
Platforms	Unix, PC
Supporting applications	PBM utilities, some other Unix utilities
Overall assessment	Excellent for interchange and translation, too bulky for storage

Advantages

Very simple to read and write, simple text encoding, large set of conversion utilities

Disadvantages

Bulky, primarily supported on Unix, binary versions only support eight bits per pixel

Overview of file structure

The Portable Bitmap Utilities are a widely used set of free utility programs written mostly by Jef Poskanzer. They include programs to read and write dozens of other bitmap file formats, as well as utilities to perform transformations on images, such as cropping, smoothing, edge enhancing, and gamma correcting. Using Unix *pipes,* users can combine these programs to do all sorts of image format conversions and transformations.

The utilities define three very simple image formats to use as a *lingua franca* among the various programs. The formats are: *Portable Bitmap* for monochrome bitmaps; *Portable Gray Map* for grayscale bitmaps; and *Portable Pixel Map* for color bitmaps. Some of the programs can handle any of the three formats, and are referred to as PNM (*Portable aNy Map*) programs.

All the format-conversion programs go either to or from one of the three formats. By combining them you can pretty much convert any supported format to any other. For example, to go from GIF to TIFF, use giftoppm to convert the GIF file to PPM, then pnmtotiff to convert the resulting PPM to TIFF. Unix pipes make it possible to do this without creating intermediate files.

Format details

Each of the three formats starts with a header, which is composed of ASCII characters followed by the pixels in the image. The header consists of a two-letter *magic number* that identifies the format type, followed by file parameters. Each parameter is a string of digits, and parameters are separated by white space—spaces, tabs, carriage returns, and new lines.

Each format has two variants, ASCII pixels and binary pixels. ASCII pixels are stored as text numbers separated by white space. For maximum portability, there should be a new line at least every 70 characters, so no line of the file is more than 70 characters wide. In either the header or within the ASCII pixels, any text from a sharp sign (#) to the end of line is ignored as a comment.

Binary pixels are stored as binary data, the details depending on the format.

Portable bitmap

Each pixel in a PBM file represents a single bit, 1 being black and 0 being white. The header of an ASCII PBM file is in Table 14-1.

ASCII PBM file header Table 14-1

Field	Description
P1	Literal magic number
	white space
width	Width of image in pixels
	white space
height	Height of image in pixels
	white space

Following the header are the bits, 1 or 0, each separated by white space. The bits are listed row by row from top to bottom, and left to right within each row.

The header of a binary PBM file is in Table 14-2.

Binary PBM file header Table 14-2

Field	Description
P4	Literal magic number
	white space
width	Width of image in pixels
	white space
height	Height of image in pixels
	white space

The white space after the height can be only a single character, typically a new line. Following that are the bits, row by row from top to bottom. The bits in each row are stored eight to a byte from left to right, the leftmost bit being the high-order bit in each byte. Each row starts in a new byte, even if the width of the image is not a multiple of eight.

Portable gray map

Each pixel in a gray map has a numeric value, from 0 for black to an image-specific maximum value for white. This is the reverse of PBM. The header of an ASCII PGM file is in Table 14-3.

Table 14-3 **Character PGM file header**

Field	Description
P2	Literal magic number
	white space
width	Width of image in pixels
	white space
height	Height of image in pixels
	white space
max	Maximum gray value
	white space

Following the header are the pixels as ASCII decimal numbers, separated by white space. The pixels are listed row by row from top to bottom, and left to right within each row.

The header of a binary PGM file is in Table 14-4.

Table 14-4 **Raw PGM file header**

Field	Description
P5	Literal magic number
	white space
width	Width of image in pixels
	white space

height	Height of image in pixels
	white space
max	Maximum gray value
	white space

Following the header are the pixels as binary values, one per byte. The pixels are listed row by row from top to bottom, and left to right within each row. Because the maximum value in an 8-bit byte is 255, the binary format cannot handle images with more than 256 gray levels. The ASCII PGM format has no such restriction.

Portable pixel map

Each pixel in a portable pixel map is represented as a triplet of red, green, and blue color values, with the values running from 0 to an image-specific maximum value. Black is 0,0,0 and white is max,max,max. The header of an ASCII PPM file is in Table 14-5.

Table 14-5 **ASCII PPM file header**

Field	Description
P3	Literal magic number
	white space
width	Width of image in pixels
	white space
height	Height of image in pixels
	white space
max	Maximum color-component value
	white space

Following that are the pixels with each component as an ASCII decimal number, separated by white space. Each pixel is written as red, green, and blue values in that order. The pixels are listed row by row from top to bottom, and left to right within each row. The header of a binary PGM file is in Table 14-6.

Table 14-6 **Raw PPM file header**

Field	Description
P6	Literal magic number
	white space
width	Width of image in pixels
	white space
height	Height of image in pixels
	white space
max	Maximum color-component value
	white space

Following the header are the pixels as binary values, one component per byte. Each pixel takes three bytes representing red, green, and blue in that order. The pixels are listed row by row from top to bottom, and left to right within each row. Because the maximum value in an 8-bit byte is 255, the binary format cannot handle images with more than 256 color levels per component. The ASCII PPM format has no such restriction.

Reference

Jef Poskanzer. "pbm (5), pgm (5), ppm (5), and pnm (5)," *PBMPLUS: Extended Portable Bitmap Toolkit*. October 1991. Public Network Distribution.

## CHAPTER 15

X Window bitmaps

Name	XBM
Image type	Monochrome bitmap
Intended use	Cursors and icons in X Window systems
Owner	MIT X Consortium
Last version/ revision/ release date	X11, 1986
Platforms	All X systems
Supporting applications	X server XReadBitmapFile, XWriteBitmapFile, and XCreateBitmapFromData operations, *bitmap editing program*, C compilers
Overall assessment	Suitable for X icons and cursors

Advantages

Directly readable

Disadvantages

Verbose, specific to X

Variants

Earlier X10 version, newer X Pixmaps

Overview of file structure

X Bitmaps are a very unusual format: they are simultaneously a bitmap format and legal C language source code. This is because the most common uses for these bitmaps are as definitions of icons and cursors that are often compiled into C programs that use X.

Each bitmap has an optional *hot spot*. If the bitmap is used as a cursor, the hot spot is the pixel within the cursor which is considered to represent the cursor's position. For example, if the cursor is an arrow the hot spot is usually the tip of the arrow. A hot spot position of 0,0 is the upper left corner of the bitmap.

Format details

The bitmap is a sequence of lines of text. The first lines define height and width and, optionally, the hot spot position of the image. Following that is the image as a C language static array of bytes. Within the array, each row is one or more bytes, with the leftmost pixel being the high bit of the first byte. If the width is not a multiple of eight, there are wasted bits in the last byte for each row. There are no explicit markers between rows.

The width and height are defined by:

```
#define name_width ncols
#define name_height nrows
#define name_x_hot xpos
#define name_y_hot ypos
```

The *name* is the name of the bitmap. If there is no hot spot defined, the *x*_hot and *y*_hot definition lines are omitted. Although the C language allows considerable flexibility in declaration formatting, X bitmaps should format the declarations without any extra spaces or comments.

The data bits are introduced by a static character-array definition, exactly as follows:

```
static char name_bits[ ] = {
```

Again, even though C allows formatting flexibility, X bitmaps should not use any extra spaces or comments. The image bytes follow, on as many lines as needed. Each byte is formatted as a C hexadecimal constant, *0xNN*, with the bytes separated by commas. There might be any number of values per line. After the end of the list of values should be a close brace and a semicolon to end the C declaration.

Example

Table 15-1 shows a typical 1616 X11 bitmap with a hot spot at (4,4).

Sample X11 XBM file Table 15-1

```
#define sample_width 16
#define sample_height 16
#define sample_x_hot 4
#define sample_y_hot 4
static char sample_bits[ ] = {
 0x00, 0x00, 0x7c, 0x00, 0x82, 0x00, 0x82, 0x00,
 0x82, 0x00, 0x82, 0x00, 0x82, 0x00, 0x7c, 0x3e,
 0x00, 0x41, 0x80, 0x80, 0x80, 0x80, 0x80, 0x80,
 0x80, 0x80, 0x80, 0x80, 0x00, 0x41, 0x00, 0x3e};
```

X10 bitmaps

The earlier X10 system used a slightly different format, Table 15-2. Image bits are grouped into 16-bit short data instead of eight-bit char data.

Table 15-2 **Sample X10 XBM file**

```
#define sample_width 16
#define sample_height 16
#define sample_x_hot 4
#define sample_y_hot 4
static short sample_bits[ ] = {
  0x0000, 0x7c00, 0x8200, 0x8200,
  0x8200, 0x8200, 0x8200, 0x7c3e,
  0x0041, 0x8080, 0x8080, 0x8080,
  0x8080, 0x8080, 0x0041, 0x003e};
```

References

Nye, Adrian. *Xlib Programming Manual*. pp. 167-68. 1989. O'Reilly and Associates, Inc.

Gettys, James, Robert W. Scheifler, et al. "Application Utility Functions" (Chapter 16), *Xlib—C Language X Interface*, *MIT X Consortium Standard*, *X Version 11*, *Release 5*, *First Revision*. August 1991.

X Window Dump

Name	XWD
Image type	Bitmap
Intended use	Save and restore screen window images
Owner	MIT X Consortium
Last version/ revision/ release date	Version 7 for X11, June 1987
Platforms	All platforms that support the X Window system, including most workstations and some PCs
Supporting applications	xwd, xwud, xloadimage, others
Similarities	Other uncompressed bitmap formats
Overall assessment	Useful with X Window applications

Advantages

Supported by many standard X Window applications

Disadvantages

Not space-efficient, not widely supported outside of X

Variants

Old X10 window dumps have a slightly different format.

Overview of file structure

The X Window system includes standard utilities *xwd* that dumps the contents of a screen window to a file, and *xwud* that displays a dumped file. Many other X utilities read and write this common format.

Format details

A file consists of a dump header, an optional color map, and the image data. Because X is designed to be as hardware-independent as possible, there are a large number (some would say an excessive number) of possible data formats that correspond to different screen formats. There are two major format variables, the visual class and the image format.

Visual classes

The *visual class* is intended to characterize the various kinds of display controllers on which X might be run. The visual class reflects (a) whether the screen supports color, (b) whether the screen has a fixed or changeable color map, and (c) whether a color screen maps the colors separately or together.

Notice that the number of colors is not part of the visual class.

- **StaticGray (code 0)** A black-and-white screen with a fixed color mapping. A StaticGray screen with one bit per pixel would be a simple monochrome display. Most black-and-white screens would be StaticGray.

- **GrayScale (code 1)** A black-and-white screen with a software loadable color map (gray map?) that controls the mapping from pixel values to screen shades. This one is uncommon.

- **StaticColor (code 2)** A color screen with a fixed hardware color map that maps pixels to screen colors. This is also uncommon, other than some low-resolution IBM CGA modes.

- **PseudoColor (code 3)** A color screen with a software-loadable color map that controls the mapping from pixel values to screen shades. Most inexpensive color displays such as IBM VGAs fall in this class, typically using 4- or 8-bit pixels.

- **TrueColor (code 4)** A color screen with a fixed mapping from red, green, and blue values to screen colors. High-end 24-bit-per-pixel full-color displays fall into this class, with the three actual 8-bit color values stored in each pixel.

- **DirectColor (code 5)** A color screen with a software loadable mapping from red, green, and blue values to screen colors, with each component mapped separately. This is relatively uncommon.

The most common visual classes are StaticGray for black-and-white and grayscale images, PseudoColor for medium-resolution color images, and TrueColor for high-resolution color images.

The visual class of an X image does not strictly reflect the screen on which it was displayed, because a more capable screen can display an image of a simpler visual class. For example, an image of a black-and-white terminal emulator might use a StaticGray visual even if it were displayed on a color screen.

Image formats

When an image requires more than one bit per pixel there are multiple ways to store the pixels. X provides three *image formats*.

- **XYBitmap (code 0)** A monochrome bitmap with the bits for each row packed into machine words. The word size and bit order within the word are both parameters.

- **XYPixmap (code 1)** A grayscale or color image with the pixels stored as independent bit planes. If, for example, the image has four bits per pixel, it is stored as four separate bitmaps. This format is a pain to use for image manipulation, but is the most efficient way to load and store images to some screens such as IBM VGAs.

- **ZPixmap (code 2)** A grayscale or color image with the pixels for each row stored as a set of bit fields.

Dump header

All fields except the image name are four-byte integers, stored in big-endian form, Table 16-1.

Table 16-1 **XWD file header**

Offset	Name	Description
0	header_size	Size of the file header
4	file_version	7
8	pixmap_format	Image format
12	pixmap_depth	Image depth
16	pixmap_width	Image width
20	pixmap_height	Image height
24	xoffset	Image x offset
28	byte_order	MSBFirst = 1, LSBFirst = 0
32	bitmap_unit	Bit map unit, 8, 16, or 32
36	bitmap_bit_order	MSBFirst = 1, LSBFirst = 0
40	bitmap_pad	Bit map scanline pad, 8, 16, or 32
44	bits_per_pixel	Bits per pixel
48	bytes_per_line	Bytes per scanline
52	visual_class	Class of color map
56	red_mask	Z red mask
60	green_mask	Z green mask
64	blue_mask	Z blue mask

68	bits_per_rgb	Bits per logical pixel
72	colormap_entries	Number of entries in color map
76	ncolors	Number of color structures
80	window_width	Window width
84	window_height	Window height
88	window_x	Window upper left X coordinate
92	window_y	Window upper left Y coordinate
96	window_bdrwidth	Window border width
100	name	Image name, null-terminated text

The header_size is the size in bytes of the header including the image name. The file_version is seven for an X11 window dump. The pixmap_format is one of the image formats described above. The pixmap_format, byte_order, bitmap_unit, bitmap_bit_order, bitmap_pad, and mask fields describe the precise arrangement of the bit image, below. The xoffset is intended to align an image to easily addressable boundaries, but it doesn't affect the window otherwise. The colormap_entries documents the size of the original color map but does not affect the image. The various window fields document the size and screen position of the original dumped image, but there is no requirement that the image be restored to the same position. The width and height are usually the same as the image width and height, but might differ slightly if the window had a border that was included in the dump. The name is an optional ASCII string that can document the original name of the window. To determine the length of the name, subtract 100, the length of the fixed header fields, from the total header length in header_size.

Color map

The *ncolors field* is the number of color map entries that follow the header. Each color-map entry is 12 bytes long, Table 16-2. Images with visual classes GrayScale, PseudoColor, and DirectColor should have color maps, while StaticGray, StaticColor, and TrueColor generally should not.

Table 16-2 **XWD color map entry**

Offset	Size	Name	Description
0	4	pixel	Entry number
4	2	red	Red value
6	2	green	Green value
8	2	blue	Blue value
10	1	flags	Not used
11	1	pad	Padding

The red, green, and blue values are each 16-bit unsigned numbers, and the values are normalized so that full brightness for each color is 65535. Each entry contains an explicit entry number that identifies the pixel value (or color-component values for DirectColor) that it maps. There is no requirement that the pixel numbers be in order, or that all possible pixel values be included.

Image data

Images are stored as rows, with the pixels within each row stored from left to right and the rows from top to bottom of the image. Each row is stored as a sequence of *units*. The units are 8, 16, or 32 bits long, determined by bitmap_unit. Within each unit, the bytes can be stored in big-endian or little-endian form, determined by byte_order, which is one (MSBFirst) for big-endian and zero (LSBFirst) for little-endian. The order of the pixels within a unit can be high bits to low bits, or low bits to high bits, determined by bitmap_bit_order, again with one (MSBFirst) for high bits first and zero (LSBFirst) for low bits first.

For example, assume one-bit pixels are packed into 32-bit units, little-endian, with the pixels stored high bit first. Then the first 32 pixels would be stored as:

```
 3  3  3  3  3  3  3  3  2  2  2  2  2  2  2  2  1  1
25 26 27 28 29 30 31 32 17 18 19 20 21 22 23 24 09 10
```

1 1 1 1 1 1 0 0 0 0 0 0 0 0 byte number
11 12 13 14 15 16 01 02 03 04 05 06 07 08 byte number

The four bytes of the unit are stored in the file low byte first (LSBFirst byte order), but once the bytes are reassembled into a word the high bit of the most significant byte is pixel one, and the low bit of the low order byte is pixel 32 (MSBFirst bit order).

The pixels of an image in ZPixmap format are packed into units as bit fields, with the order (high to low or low to high) again determined by bitmap_bit_order. The number of bits per pixel is bits_per_pixel, which should agree with pixmap_depth. For example, with 6-bit pixels packed as in the example above, the first pixel would be bits 1–6, the second 7–12, the third 13–18, the fourth 19–24, and the fifth 25–30, with the low two bits of each unit being wasted.

Each row of the image is usually padded out to a word boundary, determined by bitmap_pad, which is the size multiple to which each row is padded. If, for example, bitmap_pad is 32, then each row is padded to a multiple of 32 bits. Usually, bitmap_pad is the same as bitmap_unit.

If the image format in pixmap_format is XYBitmap or ZPixmap, the pixels for each row are stored consecutively, packed as described above. If the image format is XYPixmap, there is a separate bitmap image for each plane of the image. That is, if there are four bits per pixel there are four complete bitmaps, the first for the highest bit of each pixel, the second for the second-highest bit of each pixel, the third for the third-highest of each pixel, and the fourth for the low bit.

For TrueColor or DirectColor images, the red_mask, blue_mask, and green_mask fields identify the bits within each pixel that correspond to each color. Most typically, TrueColor pixels are 24 bits with eight bits for each color, in which case red_mask is FF0000 H, blue_mask is 00FF00 H, and green_mask is 0000FF H. Twenty-four bit images are not stored very efficiently because they have to be packed into 32-bit units, so there is one 24-bit pixel per 32-bit unit and ¼ of the space is wasted.

Conventions

The most common bit and byte order for XWD files is big-endian (MSBFirst) byte order and also MSBFirst bit order. Although XWD files can represent an enormous variety of image formats, these are the most common:

- Monochrome bitmaps, with or without a color map. The format type can be any of the XYBitmap, XYPixmap, or ZPixmap, but for images with one bit per pixel the actual image representation for the three is the same.
- PseudoColor images with four or eight bits per pixel, in ZPixmap format.
- TrueColor images with 24 bits per pixel, eight bits each of red, green, and blue, in that order.

Multiplane XYPixmap images are rare enough that many tools do not support them.

References

Nye, Adrian. *Xlib Programming Manual*, 1989, pp.165-167. O'Reilly and Associates, Inc.

MIT X Window Consortium. "*xwd.c and X11/XWDFile.h*," *X Window System Version 11 Release 5*. 1991. Network Distribution.

## CHAPTER 17

JPEG

Name	JPEG
Image type	Compressed bitmap
Intended use	Storage and display of photographic images
Owner	Joint Photographic Experts Group
Last version/ revision/ release date	1991
Platforms	Software on PC, Mac, and workstation, but intended for hardware implementation
Supporting applications	Image Alchemy and GIF2JPG/JPG2GIF, Apple QuickTime, NeXTstep 2.0. Proposed for inclusion in TIFF 6.0, ISO Office Document Architecture, CCITT color facsimile, and European ETSI videotex.
Overall assessment	Soon to be a dominant format for storage of digitized photographs.

Advantages

By far the best compression for photographic images.

Disadvantages

Slow software compression and decompression, standard still evolving; incompatible implementations exist due to options in the standard. Also, many early implementations have unique, incompatible quirks.

Variants

JPEG defines a family of compression techniques, as described below. JPEG images may be encapsulated in various ways, the most common currently being stand-alone JFIF files and JPEG-TIFF files.

Description

The Joint Photographic Experts Group is a joint effort by the ISO, the leading international standards body, and the CCITT, the body that sets standards for telephone, radio, television and the like, to define a common compression and encoding scheme for photographic images. The JPEG standard differs in several ways from all the others discussed in this book, in that it defines several different, incompatible coding schemes. In its most common modes, it is lossy; that is, the image recovered from a JPEG file is not always identical to the original. This is not necessarily bad; read on.

Lossy vs. lossless coding

Unlike nearly every other digital image-compression scheme in use today, JPEG does not necessarily reconstruct the original image bit-for-bit. It turns out, though, that the image it does reconstruct will often be a much better representation of the original photograph than one from a putatively lossless scheme.

Digitizers typically produce 24 bits per pixel, eight each of red, blue, and green. A typical compressed format, such as GIF, has a color map of 256 entries, so each pixel in the resulting image is eight bits rather than the original 24, and the resulting image uses 256 colors rather than the original 16 million. GIF further compresses the eight-bit pixels with LZW compression, but that turns out not to help very much. JPEG, on the other hand, primarily stores information on color changes, particularly variations in brightness, because the eye is very sensitive to them. As long as the reconstructed image has similar variations, to the human eye it will look very similar to the original.

Although this kind of compression is currently uncommon in digital images, it has long been used in television. NTSC, the TV transmission scheme used in the U.S., does a dreadful job of reproducing the original picture colors by any mechanical standard, but nonetheless produces pictures that look like the original because the colors it misses tend to be ones that wouldn't have been noticed.

Lossy JPEG does not do a particularly good job on images with small numbers of colors and sharp edges (e.g., computer-generated cartoons), and other compression schemes may be more effective for such images.

The space saved by JPEG compression of photographs can be quite dramatic. For example, one 727 × 525 full-color image took 1145KB in its original 24 bits per pixel form. A GIF version was 240K. A very high quality JPEG version was 155K and a standard quality JPEG version was 58K. The 58K JPEG was as high-quality as the GIF, while the 155K JPEG considerably better when viewed on a display that allowed more than 256 simultaneous colors. JPEG can usually reconstruct a full-color picture nearly indistinguishable from the original, using only about one bit per pixel for storage.

The stages of JPEG compression

Although JPEG has many encoding and compression options, the discussion below concentrates on the baseline JPEG standard, a version of JPEG that all implementations must support and that all current implementations use.

Although not strictly part of JPEG compression, most implementations start by converting the RGB image into a luminance/chrominance color space; that is, a grayscale base image plus two channels of color-difference information. The raster data may be subsampled, combining adjacent pixels into a single value. Then a discrete cosine transform (DCT) is applied to convert the raster data into rate-of-change information. Quantization truncates the results of the DCT coding to a smaller range of values. This is the step that makes JPEG lossy; the quantization coefficients determine just how much data is lost, and hence the extent of compression and the quality of the reconstructed image. Finally, the results of quantization are compressed using either Huffman or arithmetic coding to produce the final output.

Decompression reverses the above steps, decompressing the quantized results and using a reverse DCT to reconstruct the image. The low-order bits lost to quantization are not reconstructable, so the decompressor inserts zeroes for them.

Color schemes and subsampling

In a color image, JPEG compresses each color component separately. Although it would be possible to compress the usual red, green, and blue components, JPEG compression works better when applied to color data expressed as luminance (brightness) and chrominance. This is helpful because the eye is less sensitive to color changes than to brightness changes, so the chrominance channels can be coded with more loss than the luminance channel. In an RGB image, all three channels carry some brightness information, and all three would have to be coded at the same high quality.

A widely accepted color scheme known as CCIR 601 uses three components, Y, Cb, and Cr, which are roughly brightness, blueness, and redness. Y can be used directly as a black-and-white version of the image. (Sometimes Cb and Cr are called U and V, and the color scheme called YUV, although in a strict technical sense YUV is not the same thing as YCbCr.) The components are defined by:

$$
\begin{aligned}
Y &= 0.299R &&+0.587G &&+0.114B \\
Cb &= 0.1687R &&-0.3313G &&+0.5B \\
Cr &= 0.5R &&-0.4187G &&+0.0813B
\end{aligned}
$$

Notice that this is, in principle, a lossless transformation because a Y,Cb,Cr triple contains exactly the same information as the corresponding RGB. (In practice, some roundoff error is introduced, because the calculated Y,Cb,Cr values are rounded to integers; hence the reconstructed RGB values may be off by one count.)

The human eye is much less sensitive to changes in color than it is to changes in brightness. For that reason, an acceptable image can be reconstructed using many fewer Cb and Cr samples than Y samples.

JPEG allows the different components to be sampled at different rates. A fairly common choice is to use one Cb and Cr sample for each four Y samples. For each 2×2 rectangle of pixels, there are four Y samples, one Cb, and one Cr. This saves 50% of the space used (six samples rather than 12) with practically no loss in perceived image quality.

The technique of sampling some components at lower rates than others is known as *subsampling*. The sampling rate parameters, together with the quantization parameters discussed later, determine the compression rate and reconstructed image quality. In a standard JPEG file, all these parameters are included in the file header so that a decoder can reconstruct the image correctly.

DCT coding

The Discrete Cosine Transform turns an array of intensity data into an array of frequency data that tell how fast the intensities vary. JPEG applies the DCT to 8×8 rectangles of pixel data. For images with multiple components (e.g., YCbCr images), the DCT is applied separately to 8×8 blocks of data for each component. For subsampled data, there will be more blocks of some components than others; for example, for 2×2 sampling there will be four blocks of *Y* data for each block of Cb or Cr data.

The data points in each block are numbered from (0,0) at the upper left to (7,7) at the lower right, with $f(x,y)$ being the data value at (x,y). The DCT produces a new 8×8 block of transformed data using the formula:

$$F(u,v) = \frac{1}{4}C(u)C(v)\left[\sum_{x=0}^{7}\sum_{y=0}^{7} f(x,y)\cos\frac{(2x+1)u\pi}{16}\cos\frac{(2y+1)v\pi}{16}\right]$$

where $C(z) = \begin{cases} 1\backslash\sqrt{2} \text{ if } z = 0 \\ 1 \text{ if } z \neq 0 \end{cases}$

The result of the DCT is a set of *spatial frequencies*, *F(u,v)*, which, roughly speaking, indicate to what degree the values change at each of a set of rates. *F*(0,0) is the value indicating to what degree the values do not change at all; that is, the average of the 64 input values, and is known as the *DC coefficient*. The rest of the values are *AC coefficients*. For example, *F*(1,0) indicates the degree to which the values change slowly horizontally (low frequency) and not at all vertically, and *F*(7,7) indicates the degree to which the values change most quickly in both directions (high frequency.)

The DCT is, in principle, reversible, using the reverse DCT:

$$f(x,y) = \frac{1}{4}\left[\sum_{u=0}^{7}\sum_{v=0}^{7} C(u)C(v)F(u,v)\cos\frac{(2x+1)u\pi}{16}\cos\frac{(2y+1)v\pi}{16}\right]$$

although rounding errors will generally make the calculated values slightly different from the original ones.

For 8 × 8 blocks the DCT output terms have about four more bits than the input; that is, if the inputs f(*x*,*y*) are 8-bit values then the outputs *F*(u,v) are twelve-bit values. Thus, it may seem that we have expanded our data rather than compressed it. The point of changing from intensities to frequencies is that slow changes are much more noticeable than fast ones, so the low-frequency data is more important than high-frequency data for reconstructing the image. Quantization takes advantage of this fact.

Quantization

Quantization sets the precision to which each of the values resulting from the DCT is stored. JPEG uses linear quantization which means, quite simply, that each of the DCT values is divided by a quantization factor and rounded to an integer to get the value that will be stored. An 8 × 8 table of quantization factors is used, one for each DCT output term. This table is stored in the JPEG file, so an encoder may use either a standard table or one adjusted to give the desired rate of compression for a particular image. A file with multiple components may have multiple tables; most commonly, there is one table for the *Y* data and another one for the Cb and Cr.

Typical tables have a low factor, around 16, for the DC component $F(0,0)$, while the highest-frequency components will have factors around 100. Given 12-bit DCT values, this would translate to 8 bits for $F(0,0)$ and about 5.3 bits for $F(7,7)$.

When decoding, the original values are (approximately) recovered by multiplying by the quantization factor. For example, if the factor is 16, DCT values of 120 through 135 will convert to a stored value of 8, which when decompressed will convert back to 128, an approximation of the input value.

The DC component is then treated specially: since adjacent DC components tend to be similar, each DC component is stored as the difference from the DC component in the preceding block. The AC components are logically placed in a zigzag order, Fig. 17-1, that puts the lowest-frequency components first. The quantized high-frequency components will often be zero, and the final compression stage does particularly well on groups of zero values.

Figure 17-1

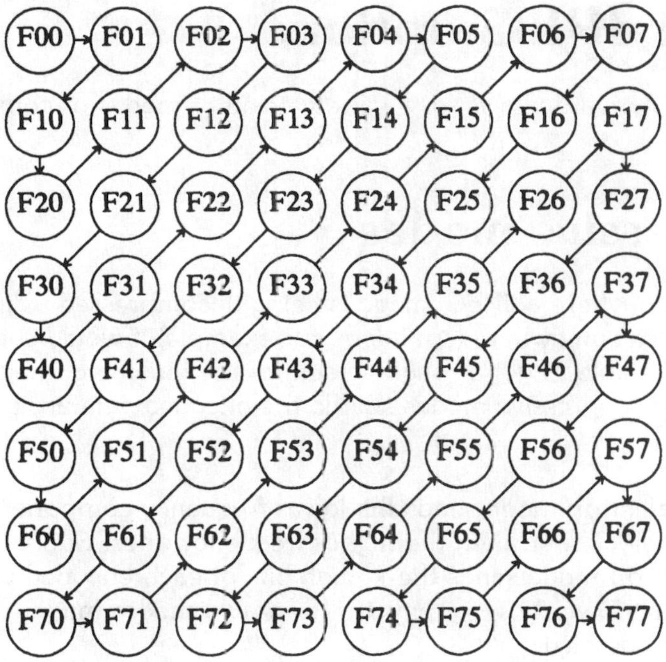

Zig-zag data order from DCT output array.

Final compression

The results of quantization are compressed (*entropy coded*) using either a modified Huffman code or arithmetic coding.

The modified Huffman code, known as a *Variable Length Code* or VLC, encodes the DC component as a 4-bit length, followed by a signed integer of the given length. The AC components are stored as an 8-bit token followed by a variable length integer. The high four bits are the number of zero values preceding this value, and the low four bits are the length of the variable length integer.

The JPEG standard allows the quantized values to be compressed using arithmetic coding, which is slightly more compact than Huffman. However, due to patent restrictions most current implementations use Huffman, which is in the public domain.

Other JPEG options

The JPEG standard allows for a variety of other modes of compression and storage.

Progressive modes

In a situation where a JPEG image is being decompressed as it is received from somewhere (a modem, for example) it would sometimes be nice to be able to get a rough version of the incoming image as it arrives. The progressive modes shuffle the encoded data around to allow this.

Spectral-selection mode sends the lower frequency components of each 8×8 block first, then the higher-frequency ones. *Successive-approximation* mode sends the N high bits of each encoded value first, then the lower bits, for any N. These two modes may be combined as needed.

No current software implementations support progressive modes, since the software all start with files on disk and—in any event—are too slow for real-time encoding or decoding. Future hardware implementations will be fast enough for progressive modes to be useful.

Hierarchical mode

In hierarchical mode, an image is stored at several increasing resolutions. For example, a 1000 × 1000 image might be stored first as a 10 × 10 thumbnail version, then 100 × 100, and finally 1000 × 1000. Each image is stored as the difference from the preceding smaller version. Current software generally doesn't implement hierarchical mode, but will probably do so in the future.

Lossless mode

A lossless compression mode is specified for JPEG users who, for some reason, require exact bit-for-bit reconstruction of their images. (The reasons tend to be more political and legal than technical.) The lossless mode stores each pixel value as a difference from the pixels immediately above or to its left, encoded using a variable-length code similar to that used for DC components above. Thus the DCT phase is not used at all; nor are subsampling and colorspace conversion, as these would also introduce loss. JPEG lossless mode thus has little in common with regular JPEG, except for the name.

The compression provided by lossless mode is nowhere near as good as is possible in the lossy mode, even at very high-quality/low-loss parameter settings. It remains to be seen whether lossless mode will become popular.

JFIF & JPEG-TIFF formats

The JPEG standard defines a standard datastream encoding of a JPEG image, but the standard allows wide variations in color encodings and other options. JFIF and JPEG-TIFF are concrete file formats that specify many details left open in JPEG.

JFIF

JFIF stands for JPEG File Interchange Format and was defined by Eric Hamilton of C-Cube Microsystems. A JFIF image is a JPEG image that uses either grayscale or YCbCr color representation. It includes a JPEG-compatible header which identifies it as a JFIF file, and also includes a version number, *X* and *Y* dots per inch or centimeter, and an optional, thumbnail RGB version of the image. JFIF is defined in detail below.

JPEG-TIFF

TIFF 6.0 will allow JPEG compressed images. TIFF Class Y defines optionally subsampled YCbCr photometric interpretation, which could be used for any pixel format but is mainly intended to support JPEG. A TIFF file can contain either a straight DCT or lossless JPEG image, or a series of JPEG-encoded strips or tiles, allowing pieces of the image to be recovered without having to read through the whole thing. Proposed *Appendix O* of TIFF 6.0 Standard defines the tags for YCbCr color, and *Appendix P* defines the tags for JPEG images. The JPEG parts of the TIFF 6.0 standard are widely considered to have enough inconsistencies that JPEG-TIFF cannot be implemented as defined. A future revision will correct the inconsistencies.

Details of JFIF format

JFIF files can contain a JPEG image compressed by any of the JPEG schemes, including progressive and hierarchical modes, but here we concentrate on files using the JPEG baseline process, which is what most actual JFIF files use.

A JFIF file, like any JPEG datastream, consists of a sequence of segments. Each segment starts with a two-byte marker that identifies the type of segment. In some cases the marker is the entire segment, while in others the marker is followed by data. All JPEG data are stored in big-endian order, with the highest-order part of the value stored first. For fields in which multiple fields are stored in a single byte, the first or most-significant field is stored in the most-significant bits of the byte. A JFIF file contains a single image typically encoded using baseline DCT compression and Huffman encoding. The image may be grayscale, in which case the data are a single component, or color, in which case the data are YCbCr. The image is encoded from the top down, with the first data in the file representing the upper left corner.

Subsampling

In a YCbCr image, the Cb and Cr components are usually subsampled; that is, a single Cb or Cr sample corresponds to a block of *Y* samples. The most common subsampling rates are 2 × 2, with each Cr and Cb sample corresponding to a block of two samples on each of two adjacent rows of the image, and 2 × 1, with each Cr and Cb sample corresponding to a pair of samples in a single row.

In a JFIF file, the subsampled components are positioned on natural boundaries. For example, if each Cb sample corresponds to a 2 × 2 block of *Y* samples, the Cb sample is positioned in the center of that block.

Markers

Each marker is two bytes. The first contains hex FF, the second the marker type. In entropy coded segments (those that contain Huffman-coded pixel data), any time a FF byte occurs in the data it is followed by a *stuffed* 00 byte to avoid having a false marker appear. The JFIF reader must discard the stuffed 00 byte. There may be multiple FF bytes in a row, in which case all but the last should be ignored.

A few segment types, SOI, EOI, and RSTn, consist solely of the marker. All other segment types except SOS segments have a length field following the marker. The length is the length of the segment, excluding the marker, but including the length field itself. This makes it easy to skip unrecognized segments. The SOS marker is followed by a parameter segment, and then by compressed image data. (See Table 17-1.)

Table 17-1 **Marker types**

Name	Value	Description
M_SOF0	0xC0	Baseline DCT frame, Huffman coded
M_SOF1*	0xC1	Extended sequential DCT frame, Huffman coded
M_SOF2*	0xC2	Progressive DCT frame, Huffman coded
M_SOF3*	0xC3	Lossless frame, Huffman coded
M_DHT	0xC4	Define Huffman table(s)
M_SOF5*	0xC5	Differential sequential DCT frame, Huffman coded
M_SOF6*	0xC6	Differential progressive DCT frame, Huffman coded
M_SOF7*	0xC7	Differential lossless frame, Huffman coded
M_JPG	0xC8	Reserved for extensions
M_SOF9*	0xC9	Extended sequential DCT frame, arithmetic coded
M_SOF10*	0xCA	Progressive DCT frame, arithmetic coded
M_SOF11*	0xCB	Lossless frame, arithmetic coded
M_SOF13*	0xCD	Differential extended sequential DCT frame, arithmetic coded
M_SOF14*	0xCE	Differential progressive DCT frame, arithmetic coded
M_SOF15*	0xCF	Differential lossless frame, arithmetic coded
M_DAC*	0xCC	Define arithmetic compression tables
M_RST0	0xD0	Restart 0
M_RST1	0xD1	Restart 1
M_RST2	0xD2	Restart 2
M_RST3	0xD3	Restart 3
M_RST4	0xD4	Restart 4

M_RST5	0xD5	Restart 5
M_RST6	0xD6	Restart 6
M_RST7	0xD7	Restart 7
M_SOI	0xD8	Start of image
M_EOI	0xD9	End of image
M_SOS	0xDA	Start of scan
M_DQT	0xDB	Define quantization tables
M_DNL	0xDC	Define number of lines
M_DRI	0xDD	Define restart interval
M_DHP*	0xDE	Define hierarchical progression
M_EXP*	0xDF	Expand reference image(s)
M_APP0	0xE0	Application specific type 0
M_APP1*	0xE1	Application specific type 1
	• • •	
M_APP15*	0xEF	Application specific type 15
M_JPG0*	0xF0	Reserved for JPEG extensions
	• • •	
M_JPG13*	0xFD	Reserved for JPEG extensions
M_COM	0xFE	Comment

* Not used in baseline JPEG files

JFIF structure

A JFIF file contains the following sequence of segments:

- An SOI (Start of Image) segment.
- An APP0 (Application type 0) segment containing JFIF header information.

- Optionally, more APP0 segments containing JFIF extension information.
- One or more DQT (Define Quantization Table) segments, containing the quantization tables used for the image.
- A SOF0 (Start of Frame type 0) segment saying that the image contains Huffman encoded baseline DCT data.
- One or more DHT (Define Huffman Table) segments containing the particular Huffman codes used.
- Optionally, a DRI (Define Restart Interval) segment defining the restart intervals used for error recovery and faster access to subparts of the image.
- At least one SOS (Start of Scan) segment that contains the actual image data.
- An EOI (End of Image) segment.

There is considerable flexibility in the order of segments. Additional COM and non-JFXX APPn segments can appear anywhere before the SOS (COM segments are widely used for ASCII annotations, although neither JPEG nor JFIF standardizes them as such). If there are multiple-quantization or Huffman tables, they may appear in one large DQT or DHT segment, or several smaller segments. DQT, DHT, DRI, COM, and APPn segments can all appear in any order before or after the SOFn marker. In a color image, the three components may be interleaved (see below) in a single SOS segment, or stored in separate SOS segments. The only ordering requirement imposed by JFIF is that the JFIF-defined APP0 segments must immediately follow the SOI marker.

Minumum coded units

A DCT JPEG image is coded as a sequence of 8 × 8 blocks of pixels. In a single component grayscale image, image data is stored as the blocks for the first eight rows of the image, then the next eight rows, and so forth. Since each DCT requires an 8 × 8 block, if the number of columns or rows is not a multiple of eight, the last block in each row and the last row of blocks may need extra padding elements for the DCT. Usually the rightmost or bottommost pixels are repeated as the padding values.

In a YCbCr image, each 8 × 8 component block is encoded separately, but the encoded blocks are usually interleaved in the file so that the decoder reads all the data for a single area of the screen together. It is valid but currently uncommon to have each component stored as separate scans, or to have one scan for *Y* and a second interleaved scan for Cr and Cb. Each interleaved group is called a *Minumum Coded Unit* or MCU. As an example, assume that there is one Cb block and one Cr block for each 2 × 2 group of *Y* data. Then an MCU would include four blocks of *Y* data, one block of Cb, and one of Cr. Each 2 × 2 group of *Y* blocks is stored by row within the group, in this case:

1 2
3 4

Although a grouping of 4 *Y*, 1 Cb, and 1 Cr is common, JPEG allows any integral multiple of groups to be used as long as an MCU contains no more than 10 blocks (a future version of JPEG will relax the 10-block minimum, so decoders should be prepared for larger MCUs). For example, each Cb block could correspond to a 2 × 3 group of *Y* blocks, and each Cr block could correspond to a 1 × 3 group of *Y*. In that case, the MCU would contain a 2 × 3 group of *Y* blocks, a single Cb block, and a 2 × 1 group of Cr blocks, or 6 *Y*, 1 Cb, and 2 Cr blocks, because that would be the smallest group containing an integral number of blocks of each component.

Restart intervals

Since the encoded data for an image can be large, there is some possibility that the image data may be corrupted during transmission or storage. Also, in a large image it can be useful just to decode a subrectangle of the image. Restart groups support both of these goals. Within an image, an integral number of MCUs may be defined as the *restart interval*.

The image data in each restart interval are encoded independently, and *restart markers* are placed between the intervals. The decoder can scan the data and find the restart marker without decoding the actual image, which allows both resynchronization after an error and quick scanning to start decoding the image in the middle.

To aid in error recovery, there are eight different restart markers. The marker after the first interval is an RST0, then RST1, ... RST7, then RST0 again. This makes it easier to tell if an error has corrupted one of the restart markers.

SOI segment

The SOI segment contains only the SOI marker, hex FF D8.

APP0 segments

The JPEG standard allows the APP0 segments to contain any application specific data, as in Table 17-2.

Table 17-2 **JPEG APPn segment**

Offset	Size	Name	Contents	Description
0	2	APP0	FF E0	APP0 marker
2	2	Length	Integer	Length of segment
4	N	Data	Arbitrary	Application data

Applications may define any desired APP0 segments. The segment data should start with a distinctive string to identify it. The initial strings JFIF and JFXX should only be used for JFIF segments, as defined here.

JFIF application segments

JFIF defines two conventional APP0 segments. The first is required and must appear once, immediately after the SOI. The second is optional, and may occur more than once. (See Table 17-3.)

Table 17-3

JFIF application segment

Offset	Size	Name	Contents	Description
0	2	APP0	FF E0	APP0 marker
2	2	Length	Integer	Length of segment
4	5	"JFIF\ 0"	JFIF marker	
9	2	Version	0x0102	JFIF version, currently 1.2
11	1	Units	Byte	0: *X* and *Y* in arbitrary units, 1: *X* and *Y* in pixels/inch, 2: in pixels/cm
12	2	X den	Integer	Horizontal pixel density
14	2	Y den	Integer	Vertical pixel density
16	1	X thumb	Integer	Width of thumbnail image
17	1	Y thumb	Integer	Height of thumbnail image
18	3N	Thumb	Pixels	Thumbnail image

The first five bytes after the length are ASCII *JFIF* and a null, identifying the segment as a JFIF marker and the file as a JFIF image. The segment may contain a thumbnail' version of the image, stored as 24-bit RGB pixels. If, as is more common, there is no thumbnail image, the *X* and *Y* thumbnail sizes are both zero. The Units field usually contains 0, with *X* and *Y* densities both 1 to indicate square pixels.

Upwardly compatible changes to the JFIF specification will use new minor version numbers, while incompatible changes will have new major version numbers. (See Table 17-4.)

If the extension type is hex 10, the extension data are a JPEG-encoded thumbnail image. The thumbnail starts with an SOI marker and ends with an EOI marker, and should not have any JFIF or JFXX markers, thus precluding thumbnails with their own thumbnails.

If the extension type is hex 11, the extension data are a thumbnail image stored as a 256-color palette and pixels. The palette is stored as 256 RGB triples, the pixels as 8-bit indexes into the palette. (See Table 17-5.)

If the extension type is hex 12, the extension data are a thumbnail image stored as RGB triples. (See Table 17-6.)

Table 17-4 **JFXX application segment**

Offset	Size	Name	Contents	Description
0	2	APP0	FF E0	APP0 marker
2	2	Length	Integer	Length of segment
4	5	Marker	"JFXX\ 0"	JFIF marker
9	1	Code	Byte	Extension type
10	N	Data	Bytes	Extension data

Table 17-5 **JFXX palette thumbnail**

Offset	Size	Name	Contents	Description
9	1	Code	11	Extension type
10	1	*X* thumb	Byte	*X* size
11	1	*Y* thumb	Byte	*Y* size
12	768	Palette	RGB	Palette for thumbnail
13	*X* X *Y*	Image	Bytes	Thumbnail image

Table 17-6 **JFXX color thumbnail**

Offset	Size	Name	Contents	Description
9	1	Code	12	Extension type
10	1	*X* thumb	Byte	*X* size
11	1	*Y* thumb	Byte	*Y* size
12	3 X X X Y	Image	RGB	Thumbnail image

There may be multiple JFXX segments containing multiple versions of the thumbnail image. Most existing JFIF files contain no thumbnail at all.

Future extensions to JFIF will define more JFXX extension codes, probably including one to hold the image gamma value.

DQT segment

The *DQT* segment(s) contain the quantization tables, values by which the encoder divides the output of the DCT to get the values stored in the file. (See Table 17-7.) Multicomponent files may contain up to four quantization tables. In a YCbCr file, typically the *Y* component uses one table and the Cr and Cb both use a second table. Each table contains 64 entries, stored in the zigzag order shown in Figure 17-1.

Table 17-7

Quantization table

Offset	Size	Name	Contents	Description
0	2	DQT	FF DE	Quantization table marker
2	2	Length	Integer	Length of segment
				Following repeats for each table
N	1	P/T	Byte	High four bits: precision, low four bits: table ID
N+1	64 or 128	Elements	Integer	Table entries

For each table the precision code is 0 for 8-bit table entries or 1 for 16-bit table entries (always 0 in baseline JPEG). The table number may be 0, 1, 2, or 3.

SOF0 segment

The *Start Of Frame* segment contains data describing the image. (See Table 17-8.)

Table 17-8 **Quantization table**

Offset	Size	Name	Contents	Description
0	2	SOF0	FF C0	Start of Frame marker
2	2	Length	Integer	Length of segment
4	1	P	Byte	Sample precision
5	2	Y	Integer	Number of rows in the image
7	2	X	Integer	Number of columns in the image
8	1	Nf	Integer	Number of components
				Following repeated for each component
N	1	Ci	Integer	Component identifier
N+1	1	H/V		High four bits: horizontal sampling factor, low four bits: vertical sampling factor
N+2	1	Tqi		Quantization table to use

For each component, the sample precision is 8 or 12 bits (always 8 in baseline JPEG). The horizontal and vertical sampling factors are the number of blocks of this component in an MCU, and determine the sizes of the blocks of image pixels represented by each component value.

JPEG allows arbitrary component identifiers, but JFIF requires that they be 1 for *Y*, 2 for Cb, and 3 for Cr, and that they be coded in that order.

DHT segments & Huffman image encoding

The *Define Huffman Table* segment describes a Huffman code used to encode the values produced by the DCT (see Table 17-9). There are at least two tables, one for the DC components (the F00 value in Figure 17-1), and one for the AC components (the rest of the values). In color images, there is usually one pair of tables for the *Y* component and a second pair of tables shared between Cb and Cr. Baseline JPEG allows no more than two DC and two AC tables.

Table 17-9

Huffman table

Offset	Size	Name	Contents	Description
0	2	DHT	FF C4	Huffman table marker
2	2	Length	Integer	Length of segment
		Following repeats for each table		
N	1	Tc/Th	Byte	High 4 bits: table class, low 4 bits: table identifier
N+1	16	Li	16 bytes	Number of codes of length 1
N+17	Varies	Vij	Bytes	Values for each code length

For each table, the table class is 0 for DC codes and 1 for AC codes. The identifier is 0 or 1 for baseline JPEG, and up to 3 for non-baseline.

The Huffman code tree is not directly represented by the DHT marker, but can be reconstructed from the list of numbers of codes of each bit length. For each bit length, the codes of that length are numerically smaller than the prefixes of all codes of longer length. No code is allowed to be all ones—that pattern can only be a prefix of a longer code.

For example, if there are no codes of length 1 or 2, two codes of length 3, and five of length 4, then the first seven Huffman codes would be 000, 001, 0100, 0101, 0110, 0111, and 1000. Longer codes would start with 4-bit sequences of 1001 or more. These first seven codes would be associated with the first seven symbols given in the Vij list.

The last byte of each segment of Huffman-coded data is padded with 1 bits. This cannot cause a false Huffman code to be recognized since no code may contain all 1 bits. The decoder will reach the next JPEG marker before obtaining a complete Huffman code.

Further details of image encoding are discussed below in the SOS segment.

DRI segment

The optional DRI segment defines the image's restart interval, (see Table 17-10). In the absence of a DRI marker, or if the interval is zero, there are no restart intervals and no restart markers.

Table 17-10 **Define Restart Interval**

Offset	Size	Name	Contents	Description
0	2	DRI	FF DD	Restart interval marker
2	2	Length	Integer	Length of segment
4	2	Length	Integer	Restart interval, number of MCU

SOS segment

The *Start of Scan* segment contains a header (see Table 17-11), followed by encoded image data.

Table 17-11 **Start of Scan**

Offset	Size	Name	Contents	Description
0	2	SOS	FF DA	SOS marker
2	2	Length	Integer	Length of header
4	1	Ns	Integer	Number of components in this scan, 1, 2, or 3
	Following two fields repeated for each component			
N	1	Cs	Byte	Component selector
N+1	1	Td/Ta	Byte	High four bits: DC coding table number, low four bits: AC coding table number
M	1	Ss	Byte	Start of spectral selection, always 0
M+1	1	Se	Byte	End of spectral selection, always 63
M+2	1	Ah/Al	Byte	Two four bits fields, high and low bits of spectral selection, always 00 in baseline JPEG

Following the header are image data, stored as blocks of components, optionally with occasional restart markers. The DC components are differentially encoded; that is, each DC value is stored as the difference from the DC value in the preceding block for this component. In the first block of the image and the first block after a restart marker, the previous value is considered to be zero. The difference value is encoded as follows: the number of bits of the magnitude of the difference is treated as a symbol and Huffman encoded. Following that is the difference value as that number of bits, the actual value if the difference is positive, or the ones complement of the absolute value if it is negative. For example, if the difference is zero the magnitude is 0, and the Huffman code for a zero is stored. If the difference is 3 the magnitude is 2 (two bits needed to represent 3), so the Huffman code for 2 is stored, followed by the two bits 1 1 to represent 3. If the difference is –5 the magnitude is 3, so the Huffman code for 3 is stored, followed by 010, the ones complement of 5.

Since many AC components are zero, the AC components are stored as a two-part value consisting of a count of zero components, and the value of the non-zero component following the zero. The count is placed in the high four bits of a byte, and the magnitude of the following non-zero value goes in the low four bits. The Huffman code for that 8-bit byte is stored, followed by the magnitude bits as above. For example, if there are four zero values followed by a –6, the Huffman code for hex 43 is stored (4 zeros, 3 magnitude) followed by the bits 0 0 1, the ones complement of 6. There are two special case codes. The byte value (before Huffman coding) 00 is End of Block, and means that all following values in this block are zero, a common situation. The byte value (before Huffman coding) hex F0 means a run of 16 zeros, and is used in the rare case when there are more than 16 consecutive zeros followed by a non-zero value. If the 63rd value in the block is non-zero, there is no EOB code.

EOI segment

The EOI segment contains only the EOI marker, hex FF D9.

References

International Organization for Standards. *Digital Compression and Coding of Continuous-Tone Still Images, Part 1: Requirements and guidelines*. 1991. New York: ANSI.

Eric Hamilton. *JPEG File Interchange Format. Version 1.02*. September 1, 1992. San Jose CA: C-Cube Microsystems, Inc.

Pennebaker, William B. and Joan L. Mitchell. *JPEG Still Image Compression Standard*. 1993. Van Nostrand Reinhold.

Wallace, Gregory K. "The JPEG Still-Picture Compression Standard." *Communications of the Association for Computing Machinery*. 34(4): 30-44. 1991.

Independent JPEG Group. *Independent JPEG Group's Software*. 1991. Available on Compuserve GRAPHSUPPORT Forum, UUNET Communications, and on many BBS Systems.

## CHAPTER 18

FITS

Name	FITS (Flexible Image Transport System)
Image type	Bitmap
Intended use	Storage and interchange of astronomical images
Owner	FITS Working Group of Commission 5 (Astronomical Data) of the International Astronomical Union.
Last version/ revision/ release date	1993
Platforms	Mainframes, workstations, and PCs
Supporting applications	Astronomy applications
Overall assessment	A bulky but very well-documented and portable file format, ubiquitous in astronomy applications.

Advantages

Well-standardized, portable, can include considerable descriptive data about images

Disadvantages

No compression at all, heavily oriented to astronomy applications

Variants

Most files are in Basic FITS format. Optional extensions are random groups, ASCII tables, and 3-D tables.

Overview of file structure

FITS (Flexible Image Transfer Format) is the file format universally used by astronomers to store and transfer astronomical images. It was introduced in the late 1970s and was quickly adopted throughout the astronomical community. Originally, FITS format was designed for magnetic tapes, but it is also used on disks and CD ROMs. There are a variety of extensions beyond the original Basic FITS format, but none are used to store images so they are not described here.

Format details

A FITS file is a sequence of 2880 byte records (the size was chosen to be an even multiple of the word sizes of all popular computers). The file starts with header records, each of which contains 36 80-byte ASCII card images, then (optionally) some number of data records (FITS files with no data are legal, but not often useful). The data in a Basic FITS file is an *N*-dimensional array. The interpretation of the data in the array is up to the applications that read and write the file. In files that contain images, the array is usually either 2-D, with the data being a grayscale image, or 3-D, with the data being a set of grayscale images.

Header

The header records are each treated as a set of 80-byte ASCII card images in a fixed format, referred to here as *cards*. If the number of cards is not a multiple of 36, the last header record is padded out to 2880 bytes with blanks.

Each card contains an 8-byte keyword starting in column one. Keywords consist of uppercase letters, digits, underscores, and hyphens. If the card assigns a value to the keyword, column nine contains an equals sign, followed by a space. Character values are enclosed in single quotes. The first quote is in column 11. Strings must be at least eight characters long, exclusive of the quotes, padded with blanks if need be. Logical values are the letters T or F, for True or False, in column 30. Numeric values are right-justified with the last character in column 30. For complex values, the imaginary part is right-justified with the last character in column 50. Integer values are optionally signed digit strings. Floating-point values must contain a decimal point and can contain an optionally signed exponent following a D or an E. All these values are intended to be easily readable by a Fortran 77 program, so they all follow Fortran data conventions.

Comments might appear after the data values in a card, or they might start in column ten in cards containing no value. By convention, each comment starts with a slash, preceded by a space if the comment follows a value.

Mandatory keywords

Every FITS file must contain SIMPLE, BITPIX, NAXIS, and END cards in that order, but can contain other records interspersed among them. If the file contains data, the NAXIS card must be followed by NAXISi cards, one for each dimension of the data. The first header card must be SIMPLE; after that, optional cards can be interspersed with the mandatory ones. The END card indicates the end of the header.

- **SIMPLE** The value is T, indicating that the file conforms to FITS format. If the first card contains XTENSION, the file is in an extended format and contains something other than an N-dimensional data array.

- **BITPIX** The value is 8, 16, 32, -32, or -64, indicating the format of the data that follows the header. If the value is 8, 16, or 32, the data are one-, two-, or four-byte signed integers in big-endian (Motorola) format. If the value is -32 or -64, the data are single- or double-precision IEEE floating-point numbers in big-endian format, with the first bit being the sign, the next eight (single) or 11 (double) bits the exponent, and the rest of the bits the fraction. Any IEEE values are allowed, including not-a-number and infinite values. The absolute value of the BITPIX value is always the number of bits per data value. Because the FITS standard predates the IEEE floating-point standard, older FITS files all have integer data.

* **NAXIS** The value is the number of dimensions in the data array. A NAXIS of zero indicates that no data follow.

* **NAXISi** If NAXIS is greater than zero, the NAXIS card must be followed by NAXIS1, NAXIS2, etc., in order, giving the extent of each dimension. Each NAXISi must be greater than zero—a zero NAXIS1 indicates a file in the relatively uncommon random groups variant format. The number of data values that follow is the product of all the NAXISi values.

* **END** The last header card is an END card, which must be filled with blanks after the END keyword.

Data

Immediately following the header records are the data. The data are in array order, with the first subscript varying the fastest. If NAXIS were 2, NAXIS1 were 2, and NAXIS2 were 3, the data would appear in the order 1,1 2,1 1,2 2,2 1,3 2,3. This peculiar order matches that for Fortran arrays. Data are packed into 2880 byte records without regard to record boundaries. The last 2880 byte record is padded out with zeros in the same format as the data.

Optional keywords

A FITS file can have any number of optional keyword cards in the header. A FITS reader can, in general, safely ignore any keywords it does not recognize. The FITS standards define the meanings of some optional keywords.

* **BSCALE** A factor to be used in conjunction with BZERO, below

* **BZERO** A constant to be added to the file data. The actual data values are actual value = BZERO + BSCALE * file value.

* **BUNIT** A string giving the units in which the data are expressed

- **BLANK** A numeric value that represents unknown or blank values. This is only allowed for integer values; for floating point the blanks must be IEEE NAN values.
- **CTYPEi** A string giving the name of the coordinate given by axis *i*
- **CRPIXi** A number giving the location of a reference point along the *i* axis, in units of the axis index. The first point in the file is index 1.
- **CRVALi** The coordinate value at the index identified by CRPIXi
- **CDELTi** The amount by which coordinate *i* increases per unit index
- **CROTAi** A rotation in degrees from some standard coordinate system for axis *i*
- **DATAMIN** The minimum valid physical value in the file
- **DATAMAX** The maximum valid physical value in the file
- **EXTEND** If the value is T, there can be an extension header and data following the image data.
- **DATE** A character string representing the date on which the file was created, in the form 'DD/MM/YY'
- **ORIGIN** A character string identifying the organization that created the file
- **BLOCKED** If the value is T, the file can be blocked on its physical medium; that is, multiple logical records per physical record (obsolescent).
- **DATE-OBS** The date on which the observation represented by the file was made; same format as the DATE card

- **TELESCOP** A character string identifying the telescope used
- **INSTRUME** A character string identifying the instrument used. Many telescopes have several instruments; for example, cameras, spectrographs, etc.
- **OBSERVER** A character string identifying the observer
- **OBJECT** The name of the object observed
- **EQUINOX** A floating-point number giving the equinox in years for the coordinate system used
- **EPOCH** An obsolescent equivalent to EQUINOX
- **AUTHOR** The name of the author if the data comes from a published paper or the like
- **REFERENC** A reference to where the data are published
- **COMMENT** A comment; there is no value field
- **HISTORY** A comment, conventionally documenting the history of the data
- **Blank keyword** A card where the first eight columns are blank is a comment.

The keywords XTENSION, PCOUNT, GCOUNT, EXTNAME, EXTLEVEL, EXTVER, PTYPEi, PSCALi, PZEROi, TFIELDS, TBCOLi, TFORMi, TSCALi, TZEROi, TNULLi, TTYPEi, TUNITi, TDISPi, TDIMi, and THEAP are used in extension headers. Extensions are not generally used to store bitmaps.

Example

Figure 18-1 shows the header records from an image taken by the faint-object camera on the Hubble Space Telescope of the supernova SN1987A. The image is 512 by 512 and has 16 bits per pixel. There are about 100 optional keyword cards, most of which are defined locally rather than in any FITS standard.

Figure 18-1

```
SIMPLE  =                    T /  FITS STANDARD
BITPIX  =                   16 /  FITS BITS/PIXEL
NAXIS   =                    2 /  NUMBER OF AXES
NAXIS1  =                  512 /
NAXIS2  =                  512 /
BLOCKED =                    T /  Tape may be blocked
EXTEND  =                    T /  There maybe standard extensions
BSCALE  =   1.2298971617786E-2 /  REAL = TAPE*BSCALE + BZERO
BZERO   =   4.030000000000E2 /
OPSIZE  =                 1152 /  PSIZE of original image
ORIGIN  = 'STScI-STSDAS'       /
FITSDATE= '21/09/90'           / Date FITS file was created
IRAFNAME= 'x0c80106t_cvt.d0h'  / NAME OF IRAF IMAGE FILE
IRAF-MAX=          8.060000E2 /  DATA MAX
IRAF-MIN=          0.000000E0 /  DATA MIN
IRAF-B/P=                   32 /  DATA BITS/PIXEL
IRAFTYPE= 'FLOATING'           /
SDASMGNU=                    1 /  Number of groups in original image
CRVAL1  =     83.8933046656671
CRVAL2  =    -69.1572568567466
CRVAL3  =     83788810.4355469
CRPIX1  =                 257.
CRPIX2  =                 257.
CD1_1   =          5.888875E-6
CD1_2   =         -1.316630E-8
CD2_1   =          1.246097E-8
CD2_2   =          6.222208E-6
DATAMIN =          0.000000E0 /  DATA MAX
DATAMAX =          8.060000E2 /  DATA MAX
MIR_REVR=                    0
ORIENTAT=           -0.1212387
FILLCNT =                    0
ERRCNT  =                    0
FPKTTIME= '24-AUG-1990 04:37:59.80'
LPKTTIME= '25-APR-1990 12:57:10.99'
CTYPE1  = 'RA---TAN'
CTYPE2  = 'DEC--TAN'
CTYPE3  = 'TIME    '

                              / GROUP PARAMETERS: OSS
```

FITS header for supernova image.

Figure 18-1 Continued.

```
                                 / FOC DATA DESCRIPTOR KEYWORDS
INSTRUME= 'FOC                ' / instrument in use
ROOTNAME= 'X0C80106T          ' / rootname of the observation set
FILETYPE= 'SCI                ' / shp, udl, sci
NSEGPGRP=                     0 / not computed - used only by OSS

                                / CALIBRATION FLAGS AND INDICATORS
OPTCRLY = 'F96                ' / optical relay: F48, F96
SMMMODE = 'NOTUSED            ' / spectro. mirror mechanism: INBEAM, NOTUSED
SHTMODE = 'NOTUSED            ' / shutter mode: INBEAM, NOTUSED
LEDMODE = 'NOTUSED            ' / led calibration status: ACTIVE, NOTUSED
PXFORMT = 'NORMAL             ' / format of the image: NORMAL, ZOOM
OPTELT1 =                     0 / filter element, wheel 1 f48: (0-7), f96: (0-11)
OPTELT2 =                    11 / filter element, wheel 2 f48: (0-7), f96: (0-11)
OPTELT3 =                     0 / filter element, wheel 3 f48: (0),   f96: (0-11)
OPTELT4 =                     0 / filter element, wheel 4 f48: (0),   f96: (0-11)
FILTNAM1= 'CLEAR1             ' / filter element name for wheel 1
FILTNAM2= 'F501N              ' / filter element name for wheel 2
FILTNAM3= 'CLEAR3             ' / filter element name for wheel 3
FILTNAM4= 'CLEAR4             ' / filter element name for wheel 4
CAMMODE = 'NOTUSED            ' / coronographic apodizer mask: INBEAM, NOTUSED
SAMPOFF =        0.2560000E+03 / sample offset (0.0-1023.75)
LINEOFF =        0.2560000E+03 / line offset   (0.0-1023.75)
SAMPPLN =                   512 / samples per line (64, 128, 256, or 512)
LINEPFM =                   512 / lines per frame  (64, 128, 256, 512, or 1024)

                                / CALIBRATION REFERENCE FILES
GRAPHTAB= 'mtab$a3c1003jm.tmg' / the HST graph table
COMPTAB = 'mtab$a3c10030m.tmc' / the HST components table
UNITAB  = 'xtab$a3f1011cx.cxu' / table of relative detective efficiency filename
BACHFILE= 'xref$91b1313sx.r0h' / background reference header file
ITFHFILE= 'xref$91b13138x.r1h' / itf reference header file
BLMHFILE= 'xref$a1m1626px.r7h' / blemish header file
UNIHFILE= 'N/A                ' / uniform de reference header file
SDEHFILE= 'N/A                ' / sde reference header file
RESHFILE= 'N/A                ' / input reseau header file
GEOHFILE= 'xref$a3f0949jx.r5h' / geometric reference header file
MODHFILE= 'N/A                ' / reseau mark model header file

                                / CALIBRATION SWITCHES: perform,omit,complete
BACCORR = 'PERFORM            ' / background subtraction correction
ITFCORR = 'PERFORM            ' / intensity transfer function correction
PXLCORR = 'OMIT               ' / split zoom-format pixels
UNICORR = 'PERFORM            ' / uniform de correction
WAVCORR = 'PERFORM            ' / compute photometric parameters
GEOCORR = 'PERFORM            ' / geometric correction
```

```
SDECORR = 'OMIT                ' / spectrograph de correction
RESCORR = 'OMIT                ' / locate reseau marks

                                 / CALIBRATION KEYWORDS
SAMPBEG =                    257 / first sample number
LINEBEG =                    257 / first line number
DNFORMT =                     16 / bits in each data number (8/16)
EXPTIME =         0.8221250E-03 / total exposure time in seconds
GEODEFV =         0.0000000E+00 / geo DN value for areas outside sci image

                                 / STATISTICAL KEYWORDS
DATE    = '24/08/90            ' / date this file was written (dd/mm/yy)
PODPSFF = '0                   ' / 0=(no podps fill), 1=(podps fill present)
STDCFFF = '0                   ' / 0=(no st dcf fill), 1=(st dcf fill present)
STDCFFP = '0000                ' / st dcf fill pattern (hex)

                                 / DISPLAY KEYWORDS
PLOTID  = 'FOC                 ' / plot title

                                 / FOC INSTRUMENT DESCRIPTOR KEYWORDS
                                 / FOC PHOTOMETRY KEYWORDS
LEDCOLOR= '                    ' / LED color (a color, blank , NONE or ERROR)

PHOTMODE= '                    ' / observation mode
PHOTFLAM=         0.0000000E+00 / Inverse Sensitivity
PHOTZPT =         0.0000000E+00 / ST magnitude zero point
PHOTPLAM=         0.0000000E+00 / Pivot Wavelength
PHOTBW  =         0.0000000E+00 / RMS Bandwidth of the Filter and Detector

                                 / DMF EXPOSURE DATA
PROPOSID= '02999               ' / PEP proposal identifier
PEP_EXPO= '4.0000000           ' / PEP exposure identifier including sequence
TARGNAM1= 'SN1987A             ' / proposer's target name (first 18 char)
TARGNAMC= '                    ' / target name continuation (last 12 char)
PLAN_EXP=  0.1000000000000E+04 / proposed time per exposure
PLAN_SN =  0.0000000000000E+00 / proposed signal-to-noise ratio
PRIORITY=                    1 / proposer's priority for exposure
RA      =        0.8386772E+02 / right ascension of the target (degrees)
DEC     =       -0.6927018E+02 / declination of the target (degrees)
EXPOSURE=        0.8221250E+03 / exposure duration (seconds)--calculated
EXPSTRT =        0.8378071E-05 / exposure start time (seconds)
EXPEND  =        0.8378868E-05 / exposure end time (seconds)
SUNANGLE=        0.9331923E+02 / angle between sun and V1 axis (degrees)
MOONANGL=        0.8664143E+02 / angle between moon and V1 axis (degrees)
END
```

References

Wells, D.C. and E.W. Greisen. *FITS: A Flexible Image Transport System. Astron. Astrophys. Suppl. Ser. 44: 363-370.* 1981.

NASA/OSSA Office of Standards and Technology. *Definition of the Flexible Image Transport System. Standard NOST 100-1.0.* June 18, 1993. Greenbelt MD: NASA Goddard Space Flight Center.

## CHAPTER 19

DXF

Name	DXF (Drawing Interchange Format)
Image type	ASCII and binary vector
Intended use	Exchange of computer-aided design (CAD) drawing data
Owner	Autodesk Inc., 2320 Marin Ship Way, Sausalito, CA. (415) 332-2344
Last version/ revision/ release date	AutoCAD Release 11
Platforms	Mostly PCs; also MacIntoshes and UNIX workstations, on applications originally developed for the PC
Supporting applications	Most PC-based CAD applications, including AutoCAD, Cadkey, Generic CADD, FastCAD. Many graphics applications, including Corel Draw; in desktop publishing: Ventura, Pagemaker
Similarities	No close similarities to any other format
Overall assessment	A de-facto standard for CAD drawing exchange; not efficient for storage; often poorly implemented; full DXF reader implementation a big job

Advantages

Because of the popularity of Autodesk's AutoCAD on the PC, the DXF exchange format is widely supported by other CAD programs, even on other computer platforms. As a published standard, it provides a valuable way for non-CAD applications to gain access to engineering drawings. It has all the advantages of a vector format (see chapter 1), plus the advantage of being a 3-D vector format and therefore capable of communicating true 3-D shapes, including wireframes and filled planes.

Disadvantages

Shapes can be assigned color codes relating them to a 256-color table, but the table is not necessarily related to the color spectrum by RGB or other color models. The ASCII form of DXF (the original and still more common form) is extremely slow to read. DXF applications must be capable of geometric calculations in at least two dimensions. Many of the features of DXF deal with text (annotation, dimensioning). A fully implemented DXF reader must be capable of font generation and manipulation as well as line and curve generation, curve fitting, and 2-D representation of 3-D shapes. In other words, it must be a CAD program.

Variants

The DXF format has two forms, ASCII and binary. The binary form, introduced with Release 10 of AutoCAD, uses binary-encoded numerical codes and data rather than ASCII numbers. The resulting file is approximately 25 percent smaller and five times faster to read than the ASCII form.

AutoCAD (and often other CAD programs) have an option for writing a DXF file that limits the DXF data to entities (shapes) only. These files are more compact and are sufficient for graphics-interchange purposes.

Overview of file structure

DXF is more of a language or graphics metafile than an image format. That is, the exact location or order of graphics data in the file is not particularly important. Like a language, however, the context in which terms appear is important; codes have different meanings, depending on what type of information is being communicated at the time. A 10 code in the context of describing a circle has a different meaning than it does when describing a line.

Everything in a DXF file is made up of pairs called groups. Each group has a group code, followed by a number or character string called the group value:

Group:
GROUP CODE
GROUP VALUE

The *group code* is an ASCII integer (binary in binary DXF) that indicates what type of value follows. Certain ranges of group codes are reserved for certain types of data. For instance, group codes in the range of 0–9 indicate that an ASCII character string follows; the specific code indicates what that string is used for. Group codes and values are delimited by a carriage-return/line-feed character pair. Data in a DXF file are organized in the following way:

- **HEADER section** Mostly contains information of little value to non-CAD applications, much of it relating to text and dimensioning. Sometimes it is omitted altogether.

- **TABLES section** Defines certain universal constants, such as drawing layers, viewing angles and distances, coordinate systems, and styles of dimensioning. Like the header section, the tables section can sometimes be omitted.

- **BLOCKS section** Defines groups of entities by name, and can also contain entities. It is not broadly used at this time, but it is becoming increasingly popular because it allows modularization of drawings.

- **ENTITIES section** Defines actual 3-D or 2-D geometries (entities) through the use of points, lines, circles, arcs, etc., and includes data linking the entity to a layer and/or a block.

For many purposes, the HEADER and TABLES sections can be skipped. The principal section for communicating geometric shapes (called *entities*) is the ENTITIES section; however, the BLOCKS section can also contain entities. The HEADER, TABLE, and BLOCKS sections are generally given, even if empty, simply because many applications expect them. When used, the sections appear in the order given above.

Format details

In this book, we will deal only with communicating standard geometric and graphic information using a single DXF data file. This excludes all portions of DXF that deal with text (dimensioning, annotation, special attributes), data that are part of another file and is referenced by the drawing file (inserts and shapes), and custom data for special applications.

The DXF characteristics discussed here roughly follow the 80/20 rule; that is, 80 percent of the information is used only 20 percent of the time! This is especially true of non-AutoCAD implementations, which give scant attention to the fine points of DXF, generally providing just basic 3-D entities.

Much of the following information is abstracted from the AutoCAD Reference Manual, and appears here by courtesy of Autodesk.

Structure of a CAD drawing

Although the DXF file format is not rigorously structured, the data itself can be structured. For instance, entities can be tagged as belonging to a named or numbered *block*. Furthermore, CAD drawings are generally divided into *layers* (also called *levels*) analogous to a set of paper drawings. Entities and blocks, therefore, are generally tagged with a layer name or number.

Although blocks can often be ignored for non-CAD applications, a DXF-reading application might need to be aware of layers. For instance, usually each layer contains a drawing for a different part of a mechanical assembly, so if all that is wanted from a DXF file is just one region of an assembly, the reading program might need the ability to distinguish layers. Layers are defined in the TABLES section. (Certain layers can be *frozen*, indicating that they were not visible in the CAD application when the file was stored.) If all that is wanted is a single component of an assembly, the DXF reader might need the ability to distinguish blocks, as well.

Views and viewports

A DXF-reading application might need to be aware of views. A view defines a viewer position—an angle and distance from some point on an object. This information is sometimes present in the DXF file (TABLES section), representing the view that the originator of a 3-D CAD drawing had in mind; a reading application would therefore be well advised to use that view. While DXF for AutoCAD Release 11 allows multiple viewports (windows offering different views), most non-CAD applications can safely ignore all but the current viewport, the first active one defined. If none is given, a reasonable (if often uninteresting) default view is a simple 2-D projection onto the XY plane. Active viewports are denoted by a group value, *ACTIVE.

Coordinate systems

Certain CAD concepts might be unfamiliar to non-CAD users, causing problems in translating DXF files. Foremost among these concepts is multiple-coordinate systems. In a CAD drawing, several coordinate systems (orientations of X, Y, and Z) are often used. In AutoCAD these are the world, user, and entity coordinate systems, called WCS, UCS, and ECS, respectively. The Z direction is often called the extrusion dimension in 3-D drawings, reflecting the fact that 3-D shapes in AutoCAD are often created by sweeping a 2-D shape in the Z direction. AutoCAD X and Y axes, visualized on paper, would always appear with $+X$ to the right and $+Y$ up; $+Z$ comes out of the page, toward the viewer. X cross $Y = Z$, in vector algebra, following the righthand rule. For vectors A and B, for instance, to visualize the result of A cross B, first visualize the vectors joined at their tails. Now align your right hand with vector A, fingers together, hand flat, and thumb extended; curl your fingers to point toward (not along) vector B. Rotate your hand at the wrist if necessary. Your thumb now points in the direction of the resulting vector. Note that $(A \times B) = -(B \times A)$.

WCS is the single, master-reference-coordinate system. UCS and ECS are defined with respect to WCS. All Line and Point entities are given exclusively in WCS coordinates, as are the following 3-D entities: 3-D Faces, 3-D Polylines (contiguous lines), 3-D Vertexes, 3-D Meshes (grids), and 3-D Mesh Vertexes.

There can be more than one UCS; each is defined in the TABLES section. Only one of these is *current* and is named and defined by the HEADER. No entities are defined in UCS coordinates, however, so the UCS concept is of little value for data-exchange purposes. The current UCS can, however, roughly substitute for a viewport if no viewport is given.

Entities that are planar in nature have their own, local ECS; their coordinates are given in this ECS. Planar entities include Circles, Arcs, Solids (filled planar, not 3-D, shapes of three or four sides), Traces (2-D filled lines of defined width), 2-D Polylines, and 2-D Vertexes. Other entities using ECS are Text, Attrib, Attdef, Shape, and Insert. These are not considered here.

To relate the ECS to the WCS, each entity can include an offset (code 38), called the *elevation*, between the origin of its ECS and the origin of the WCS, along the *Z* axis of the WCS. If no elevation code and value are given, the offset is zero.

Each ECS might also include a rotation from the WCS (as of AutoCAD Release 11). The rotation is given by a unit-length 3-D vector in world-coordinate space, defining the extrusion direction (*Z* axis) of the entity. The vector is defined by three groups (codes 210, 220 and 230) for *X*, *Y*, and *Z* respectively. If these groups are absent, there is no rotation.

The orientation of the *X* and *Y* axes is determined from the *Z* vector by AutoCAD's *Arbitrary Axis Algorithm*. If the unsigned values of the *X* and *Y* components of the entity's *Z* vector (the values following codes 210 and 220) are both less than $\frac{1}{64}$, then the *X* direction is given by Y_w cross Z_e. Otherwise it is Z_w cross Z_e, where the subscripts $_w$ and $_e$ indicate WCS and ECS, respectively. The *Y* axis is then oriented according to the righthand rule.

Header variables

More than 150 variables in Release 11 of AutoCAD can be defined in the header section of a DXF file. Only a relative few of these relate directly to communicating purely graphical data, and those are the variables given in Table 19-1. Programs other than AutoCAD make minimal use of header variables, often listing only entity color ($CECOLOR). Some programs omit the header altogether. All header variables are ASCII values preceded by group code 9.

DXF header variables Table 19-1

Variable	Subsequent group code	Interpretation of subsequent group value
CECOLOR	62	Color number for entity; 256=> BYLAYER; 0=> BYBLOCK
$CELTYPE	6	Line type for entity; ASCII descriptor, e.g., CONTINUOUS; also BYBLOCK or BYLAYER.
$EXTMAX	10, 20, 30	X,Y,Z maximums; actual extent of drawing.
$EXTMIN	10, 20, 30	X,Y,Z minimums; actual extent of drawing.
$PLINEWID	40	Default width of polyline.
SHADEDGE	70	0—Faces shaded
		1—Faces shaded, edges black
		2—Faces not filled, edges in entity color
		3—Faces in entity color, edges black
$TRACEWID	40	Default width of Trace entity.
$UCSNAME	1	Current UCS name.
$UCSORG	10, 20, 30	X,Y,Z; Current UCS origin (in WCS).
$UCSXDIR	10, 20, 30	X,Y,Z; Current UCS X axis vector (in WCS).
$UCSYDIR	10, 20, 30	X,Y,Z; Current UCS Y axis vector (in WCS).
$VIEWCTR	10, 20	X,Y; Current view center before Release 11
$VIEWDIR	10, 20, 30	X,Y,Z; Current view direction before Release 11

Table 19-1 **Continued**

Variable	Subsequent group code	Interpretation of subsequent group value
$VIEWSIZE	40	Current view height before Release 11 (Note: these variables superceded by Viewports; see Tables discussion)

Adapted from *AutoCAD Reference Manual* (Release 11). 1990. Autodesk, Inc.

A typical DXF file will begin with a HEADER section, something like the following:

```
  0
SECTION
  2
HEADER
  9
$CECOLOR
  62
  0
  0
ENDSEC
```

A DXF file generated by AutoCAD will have many more header variables defined. The word HEADER is preceded by a group code of 2, as is every section name—TABLES, ENTITIES, BLOCKS, and so on.

Group code type categories

Group codes fall into various functional types. Table 19-2 indicates what data (group value) follows each group code. Additional explanations follow in subsequent discussions of TABLES, BLOCKS, and ENTITIES. Parentheses indicate codes not relevant to communicating graphical data.

Table 19-2 **DXF group codes**

Group code	Group code interpretation
0	General-purpose beginning and end delimiting mark for files, entities, blocks, and tables. Text follows, indicating what is being delimited (e.g., "EOF" for end of file).
(1)	(Entity text value follows.)

2	Name, e.g., block name (or attribute tag), follows.
(3–4)	(Additional names or text follows.)
(5)	(Entity "handle" follows: hexadecimal code for external access).
6	Line type follows: CONTINUOUS, DASHED, CENTER, DASHDOT; also BYLAYER and BYBLOCK.
(7)	(Text style follows.)
8	Layer name follows.
9	Header variable name follows; HEADER section only.
10	First *X* coordinate of an entity follows, e.g., center of circle; see ENTITIES, following.
11–18	Other *X* coordinate follows; see details.
20	First Y coordinate of an entity follows; goes with first *X* coordinate.
21–28	Other *Y* coordinate follows; 11 and 21 form one *X,Y* coordinate, 12 and 22 form another, etc.
30	First *Z* coordinate of an entity follows; 10, 20 and 30 form *X,Y,Z* coordinate.
31–37	Other *Z* coordinate follows; 11, 21 and 31 form an *X,Y,Z* coordinate.
38	Elevation of entity follows; often deleted since Release 11, defaulting to zero.
39	Thickness of entity follows; defaults to zero if omitted.
(40–48)	(Floating-point value follows; generally text-related.)
49	Repeated value follows; always preceded by a count given by a 70-78 group.
50–58	Angle follows.
62	Color number follows; integer.
70–78	Integer follows for repeat count, flag, or mode.
210, 220, 230	*X*, *Y*, and *Z* terms in WCS for *Z* axis vector (extrusion direction) of entity.
999	Comment follows.

Adapted from *AutoCAD Reference Manual (Release 11)*. 1990. Autodesk, Inc.

To familiarize you with the appearance of DXF files, the following section on TABLES shows DXF groups, line-by-line, the way they appear in the file. Note, however, that the order in which groups appear is arbitrary. The DXF specification does not specify any particular order of groups within a table, block, or entity.

TABLES section

There are various types of tables in the TABLES section of a DXF file. Those that are used to communicate graphical information are the LTYPE, LAYER, VIEW, UCS, and VPORT tables. There can be any number of these tables, and they can appear in any order. A TABLES section will be structured as follows:

```
0
SECTION
2
TABLES
•
•
•
(individual tables)
•
•
•
0
ENDSEC
```

Individual tables are structured as follows; blank lines have been added to help you visualize the groups more easily:

```
0
TABLE

2
(table type name, e.g., LAYER)

70
(maximum number of table entries to follow.)

0
```

(table type name, e.g., LAYER, again!)

2
(user-assigned name or number, e.g., WIRING)

(various group codes and values)
•
•
•
0
ENDTAB

The table type names of interest are LTYPE, LAYER, VIEW, UCS, and VPORT. Each table type name inexplicably appears twice for each instance of a table! Once, after a 2 code, to introduce a 70 group; then again, following a 0 code, to introduce subsequent data. The 70-group value is a number greater than or equal to the number of table entries that follow.

After the second appearance of the table type name (e.g., LAYER), another 2-group provides a user-assigned name for the individual instance of that table type (e.g., WIRING for the wiring layer of a building drawing). The subsequent groups comprise a variety of group codes, whose significance differs with the table type. For instance, the 10, 20, and 30 groups used in a VIEW type table represent the view center point (*X*,*Y*,*Z*); when used in a UCS type table, they represent the UCS origin *X*, *Y*, and *Z* (in WCS units).

LTYPE tables

LTYPE tables describe a line type (e.g., dashed, dotted) by name. These names will be used in the entity or layer descriptions. The following groups, with blank lines added for clarity are of interest in an LTYPE table; they can appear in any order:

2
LTYPE

70

(flags—ignore)

0
LTYPE

2
(user-assigned line type name, in ASCII, e.g., DOTDASH)

73
(number of dash-length definitions that follow, e.g., 2)

40
(physical length of repeated dash pattern, e.g., 0.0 units)

49
(first dash length, e.g., 0.005)

49
(second dash length, e.g., 0.025)

(additional 49 groups as needed)

LAYER tables

LAYER tables associate a distinguishing line type and color with a particular layer name, and indicate whether a layer is frozen, thawed, unused, or exclusively "owns" a particular viewport. They include any of the following groups:

2
LAYER

70
(flags, bit coded—see below)

0
LAYER

2

(user-determined layer name, often a number, in ASCII)

62
(color number associated with drawings on this layer)

6
(linetype name associated with drawings on this layer)

The value following a 70 code is always bit-coded. In the LAYER table, the following bits are of interest:

1-bit: 0 = layer on and thawed; 1 = layer frozen.

4-bit: 1 = only this layer appears in the current viewport.

VIEW tables

VIEW tables establish certain named viewpoints of the 3-D model, from which 2-D images can be derived. They include the following groups (blank lines added for clarity here, and subsequently):

2
VIEW

70
(ignore)

0
VIEW

2
(user-determined view name, e.g., UNDERSIDE)

40
(view height)

41
(view width)

10
(view center, *X* in WCS)

20
(view center, *Y* in WCS)

11
(direction of view from target, *X* component)

21
(direction of view from target, *Y* component)

31
(direction of view from target, *Z* component)

UCS tables

These define any User-Coordinate Systems that have been created, with respect to World Coordinates. If no UCSs have been created, there will be only a 70 group following the type name, UCS. Groups unessential to graphics exchange have been omitted.

2
UCS

70
(ignore)

0
UCS

2
(user-defined UCS name)

10
(origin *X*)

20
(origin *Y*)

30
(origin *Z*)

11
(*X* component of UCS *X*-axis vector)

21
(*Y* component of UCS *X*-axis vector)

31
(*Z* component of UCS *X*-axis vector)

12
(*X* coordinate of target point in WCS)

22
(*Y* coordinate of target point in WCS)

32
(*Z* coordinate of target point in WCS)

43
(front clipping plane: offset distance along sight vector from target; 0 = no clipping)

44
(back clipping plane: offset distance along sight vector from target; 0 = no clipping)

VPORT tables

Viewports are windows of particular orientation with respect to the 3-D model. They are similar to named views (see VIEW tables), but whereas named views are optional, there is always at least one viewport. For graphics-exchange purposes, the most important viewport is the current viewport, which is always the first "active" viewport listed in a DXF file. In Release 11 of AutoCAD, Viewports generated when TILEMODE is off (paper-space mode) are recorded as VIEWPORT entities in paper space; these are not documented here.

An active viewport will appear as follows. There are many group codes not of interest for graphics-exchange purposes, and they are omitted.

2
VPORT

70
(ignore)

0
VPORT
2

*ACTIVE

16
(*X* component of view vector from target point)

26
(*Y* component of view vector from target point)

36
(*Z* component of view vector from target point)

17
(*X* coordinate of target point)

27
(*Y* coordinate of target point)

37
(*Z* coordinate of target point)

43
(front clipping plane: offset distance along sight vector from target)

44
(back clipping plane: offset distance along sight vector from target)

BLOCKS section

The BLOCKS section of a DXF file serves only to organize entities into named groups. Entities that are part of a block are recorded here, rather than in the ENTITIES section. A BLOCKS section is organized as follows:

```
0
SECTION

2
BLOCKS

0
BLOCK

2
(user-assigned block name)

70
(ignore)

•
•
•
(individual entities)
•
•
•
0
ENDBLOCK

0
ENDSEC
```

ENTITIES section

This section is where the real geometric information exists, and comprises the bulk of a DXF file. The ENTITIES section is organized as follows:

```
0
SECTION
2
ENTITIES
•
•
•
(individual entities)
•
•
•
0
ENDSEC
```

The geometric entities of interest are: POINT, LINE, CIRCLE, ARC, TRACE, SOLID, POLYLINE, VERTEX and SEQUEND, and 3DFACE. Other entities, not covered here, include TEXT, SHAPE, INSERT, ATTDEF, ATTRIB, and VIEWPORT.

Individual entities take the form:

```
0
(entity name, e.g., LINE)

8
(layer name or number in ASCII, e.g., 0)

(associated group codes and values)
•
•
•
```

All entities can include any of the groups shown in Table 19-3.

Common entity groups Table 19-3

Group code	Meaning of subsequent group value
6	Line type name (e.g., CONTINUOUS), or BYLAYER or BYBLOCK.
38	Elevation (*Z*), for implementations prior to Release 11; default is zero.
39	Thickness of line.
62	Color number, or BYLAYER, or 0 to indicate BYBLOCK.
67	0 or omitted indicates model space entity; 1 indicates paper space.
210, 220, 230	(*X*,*Y*,*Z*) extrusion (*Z*) direction vector for ECS of planar entities; omission indicates *Z*-axis parallel to *Z*-axis of WCS.

Adapted from: *AutoCAD Reference Manual (Release 11)*. 1990. Autodesk, Inc.

Remember that planar entities (CIRCLE, ARC, TRACE, SOLID, and POLYLINE) are recorded in their own Entity Coordinate Systems (see the section on coordinate systems, preceding). Other entities are in the World Coordinate System.

At this point in the discussion of DXF, we will stop giving a line-by-line account of group codes and values and simply list them for each entity. Bear in mind that groups appear in no particular order in DXF files.

Basic geometric entities

POINT entity groups

10, 20, 30: (*X*,*Y*,*Z*) location

LINE (or 3DLINE) entity groups

10, 20, 30: (*X*,*Y*,*Z*) start point
11, 21, 31: (*X*,*Y*,*Z*) stop point

✻ CIRCLE entity groups

10, 20, 30: (*X*,*Y*,*Z*) center
40: radius

✻ ARC entity groups

10, 20, 30: (*X*,*Y*,*Z*) center
40: radius
50: start angle
51: end angle

✻ TRACE entity groups

10, 20, 30;
11, 21, 31;
12, 22, 32;
13, 23, 33: corners of trace (rectangle)
TRACE entities are essentially wide lines.

✻ SOLID entity groups

10, 20, 30;
11, 21, 31;
12, 22, 32;
13, 23, 33: corners of solid (can be triangular, in which case third and fourth groups are identical). All *Z* coordinates of TRACE and SOLID entities must currently be identical, because all points are in local space.

✻ POLYLINE entity groups

66: always followed by 1, indicating that a VERTEX list follows the POLYLINE entity.
70: bit-coded flag (see below)
71, 72: (*M*, *N*) for polygon mesh of *M* X *N* vertices; or, if polyface mesh (see 64 bit of 70 group value), *M* is count of vertices, *N* is count of faces.
73, 74: (*M*, *N*) for smooth surface of *M* X *N* densities.
75: type of surface if smooth; 0 = no smooth surface; 5 = quadratic B-spline; 6 = cubic B-spline; 8 = Bezier.

(POLYLINES are contiguous lines or arcs, sometimes forming a mesh, whose vertices or intersections are given by a subsequent VERTEX entity. Polyface meshes are a type of POLYLINE, comprising filled, opaque planes or curved surfaces.)

The 70 group value of a POLYLINE entity is bit-coded, as follows:

1-bit: entity is a closed polyline
2-bit: includes curve-fit vertices
4-bit: includes spline-fit vertices
8-bit: entity is a 3-D polyline
16-bit: entity is a 3-D polyline mesh
32-bit: polygon mesh is closed in *N* direction
64-bit: entity is a polyface mesh.

POLYLINE entities are always followed by a sequence of VERTEX entities, which is a list of vertices for the POLYLINE, terminated by the SEQEND entity.

If the POLYLINE is actually a polyface mesh, things get quite complicated. We have not tested this capability, but from the specification it appears that two groups of VERTEX entities follow the POLYLINE entity. The first group gives the corners of the faces, the second group gives the characteristics of each face. These characteristics are associated with the preceding locations by treating the first group as an indexed list; each face definition has four index pointers (71, 72, 73, and 74-groups) to the earlier group of vertex locations, defining the boundaries of the face.

✳ VERTEX entity groups

10, 20, 30: (X,Y,Z) location; 0 (ignore) if polyface.
42: "bulge"; = tan (0.25*included angle) for arc, negative if arc is clockwise from start to endpoint; 0= straight line; 1= semicircle.
50: curve-fit tangent direction
70: bit-coded flag, as follows:
  1-bit: additional vertex due to curve fitting
  2-bit: there is a curve-fit tangent for this vertex (group 50)
  4-bit: not used
  8-bit: spline-fit vertex

16-bit: spline frame control point
32-bit: vertices are for a 3-D polyline
64-bit: vertices are for a 3-D polygon mesh
128: entity is a polyface; ignore 10, 20, 30 groups. Face bounded by vertices listed earlier; 71, 72, 73, and 74 groups are indices into vertex list.

* **SEQEND entity** No data groups. Marks end of vertex list.

* **3DFACE entity groups**

10, 20, 30;
11, 21, 31;
12, 22, 32;
13, 23, 33: (*X*,*Y*,*Z*) coordinates of corners of a 3-D face.
70: invisible edge flags (1-bit= 1st edge is invisible; 2-bit= 2nd; 4-bit= 3rd; 8-bit= 4th).
3-D faces might have only three corners, in which case the third coordinate is duplicated in the fourth.

Extended entity data

DXF supports a number of special group codes starting at 1000. These codes implement special drawing or modeling applications, or third-party extensions of AutoCAD, and are not covered here.

Binary DXF files

A more compact, binary version of DXF was created with Release 10 of AutoCAD. The differences are: ASCII group codes are replaced with 1-byte binary group codes; ASCII integers become 2-byte binary integers (lsb first); ASCII floating point numbers become binary, 8-byte IEEE double-precision numbers (lsb first); ASCII strings are terminated only with a zero (null) byte.

Binary DXF files begin with a 22-byte ASCII header (called a sentinel by Autodesk), as follows:

AutoCAD Binary DXF[CR][LF][SUB][NUL]

[CR] is 0D H
[LF] is 0A H
[SUB] is 1A H
[NUL] is 00

Example

Figure 19-1 shows a simple example of a line drawing that was stored in DXF format. Figure 19-2 lists the DXF file. To show typical implementation, the drawing was created using a non-AutoDesk solids modeling CADD program; hence the widespread use of the 3DFACE entity and minimal use of header variables.

Figure 19-1

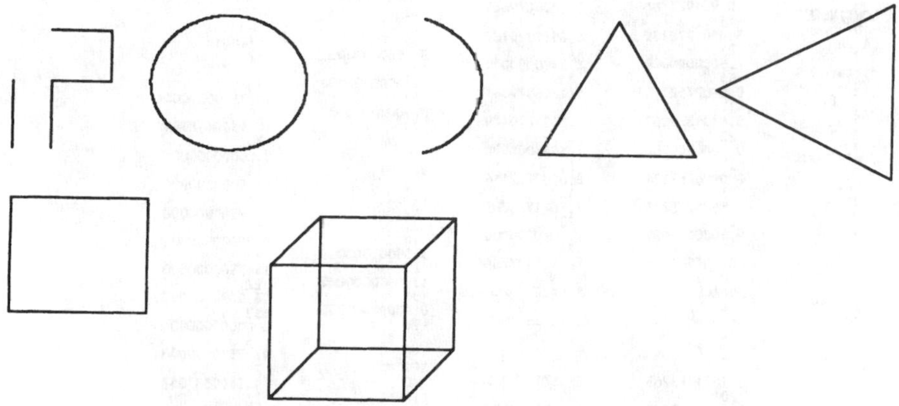

Example drawing of planar and 3-D figures.

Figure 19-2

```
  0
SECTION
  2
HEADER
  9
$CECOLOR
 62
     0
  0
ENDSEC
  0
SECTION
  2
TABLES
  0
TABLE
  2
LAYER
  0
LAYER
  2
0
 70
     0
 62
     7
  6
CONTINUOUS
  0
LAYER
  2
squares
 70
     0
 62
     7
  6
CONTINUOUS
  0
LAYER
  2
triangs
 70
     0
 62
     7
  6
CONTINUOUS
  0
LAYER
  2
circarc
 70
     0
 62
     7
  6
CONTINUOUS
  0
LAYER
  2
lines
 70
     0
 62
     7
  6
CONTINUOUS
  0
LAYER
  2
skewcub
 70
     0
 62
     7
  6
CONTINUOUS
  0
LAYER
  2
planars
 70
     0
 62
     7
  6
CONTINUOUS
  0
ENDTAB
  0
ENDSEC
  0
SECTION
  2
ENTITIES
  0
3DFACE
  8
planars
 62
     7
 10
7.5621778265
 20
7.5000000000
 30
-0.9019237886
 11
7.5621778265
 21
9.5000000000
 31
-0.9019237886
 12
5.8301270189
 22
9.5000000000
 32
0.0980762114
 13
5.8301270189
 23
7.5000000000
 33
0.0980762114
  0
3DFACE
  8
skewcub
 62
     7
 10
7.5621778265
 20
7.5000000000
 30
-0.9019237886
 11
5.8301270189
 21
7.5000000000
 31
0.0980762114
 12
5.8301270189
 22
9.5000000000
 32
0.0980762114
 13
7.5621778265
 23
9.5000000000
 33
-0.9019237886
  0
3DFACE
  8
skewcub
 62
     7
 10
8.1871778265
 20
8.2500000000
 30
0.1806079661
 11
8.1871778265
 21
10.2500000000
 31
0.1806079661
 12
6.4551270189
 22
10.2500000000
 32
1.1806079661
 13
6.4551270189
 23
8.2500000000
 33
1.1806079661
  0
3DFACE
  8
skewcub
 62
     7
 10
6.4551270189
 20
8.2500000000
 30
1.1806079661
 11
6.4551270189
 21
10.2500000000
 31
1.1806079661
 12
5.8301270189
 22
9.5000000000
 32
0.0980762114
 13
5.8301270189
 23
7.5000000000
 33
0.0980762114
  0
3DFACE
  8
skewcub
 62
     7
 10
8.1871778265
 20
8.2500000000
 30
0.1806079661
 11
6.4551270189
 21
8.2500000000
 31
1.1806079661
 12
5.8301270189
 22
7.5000000000
 32
0.0980762114
 13
7.5621778265
 23
7.5000000000
 33
-0.9019237886
  0
3DFACE
  8
skewcub
 62
     7
 10
8.1871778265
 20
10.2500000000
 30
0.1806079661
 11
8.1871778265
 21
8.2500000000
 31
0.1806079661
 12
7.5621778265
 22
7.5000000000
 32
-0.9019237886
 13
7.5621778265
 23
9.5000000000
 33
-0.9019237886
  0
3DFACE
  8
skewcub
 62
     7
 10
6.4551270189
 20
10.2500000000
 30
1.1806079661
 11
8.1871778265
 21
10.2500000000
 31
0.1806079661
 12
7.5621778265
 22
9.5000000000
 32
-0.9019237886
 13
5.8301270189
 23
9.5000000000
 33
0.0980762114
  0
3DLINE
  8
lines
 62
     7
 10
2.5000000000
 20
12.2500000000
lines
 62
     7
 10
3.7500000000
 20
13.0000000000
 30
0.0000000000
 70
    32
  0
VERTEX
  8
lines
 62
     7
 10
3.0000000000
 20
13.0000000000
 30
0.0000000000
 70
    32
  0
SEQEND
  0
CIRCLE
  8
circarc
 62
     7
 10
5.2500000000
 20
12.2500000000
 30
0.0000000000
 40
1.0000000000
  0
ARC
  8
circarc
 62
     7
 10
7.4583333333
 20
12.2500000000
 30
0.0000000000
 40
1.0416666667
 50
-73.7397952917
 51
73.7397952917
  0
3DFACE
  8
triangs
 62
     7
 10
11.2500000000
 20
11.2500000000
 30
0.0000000000
 11
10.2500000000
 21
13.2500000000
 31
0.0000000000
 12
9.2500000000
 22
11.2500000000
 32
0.0000000000
 13
9.2500000000
 23
11.2500000000
 33
0.0000000000
  0
3DFACE
  8
triangs
 62
     7
 10
13.7500000000
 20
10.9509618943
 30
0.0000000000
 11
11.5000000000
 21
12.2500000000
 31
0.0000000000
 12
13.7500000000
 22
13.5490381057
 32
0.0000000000
 13
13.7500000000
 23
13.5490381057
 33
0.0000000000
  0
3DFACE
  8
squares
 62
     7
 10
4.2500000000
 20
10.5000000000
 30
0.0000000000
 11
4.2500000000
 21
8.7500000000
 31
0.0000000000
 12
2.5000000000
 22
8.7500000000
 32
0.0000000000
 13
2.5000000000
 23
10.5000000000
 33
0.0000000000
  0
ENDSEC
  0
EOF
```

DXF code for Fig. 19-1.

References

Autodesk, Inc. *AutoCAD Reference Manual*. 1990.

Bourke, Paul. *Minimum Requirements for Creating a DXF File of a 3D Model*. 1991. Auckland, NZ: School of Architecture, Property, and Planning, Auckland University, Private Bag.

CHAPTER 20

HPGL

Name	HP-GL (Hewlett-Packard Graphics Language)
Image type	Line drawing
Intended use	Originally, control of pen plotters, now also laser printers
Owner	Hewlett-Packard Co., San Diego Printer Operations, 16399 W. Bernardo Drive, San Diego CA 92127-1899
Last version/ revision/ release date	HP-GL/2, 1990
Platforms	HP Pen plotters, many other plotters and laser printers. See Table 20-1.
Supporting applications	All CAD programs, many charting programs and word processors
Similarities	CAD formats
Overall assessment	The standard language for printing line drawings; also usable as a low-level vector picture format

Table 20-1 **Plotters and printers supporting HP-GL**

HP-GL Plotters	HP 7220, 74xx, 75xx, Color Pro, DraftPro, and DraftMaster I and II
	IBM 737x, 618x
	Most clone implementations before 1990
HP-GL Printers	IBM 4019, many other PCL 4 clones have HP-GL modes.
HP-GL/2 Plotters	HP 7550 Plus, most 7600 models, DraftMaster MX/RX/SX and Plus, DesignJet
	Most clone implementations since 1990
HP-GL/2 Printers	HP Laserjet III, IIID, IIIP, IIISi, PaintJet XL PCL 5 clones

Advantages

Widely used, easy to produce, independent of paper size, although very large images might have to be drawn in pieces.

Disadvantages

Few, if you want to print a line drawing. Very low-level as a picture format.

Variants

The original HP-GL had many minor variations in 25 implementations at HP alone. HP-GL/2 is better standardized and has optional modules that can be present or absent.

Overview of file structure

HP-GL is the command language for Hewlett-Packard pen plotters. Due to the wide acceptance of HP plotters, HP-GL has become the *de facto* standard plotter control language and is widely implemented both on pen plotters and laser printers. Unlike most other drawing formats, HP-GL consists almost entirely of readable ASCII characters, making it easy to produce and to debug. (The HP-GL/2 Polyline Encoded command is a major exception, as it encodes numeric values using the binary values of characters, but it is not yet in wide use.)

HP-GL was originally implemented in 1976 for HP's 7400 series pen plotters. Over the years, it was re-implemented many times, both at HP and elsewhere, on pen plotters and other kinds of printers. Although the core language was quite stable, many extensions appeared. In 1990 HP released HP-GL/2, a mostly upward-compatible extension of HP-GL. HP-GL/2 has a core language and several extension sets. The *Technical Graphics* extension provides better control over drawing details, and is present in nearly all implementations of both HP-GL and HP-GL/2. The *Palette* extension supports color inkjet and similar printers. The *Dual Context* extension supports HP-GL/2 embedded in PCL laser printer data streams. The *Digitizing* extension supports using a pen plotter as a digitizer. Any particular implementation of HP-GL/2 is supposed to include the entire core language, and either to completely include or completely exclude each extension. For example, a laser printer would include Technical Graphics and Dual Context, but not Palette or Digitizing.

The complete set of all HP-GL and HP-GL/2 commands would take several hundred pages to present, so we concentrate here on the commands that are common to most implementations of HP-GL and HP-GL/2. All the commands here are in the HP-GL/2 core language.

Format details

An HP-GL file is a sequence of commands to draw a picture. First come initialization commands to set the size of the image, and other parameters, then commands to draw lines, figures and strings, and usually a command or two to finish up. Each command is a two-letter command (CI for circle), followed by a number of parameters; for example, the radius of the circle. Parameters are usually numbers, but for a few commands they are text strings.

The drawing model is based on that of a pen plotter. There is a set of pens, each of which is typically a different color or, on a monochrome printer, a different width, which can be used for drawing. Drawing can be *pen up*, in which case the pen moves but does not draw anything, or pen down, in which case the path the pen takes becomes part of the image. On an actual pen plotter, the types and colors of the pen are set by physically loading pens into the plotter. On a laser or inkjet printer, the pens are simulated in software. The conventional pen colors are 0 white, 1 black, 2 red, 3 green, 4 yellow, 5 blue, and 6 purple or cyan. Selecting pen 0 on a pen plotter tells the plotter to put the current pen away. White pens are transparent, so drawing with a white pen has no visible effect. On a monochrome printer, such as a laser printer, only pens 0 and 1 are usually available. Higher numbered pens might be black pens of different widths.

Characters are typically drawn using simple stroke fonts, so they can be scaled, rotated, and slanted.

Some commands that take numeric arguments require integer values, while others allow real numbers with a decimal point. Negative numbers are preceded by a sign. The maximum numeric value varies from implementation to implementation, and can be as low as 2^{14} on older HP/GL plotters, but is always at least 2^{23} on HP-GL/2 plotters. At least four digits to the right of the decimal point are significant.

Some commands send results back to the host computer; for example, OI reports the model identification of the plotter. These commands only work on plotters that are connected by a bi-directional interface, such as RS-232 serial or GP-IB. They do not work on the common Centronics parallel interface nor on plotters connected through a network. These commands are not usually present in files of HP-GL data, because they make sense only in the context of a program that is prepared to read back the results, and they are not discussed further here.

Geometry

The HP-GL drawing area is a rectangle with the origin usually at the lower left corner. *X* increases to the right, and *Y* increases upward.

The physical unit for HP-GL is typically $\frac{1}{1000}$ inch. For HP-GL/2, each physical unit is $\frac{1}{40}$ mm, which is $\frac{1}{1016}$ inch. Logical units are set by mapping points in logical units onto points in physical units. There are two physical reference points known as P1 and P2. By default, P1 is at the lower left corner of the printable area of the page, and P2 is at the upper right, the "hard clip" limits. On most HP-GL plotters, the default origin is in the center of the page. On HP-GL/2 plotters, the default origin is at P1, the lower left corner. The IP command sets the P1 and P2 in terms of physical units; most typically the P1 point is set in order to put the origin at some other place, such as the middle of the page. The SC scaling command sets the logical coordinates that correspond to the P1 and P2 points. Because the default P1 and P2 are at the extreme corners of the page, the usual arguments of SC are the limits of the logical coordinates used, so the plot fills the page, whatever the page size is. Various combinations of IP and SC can set any desired scaling, including mirroring the coordinates. In HP-GL/2, there are extra arguments to SC that can force isomorphic scaling; that is, equal scales on the two axes.

The default logical coordinates are identical to the physical coordinates, and many plots are drawn using these physical coordinates.

All pictures are clipped to the physical paper limits. The IW Input Window command can be used to set a logical clipping rectangle that further clips output.

In the commands below, all coordinate values are expressed in logical units unless otherwise indicated.

Command encoding

HP-GL was designed to be easy to generate, even in programming languages with limited output-formatting abilities, such as microcomputer versions of Basic. Each command starts with a command mnemonic consisting of two uppercase letters; for example, PA for Plot Absolute. The mnemonic can be followed by some number of arguments. Numeric arguments are separated by spaces or commas. String arguments are delimited by a terminator character, by default ASCII ETX or hex 03. Commands are terminated by a semicolon, which for most commands can be omitted if another command immediately follows. For example:

```
PA 1000,2000;
```

is a command to move to position (1000,2000). In most cases, any optional characters should be omitted to save space and minimize transmission time. The commands:

```
PA 100,200; SP 3; PA 200,200; PA 200,300;
```

could be written as:

```
PA100,200SP3PA200,200PA200,300;
```

or, because the PA command can take any number of arguments, as:

```
PA100,200SP3PA200,200,200,300;
```

Outside of character strings, carriage returns and line feeds are separator characters (like spaces) but are otherwise disregarded. Within character strings, they perform their usual formatting function of starting a new line.

The HP-GL/2 PE (Polyline Encoded) command, unlike any other command, uses character-encoded binary data described later.

Starting & ending a picture

- **IN (Initialize)** Set all parameters to defaults, move the pen to the origin, and prepare for a new plot. Many HP-GL picture files do not begin with IN, so they can be embedded in larger pictures.

- **DF (Defaults)** Set all parameters to defaults, but do not change P1 or P2.

- **SC (Scale) *X0,X1,Y0,Y1*** Set the scale of the plot. (*X0*,*Y0*) is the lower left corner and (*X1*,*Y1*) is the upper right. The plot can be flipped left to right or top to bottom by making *X1* less than *X0* or *Y1* less than *Y0*. (Flipping is not supported on some older HP/GL plotters.)

- **IP (Input Points) *X1,Y1,X2,Y2*** Change the scaling points. (*X1*,*Y1*), expressed in physical units, becomes the new P1 scaling point, and (*X2*,*Y2*), expressed in physical units, becomes the new P2 scaling point. If *X2* and *Y2* are omitted, P2 is moved so that the scale is unchanged, in which case this command just shifts the origin.

* **IW (Input Window) *X0,Y0,X1,Y1*** Set clipping limits. Subsequent output is clipped to the rectangle defined by (*X*0,*Y*0) and (*X*1,*Y*1). An IW; with no arguments turns off clipping.

* **RO (Rotate) Angle** Rotate the coordinate system the given number of degrees counterclockwise. The angle in HP-GL must be 0 or 90, and in HP-GL/2 can also be 180 or 270. Rotation causes a different transformation than the mirroring available with the SC command. Text drawn rotated 180 degrees appears upside down, while text drawn with negative *X* scaling is backwards.

* **PG (Page)** Eject the paper, or advance roll-fed paper to the next frame. This marks the end of a plot. Disregarded on LaserJet III and on some older HP/GL plotters.

Lines

To draw lines, one selects a pen, lifts the pen with PU, moves to the beginning of the line, puts the pen down with PD, and draws the line. A few commands automatically put the pen up or down, as noted.

* **SP (Select Pen) PenNo ...** Select the given pen for subsequent drawing. At the beginning of the picture, transparent white pen 0 is selected, so for drawing to have any effect, some other pen must be selected.

* **PU (Pen Up) *X1, Y1*, ...**

* **PD (Pen Down) *X1, Y1*, ...** Remove the pen from the paper for PU, or put the pen down on the paper for PD. Then move the pen to (*X*1,*Y*1), and so forth. The (*X*,*Y*) pairs are interpreted as absolute or relative coordinates, depending on whether a PA or PR command was most recently executed.

* **PA (Plot Absolute) *X1, Y1, X2, Y2*, ...** Move to (*X*1,*Y*1), then (*X*2, *Y*2), and so forth. If the pen is down, draws a series of lines.

* **PR (Plot Relative) *X1*, *Y1*, *X2*, *Y2*, ...** Move to the current position plus (*X1*,*Y1*), then that position plus (*X2*, *Y2*), and so forth. If the pen is down, draws a series of lines.

* **LT (Line Type) Type** Set the type of line drawn. The default is a solid line. Type 0 is only a dot at the end of the line. Type 1 is dotted, 2 short dash, 3 long dash, 4 dash and dot, 5 long dash/short dash, 6 long dash/two short dashes. Negative values define adaptive line types that adjust the dash lengths so there is a whole number of dashes in each line. Type 99 restores the line type before the previous LT.

* **SM (Symbol Mode) Character** Draw the given character at the end of each line, even if the pen is up. If the character is omitted, turn off symbol mode.

* **PE (Plot Encoded, HP-GL/2 only) encoded string** Draw a series of lines. Because HP-GL pictures typically include huge numbers of pen motions, this special function provides an efficient way to send a set of motion commands. The encoded string is a stream of flag bytes and data values, terminated with a semicolon. For this command, the semicolon cannot be omitted.

  In the absence of flags, pairs of data values are taken to be (*X*,*Y*) relative motions as in the PR command and are drawn pen down. An equals sign (=) treats the next pair as absolute coordinates. A less-than sign (<) treats the next pair as a pen up move. A colon (:) treats the next single value as the pen number for subsequent drawing.

  Values are encoded in 6-bit or 5-bit chunks. If the data path to the plotter is 8 bits wide, the default 6-bit chunks are appropriate. If the operating system preempts the high bit of each character for parity, 5-bit chunks are appropriate. A 7 following the PE command says that 5-bit chunks follow. Each value can have zero or more fraction bits. By default, values are integral, i.e., there are no fraction bits. A > flag followed by a single value sets the number of fraction bits for subsequent values.

In each value, the low bit of the encoded value is the sign, 0 for positive or 1 for negative. To the left of the sign are the fraction bits, and to the left of the fraction bits is the integer value. For example, if there were two fraction bits, the value 11.5 would be binary 1011 10 0. The spaces show the boundaries between the integer, fraction, and sign. The binary value is broken up into 5- or 6-bit chunks starting at the right and encoded into characters. Each chunk other than the last for a value is encoded by adding 63 (3F H.) The last chunk for a value is encoded by adding 191 (BF H) for 6-bit chunks or 95 (5F H) for 5-bit chunks. To finish encoding 11.5 as 5-bit chunks, for example, regroup the bits as chunks 10 and 11100, (2 H and 1C H). First transmit the low chunk as 1C+3F or 5B. Then transmit the high chunk as 2+5F or 61. A single value might take up to eight bytes to encode depending on its magnitude and the number of fraction bits.

Arcs & circles

HP-GL approximates arcs and circles with short line segments, with each segment typically being five degrees of a circle. This occasionally causes trouble when using polygon mode (below) if the number of segments overflows the polygon buffer, and when using adaptive line types, because the adaptation is done for each segment, not for the whole circle or arc. If anisotropic scaling is in effect (i.e., the *X* and *Y* scaling factors are different), circles are drawn as ellipses and arcs are elliptical arcs.

- **AA (Arc Absolute) *X*, *Y*, Angle** Draw an arc of the circle whose center is at (*X*,*Y*) and that passes through the current position. The arc starts at the current position and continues for *Angle* degrees counterclockwise (clockwise for a negative Angle).

- **AR (Arc Relative) *X*, *Y*, Angle** Draw an arc of the circle whose center is distance (*X*,*Y*) from the current position and that passes through the current position. The arc starts at the current position and continues for *Angle* degrees counterclockwise (clockwise for a negative Angle).

✳ **CI (Circle) Radius, Angle** Draw a circle centered at the current point with the given *Radius*. The circle is always drawn with the pen down. The optional Angle specifies what angle each line segment that approximates the circle should cover. For example, an Angle of 60 would draw a hexagon.

Polygons

Some HP-GL and all HP-GL/2 devices have a polygon buffer that stores the vertices of a polygon to be drawn. One initializes the buffer with PM, then draws the polygon using AA, AR, CI, PA, PD, PE, PR, and PU, terminates the polygon with PM2, then uses primitives to outline or fill the polygon. The pen position when the PM is executed becomes the first vertex of the polygon. More than one polygon can be defined simultaneously to describe nonsimple areas; for example, one polygon inside another to describe a hollow area. A few commands draw a figure and enter it into the polygon buffer: EA,ER,EW,RA,RR, and WG.

In implementations without a polygon buffer, the PM and FP commands are omitted.

✳ **PM (Polygon Mode) Flag** If the flag is 0 or omitted, flush the polygon buffer and start a new polygon. If the flag is 1, close the current polygon if necessary (add an edge to the first vertex) and start a new polygon with the next drawing command. If the flag is 2, close the current polygon.

✳ **FP (Fill Polygon)** Fill the current polygon. The FT command sets the fill pattern.

✳ **EP (Edge polygon)** Outline the current polygon.

✳ **EA (Edge rectangle Absolute) *X,Y*** Outline the rectangle defined by the current position and (*X*,*Y*) and enter that rectangle into the polygon buffer.

* **ER (Edge rectangle Relative) *X,Y*** Outline the rectangle defined by the current position and the current position plus (*X*,*Y*) and enter that rectangle into the polygon buffer.

* **EW (Edge wedge) Radius, Start, Sweep** Outline a pie-shaped wedge. Draw an arc of the circle with the center at the current point and the given radius, starting at *Start* degrees and sweeping for *Sweep* degrees. Start is measured counterclockwise (clockwise if negative) from the point (Radius,0) from the center. Sweep is measured counterclockwise from Start (clockwise if negative). Lines are drawn from the ends of the arc to the center.

* **RA (Rectangle Absolute) *X,Y*** Fill the rectangle defined by the current position and (*X*,*Y*) and enter that rectangle into the polygon buffer.

* **RR (Rectangle Relative) *X,Y*** Fill the rectangle defined by the current position and the current position plus (*X*,*Y*) and enter that rectangle into the polygon buffer.

* **WG (Fill wedge) Radius, Start, Sweep** Fill a pie-shaped wedge. The arguments are the same as for EW.

* **FT (Fill Type) Type, A, B** Set the fill type for subsequent filled polygons. Fill types 1 and 2 are solid color, and A and B are ignored. On pen plotters, type 2 is drawn unidirectionally for purer pen color. Fill types 3 and 4 are hatched and crosshatched. A is the spacing of the lines and B is the angle in degrees of the lines, measured counterclockwise from horizontal.

Text

HP-GL provides the ability to include text strings in a picture. The set of characters available varies from one implementation to another, but always includes at least the usual ASCII set. Characters can be drawn at any size, in any direction. They can also be slanted to create an italic effect.

✳ **LB (Label) String** Draw the string, starting at the current position. The string ends with an ETX (03 H) unless DT has set another terminator.

✳ **CP (Character Position) *X, Y*** Move to the point (*X*,*Y*) character spaces from the current position. CP is similar to PR except that the values are in terms of character sizes. CP always moves with the pen up.

✳ **DI (Absolute Text Direction) *X, Y***

✳ **DR (Relative Text Direction) *X, Y*** DI and DR set the angle at which text is drawn. DR is relative to the current P1 and P2, while DI is independent of them. The angle is set to arctan(*Y*/*X*). Common values include 1,0 for horizontal, 0,1 for vertical heading up, –1,0 for upside down, and 0,–1 for vertical heading down.

✳ **DT (Define Terminator) C** The character immediately after the DT becomes the new label terminator. If the character is missing, the terminator is reset to ETX (03 H). This command always requires a semicolon.

✳ **ES (Extra Space) W,H** Leave extra space of W units horizontally and H units vertically between characters. W and H may be negative to get closer than usual spacing.

✳ **SA (Alternate Font)**

✳ **SS (Standard Font)** Switch between two internal plotter fonts.

✳ **SI (Absolute Character Size) *X, Y*** Set the size of characters drawn, in units of centimeters.

✳ **SR (Relative Character Size) *X, Y*** Set the size of characters drawn, in units of percent of the page. A size of 1,1 would make the height and width of each character 1% of the vertical and horizontal page size, respectively.

✻ **SL (Slant) Tan** Set the slant of characters drawn. Tan is the tangent of the slant angle. Common values include 0 for vertical, 1.0 for a 45-degree forward slant, and –1.0 for a 45-degree backward slant.

Interaction with PCL 5

PCL 5 printers, such as the HP LaserJet III, all implement HP-GL/2. Using PCL commands, it is possible to define a subrectangle on the page in which the HP-GL/2 picture is drawn, so that HP-GL/2 pictures can be embedded in PCL 5 documents. See the *HP PCL 5 Printer Language Technical Reference Manual* for details.

Examples

These examples are formatted to be readable by people; real HP-GL files usually squeeze out extra spaces and punctuation. Real HP-GL files are often structurally very simple. Many use only SC, SP, PU, PD, PA, and PR, drawing shapes and filling figures explicitly.

Table 20-2 shows the commands to draw Fig. 20-1. First it outlines and fills two squares using ER and RR. Then it outlines three wedges in a pie chart using EW, and fills the second and third ones with WG.

Table 20-2 **Commands for HP-GL example**

```
IN; SP1;
PA 1000,1000 FT3,100,45 ER 1000,1000 RR 1000,1000;
PA 2200,1000; FT 4,100,0; ER 1000,1000 RR 1000,1000;
PA 3000,3000 EW 500,0,120 EW 500,120,120 WG 500,120,120;
PR 100,-100 EW 500,0,-120 FT 3,45 WG 500,0,-120;
```

Table 20-3 shows the commands to draw Fig. 20-2, a more typical HP-GL file that uses only a few different commands. It draws a spiral as a long series of short line segments.

Figure 20-1

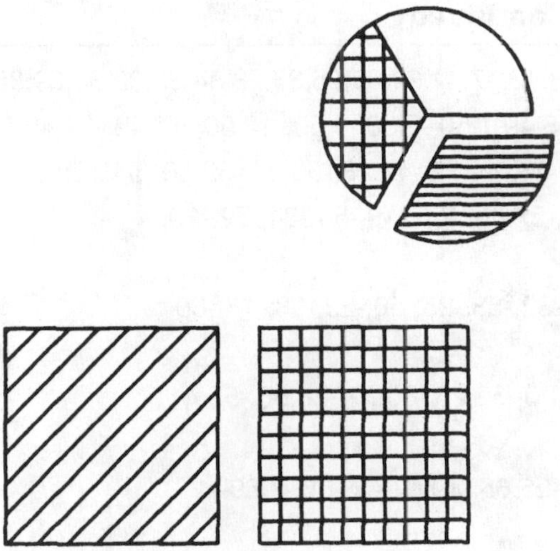

Sample HP-GL picture.

Table 20-3

Commands for HP-GL spiral figure

```
IN;SP1;PU;
PA4000,3000PRPD,0,0,3,0,3,1,3,1,3.2,3,2,2,3,2,4,1,4,0,4,0,5,-1,5,-2,5,-3,5;
PD-3,5,-4,5,-5,5,-6,4,-6,4,-7,3,-8,3,-8,2,-9,1,-9,0,-10,-1,-10,-2,
-10,-3;
PD-10,-4,-10,-5,-10,-6,-9,-7,-9,-8,-8,-9,-8,-10,-7,-11,-6,-12,
-5,-13,-4,-13;
PD-3,-14,-1,-14,0,-15,1,-15,3,-15,4,-15,6,-15,7,-15,9,-14,10,-14,11,
-13;
PD13,-12,14,-11,15,-10,16,-8,17,-7,18,-5,19,-4,19,-2,20,0,20,2,20,4,20,6;
PD19,7,19,9,18,11,17,13,16,15,15,17,14,18,12,20,10,21,9,22,7,23,5,24,2,25;
PD0,25,-2,26,-5,26,-7,26,-9,25,-12,25,-14,24,-17,23,-19,22,-21,20,-23,19;
PD-25,17,-27,15,-28,12,-29,10,-31,7,-32,5,-32,2,-33,-1,-33,-4,-33,-6,
-32,-9;
PD-32,-12,-31,-15,-30,-18,-29,-21,-27,-23,-25,-26,-23,-28,-21,-30,
-18,-32;
PD-15,-34,-12,-36,-9,-37,-6,-38,-3,-38,1,-39,4,-39,7,-39,11,-38,14,
-37,18,-36;
PD21,-35,24,-33,27,-31,30,-29,33,-26,35,-23,37,-20,39,-17,41,-14,42,
-10;
```

Table 20-3 **Continued**

```
PD43,-6,44,-3,44,1,44,5,44,9,43,13,42,17,41,21,39,25,37,28,34,32,32,35,29,38;
PD25,41,22,43,18,45,14,47,10,48,6,49,1,50,-3,50,-8,50,-12,50,-17,49,-21,48;
PD-25,46,-30,44,-34,41,-37,39,-41,35,-44,32,-47,28,-50,24,-52,20,-54,15;
PD-56,11,-57,6,-57,1,-58,-4,-57,-9,-57,-14,-56,-19,-54,-24,-52,-29,
-50,-33;
PD-47,-38,-44,-42,-40,-46,-36,-49,-32,-53,-28,-56,-23,-58,-18,-60,
-13,-62;
PD-7,-63,-2,-64,4,-64,9,-64,15,-63,20,-62,26,-60,31,-58,36,-55,41,
-52,46,-48;
PD50,-44,54,-40,57,-35,60,-30,63,-25,65,-19,67,-13,68,-7,69,-1;
PUPA4000,5000;CP-20,0;
PG;
```

Figure 20-2

Sample HP-GL spiral figure.

References

Hewlett-Packard. *The HP-GL/2 Reference Guide: A Handbook for Program Developers*. 1990. Reading, MA: Addison-Wesley.

Hewlett-Packard. *HP-GL vs. HP-GL/2 Language Comparison Guide, Rev 1.0*. 1991. San Diego: Hewlett-Packard.

Hewlett-Packard. *The HP-GL/2 Product Comparison Guide, Pub. No. 5959-9734*. 1990. San Diego: Hewlett-Packard.

Hewlett-Packard. *HP PCL 5 Printer Language Technical Reference Manual, Pub. No. 33459-90903*.1990. Boise, ID: Hewlett-Packard.

## CHAPTER 21

Lotus PIC

Name	Lotus PIC
Image type	Line drawing
Intended use	Intermediate file between Lotus 1-2-3 and graph printing programs
Owner	Lotus Development Corp., 55 Cambridge Parkway, Cambridge MA 02142
Last version/ revision/ release date	1986
Platforms	IBM PC, Sun Workstations
Supporting applications	Lotus 1-2-3 and Symphony, Javelin, MS Word, WordPerfect, many other word processors and graphics programs
Similarities	Unix Plot, HP GL
Overall assessment	An extremely simple but surprisingly ubiquitous format

Advantages

Easy to generate and read

Disadvantages

Very low level and inflexible

Variants

There are no variants.

Overview of file structure

Lotus 1-2-3 generates PIC files to be fed to the Lotus print graph auxiliary program. Because the format is so simple, many competing programs such as Javelin also generate PIC files, and word processors are able to read PIC files to embed graphs in documents. The PIC file has become a *lingua franca* for business charts, albeit a very simple and somewhat obsolescent one. Recent versions of 1-2-3 since version 3.0, by default, generate CGM files instead, although they can still also generate PIC.

Format details

A PIC file has a fixed 16-byte header followed by a series of drawing commands. PIC files have a fixed geometry. The lower left corner of the picture is (0,0) and the upper right is (3200,2311). The picture is scaled to fit in this area.

Header

The header consists of the following 17 hex bytes:

01 00 00 00 01 00 08 00 44 00 00 00 00 0C 7f 09 06

Commands

Each drawing command is a 1-byte opcode followed by arguments if necessary. *X* and *Y* coordinate values are all stored as 16-bit signed integers. Values are stored with the high byte first, the Motorola convention, even though nearly all programs that handle PIC run on

Intel machines. Some commands also take 1-byte values, and a few commands encode an argument into the opcode itself.

- **Color (Bx H)** The low byte of the opcode sets the color for subsequent drawing. On a monochrome device, different colors are simulated by different crosshatch patterns.

- **Move (A0 H)** *X*, *Y*. Make (*X*,*Y*) the current position.

- **Draw (A2 H)** *X*, *Y*. Draw a line to location (*X*, *Y*) and make that the current position.

- **Fill (30 H) and Fill outlined (D0 H) *N*, *X*0, *Y*0,** Draw a filled polygon. The opcode is followed by a 1-byte vertex count, which is stored as one less than the number of vertices (e.g., for a rectangle the count byte contains three). The count is followed by (*X*, *Y*) pairs for all the vertices for the polygon. Pie wedges are simulated with polygons containing several dozen vertices.

  Both opcodes draw the filled polygon and also draw the border of the polygon.

- **Size (AC H) *X*, *Y*** Set the size of subsequently drawn text. *X* and *Y* are the size of a character cell.

- **Font (A7 H) *N*** The opcode is followed by a single byte, *N*, that sets the font to use when drawing text. Only two fonts are used, numbered 0 and 1.

- **Text (A8 H) *N*, String** Draw some text at the current position. The opcode is followed by a single byte, *N*, which controls the direction and position of the text, followed by the text itself, terminated by a zero byte. The high four bits of *N* are drawing direction, with 00 H horizontal, 10 H vertical heading up, 20 H upside down, and 30 H vertical heading down. The low four bits of *N* control the alignment of the text string relative to the current point. The string is considered to be enclosed in a box, and some point on the box is aligned at the current point. Alignment values are 0 for the center of the box, 1 for left center, 2 for top center, 3 for right center, 4 for bottom center, 5 for top left, 6 for top right, 7 for bottom left, and 8 for bottom right.

* **End (6x H)** Any opcode in the range 60 to 6F marks the end of the picture.

Examples

Individual commands are encoded very simply; for example, a Move to location 1000,2000 or 3E8,7D0 H is encoded as:

A0 03 E8 07 D0

A filled triangle with vertices (100,100), (200,200), and (100,300) or (64,64) H, (C8,C8), and (12C,64) H is:

48 02 00 64 00 64 00 C8 00 C8 00 64 01 2C

Table 21-1 shows the PIC commands for the chart in Fig. 21-1 (page 290) which came from Lotus 1-2-3, Version 3.0. Rather than show literal PIC bytes, the PIC commands are decoded into a readable form. The chart boundaries and scale ticks are drawn with Move and Draw commands, using Text commands for the scale values. Then the bars are filled with Fill commands and outlined with Move and Draw. Finally PIC draws the caption.

Reference

Lotus File Formats for 1-2-3, Symphony, and Jazz. 1986. Reading, MA: Addison-Wesley.

Sample PIC commands

Table 21-1

```
Move(123,3)
Color(0)
Move(180,62)
Draw(180,2000)
Draw(3150,2000)
Move(3150,2000)
Draw(3150,62)
Draw(180,62)
Font(1)
Size(40,59)
Move(155,62)
Text(0,3,"0")
Move(155,385)
Text(0,3,"50")
Move(155,708)
Text(0,3,"100")
Move(155,1031)
Text(0,3,"150")
Move(155,1354)
Text(0,3,"200")
Move(155,1677)
Text(0,3,"250")
Move(155,2000)
Text(0,3,"300")
Move(180,62)
Draw(221,62)
Move(180,385)
Draw(221,385)
Move(180,708)
Draw(221,708)
Move(180,1031)
Draw(221,1031)
Move(180,1354)
Draw(221,1354)
Move(180,1677)
Draw(221,1677)
Color(1)
Move(-1,1)
Fill(4, 354,62, 878,62, 878,708, 354,708)
Move(-1,-1)
Color(0)
Move(354,62)
Draw(354,708)
Draw(878,708)
Move(878,708)
Draw(878,62)
Draw(354,62)
Move(-1,-1)
Color(1)
Move(-1,1)
Fill(4, 1053,62, 1577,62, 1577,1354, 1053,1354)
Move(-1,-1)
Color(0)
Move(1053,62)
Draw(1053,1354)
Draw(1577,1354)
Move(1577,1354)
Draw(1577,62)
Draw(1053,62)
Move(-1,-1)
Color(1)
Move(-1,1)
Fill(4, 1752,62, 2276,62, 2276,1677, 1752,1677)
Move(-1,-1)
Color(0)
Move(1752,62)
Draw(1752,1677)
Draw(2276,1677)
Move(2276,1677)
Draw(2276,62)
Draw(1752,62)
Move(-1,-1)
Color(1)
Move(-1,1)
Fill(4, 2451,62, 2975,62, 2975,1031, 2451,1031)
Move(-1,-1)
Color(0)
Move(2451,62)
Draw(2451,1031)
Draw(2975,1031)
Move(2975,1031)
Draw(2975,62)
Draw(2451,62)
Move(-1,-1)
Font(0)
Size(180,269)
Move(1665,2273)
Text(0,2,"Sample bar chart")
End(0)
```

Figure 21-1

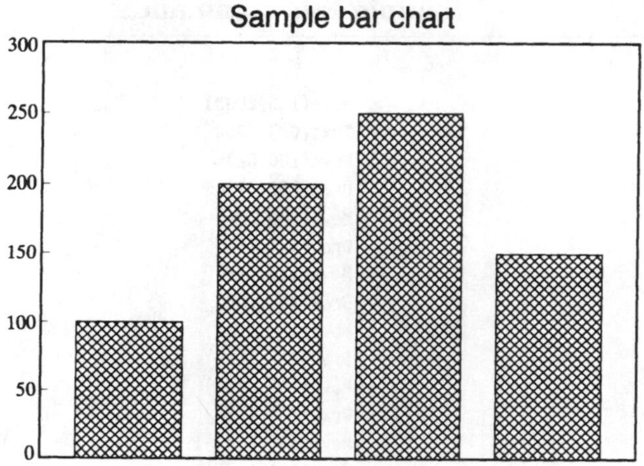

Sample bar chart.

## CHAPTER 22

UNIX plot format

Name	UNIX plot format
Image type	Line
Intended use	Common format for UNIX image drawing programs
Owner	UNIX System Labs, owners of UNIX
Last version/ revision/ release date	System V Release 4, 1989, although basic format is unchanged since the late 1970s
Platforms	Any Unix system
Supporting applications	UNIX graph, spline, sag, and tplot programs, and plot library. Output filters support DASI and Tektronix 4014 terminals (and the xterm terminal emulator under X windows, which emulates a 4014) and Versatec D1200A printer. Other vendors have written output filters for other devices.
Similarities	Unix Plot, HP GL
Overall assessment	A simple, fairly portable, low-level line-graphics language

Advantages

Simple to describe and use, universal low-level support on Unix systems

Disadvantages

Very low-level, limited application support; byte-order problems when moving among incompatible machines

Overview of file structure

The UNIX plot file is a simple format for describing line drawings. It is not particularly powerful, but it is very easy to generate and interpret. Because the format has been around for nearly 15 years, a lot of programs that support it are floating around in the UNIX community.

A plot file consists of a sequence of plotter instructions. Each instruction is a lowercase ASCII letter, usually followed by some parameters. A string parameter is ASCII text, terminated by a newline (0A H) byte. A numeric parameter is a two-byte signed integer, with the bytes in the local byte order.

Geometry

Coordinates are 16-bit integers. The origin and extent of the drawing area are set by the *Space* command, which should be the first one in the file. The origins are at the lower left corner, with *X* increasing to the right and *Y* increasing upward, which is the reverse of the *Y* conventions in many other formats.

Format details

The first command in a plot file should be a *Space*. After that, commands can be in any order with an *Erase* between images.

- **Space** The letter s followed by four numeric parameters. The first two parameters are the *X* and *Y* coordinates of the lower left corner of the drawing area. The next two parameters are the *X* and *Y* coordinates of the point just above and to the right of the drawing area. For example, if the four parameters were 0, 0, 1000, 1000, the *X* and *Y* dimensions each run from 0 to 999.

- **Erase** The letter e. Erase the screen, or start a new page on the printer.

- **Move** The letter m followed by two numeric parameters, *X* and *Y*. Make (*X* ,*Y*) the current point.

- **Line** The letter l followed by two numeric parameters, *X*0, *Y*0, *X*1, and *Y*1. Draw a line from (*X*0,*Y*0) to (*X*1,*Y*1) and make (*X*1,*Y*1) the current point.

- **Continue** The letter n followed by two numeric parameters, *X* and *Y*. Draw a line from the current point to (*X* ,*Y*) and make (*X* ,*Y*) the new current point.

- **Point** The letter p followed by two numeric parameters, *X* and *Y*. Draw a single point at (*X*,*Y*), and make (*X*,*Y*) the current point.

- **Circle** The letter c followed by three numeric parameters, *X*, *Y*, and *R*. Draw a circle of radius *R* with center at (*X*,*Y*).

- **Arc** The letter a followed by six numeric parameters, *X*, *Y*, *X*0, *Y*0, *X*1, and *Y*1. Draw an arc of the circle whose center is (*X*,*Y*) from point (*X*0,*Y*0) to (*X*1,*Y*1).

- **Label** The letter t followed by a string. Draw the string starting at the current point.

- **Line type** The letter f followed by a string. The string defines the way subsequent lines are drawn. It must be one of these literal strings: dotted, solid, long-dashed, short-dashed, or dot-dashed.

Conventions

Most programs that produce plot format output send their results to the standard output file. The standard output can be redirected into a file for later use, or piped directly into a plot output filter for immediate display.

Reference

AT&T. "Plot (4)," *Unix System V/386 Release 3.2 Programmer's Reference Manual*. 1988. Prentice-Hall.

## CHAPTER 23

PCL

Name	PCL (Hewlett-Packard Printer Control Language)
Image type	Printer data stream with embedded bit images
Intended use	Control of Hewlett-Packard Laserjet and Deskjet printers
Owner	Hewlett-Packard
Last version/ revision/ release date	PCL 5, 1990/
Platforms	Hewlett-Packard and many compatible laser printers, Table 23-1
Supporting applications	Many
Similarities	Encapsulated PostScript, slightly
Overall assessment	Excellent for sending images to laser printers

PCL compatible printers Table 23-1

Model	Level
PCL 3	Original LaserJet, LaserJet Plus, Laserjet 500
PCL 3	LaserJet II, LaserJet IID, Deskjet
PCL 4	LaserJet IIP, Deskjet Plus, Deskjet 500, most clones
PCL 5	Laserjet III, IIID, IIISi, and IIIP

Advantages

The most widely supported laser printer command language, and one of the most compact for bit images

Disadvantages

Monochrome only. Recovering an image can, in the worst case, require simulating the entire printer imaging model.

The most widely supported laser printer command language, and one of the most compact for bit images

Overview of file structure

PCL is the data stream used to control the Hewlett-Packard LaserJet and compatible printers. Because the LaserJet series has been so successful, many other printer vendors have made their printers accept PCL as well.

Variants

PCL has evolved over the years. Each new version is a superset of the previous ones. The current version is PCL 5, which includes all of PCL 1 through 4. The original LaserJet supported PCL 3. The LaserJet III supports PCL 5, and the other models such as the LaserJet IIP and DeskJets were PCL 4 or PCL 3 "plus extensions' such as Delta Row from PCL 5. For raster images, the most important difference is that PCL 4 and 5 allow compressed raster images. PCL 5 also permits embedded HP-GL, the command language for HP pen plotters. See chapter 20 for details on HP-GL.

The entire PCL language is very large and includes commands to format text on a page, switch fonts, download soft fonts, and perform many other printer operations. The discussion in this chapter concentrates on the parts of the language that concern raster graphics and line drawing.

In its simplest form, a PCL data stream is just a stream of ASCII characters that are sent to the printer. Embedded in the data stream can be escape sequences—sequences of characters, starting with the

ASCII *Escape* character (decimal 27 or 1B H), which specify various printer operations. Escape sequences are also sometimes referred to as printer commands. In the description that follows, the nonprinting Escape character is written ESC, and spaces are used in the examples to make them easier to read. The actual PCL uses the ASCII escape character and does not include the spaces.

To print raster graphics in PCL, a data stream must include:

- Initialization command to reset the printer (not required, but recommended)
- Print-positioning command to position the image on the page
- Raster commands to transfer the actual image.

Format details

PCL commands are of two consistent forms. The simplest commands are two characters, an ESC followed by a letter or digit. For instance, ESC E resets the printer.

More complicated commands are referred to as parametrized commands. Such a command includes an ESC, a punctuation character, and a lowercase letter that together identify the category of the command, a numeric parameter as an optionally signed decimal number, and an uppercase letter that identifies the particular command. For example, ESC & a 13 R sets the print position to row 13, and ESC & a 20 C sets the print position to column 20.

It is often necessary to send several commands in a row to the printer. If two or more consecutive commands are in the same category (that is, have the same two characters after the ESC), the commands can be combined. In the combined command, the ESC and two common characters are omitted from all but the first command, and the final command letter of all but the last command are in lowercase. The two commands in the previous example could be combined as ESC & a 13 r 20 C. There is no limit to the number of commands that can be combined, although in practice it is rare to have more than two or three.

Some commands, notably the ones for raster graphic images, are followed by binary image data. Because any bit pattern can occur in binary data, the number of bytes of binary data to read is set by the command that the data follow.

Paper geometry

HP printers use a straightforward geometry model with the origin at the upper left corner. There are three units in which print cursor positions can be specified: dots, decipoints, and rows or columns. A dot is 1⁄300 inch, the basic resolution of LaserJet printers. A decipoint is a tenth of a printer's point, or 1⁄720 inch. The width and height of a row or column depends on the horizontal and vertical spacing that has been set. By default, a column is 1⁄10 inch, corresponding to ten characters per inch, and a row is 1⁄6 inch, corresponding to six lines per inch.

LaserJets have a *logical page*, which is smaller than the physical paper in the printer. By default, it is the full height of the page and 1⁄4 inch narrower on each side than the physical paper. Within the logical page, there are also margins, which by default are 1⁄2 inch at the top and bottom of the page, so the printable area on an 8½ by 11-inch sheet is 8 by 10 inches. Laser printers cannot physically print all the way to the edge of the page, so it is generally advisable to limit your images to 8 by 10.

A LaserJet can either print with the narrow side of the paper at the top of the image (portrait) or with the wide side of the paper at the top (landscape). In PCL 3, all raster data are printed in portrait orientation, even if text is being printed in landscape orientation, so any raster image to be displayed in landscape orientation must be transposed before being sent. PCL 5 allows images to be printed in the prevailing orientation.

Raster resolution

Raster images can be displayed at 300, 150, 100, or 75 dots per inch (dpi). Because the physical resolution of the printer is 300 dpi, at lower resolutions the printer displays each pixel as a square two, three, or four dots on a side. The advantage of using lower resolutions is that the number of bits in the image is smaller so it takes less time to send to the printer. A full-page 300-dpi image is 7.2 million bits, or 900K bytes, so even with a fast parallel interface it can take several minutes to send an image to the printer. A 75-dpi image is 1⁄16 the number of bits as a 300-dpi image of the same size, so it takes about 1⁄16 the time to send.

Some LaserJet printers do not have enough internal memory to buffer a full page 300-dpi image, so for maximum portability you should restrict 300-dpi images to about half a page.

Image-compression techniques

Because bit images can be large, PCL provides a variety of image-compression techniques. PCL 3 provided no compression per se, although because each row of an image is sent separately, some compression was possible by not sending trailing zero bytes in each row. PCL 4 provided two new compression schemes, and PCL 5 provides two more:

- Uncompressed data, raster image sent as is (PCL 3).
- Run-length encoded, image sent as pairs of count and data (PCL 4).
- PackBits encoding (referred to as *TIFF encoding* by HP) with strings of literal or repeated bytes (PCL 4).
- Delta row compression, which sends only the changes from one row to the next (PCL 5).
- Adaptive compression, which combines the other four modes, row skipping, and row duplication (LaserJet IIIP only).

Different compression methods can be specified for different rows in the same raster image. The most efficient compression is generally PackBits, unless adjacent rows are very similar, in which case Delta row compression is better.

PCL 5 also introduces the concepts of transparency and a *raster area*. Normally, white pixels are really transparent; that is, any previous image in the same place shows through white pixels. On a PCL 5 printer, you can set white pixels so they are opaque and they "white out" anything underneath them. To turn transparency on or off:

```
ESC * v N O
```

An *N* of zero makes white pixels transparent; one makes them opaque.

The raster area for an image can be set before sending a raster image. The image is clipped to the raster area, and parts of the area not otherwise specified by raster data will be whited out if in opaque mode. Raster areas are not very useful for pure raster images, because the default background is white anyway, but they can be useful when mixing raster images with other kinds of data on the page. Raster areas are important for print files that use opaque mode because, in the absence of an explicit raster area, each image is considered to be the full width of the page and might inadvertently erase any material to the right of a bit image.

Image formats

The full set of commands to draw an image is *printer reset*, *set page orientation and position*, *set presentation*, *set resolution*, *set raster area*, *start raster graphics*, the image data row by row, and *end raster graphics*. Only the last three of these are required.

A LaserJet raster image can be printed directly (a stand-alone image), or it can be embedded in a larger page image created by a word processor or other program. In the first case, it is generally a good idea to position the image on the page and set the resolution, because the default, *print at the upper left corner at 75-dpi*, is rarely the best choice. In the second case, the program creating the larger image generally sets the position and resolution, so the image file should not contain positioning or resolution commands.

✳ **Printer reset** The command to reset the printer to a standard default state with default margins, portrait orientation, position (0,0) at the upper left corner is:

```
ESC E
```

Stand-alone images should always start with this command.

✳ **Set orientation** The default page orientation is portrait. The command

```
ESC & l 1 O
```

sets the orientation to landscape. Raster images usually print in portrait orientation even when the overall image is landscape.

The command (PCL 5 only)

```
ESC & r 0 F
```

sets the raster orientation to match the overall orientation. For maximum portability to PCL 4 printers, images should be printed in the default portrait orientation. Changing the page orientation starts a new page, so embedded images should never use these commands.

✳ **Position** The cursor position can be set in terms of dots, decipoints, or character rows and columns. To set the horizontal position:

```
ESC & a N C
ESC & a N H
ESC * p N X
```

These set the cursor in terms of columns, decipoints, and dots, respectively. If the number *N* is signed, the new position is set relative to the current position. If unsigned, it is relative to the left margin.

To set the vertical position:

ESC & a N R
ESC & a N V
ESC * p N Y

These set the cursor in terms of rows, decipoints, and dots, respectively. If the number *N* is signed, the new position is set relative to the current position. If unsigned, it is relative to the top margin.

These two commands are usually combined. For example, to set the cursor position to the center of the page, with the position given in dots, the command is:

ESC * p 1200x1500 Y

The logical page is 8 by 10 inches, so the center is four inches or (1200 dots) from the left, and 5 inches (or 1500 dots) from the top.

When positioning by rows and columns, keep in mind that, in an embedded image, the enclosing document might have changed the row or column spacing from the default ⅙ and ⅒ inch. Positioning by dots or decipoints is more reliable. Embedded images can use relative positioning if an image is sent as multiple raster areas, but should let the enclosing document set the absolute position.

Resolution The command to set raster image resolution is:

ESC * t N R

The value *N* can be 75, 100, 150, or 300. Stand-alone images should set the resolution. Embedded images might or might not, depending on the expectations of the enclosing document.

Raster area These commands set the height and width of the raster area (PCL 5 only):

ESC * r H T
ESC * r W S

The height and width are specified in dots. These commands are invariably combined, so to set an area 100 dots high and 200 dots wide the command would be:

```
ESC * r 100 t 200 S
```

If the subsequent raster data is wider or longer than the raster area, the image is clipped to the raster area. If the raster image is overlaid on some other material, normally any black parts of the other material show through the white parts of the raster. If an enclosing document has set the *source transparency mode* to opaque, white parts of the raster area appear white regardless of what might have been there before.

PCL 4 has no concept of a raster area, so for maximal portability, do not set a raster area.

✳ **Image data** The image consists of a *start graphics* command, an *image data* command for each row in the image (optionally with *set compression mode* commands intermixed), and an *end graphics* command. The *start graphics* command is:

```
ESC * r 1 A
```

If the command contains a zero instead of a one, the graphics start at the left margin rather than at the current position.

The command to transfer a row of data is:

```
ESC * b N W image data
```

where *N* is the count of bytes of image data that follow. Even though each row is logically the same length, the number of image bytes sent per row can vary, because compressed rows will come out in different lengths. Even in uncompressed data there is no need to send bytes for trailing white space at the end of a row. Image data is an exception to the rule that all commands with common prefixes can be combined. It is safe to combine an image data command with a preceding command, but not to combine one with a following command.

If there are several consecutive blank rows, they can be skipped with a *Raster Y Offset* command (PCL 5 only):

```
ESC * b N Y
```

This is equivalent to sending *N* rows of all-zero raster data. The value *N* must be an unsigned integer.

If the image is compressed (PCL 5 only), the compression mode can be changed before each row:

```
ESC * b N M
```

where *N* is 0 for unencoded data, 1 for run-length encoded, 2 for PackBits, and 3 for delta-row compression. This command is generally combined with the following row of data. To set the mode to unencoded and then send a 5-byte row:

```
ESC * b 0 m 5 W x x x x x
```

At the end of the image, the *end graphics* command is:

```
ESC * r B
```

If a raster area was specified, this sets the cursor to the lower left corner of the area.

Image data encoding

PCL 3 images are all sent unencoded. PCL 4 and 5 add four compression modes that can greatly decrease the number of bytes that have to be sent to the printer, at the cost of extra programming when the image is created.

✳ **Unencoded: (Mode 0)** Unencoded images are sent as a set of binary bytes. The high bit in the first byte corresponds to the leftmost pixel in the row. Trailing zero bytes need not be sent.

⁂ **Run-length encoded: (Mode 1)** Image data are sent as byte pairs. The first byte in each pair is the repeat count, and the second byte is the data byte to repeat. The number of repetitions is one more than the repeat count, so a count of zero means to use the data byte once, and a count of 255 means to use the data byte 256 times. For example, a row with 80 black bits, 40 alternating black and white bits, and 64 more black bits would be sent as:

```
ESC * b 1 m 6 W 09 FF 04 AA 07 FF
```

The compression mode is switched to mode 1 (not necessary if the previous row was in mode 1). The first count is 09, meaning 10 bytes (80 bits) with the value FF, all black bits. The second count is 04, meaning five bytes with alternating ones and zeros, hex AA. The third pair is eight more bytes (64 bits) of FF.

This scheme is primarily useful for very stylized images where a single byte is repeated across a large part of the image. If a byte value occurs only once, it must still be sent as a byte pair, so this scheme can easily end up making the compressed image larger than the original. For most images, PackBits will compress the image better.

⁂ **PackBits: (Mode 2)** Image data are sent as a series of *subrecords*, each consisting of a control byte followed by one or more data bytes. If the control byte *C* has the value 0 through 127 (0 through 7F H), the following *C* +1 bytes are taken as literal data. For example, the control byte 04 means to take the next 5 bytes as literal data. A control byte of 128 (80 H) is a no-op, and the next byte in the data stream is the next control byte. If the control byte *C* has the value 129 to 255 (81 H to FF H), the following data byte is repeated 257-*C* times. For example, the subrecord F8 99 would mean 9 occurrences of a 99 byte, because F8 is decimal 248 and 257–248 is 9.

To send a row consisting of 80 black bits, then the 64 bits AABBCCDDEEFF, then 64 more black bits:

```
ESC * b 2 m 11 W F7 FF 05 AA BB CC DD EE FF FB FF
```

The first control byte, F7 or decimal 247, means 257–247 or 10 bytes of FF. The next control byte, 05, means 6 literal bytes. The last control byte, FB or 251, means 257–251 or 6 bytes of FF.

For most images PackBits provides good compression and is not too hard to implement.

- **Delta row compression: (Mode 3)** Many images have only small changes from one row to the next. Delta-row compression sends only the changes for each row. It offers the possibility of dramatic compression at the cost of a much more complicated encoding than any of the previous modes.

For each row, the *seed row* is the previous row in the image, to which updates are made to produce the new row. At the beginning of the image and after a *Raster Y Offset* command, the seed row is zero. After the image data for a row, whether the row is encoded with delta-row compression or any other mode, that row is the seed for the next row.

The data for each row consists of subrecords, each of which includes one or more control bytes that specify the position and length of the bytes in the seed row to be updated, and one to eight data bytes of update information. The control byte is divided up into two fields, bitwise:

```
LLLPPPPP
```

The 3-bit LLL field is the length of the update, with 000 meaning one byte and 111 meaning eight bytes. An update more than eight bytes long must be sent as multiple subrecords. The PPPPP is the distance from the end of the previous update, or for the first subrecord, from the beginning of the row. A PPPPP of 00000 means that the update starts immediately after the previous one (or at the beginning of the row if it's the first subrecord), and a PPPPP of 11110 means the update starts 30 bytes after the previous one.

A PPPPP of all ones is an escape sequence for distances of 31 bytes or greater, in which case the value of the following byte is added to 31 to get the distance (e.g., a PPPPP of all ones followed by a byte of decimal 100 means a distance of 131 bytes). If the following byte has the value 255, then the byte after that is added to 31 + 255. There can be any number of 255 bytes to get arbitrarily large distances.

Following the control byte(s) are the *update data* bytes, which replace the corresponding bytes in the seed row to get the updated row. For example, assume that two rows in an image are, in hex:

```
11 22 33 44 55 66 77 88 99 11 22 33 44 55
11 22 AA BB 55 66 77 88 99 CC DD EE 44 55
```

The second row in delta-row compressed form (for ease of reading, the control bytes are displayed in binary, while the data bytes are in hex) is:

```
ESC * b 7 W 0010010 AA BB 01000101 CC DD EE
```

The first control byte has an LLL of 001, meaning a 2byte update, and a PPPPP of 00010 for a position of two bytes from the beginning of the row, followed by two bytes of update data. The second control byte has an LLL of 010, meaning a 3-byte update, and a PPPPP of 00101 for a position of five bytes beyond the previous update, followed by the three data bytes.

An image row that is identical to the previous row is sent as:

```
ESC * 0 W
```

because no updates are necessary.

- **Adaptive compression: (Mode 5)** The LaserJet IIIP adds yet another compression mode. Unlike all the other modes, a single block of data can contain more than one image row. A data block consists of a series of groups, with each group containing a command byte, a 2-byte binary length, and perhaps some data. The command byte specifies the type of coding for the row, and the length bytes (high order byte first) contain either the length of the following data or else the number of affected rows. A command byte of 0, 1, 2, or 3 means that there is following data that is a row of bits compressed using mode 0,1,2, or 3 respectively. A command byte of 4 means empty (white or transparent) rows, with the length bytes being the number of blank rows. A command byte of 5 means to duplicate the previous row, with the length bytes being the number of times to duplicate the bit.

A single data block is limited to 32,767 bytes, so an adaptively compressed image longer than that must be sent as more than one data block.

The adaptive compression scheme can be quite compact, but because it is specific to only one model of printer, it is not at all portable or general.

A sample image

Here is an annotated complete sample PCL data stream for a raster image that is 24 by 24 bits, consisting of alternating black and white pixels:

```
ESC E
ESC * p 1200x1500 Y
ESC * t 100 R
```

Reset the printer, position the cursor to the center of the page, and set the resolution to 100 DPI. (These commands would be omitted for an embedded image.)

```
ESC * r 1 A
```

Start the image.

```
ESC * b 3 W AA AA AA
ESC * b 3 W 55 55 55
```

Repeat previous two commands 11 more times each. Image data, three bytes or 24 bits per row, totals 12 rows. Because no compression mode has been set, the default PCL 3-compatible, uncompressed-image mode is used.

ESC * r B

End graphics image.

Image hints & conventions

The most portable PCL images are encoded using the convention above, using only the simplest PCL 3 commands as in the example. For images to be printed on a PCL 5 printer, setting the raster area in an embedded image is a good idea for two reasons. First, it makes the image somewhat more robust so that an error in transmission of the image data won't draw garbage all over the page. Second, a program reading the image file can scan for the commands that set the raster area to determine the image size. Otherwise, it would have to interpret all the raster data commands, potentially a very complex task if complex image-compression modes are used.

It is usually possible for a program to extract the raster image from a PCL raster file without having to understand the full set of PCL commands. Because the syntax of all PCL commands is consistent, the program can skip over unknown printer commands without having to interpret them. The program need interpret only the *start image*, *end image*, and *raster data* commands to extract the image.

Box & line drawing

PCL levels 4 and 5 provide the ability to draw shaded or patterned boxes. A long thin black box looks like a line, so this feature can also be used for line drawing. To draw a box, one moves to the upper left corner of the box, specifies the height and width of the box in dots or decipoints, sets the shading darkness for shaded boxes or the pattern to use for patterned boxes, and then specifies the box type, which actually draws the box.

To set the box height:

ESC * c N V
ESC * c N B

These set the height in terms of decipoints and dots, respectively.

To set the box width:

```
ESC * c N H
ESC * c N A
```

These set the width in terms of decipoints and dots, respectively.

To set the shading darkness or pattern:

```
ESC c N G
```

For shaded boxes, *N* is taken as a darkness percentage with 0 being completely white and 100 being completely black. Printers typically can generate only six or eight different shades, so the value specified is rounded to an available shade.

For patterned boxes, *N* is the pattern number. Pattern 1 is horizontal lines, 2 is vertical lines, 3 is diagonal lines rising to the right, 4 is diagonal lines rising to the left, 5 is horizontal and vertical crosshatch, and 6 is diagonal crosshatch.

To draw the box:

```
ESC * c N P
```

The value of *N* determines the type of box. Type 0 is all black (suitable for line drawing), 1 is white (PCL 5 only), 2 is shaded, 3 is patterned, and 5 is *current pattern fill* (PCL 5 only). PCL 5 printers can have a current pattern used for several boxes set by ESC * v N T, with *N* taking the values from 0 to 3, meaning the same as the box types above. Both black and white boxes disregard the shading darkness or pattern type.

Box & line examples

To draw a 3 × 4 inch box shaded 30 percent at the position two inches from the top and one inch from the left:

```
ESC * p 600 y 300 X
```

(set position in dots)

```
ESC * c 900 a 1200 B
```

(set size in dots)

```
ESC * c 30 g 2 P
```

(set 30 percent shading and draw a shaded box). The last two pairs of commands could also have been combined to make the sequence three bytes shorter.

References

Hewlett-Packard. *PCL 5 Printer Language Technical Reference Manual*, Part No 33459-90903. 1990.

Hewlett-Packard. *PCL 5 Developer's Guide, Third Edition*, Part No 5002-1847. 1991.

Hewlett-Packard. *PCL 5 Comparison Guide, Third Edition*, Part No 33481-90968. 1991.

Hewlett-Packard. *LaserJet Series II Printer Technical Reference Manual*, Part No 33440-90905, 1987.

Hewlett-Packard. *LaserJet IIP Printer Technical Reference Manual*, Part No 33471-90905. 1989.

Hewlett-Packard. *LaserJet IID Printer Technical Reference Manual*, Part No 33447-90905. 1988.

## CHAPTER 24

Basic PostScript graphics

Name	PostScript
Image type	Vector and bitmap; page-description language
Intended use	Originally for printers and other output devices; now also used for image storage and exchange, especially in encapsulated PostScript (EPS) form
Owner	Adobe Systems, Inc.
Last version/ revision/ release date	Level 2
Platforms	Primarily Macintosh & Mac peripherals; now also PCs and UNIX
Supporting applications	Nearly all Macintosh applications; many PC word-processing and desktop-publishing programs; some high-end PC graphics and CAD applications; UNIX applications translated via Adobe TranScript and others
Similarities	FORTH programming language
Overall assessment	Excellent for ensuring consistency across various platforms and media, for color or monochrome images; usually not efficient for bitmaps. PostScript readers are complex; writers are less so.

Advantages

Postscript is the de facto standard for desktop publishing, and incorporates many advanced graphics features such as 36-bit RGB, monochrome and color standardization and correction, vector and bitmap images, vector fonts, and linear transformations of images.

Disadvantages

Because images can be expressed in many different ways, implementation of a general-purpose PostScript reader (translator) is a large job. (The full definition of PostScript is given in Adobe's *PostScript Language Reference Manual, Second Edition*, a tome of over 700 pages.) Also, PostScript is generally recorded in ASCII (although Display and Level 2 PostScript also support binary and compressed data), which makes bitmap files large and/or slow to display.

Variants

PostScript has four variants: *Level 1*, *Level 2*, *Encapsulated*, and *Display PostScript*. Level 1 is the original language set, predominantly used for monochrome graphics and images up to eight bits deep, but capable of delivering RGB or CMYK color.

Level 2 includes Level 1, but adds a number of improvements, including optional use of binary code instead of ASCII, various filters for compression, use of colorimetry and various color spaces, and color bitmap image depth of up to 32 bits.

Encapsulated PostScript (EPS) files are PostScript descriptions of a single page, designed to be incorporated into a larger PostScript document without modification. They are distinguished from regular PostScript files by the inclusion of certain *comment* fields, the exclusion of certain *operators*, and the avoidance of certain actions that would affect the larger document. EPS is the variant of PostScript designed to support graphics exchange.

Display PostScript interpreters act as real-time device-independent interfaces for computer monitors. These interpreters support multitask execution of PostScript programs, binary encoding of names, use of windowing systems, and the use of bitmap fonts. The Display PostScript language employs certain extensions appropriate to these tasks.

Overview of file structure

PostScript is a programming language and, as such, it demands no particular structure beyond observing proper syntax and semantics. A certain logical sequence is, however, inherent in communicating information efficiently and in a page-independent, device-independent manner, as PostScript intends to do. Adobe has formalized such a sequence by specifying certain conventions called the *Document Structuring Conventions* (DSC) (Version 3.0). Files that conform to these conventions begin with a prolog section, followed by a script section.

The structuring imposed by DSC helps ensure that PostScript files are properly handled by print spoolers, post-processors, and other resources, called *document managers*. To further control such resources, Adobe has also created a sort of second language, as part of the DSC, called *DSC comments*. Terms of this language appear within the PostScript-language program. They appear to the PostScript interpreter as comments, so they are ignored by that processor but are read by the document manager. As part of their job of controlling document managers, they serve to delimit structures within the file, such as prologs and pages.

PostScript files do not have to conform to DSC guidelines of structure or contain DSC comments to be executed properly by the PostScript interpreter. If they don't conform, however, they might not be properly handled by document managers. EPS files and other PostScript variants require certain DSC comments.

The general structure of a PostScript file under Version 3.0 of the DSC is as follows:

Prolog
  Header
  Defaults (optional)
  Procedures
Script
  Document setup
  Page(s) of PostScript code

•
•
•
Document trailer

This structure is implemented by using DSC comments, which generally begin with a double percent sign (%%), contain no more than 255 characters, and terminate at the first CR (carriage return) or CR/LF (linefeed) pair. DSC comments generally contain a keyword and various arguments. The entire line is case-sensitive. Many terms include a terminating colon, which should not be overlooked. Arguments are delimited by white space.

A subset of DSC comments, called *body comments*, delimit the beginning and end of each section listed above. For example, the DSC comments %%BeginSetup and %%EndSetup delimit the document setup section.

Only the DSC comments that are most useful to the purpose of this chapter (i.e., using simple graphics on a single page, with no text) are discussed. The resulting simplified structure is:

Prolog
  Header
  Procedures
Script
  PostScript code
  Document trailer

Prolog

The prolog is the first part of a conforming file. It contains a header, an optional defaults section, and a procedures section, also called the *prolog proper*. The defaults section will not be covered.

Prolog header section The header section contains no PostScript code, just comments. In some instances, header information, such as *bounding box* can be deferred to the trailer; this is indicated by the use of the keyword (*atend*) as an argument. The critical header comments for the purposes of this chapter are as follows. Arguments are shown in italics.

%!PS-Adobe-3.0: *keyword*

This is the PostScript file identifier which must begin the file. It is the only comment to begin with the %! symbol. The keyword designates variations; the only keyword of interest here is EPSF-3.0, used for encapsulated PostScript. The "3.0" in both terms reflects the current version number; earlier versions have lower numbers. All DSC features listed were also present in version 2.0 unless otherwise specified.

%%BoundingBox: *Xlowleft Ylowleft Xupright Yupright* The bounding box defines a rectangular region in user space (defined later) where the ensuing PostScript code will make its marks. This region must allow for line widths if vector-type graphics are used. The four arguments define the lower-left and upper-right coordinates at opposite corners of this rectangle.

%%LanguageLevel: *level* This line is necessary only if PostScript Level 2 operators are used, for which case level is the unsigned integer two.

%%Extensions: *CMYK* This line is needed if Level 1 PostScript is being used with the CMYK color space extension.

%%DocumentData: *Binary* This line is necessary only if eight-bit data are used. The data referred to can be delimited by %%BeginData and %%EndData comment lines in the script section.

%%EndComments Terminates the header portion of the prolog; optional.

- **Prolog procedure section** This section contains user-defined procedures. These procedures are defined in the fashion described later in this chapter. The section is bracketed by the following DSC comments:

%%BeginProlog

begins the *prolog proper* or procedures-definition section; optional.

%%EndProlog

terminates the procedures definition section and the entire prolog. The main body of the PostScript program begins after this comment.

PostScript code

This is the main body of code as described in the following section, PostScript details. This code might also contain certain DSC comments.

Trailer

This section, if included, contains a mix of DSC comments and PostScript code intended to perform various cleanup operations. It might also contain important DSC header information that has been deferred to the trailer by the comment keyword atend. The start of the trailer is indicated by the DSC comment %%Trailer.

Encapsulated PostScript (EPS)

Encapsulated PostScript, or EPS, is the principal form of PostScript used for graphics exchange. It can contain no more than a single page of information, and its header must include two of the DSC comments previously described:

%!PS-Adobe-3.0 *EPSF-3.0*

and

%%BoundingBox: *Xlowleft Ylowleft Xupright Yupright*

If features beyond basic Level 1 PostScript are required, the header comments %%LanguageLevel: or %%Extensions: might be required as well.

EPS files in general must avoid actions that would affect an entire document, such as clearing the stacks or resetting the transformation matrix (CTM). The existing graphics state should be saved at the start of an EPS file and restored at the end. Operators related to these actions are discussed in the following section.

PostScript details

Fully detailing the PostScript language requires far more space than is available here. You should refer to the *PostScript Language Reference Manual* to implement a full PostScript writer or reader. It is our intention here to provide only the information you would generally need to create and read a simple, one-page PostScript or Encapsulated PostScript graphics file, especially one that contains bitmap data.

PostScript execution

It is essential that we begin by explaining the unique way the PostScript language executes. This is because, even though PostScript generally comprises ASCII words and numbers, its manner of execution does not become apparent simply by examination (as is often the case with other languages).

- **Objects** As a file is scanned by the PostScript interpreter, the ASCII code is first parsed into *objects*. Objects can be executable or nonexecutable. Executable objects are the commands of PostScript; nonexecutable objects (called *literals*) are the data. Executable objects might be terms built into PostScript, called *operators*, or names of procedures created by users. The basic nonexecutable objects include numbers (signed integer or real), strings, and booleans. Comments are denoted by a preceding % character.

- **Stack-based execution** PostScript executes by using stacks. Depending on their natures, objects are either pushed onto a stack or immediately executed as commands. There are four stacks: the *operand*, *dictionary*, *execution*, and *graphics state* stacks.

  When a nonexecutable (data) object is encountered, such as a number, string, or data array (indicated by brackets, [ ]), the object is pushed onto the operand stack.

When an operator or other executable object is encountered, it is executed, and it begins by popping input data (if any) off the operand stack. Because of this, the data for an executable object appear before the executable itself. Similarly, an executable object generally pushes its result onto a stack. In this way, executables can appear in sequence, passing data from one to the next by means of the stack instead of by using named variables, as is often done in other languages.

For example, a PostScript operator to fill a rectangle, whose lower left-hand corner is at *x,y* and whose dimensions are *height* and *width*, would appear as:

x y width height rectfill.

The operands *x*, *y*, *width*, and *height* would be pushed onto the operand stack. The command rectfill would then be executed, which would pop the operands off the stack.

The stacks are sometimes manipulated directly, especially the operand stack. Often, objects are popped off and discarded using the pop operator; or, the top element might be duplicated (once) using the dup operator. The entire operand stack can be cleared with the *clear operator* (never used in EPS).

✳ **Names** When the interpreter encounters a series of regular symbols, such as letters and numbers (delimited by white space characters or punctuation), and that series cannot be interpreted as a number, it is considered a name object. Names are unique identifiers used for operators, strings, variables, procedures, and the like.

If the name represents an operator or user-defined procedure known to PostScript, the operator is executed as soon as it has been parsed. If the name represents data, the data is pushed onto the operand stack. If, however, the name is prefixed by the / (slash) character, the name is treated as data (a literal) and the name is pushed on the operand stack. The / prefix is used for passing names as arguments to operators and procedures, for example.

User-named objects are created by the operator *def*, which has the following form:

key value def

where *key* is a slash-prefixed name and *value* is a number, string, procedure, or other object.

✻ **Executable objects (operators)** The commands of PostScript are either built-in operators, like rectfill, or user-defined procedures, like *subroutines*. Operators are English-like terms in ASCII, which PostScript "knows" because their names are entered in the system dictionary portion of the dictionary stack. Similarly, the names of user-defined procedures are placed into the user portion of the dictionary stack.

User-defined procedures can be created by enclosing the desired operators and their data in braces, { }, preceding them with */name*, where name is your name for the procedure, and ending with the operator def. The braces define an "executable array" whose execution is to be deferred.

It is important to understand what occurs when such a line is executed. The interpreter initially treats the operators as data, in a process called deferred execution. The / symbol indicates that a literal object (data) follows, so the name is pushed on the operand stack. The enclosure of operators in braces, { }, likewise causes them to be treated like an array of data when they are first read; that is, they are pushed onto the operand stack. The def operator then pops all these objects off the operand stack and creates an entry in the user dictionary.

For example, the following line:

```
/square {50 50 rectfill} def
```

creates a procedure in the dictionary stack called *square* that generates a 50 x 50 filled rectangle. If the PostScript interpreter encounters the term square, an *x* and *y* location will be popped off the operand stack and a filled square will be created at those coordinates.

✻ **Types of data** Integers and real numbers take conventional signed form. Real numbers can have any number of decimal points (e.g., 2.0 or 1.599) or use signed exponential notation (e.g., 235.667^{10} or 1.56^{-15}).

Literal strings are recorded primarily as text enclosed in parentheses ( ). They can alternatively be found in hex form enclosed in ~, or in ASCII base-85 in ~.) Nonprinting characters, such as line-feeds and carriage returns, can be included either in ASCII or, more commonly, in a specially encoded form. The latter form uses the \ (backslash) symbol as a prefix followed by the following characters: b = backspace; f = formfeed; n = newline (LF); r = carriage return (CR); t = tab; nnn = octal character code. Embedded parentheses and backslashes use the same scheme: \(, \), and \\. Strings can alternatively contain the actual ASCII characters represented by this set, including parentheses if used in balanced pairs. A line break (CR or CR/LF) in a string is ignored if immediately preceded by a backslash; this feature allows long strings to be conveniently broken up in program listings.

Strings can also be used as buffers in the operand stack. They can be allocated by the using the operator string, which takes the following form:

stringsize string

where stringsize is an integer. This operator pushes stringsize bytes, filled with zero, onto the top of the operand stack.

Multiple numbers and strings can be made part of a single composite object, called an array, by enclosing them in brackets, [ ]. Any executable objects in such an array will be executed as they are parsed, unless they are prefixed by a / to make them literal, as previously noted.

Graphics state

When a PostScript interpreter executes a graphic, it relies on certain system parameters, such as the *current color* or other "current" settings. Collectively, these comprise the current graphic state. A few of the most essential parameters for our purposes here are listed in Table 24-1. There are nearly two dozen such parameters; some of them, not shown in Table 24-1, are device-specific and therefore generally set up during system configuration, rather than in the image or graphic data file.

Table 24-1 **Basic, device-independent graphics-state parameters**

Parameter	**Principally controlled by**	**Specifies**
CTM	setmatrix, translate,	Coordinate transformation matrix
	rotate, scale	
path	path construction op.s	Where lines, arcs, etc. are drawn
line width	setlinewidth	Width of drawn lines
color*	setcolor	Painting color
color space*	setcolorspace	Interpretation of painting color

*These two parameters can be set with a single operator in Level 2 PostScript. See *Color*, following. Path-construction operators are discussed in the following section, Vector-type graphics.

A variety of graphic states can be stored on the graphics-state stack and restored to currency as needed, using the gsave and grestore operators. Often, especially in EPS, a PostScript program will gsave the current state, alter some parameters to create a new current state, display an image, and then grestore the original state. In Level 2 PostScript, such states can also be stored as named objects.

Of those parameters listed in Table 24-1, only the CTM and color space pertain to bitmap images. The rest influence vector-type images.

✳ **Coordinate systems** The metaphor for PostScript graphics is the placement of opaque "ink" on a virtual white page called the *current page*. The PostScript coordinate system, called *user space*, applies to this page. A second coordinate system, called *device space*, is mapped to user space by means of a coordinate transformation matrix (CTM).

Through the CTM, the actual output can be moved, rotated, scaled, sheared, or otherwise linearly transformed. The default CTM uses conventionally oriented, orthogonal *X* and *Y* axes, scaled to 1 unit = 1/72 inch (1 point), and placed so that the user-space origin aligns with the device space origin. The CTM can be set directly, using matrix algebra and the setmatrix or concat operator, but is more often modified through the operators translate, rotate, or scale. Matrix algebra operations on the CTM are too complex to discuss here. The other principal CTM operators are as follows:

- *xdistance ydistance* translate, where *xdistance* and *ydistance* are the desired motion along the axes of the user space (and in user space units), moves the user space with respect to its former position.
- *Angle* rotate, where *angle* is expressed in degrees, rotates the current user coordinate system counterclockwise about its origin.
- *xscale yscale* scale specifies the scaling of the user coordinate system relative to its former size.

All three of these operators have an alternative form in which they accept matrices as input and output.

✳ **Color** PostScript supports both grayscale and color images. Color is generally specified using RGB, CMYK, or CIE color space as described in chapter 1. CMYK color is not supported in all Level 1 implementations, however. PostScript also supports HSI (called HSB by Adobe, for *Hue*, *Saturation*, *Brightness*) as an alternate coordinate system in RGB space. Adobe refers to the RGB/HSB and CMYK color spaces as *device space*.

Color space can be set independently of other parameters by the following operator:

operand setcolorspace, where *operand* is either an array or a single literal name, /DeviceGray, /DeviceRGB, or /DeviceCMYK.

There are also *Pattern*, *Indexed* (palette), and *Separation* color spaces, too complex for discussion here. The initial color space is /DeviceGray, or grayscale. The initial state is /DeviceGray.

Besides color space, another important parameter is *CurrentColor*, used for vector-type graphics, but not bitmaps. The current color is used for drawing lines of all types and for filling (painting) areas. The principal operator for setting this color is the following:

operand(s) setcolor, where the operands are the three values, red, green, and blue for RGB space, four values for CMYK, or one value for grayscale. The range is 0 (black) to 1 (white), inclusive, initially set to 0.

Both current color and color space can be set concurrently by the following operators:

operand(s) setgray setrgbcolor sethsbcolor, or setcmykcolor. These operators set both the color space and current color in one operation. The *operand(s)* specify the current color, as in setcolor.

Vector-type graphics

The following is a simple example of vector-type graphics code in PostScript:

```
  0 3.5 moveto
  4.0 3.5 lineto
  4.0 4.5 lineto
  3.0 4.5 lineto
stroke
```

This code would define a square box with its lower left-hand corner at user coordinates (3.0, 3.5).

PostScript creates such graphics in a two-step process. First, a *current path* is created using coordinates in user space and operators like lineto; then *painting* operators (such as stroke) act upon the current path using the current color. The resultant output is subject to modification (scaling, shearing, rotating, etc.) by the CTM.

There are many path operators. A few of the most basic are the following:

- ***x y* moveto** Here *x* and *y* are user coordinates (real numbers). This operator establishes a current point where a path may begin, but does not extend the path; analogous to a plotter move with the pen up.

- ***dx dy* rmoveto** Here *dx* and *dy* are increments relative to the current point. This operator works like moveto, but uses relative, not absolute terms.

- ***x y* lineto** Extends the path in a straight line from the current point to the location *x*,*y*. The new current point is at *x*,*y*. *dx dy* rlineto is a relative lineto.

- ***x y r* angle1 angle2Arc** This describes an arc, where *x*,*y* is the center of a radius, r, *angle1* and *angle2* are the arc start and finish points, respectively, measured counterclockwise with respect to the positive *x* axis of the user coordinate system. Before the arc is added to the path, a straight line is added to connect the current point to the start point of the arc.

- **xlowleft ylowleft xupright yuprightSetbbox** Where the arguments define the lower left and upper right corners of a rectangle, this establishes a boundary box for a path. It is most commonly used in *user paths* (i.e. procedures comprising path operations) in which it must precede the sequence of path operators.

* **closepath** Makes the current path into a closed shape by connecting the current point to the starting point with a straight line.

* **newpath** Erases the current path and leaves the current point undefined.

Painting operators use the path to actually create the graphic by drawing lines or filling in shapes. Two of the principal operators follow:

* **fill** Paints an area bounded by the current path, using the current color (and overwriting any previous marks in the area). If the current path is not yet closed, the fill operator closes it.

* **stroke** Paints a line along the current path, using the current color (and overwriting any previous marks). The line type (solid or broken), the joints between lines, and the shape of line ends (caps) can take various alternative forms not discussed here. The defaults are a solid line with simple, unmitered joints and squared ends. The stroke width is set by the operator width setlinewidth, where width is in user space units.

Grayscale bitmap images

The following is a simple example of code for a monochrome (black-and-white) bitmap image, 16 by 16 pixels:

```
/pixbuf 2 string def
gsave
298.32 373.32 translate
15.36 15.36 scale
16 16 1 % width, height, bits per sample
[16 0 0 -16 0 16] % image matrix denotes scan order.
{currentfile image pixbuf readhexstring pop} % data source procedure
image
% hex image data in ASCII follows; line breaks are ignored.
fffffefffeffeeef
f6dffabffd7f8383
fdffabff6dfeeeff
efffefffffffffff
grestore
```

This segment of code first defines a pixel-data buffer, two bytes long, called *pixbuf*.' It then protects the current graphics state by pushing it onto the graphics stack with gsave. Next, it specifies a position and scale for the image. Then, data begins for the image operator. Actual bitmap data follows the image operator, and finally, the original graphics state is restored.

The image operator and the related colorimage operator are the generators of bitmap images. The image operator of Level 1 PostScript supports grayscale with one, two, four, or eight bits per sample. In Level 2, it also supports 12-bit depth and color. The basic, grayscale form for the image operator, usable in both levels, is:

width height bits/sample matrix datasource image

Width and *height* give the number of columns and rows, respectively, in the original pixel plane.

Bits/sample gives the image depth of 1, 2, 4, 8, or 12.

Matrix is a special, six-element image matrix, analogous to but not substituting for the CTM. It can be used for linear transformations like those of the CTM, but is mostly used for specifying the scan order of the bitmap image. For images scanned left to right, top to bottom, the matrix is [width 0 0 height 0 height]. For left to right, bottom to top, the matrix is [width 0 0 height 0 0]. Either of these matrices will produce an image that is one unit by one unit, before scaling.

Datasource is a source of binary bitmap data; conventionally, it is a procedure that fills a string of arbitrary length with data. In Level 2, it might also be a file such as *currentfile* or a filtered file (see the following section on direct file reading and filtering). The procedure, called repeatedly by the image operator until the image is complete or an end-of-file is found, leaves a string of data on top of the stack each time it is called. The datasource will be examined more closely under *Bitmap data*, following.

✳ **Bitmap data** In the preceding example, and in most instances, the data used by the image operator are located in the PostScript program file itself, which is denoted by the name *currentfile*. The image operator can, however, also accept bitmap data from a variety of locations, including files other than currentfile.

As in the example, the *datasource* for the image operator is usually a procedure; that is, a procedure that reads data from a location, converts them to binary if necessary, and puts them on the stack for the image operator. In the preceding example, the procedure {currentfile pixbuf readhexstring pop} is the datasource—the last object before the image operator. The image operator repeatedly calls this procedure to obtain binary data and place them on the stack. This operation is discussed in the following section.

The datasource could conceivably be a file containing properly ordered 8-bit binary data; that is, after all, what image requires. But PostScript files are designed for maximum portability and so are generally encoded in 7-bit ASCII. Files that do contain 8-bit data will have a DSC comment %%DocumentData: Binary.

✳ **Reading ASCII hexadecimal data** Usually, bitmap data are encoded using ASCII characters to represent hexadecimal values. In such instances, the heart of a procedure used as a data source for image is the operator readhexstring. The operator takes the form:

file string readhexstring

in which *file* is the location of the data, and *string* is a buffer into which data will be read. The operator reads pairs of ASCII characters as hexadecimal numbers and converts them into 1-byte binary values. White space and nonhex data are ignored. The length of string is not critical, as long as it exceeds *bits/sample*; data will be read until the string is filled or an end-of-file is encountered. This operator pushes two results onto the operand stack: a resultant string of binary data and a boolean. The boolean is "true" unless an end-of-file was encountered.

In the example, this operator is employed as follows: the file for readhexstring is *currentfile* and the string is *pixbuf*. Because the readhexstring operator leaves a boolean on the top of the stack that image does not use, the pop operator is used to remove the boolean.

Once the image operator is executed, the file pointer for the currentfile is at the beginning of the bitmap data, so readhexstring begins to read data at that point. This is a common approach to reading bitmap data, so you can generally find bitmap data by looking immediately after the image operator in a PostScript file. Most of the time, the data will be ASCII hex, and will represent 1-bit or 8-bit grayscale pixels.

Color bitmap images

In Level 2 PostScript, the image operator can take another, more flexible form that, among other features, allows the use of color. It is the "single argument" or "image dictionary" form, as follows:

imagedictionary image

Imagedictionary is a special type of array called a "dictionary" array containing name and value pairs that define the following image parameters: image dimensions and depth, data source, matrix, and type of coding used for the bitmap data. The interpretation of data as grayscale or color depends on the ColorSpace parameter.

An example of the use of this form is the following code:

```
/DeviceRGB setcolorspace
<<
/ImageType 1
/Width 16
/Height 16
/BitsPerComponent 8
/Decode [0 1 0 1 0 1]
/ImageMatrix [16 0 0 -16 0 16]
/DataSource currentfile
/ASCIIHexDecode filter
>>
image
```

The image dictionary array is delimited by the characters << and >>. The principal entries required are those shown in the example. The ImageType entry is always 1; Width and Height are the image dimensions in pixels; BitsPerComponent is the sample size for each primary color (R, G, and B because DeviceRGB is the color space). The Decode array maps the range of each color component (R, G, and B in the example) to a range of 0 to 1 (or 1 to 0 for color inversion). The ImageMatrix is the same as matrix in the earlier form of image. The DataSource entry specifies a data source object, typically currentfile, with a "filter" applied.

✻ **Direct file reading and filtering** There are two previously undiscussed Level 2 actions taking place with DataSource in the preceding example. First, the image operator is reading a data file directly; specifically currentfile, the same file containing the commands. In Level 1, a procedure was required. Second, the data from that file are being translated into binary, as they are read, by a filter. Previously, the readhexstring operator was employed.

"Filtered reading" is a Level 2 feature that can be used when an operator directly reads a data source object. The filter operator takes the following form for reading data:

source parameter readfilter filter, where *source* is typically a file object such as currentfile, and *readfilter* is the name of a reading-type filter. Some filters require additional parameters for control; most do not require a *parameter* operand. The output is a data source.

Among the available *readfilter* names are /ASCIIHexDecode, /ASCII85Decode, /LZWDecode, /RunLengthDecode, and /CCITTFaxDecode.

There is an equivalent system for filtered writing, wherein the source becomes a target, and *readfilter* becomes *writefilter*. The filters for writing are: /ASIIHexEncode, /ASCII85Encode, /LZWEncode, /RunLengthEncode, and /CCITTFaxEncode. The CCITTFax encode and decode filters require additional parameters not covered here; so does the /RunLengthEncode filter. The rest do not.

This approach of directly reading data from files and filtering them can also be used with the earlier (5-operand) form of image in Level 2 PostScript. In the earlier example, the procedure {currentfile pixbuf readhexstring pop} could be replaced by currentfile /ASCIIHexDecode filter.

✻ **ColorImage operator** The operator colorimage is analogous to the image operator. It is a Level 1 extended feature (usually found in Level 1 implementations on color printers), and remains present in Level 2. Its standard form is:

width height bits/component matrix datasource(s) multisources ncomponents

colorimage

The *width*, *height*, and *matrix* operands are the same as for image.

Bits/component gives the bits per sample per component; for instance "24-bit" RGB uses *bits/component* of eight.

Datasource(s) is one or more sources of the type described for the image operator. For image plane organization, where the component values for a pixel appear consecutively, there is one source. For color-plane organization there are three or four.

Multisources is a boolean that, if true, indicates that multiple data sources are used.

Ncomponents is the number of color components, and therefore is the integer value 1 (for grayscale), 3 (for RGB/HSB), or 4 (for CMYK).

Multisources is true if there are separate *proc* arguments for each color, and false if there is one procedure that returns interleaved color data. *Ncomponents* is 1, 3, or 4. If 1, the bitmap is grayscale and colorimage behaves essentially the same as image. If 3, the image is RGB color, and if 4 the image is CMYK subtractive color.

If there are three colors and multisources is false, the single procedure must return the red, green, and blue components for each pixel in order, with the appropriate number of bits per component. The bits are packed into bytes without regard for pixel boundaries. If multisources is true there are three datasource arguments for red, green, and blue data respectively. If the sources are procedures rather than files, each procedure is called in turn as color data are needed. See the end of this chapter for a color-image example.

Page printing

As PostScript code is executed, lines, bitmaps, and other image data are added to a page image that is being built in memory. The command:

```
showpage
```

tells PostScript that the page is done. It prints or displays the page, then clears the page image.

As a special case, showpage commands in EPS files are ignored. (The enclosing PostScript code typically redefine showpage to a no-op around the EPS file.)

An EPS file should generally end with a showpage, so that it can be sent directly to the printer and will print normally.

EPS preview

EPS files can contain preview images that allow an application to display an approximation of the EPS image without having to interpret the full PostScript language.

Macintosh PICT preview

In an EPS file stored on an Apple Macintosh computer, the resource fork of the file can contain a PICT image stored as resource number 256. See chapter 26 for details on PICT.

MS-DOS WMF or TIFF preview

An EPS file on a DOS computer can contain a WMF or TIFF preview image. If it does, the EPS file must start with a special binary header, Table 24-2.

Table 24-2

DOS preview header

Offset	Size	Contents
0	4	ID string C5D0D3C6 H
4	4	Location of PostScript
8	4	Length of PostScript
12	4	Location of WMF
16	4	Length of WMF
20	4	Location of TIFF
24	4	Length of TIFF
28	4	XOR checksum or FFFF H

The header starts with a 4-byte ID string that marks the file as an EPS file with a preview image. The three *location,length* pairs identify the parts of the file that contain PostScript, WMF, and TIFF, respectively. The location is the byte offset from the beginning of the file, and the length is the section length in bytes. The *checksum* is the XOR of the preceding seven 4-byte words, or else FFFF H. A single file should not contain both a WMF and a TIFF preview image. See chapter 25 for more information on WMF and chapter 6 for more information on TIFF.

Device-independent preview

Any EPS file can contain a preview bitmap stored as hex data in comments. Such a file is called *Encapsulated PostScript Interchange*, or EPSI. The preview, if present, must immediately follow the %%EndComments line. It has the following structure:

```
%%BeginPreview: width height depth lines
%hex data
• • •
%%EndPreview
```

The *width*, *height*, and *depth* describe the preview bitmap. Depth should be 1, 2, 4, or 8; *lines* is the number of text lines in the file that the hex data occupy.

The image is stored row by row, from the bottom of the image to the top, left to right within a row. The hex data are in the same format as used by the image operator, with pixels packed into bytes from high to low. Each row starts on a byte boundary, with zero padding if the row size is not an even number of bytes. Each hex data line must start with a % to mark it as a PostScript comment, and must obey the DSC convention that no line is longer than 255 bytes.

Examples

Here are some simple complete examples of a monochrome and a color EPS bitmap file.

EPS monochrome bitmap

Figure 24-1 shows a complete EPS file that displays a simple 16 × 16 bitmap, printed at about 72 dpi, with EPS comments. First comes the EPS header, giving the name of the image, and the facts that it is one page long and fits in the rectangle between (298,314) and (373,389). Then comes the PostScript code, similar to what we saw earlier. Calls

Figure 24-1

```
%!PS-Adobe-3.0 EPSF-3.0
%%Creator: someprogram
%%Title: sample.ps
%%Pages: 1
%%BoundingBox: 298 373 314 389
%%EndComments

/readstring {
  currentfile exch readhexstring pop
} bind def
/picstr 2 string def
%%EndProlog
gsave
298.32 373.32 translate
15.36 15.36 scale
16 16 1
[ 16 0 0 -16 0 16 ]
{ picstr readstring }
image
ffff ffff ffff fc3f
f00f f00f e007 e007
e007 e007 f00f f00f
fc3f ffff ffff ffff
grestore
showpage
%%Trailer
```

Monochrome color EPS document.

to gsave and grestore surround the code so that the scale and translate operators will only affect the image operator and not anything that might happen to follow lately. (The scaling factor is 15.36 rather than 16, so it fits neatly inside a 16 ×16 box.)

This version defines the procedure readstring in the prolog and refers to it in the *datasource* argument to image. The exch in the procedure exchanges the currentfile argument with the name of the buffer, *picstr* in this case, which is assumed already to be on the stack, so they are in the correct order for readhexstring. Finally, there is a showpage and a one-line EPS trailer.

```
%!PS-Adobe-3.0 EPSF-3.0
%%Creator: someprogram
```

```
%%Title: sample.ps
%%Pages: 1
%%BoundingBox: 298 373 314 389
%%EndComments
/readstring {
currentfile exch readhexstring pop
} bind def
/picstr 2 string def
%%EndProlog
gsave
298.32 373.32 translate
15.36 15.36 scale
16 16 1
[ 16 0 0 -16 0 16 ]
{ picstr readstring }
image
ffff ffff ffff fc3f
f00f f00f e007 e007
e007 e007 f00f f00f
fc3f ffff ffff ffff
grestore
showpage
%%Trailer
```

EPS color bitmap

A color bitmap is only slightly more complicated than a monochrome one. Figure 24-2 shows a 4 × 4 color image with four bits per pixel. The EPS header is much the same as in the monochrome case, except that it defines separate red, green, and blue string buffers. The arguments to colorimage are similar to those for image, except that there are three separate *datasource* procedures, because *multisource* is true.

Figure 24-2

```
%!PS-Adobe-3.0 EPSF-3.0
%%Creator: pnmtops
%%Title: feep.ps
%%Pages: 1
```

Monochrome color EPS document.

Because each string buffer is two bytes long, each procedure will return two bytes or four hex digits of data per call, so the data after the colorimage operator is four digits of red, four digits of green, four digits of blue, for each set of four pixels. There are many possible ways to organize color pixel data, but this is a fairly common one.

Again at the end are grestore, showpage, and the EPS trailer.

```
%!PS-Adobe-3.0 EPSF-3.0
%%Creator: pnmtops
%%Title: feep.ps
%%Pages: 1
%%BoundingBox: 304 379 308 383
%%EndComments
/readstring {
currentfile exch readhexstring pop
} bind def
/rpicstr 2 string def
/gpicstr 2 string def
/bpicstr 2 string def
%%EndProlog
gsave
304.08 379.08 translate
3.84 3.84 scale
4 4 4
[ 4 0 0 -4 0 4 ]
{ rpicstr readstring }
{ gpicstr readstring }
{ bpicstr readstring }
true 3
colorimage
000f 0000 000f 0000
0f00 0700 0000 00f0
070 f000 0000 f000
grestore
showpage
%%Trailer
```

Reference

Adobe Corporation. *PostScript Language Reference Manual, Second Edition*. 1990. Reading, MA: Addison-Wesley.

## CHAPTER 25

WMF

Name	WMF (Microsoft Windows Metafile)
Image type	Display list
Intended use	Storage and interchange under MS Windows
Owner	Microsoft Corp., 1 Microsoft Way, Redmond WA 98052-6399, 1-800-426-9400
Last version/ revision/ release date	Windows 3.0, 1990
Platforms	IBM PCs and clones
Supporting applications	Visual Basic, Word for Windows, PageMaker, Ventura for Windows, Corel Draw, Drafix Windows CAD, and others. Most applications other than Visual Basic require the placeable metafile header.
Similarities	CGM, somewhat
Overall assessment	Best device-independent format under Windows

Advantages

Device-independent, files can be well-structured, files can be much smaller than corresponding bitmaps due to higher-level feature descriptions.

Disadvantages

Semantics are closely tied to Windows imaging model; files are relatively complex.

Variants

Windows 3.x adds new record types to the Windows 2.x metafile format, but metafiles that avoid the new types should be backward-compatible. Placeable metafiles have a prefix header containing size and scaling information.

Overview of file structure

A Windows Metafile stores a list of Microsoft Windows graphical function calls. Only a subset of the Windows functions are allowed in metafiles, but it is a large subset containing most of the drawing calls. Although the metafile was originally intended as a sort of a graphical macroinstruction, it turns out to be more generally useful and is now often used as a general image-interchange format among Windows applications.

A metafile consists of a short header followed by some number of records. An optional *placement* header can precede the file header. Each record corresponds to a Windows graphics device interface (GDI) call, and contains a size, a function number, and some argument data. In most cases, the argument data words are just the values that would be passed to the corresponding Windows GDI routine, although for some of the more complicated routines there are somewhat more complex data encodings.

Windows imaging model

Here is a brief overview of Windows graphics programming. For more details, consult the *Microsoft Windows Programmer's Reference*.

Geometry

All graphics in Windows are drawn in a *display context*, which contains a set of parameters, such as colors, scaling, defined drawing objects, etc. Drawing coordinates are relative to a logical window, which is mapped into a physical viewport on a screen or printer. Normally, coordinates in the window correspond to the viewport one to one, with one unit being one pixel, although it is possible to scale and move both the window and the viewport. All coordinates are expressed as 16-bit signed integers.

Drawing is done with "objects," which are pens, brushes, bitmaps, fonts, and regions. A pen draws a line of some width that might be solid, dashed, or dotted. A brush lays down repeated copies of an array of pixels. A brush can use a built-in solid color or crosshatch brush pattern, or an arbitrary bitmap. One might outline a rectangle or circle with a pen, then use a brush to fill it in with a desired color or pattern. A region defines a clipping area—when a region is in effect, all graphics are clipped so that only material within the region is actually drawn.

All the defined objects are assigned object numbers, starting at zero. When a new object is defined, it is assigned the lowest unused number. After an object is deleted, its number is reused. Only one object of a particular kind is active at a time. The file header contains the maximum count of simultaneously defined objects, which is one more than the highest object number used.

To draw text, one first defines a font in terms of size, character style, color, and other attributes. Then a separate *call* draws the text, giving the position, the string, and some formatting options.

The color model uses a standard color map that is shared among all windows on the screen. Twenty entries are pre-allocated for standard colors. Windows compete for the rest of the entries. A set of color entries is known as a logical palette, which is realized when a window becomes visible by assigning the palette entries to entries in the physical color map. Within a palette entry, colors are specified as three values for red, green, and blue, with each value in the range 0 to 255 with 255 being the brightest. Colors in GDI calls are generally given as entry numbers in the active logical palette.

Color references

Many calls take as arguments a color reference, a 32-bit number in one of several forms. If the high byte is zero, it is an absolute color reference and the form is hex 00RRGGBB with RR, GG, and BB being red, green, and blue direct color values. If the high byte contains 1, the form is 0100NNNN where NNNN is a color index in the current logical palette. If the high byte contains 2, the form is 02RRGGBB where RRGGBB are again color values, but the system is to choose the closest existing color in the current logical palette.

Format details

Intel little-endian format is used for all data. Most values are 16-bit integers. All sizes are given in terms of 16-bit words, not bytes.

Header format

Every metafile starts with a file header (see Table 25-1).

Table 25-1 **WMF file header**

Offset	Size	Description
0	2	Metafile type, always 1 for a disk file
2	2	Header size in words, generally 9.
4	2	Version number, hex 0300 for Windows 3
6	4	File size in words
10	2	Number of object handles used
12	4	Size in words of largest record
16	2	Unused

The file header gives the maximum record size and the number of simultaneously declared objects, so that a program that reads the file can pre-allocate space.

Record format

Each record, Table 25-2, starts with a header containing a size word, followed by the code that defines the function and as many parameters as the function requires. The shortest possible record, with no parameters, is three words long.

Table 25-2 **WMF record format**

Offset	Size	Description
0	4	Size in words of the record
4	2	Function code
6	2**N*	Function parameters

Metafile record types

Each record starts with the record size and function code as above. Function codes are all specified in hexadecimal. The parameters are usually the arguments to the corresponding Windows GDI function, in reverse order for some reason. For some of the functions the parameters are more complicated, usually because the Windows function takes as a parameter a data structure more complex than a single value. In the descriptions below, if the parameters are all single words, they are merely listed in the order they appear in the record. If they are more complex, a structure description appears.

✳ AnimatePalette

Code: 436 (new in Windows 3.x)
Parameters: See Table 25-3.

AnimatePalette parameters Table 25-3

Offset	Size	Description
6	2	Starting palette entry number
8	2	Number of entries to animate
10	4*N	New palette entries

The new palette entries in the parameters immediately replace the given entries in the active logical palette.

Each entry is an absolute color reference.

Arc

Code: 817
Parameters: *Y4*, *X4*, *Y3*, *X3*, *Y2*, *X2*, *Y1*, *X1*

Draw an elliptical arc using the currently selected pen. The center of the ellipse is the center of the bounding rectangle, with corners at (*X1*,*Y1*) and (*X2*,*Y2*). The arc is drawn counterclockwise from (*X3*,*Y3*) to (*X4*,*Y4*).

BitBlt

Code: 922 (obsolete, Windows 2.x only)
Parameters: See Table 25-4.

Old BitBlt parameters Table 25-4

Offset	Size	Description
6	2	Type of operation
8	2	Bitmap *Y* origin
10	2	Bitmap *X* origin
12	2	Destination area height
14	2	Destination area width
16	2	Destination *Y* origin
18	2	Destination *X* origin

Table 25-4 **Continued**

Offset	Size	Description
20	2	Bitmap width in pixels
22	2	Bitmap height in pixels
24	2	Bitmap width in bytes
26	2	Bitmap number of planes
28	2	Pixel bits per plane, always 1
30	*N*	Bitmap data

Transfer a rectangle of bits into the image. The source and destination rectangles need not be the same size; if they are not, the mode from the most recent SetStretchBltMode controls how the source image is resized. The source *X* and *Y* origins are disregarded and are usually zero.

The source bitmap is stored by plane by scan line, with the most-significant plane first for each pixel row. Each scan line is padded out to a multiple of 16 bits, and the width in bytes at offset 24 reflects this padding. Color bitmaps depend on the target device, but usually store triples of red, green and blue planes in that order. (The new BitBlt3 operator below handles color images in a device-independent way.)

The type of operation controls how the source bitmap is merged with the existing contents of the destination rectangle. Type 0020 means *source overwrites destination*. Type 0086 logically ORs the source with the destination. Type 00C6 logically ANDs the source with the destination. Type 0046 logically XORs the source with the destination. Other types exist but are less often used.

✳ BitBlt3

Code: 940 (new in Windows 3.x)
Parameters: See Table 25-5.

Table 25-5 **New BitBlt parameters**

Offset	Size	Description
6	2	Type of operation
8	2	Bitmap *Y* origin
10	2	Bitmap *X* origin

12	2	Destination area height
14	2	Destination area width
16	2	Destination *Y* origin
18	2	Destination *X* origin
20	40	BITMAPINFOHEADER
60	4*N*	color map
60+4N	S	bits

The Windows 3 BitBlt operation is the same as the Windows 2 version, except that the bitmap is specified in a device-independent format. The BITMAPINFOHEADER, color map, and image bits are identical to those in the Windows Bitmap file described in chapter 11.

Chord

Code: 830
Parameters: *Y4*, *X4*, *Y3*, *X3*, *Y2*, *X2*, *Y1*, *X1*

Draw a chord, the intersection of an ellipse and a line. An elliptical arc is drawn the same way that Arc draws it, then the endpoints are connected using the selected pen and the chord is filled using the selected brush.

CreateBrushIndirect

Code: 2fc
Parameters: See Table 25-6.

CreateBrushIndirect parameters Table 25-6

Offset	Size	Description
6	2	Brush style
8	4	Brush color
12	2	Cross-hatch line type

Create a new brush type and add it to the object table. The brush style is 0 for solid color, 1 for "hollow'" (background color shows through), or 2 for crosshatched. If the brush is crosshatched the line types are 0 for horizontal, 1 for vertical, 2 for diagonal rising to the right, 3 for diagonal rising to the left, 4 for horizontal and vertical, and 5 for both diagonals.

The color of a solid or crosshatched brush is a 32-bit color reference.

✳ CreateFontIndirect

Code: 2fb
Parameters: See Table 25-7.

Table 25-7 **CreateFontIndirect parameters**

Offset	Size	Description
6	2	Height
8	2	Width
12	2	Escapement
14	2	Orientation
16	2	Weight
18	1	Italic
19	1	Underline
20	1	Strikeout
21	1	Character set
22	1	Output precision
23	1	Clipping precision
24	1	Output quality
25	1	Two low bits: pitch, four high bits: font type
26	32	Typeface name

Select a font that best matches the attributes given and add it to the object table. Height is the character cell height if positive, average character height if negative, or selects a default size if zero. Width is the average character width, or a default if zero.

Slant specifies in tenths of degrees the angle of slanted (pseudo-italic) characters, with positive being clockwise from horizontal. Orientation specifies in tenths of degrees the angle at which the font is drawn, with positive being clockwise from horizontal. Weight is in the range of 0 to 1000, with typical values being 400 for normal and 700 for bold characters. Italic, Underline, and Strikeout if nonzero specify the corresponding font attributes. Character set contains a character set code, typically 0 for ANSI. Output precision says how closely the character sizes and angles must match the ones specified, 0 for default, 1 for matching at the string level, and 2 for matching at the character level. Clip precision says how precisely to clip characters that are partially contained in the clipping region. Both are typically zero to use a default precision. Output quality is 0 for default pitch, 1 for draft, and 2 for proof quality. The two low-order bits of the pitch and family byte are 0 for default, 1 for fixed, and 2 for variable. The high four bits set the font family, 0 for a default or 10 H for Roman, 20 for Sans-Serif, 30 for Typewriter, 40 for Script, and 50 for Decorative font. Typeface name is the null-terminated ASCII name of the desired typeface.

✻ CreatePalette

Code: 0f7 (new in Windows 3.x)
Parameters: See Table 25-8.

CreatePalette parameters Table 25-8

Offset	Size	Description
6	2	Version
8	2	Number of entries
10	4*N	Palette entries

Create a color palette with the desired entries and add it to the object table. The palette has one or more entries, each specified by a 32-bit color reference. Version is 300 H for Windows 3.x.

✳ CreatePatternBrush

Code: 1f9 (obsolete, Windows 2.x only)
Parameters: See Table 25-9.

Table 25-9 **CreatePatternBrush parameters**

Offset	Size	Description
6	2	Width in bits
8	2	Height in bits
10	2	Width in bytes
12	2	Number of planes
14	2	Pixel bits per plane, always 1
16	2	Pointer to bits, unused
18	N	Bitmap bits

Create a brush using the specified bitmap and enter it in the handle table. Each bit row is stored as an integral number of words, so the width in bytes must be a multiple of two, with part of the last word in each row possibly unused. A monochrome bitmap is stored as a series of rows, from top to bottom, with the bits in each row stored from left to right. A color bitmap is stored by row, so for a 9-bit deep-bitmap, the first row of each plane is stored in the order red0, red1, red2, green0, green1, green2, blue0, blue1, blue2. Then the second row of each plane is stored, in the same order, and so forth.

✳ CreatePatternBrush3

Code: 142 (new in Windows 3.x)
Parameters: See Table 25-10.

Table 25-10 **CreatePatternBrush3 parameters**

Offset	Size	Description
6	2	Type
8	2	Usage
10	N	BITMAPINFO describing the bitmap
10+*N*	M	bits

Create a brush using the given bitmap and enter it in the handle table. Type field should be 5 to indicate that a device-independent bitmap follows, and Usage should be 0 to indicate that its palette contains explicit RGB values.

The BITMAPINFO and bits are identical to those in a Windows bitmap file, as described in chapter 11.

✳ CreatePenIndirect

Code: 2fa
Parameters Style, Width, unused, Color

Create a logical pen and enter it in the handle table. The style can be 0 solid, 1 dashed, 2 dotted, 3 alternating dot and dash, 4 alternating dash and two dots, 5 none, and 6 inside frame. The *inside frame* style is a variety of solid that draws the interior, but not the boundary, of primitive objects. *Width* is the stroke width in logical units. *Color* is a 32-bit color reference.

✳ CreateRegion

Code: 6ff
Parameters Unspecified

Create a region and enter it in the handle table. This function is not often used and its arguments are not documented.

✳ DeleteObject

Code: 1f0
Parameters: Index

Delete the object identified by the handle table index, and free the entry in the handle table.

✳ DrawText

Code: 62f
Parameters: See Table 25-11.

Table 25-11 **DrawText parameters**

Offset	Size	Description
6	2	Format method
8	2	Character count, or zero for null-terminated string
10	2	*X*1
12	2	*Y*1
14	2	*X*2
16	2	*Y*2
18	N	Character string

Draw the given text within the rectangle defined by (*X*1,*Y*1) and (*X*2,*Y*2). The format method is the logical OR of several sets formatting option bits.

Horizontal alignment 2 H for right aligned, 1 for centered, 0 for left aligned.

Vertical alignment 8 H for bottom of the rectangle, 4 for centered, 0 for the top.

Single line 20 H says to treat the text as a single line, even if it contains carriage returns or line feeds.

Word Break 10 H says to break into multiple lines at spaces rather than always at the right boundary. Carriage returns and line feeds also force a new line, unless the single-line bit is set.

Tabs 40 H says to expand tab characters, and 80 H says to use the high byte as the format word as the number of spaces per tab stop (default 8).

Clipping 400 H says to extend the rectangle at the right for single lines, or at the bottom for multiple lines to make the text fit. 100 H says to draw the text without clipping.

Miscellaneous 200 H says to include the "external leading" of a font in size calculations, and 800 H suppresses the special treatment of the & character, which normally means to underscore the following character.

✻ Ellipse

Code: 418
Parameters: *Y*2, *X*2, *Y*1, *X*1

Draw an ellipse bounded by the rectangle defined by (*X*1,*Y*1) and (*X*2,*Y*2).

✻ Escape

Code: 626
Parameters: See Table 25-12.

Escape parameters Table 25-12

Offset	Size	Description
6	2	Escape number
8	2	Number of bytes of escape data
10	*N*	Escape data

Call an escape function defined by the output-device driver.

✻ ExcludeClipRect

Code: 415
Parameters: *Y*2, *X*2, *Y*1, *X*1

Create a new clipping region, consisting of the current region minus the rectangle defined by (*X*1,*Y*1) and (*X*2,*Y*2).

✻ ExtTextOut

Code: a32
Parameters: See Table 25-13.

Table 25-13 **ExtTextOut parameters**

Offset	Size	Description
6	2	*Y* character origin
8	2	*X* character origin
10	2	Option bits
12	2	*X*1
14	2	*Y*1
16	2	*X*2
18	2	*Y*2
20	*N*	Text string
20+*N*	M	Optional character spacings

Draw the text string in the rectangle defined by (*X*1,*Y*1) and (*X*2,*Y*2). Option bit 4 H clips the text to fit in the rectangle, and 2 fills the rectangle with the current background color. If neither bit is set, the rectangle data are ignored. The text string must be padded to an even boundary. If the character spacings are present, they are an array of words giving the width of each character cell.

✻ FloodFill

Code: 419
Parameters: Color, *Y*, *X*

Fill an area using the current brush, starting at (*X*,*Y*) and extending out to a boundary whose color is given by the 32-bit color reference, *Color*.

✻ IntersectClipRect

Code: 416
Parameters: *Y*2, *X*2, *Y*1, *X*1

Create a new clipping region consisting of the intersection of the current region and the rectangle defined by (*X*1,*Y*1) and (*X*2,*Y*2).

✳ LineTo

Code: 213
Parameters: *Y*, *X*

Draw a line using the current pen from the current position to (*X*, *Y*).

✳ MoveTo

Code: 214
Parameters: *Y*, *X*

Set the current position to (*X*, *Y*).

✳ OffsetClipRgn

Code: 220
Parameters: *Y*,*X*

Move the current clipping region by the distance (*X*, *Y*).

✳ OffsetViewportOrg

Code: 211
Parameters: *Y*, *X*

Move the viewport origin by adding (*X*, *Y*) to the current origin. *X* and *Y* are in *device* coordinates.

✳ OffsetWindowOrg

Code: 20f
Parameters: *Y*, *X*

Move the window origin by adding (*X*, *Y*) to the current origin. *X* and *Y* are in *logical* coordinates.

✳ PatBlt

Code: 61d
Parameters: Op, Height, Width, *Y*, *X*

Create a pattern in the rectangle with origin (*X*,*Y*) and the given Height and Width by combining the current brush with the existing contents in a manner defined by the 32-bit Op parameter. Values of Op are 00F00021 H to replace the contents with the rectangle with the brush pattern, 005A0049 H to XOR the brush pattern with the existing contents, 00550009 H to logically invert the existing contents disregarding the brush, 00000042 H to make the rectangle entirely black, and 00FF0062 H to make the rectangle entirely white.

✳ Pie

Code: 81a
Parameters: *Y*4, *X*4, *Y*3, *X*3, *Y*2, *X*2, *Y*1, *X*1

Draw a pie-shaped area bounded by an elliptical arc. The center of the ellipse is the center of the bounding rectangle, with corners at (*X*1,*Y*1) and (*X*2,*Y*2). The arc is drawn counterclockwise from (*X*3,*Y*3) to (*X*4,*Y*4), then lines are drawn from the endpoints to the center and the area is filled with the current brush.

✳ Polygon

Code: 324
Parameters: See Table 25-14.

Table 25-14 **Polygon and Polyline parameters**

Offset	Size	Description
6	2	Count
8	2	*X*1
10	2	*Y*1
•••		

Draw a polygon. Count is the number of (*X*,*Y*) pairs that follow, each defining a vertex of the polygon. The polygon is filled with the current brush using the mode set by SetPolyFillMode.

Polyline

Code: 325
Parameters: See Table 25-14.

Draw a polyline. Count is the number of (*X*,*Y*) pairs that follow, each defining the end of a line segment. Lines are drawn from (*X*1,*Y*1) to (*X*2,*Y*2), then from (*X*2,*Y*2) to (*X*3,*Y*3), etc.

PolyPolygon

Code: 538 (new in Windows 3.x)
Parameters: See Table 25-15.

PolyPolygon parameters Table 25-15

Offset	Size	Description
6	2	Point count
8	N	Polygon counts
8+*N*	2	*X*1
10+*N*	2	*Y*1
•••		

Draw a set of polygons. *Point count* is the total number of (*X*,*Y*) pairs provided. *Polygon counts* is a list of words, each specifying the number of points that define a single polygon. The sum of the polygon counts must equal the point count.

RealizePalette

Code: 035 (new in Windows 3.x)
Parameters: none

Realize the current logical palette; that is., select colors in the current display that correspond to those in the logical palette.

⁂ Rectangle

Code: 41b
Parameters: *Y*2, *X*2, *Y*1, *X*1

Draw the rectangle defined by (*X*1,*Y*1) and (*X*2,*Y*2) using the current pen.

⁂ ResizePalette

Code: 139 (new in Windows 3.x)
Parameters: Number of entries

Change the current logical palette so it contains the specified number of entries. Entries are added or deleted at the end, and new entries are all black.

⁂ RestoreDC

Code: 127
Parameters: Context, Handle

Restore a context saved by SaveDC from the context stack. Handle identifies the object to restore. Context should be –1 to specify the context at the top of the stack.

⁂ RoundRect

Code: 61c
Parameters: *Y*3, *X*3, *Y*2, *X*2, *Y*1, *X*1

Draw the rectangle defined by (*X*1,*Y*1) and (*X*2,*Y*2) with rounded corners, using the current pen, and fill it with the current brush. *X*3 and *Y*3 define the width and height of the ellipse to use for the corners.

⁜ SaveDC

Code: 01e
Parameters: Handle

Save a copy of the object identified by *Handle* on the context stack.

⁜ ScaleViewportExt

Code: 412
Parameters: *Y*1, *X*1, *Y*0, *X*0

Change the size of the viewport by multiplying its size by (*X*0/*X*1, *Y*0/*Y*1).

⁜ ScaleWindowExt

Code: 400
Parameters: *Y*1, *X*1, *Y*0, *X*0

Change the size of the window by multiplying its size by (*X*0/*X*1, *Y*0/*Y*1).

⁜ SelectClipRgn

Code: 12c
Parameters: Handle
Select the clipping region identified by *Handle*.

⁜ SelectObject

Code: 12d
Parameters: Handle

Select the bitmap, pen, brush, font, or region identified by *Handle*.

SelectPalette

Code: 234
Parameters: Handle

Select the palette identified by *Handle*.

SetBkColor

Code: 201
Parameters: Color
Set the background color identified by 32-bit color reference *Color*.

SetBkMode

Code: 102
Parameters: Mode

If *Mode* is 2, fill the background with the current color before a pen, brush, or text is drawn. If *Mode* is 1, leave the background alone.

SetDIBitsToDevice

Code: d33 (new in Windows 3.x)
Parameters: See Table 25-16.

Table 25-16 **SetDIBitsToDevice parameters**

Offset	Size	Description
6	2	Usage
8	2	Number of scan lines
10	2	First scan line
12	2	Bitmap *Y* origin
14	2	Bitmap *X* origin
16	2	Bitmap height
18	2	Bitmap width
20	2	Destination *Y* origin

22	2	Destination X origin
24	N	BITMAPINFO structure
24+N	M	bitmap data

Transfer the given bitmap directly to the output device. The source bitmap is the rectangle in the given bitmap defined by the bitmap X and Y origins, width, and height. Data can be transferred a band at a time using the First scan line and Number of scan lines to limit the amount of data transferred. Usage is 1 to say that the palette in the BITMAPINFO contains 16-bit indices into the current logical palette, or zero to say that the palette contains explicit RGB values.

The BITMAPINFO and bits are identical to those in a Windows bitmap file, as described in chapter 11.

✻ SetMapMode

Code: 103
Parameters: Mode

Set the units used to transform logical to physical device coordinates. Mode 1 maps units directly to pixels, 2 makes a logical unit 0.1 mm, 3 makes it 0.01 mm, 4 makes it 0.01 inch, 5 makes it 0.001 inch, 6 makes it 1⁄1440 inch, 7 and 8 make it arbitrary units defined by SetWindowExt and SetViewportExt, with mode 7 forcing equal scaling on the two axes. In mode 1 the Y origin is at the bottom of the screen with increasing values toward the top; in modes 2 through 6 the Y origin is at the top of the screen with increasing values toward the bottom; and in modes 7 and 8 the origin and orientation depend on the scaling set.

✻ SetMapperFlags

Code: 231
Parameters: Flag

Flag is a 32-bit value. If its high bit is 1, fonts will be mapped only if the X and Y aspect ratio of a logical font exactly matches the physical font.

✳ SetPaletteEntries

Code: 037
Parameters: See Table 25-17.

Table 25-17 **SetPaletteEntries parameters**

Offset	Size	Description
6	2	First entry
8	2	Number of entries
10	4*N	Entries

Set the given entries in the current logical palette. Each entry is a 32-bit color reference. Changes are not visible until the next RealizePalette.

✳ SetPixel

Code: 41f
Parameters: Color, *X*, *Y*

Set the pixel at (*X*,*Y*) to Color, a 32-bit color reference.

✳ SetPolyFillMode

Code: 106
Parameters: Mode

If *Mode* is 1, nonsimple polygons are filled only in simply enclosed areas; if mode is 2 the entire polygon is filled. For example, in a five-pointed star, mode 1 fills only the points while mode 2 fills the entire star.

✳ SetROP2

Code: 104
Parameters: Mode

Set drawing mode, the way that pen and display data are combined during drawing. The mode is computed as follows: Start with a mode value of 1. Add 1 to the mode if bits where the pen and display were both 0 should be 1. Add 2 to the mode if bits where the pen was 0 and the display was 1 should be 1. Add 4 to the mode if bits where the pen was 1 and the display was 0 should be 1. Add 8 to the mode if bits where the pen and display were both 1 should be 1. Common values are 13 to have the pen overlay the existing contents and 7 for XOR drawing.

✳ SetStretchBltMode

Code: 107
Parameters: Mode

Set the disposition of deleted scan lines when a bitmap is compressed in a StretchBlt function. Mode 1 ANDs the eliminated lines with adjacent lines. Mode 2 ORs the eliminated lines with adjacent lines. Mode 3 simply discards the eliminated lines. Modes 1 and 2 can be useful to preserve significant foreground or background pixels in monochrome bitmaps.

✳ SetTextAlign

Code: 12e
Parameters: Flags

Set text-alignment options, based on bits in Flags. 01 H says to update the current graphics position after each TextOut or ExtTextOut call. The default is not to update.

By default, horizontal text alignment is based on the left side of the character bounding rectangle. 02 H says to align on the right side and 06 H says to align on the center of the rectangle.

By default, vertical text alignment is based on the top side of the character-bounding rectangle. 08 H says to align on the bottom, and hex 18 says to align on the text baseline.

✻ SetTextCharExtra

Code: 108
Parameters: Width

Set the amount of extra space between characters to Width logical units.

✻ SetTextColor

Code: 209
Parameters: Color

Set the foreground color of text to Color, a 32-bit color reference.

✻ SetTextJustification

Code: 20a
Parameters: BreakCount, BreakExtra

Horizontally justify subsequent output text. *BreakExtra* is the distance in logical units to be distributed among the break characters in the line. *BreakCount* is the number of break characters (typically spaces) in the line. A BreakExtra of zero turns off justification.

✻ SetViewportExt

Code: 20e
Parameters: *Y*, *X*

Make the viewport extent (*X*, *Y*), expressed in device units. Ignored if the mode set by SetMapMode is not 7 or 8.

✻ SetViewportOrg

Code: 20d
Parameters: *Y*, *X*

Make the viewport origin (*X*, *Y*) expressed in device units.

SetWindowExt

Code: 20c
Parameters: *Y*, *X*

Make the window extent (*X*,*Y*) expressed in logical units. Ignored if the mode set by SetMapMode is not 7 or 8.

SetWindowOrg

Code: 20b
Parameters: *Y*, *X*

Make the window origin (*X*,*Y*) expressed in logical units.

StretchBlt

Code: b23 (obsolete, Windows 2.x only)
Parameters: See Table 25-18.

StretchBlt parameters Table 25-18

Offset	Size	Description
6	4	Operation
10	2	Source height
12	2	Source width
14	2	Source *Y* origin
16	2	Source *X* origin
18	2	Destination height
20	2	Destination width
22	2	Destination *Y* origin
24	2	Destination *X* origin
26	2	Bitmap width in pixels
28	2	Bitmap height
30	2	Bitmap width in bytes
32	2	Bits per pixel per plane, always 1
34	*N*	Bitmap

Move a source rectangle from the bitmap to a destination rectangle, stretching or shrinking it to fit. The height and width values might be of opposite signs to produce mirror-image transfers. The bitmap is stored the same way as for the BitBlt operator, above. The Operation type determines how the source and destination are combined. Type 00CC0020 H means source overwrites destination. Type 00EE0086 H logically ORs the source with the destination. Type 008800C6 H logically ANDs the source with the destination. Type 00660046 H logically XORs the source with the destination. Other types are possible but less common.

The source and destination bitmaps need not have the same depth. Black and white pixels in monochrome bitmaps are converted to the foreground and background colors in color bitmaps, and vice versa.

✳ StretchBlt3

Code: b41 (new in Windows 3.x)
Parameters: See Table 25-19.

Table 25-19 **StretchBlt3 parameters**

Offset	Size	Description
6	4	Operation
10	2	Source height
12	2	Source width
14	2	Source *Y* origin
16	2	Source *X* origin
18	2	Destination height
20	2	Destination width
22	2	Destination *Y* origin
24	2	Destination *X* origin
26	2	BITMAPINFO structure
26+*N*	*N*	Bitmap data

Move a source rectangle from the bitmap to a destination rectangle, stretching or shrinking it to fit. The height and width values might be of opposite signs to produce mirror-image transfers. The Operation values are the same as for StretchBlt, earlier.

The BITMAPINFO and bits are identical to those in a Windows bitmap file, as described in chapter 11.

StretchDIBits

Code: f43 (new in Windows 3.x)
Parameters: See Table 25-20.

StretchBlt3 parameters Table 25-20

Offset	Size	Description
6	4	Operation
10	2	Usage
12	2	Source height
14	2	Source width
16	2	Source *Y* origin
18	2	Source *X* origin
20	2	Destination height
22	2	Destination width
24	2	Destination *Y* origin
26	2	Destination *X* origin
28	2	BITMAPINFO structure
28+*N*	*N*	Bitmap data

Move a source rectangle from the bitmap to a destination rectangle, stretching or shrinking it to fit. The height and width values may be of opposite signs to produce mirror-image transfers. The Operation values are the same as for StretchBlt, above. Usage is 1 to say that the palette in the BITMAPINFO contains 16-bit indices into the current logical palette, or zero to say that the palette contains explicit RGB values.

The BITMAPINFO and bits are identical to those in a Windows bitmap file, as described in chapter 11.

✳ TextOut

Code: 521
Parameters: See Table 25-21.

Table 25-21 **TextOut parameters**

Offset	Size	Description
6	2	String length
8	*N*	String
8+*N*	2	*Y* origin
10+*N*	2	*X* origin

Draw the string starting at (*X*,*Y*). The text string must be padded to an even boundary.

Placeable metafiles

Placeable metafiles contain a header preceding the file header, Table 25-22.

Table 25-22 **Placeable Metafile header**

Offset	Size	Description
0	4	ID word, 9AC6CDD7
4	2	Unused, must be zero
6	2	Top left *X*
8	2	Top left *Y*
10	2	Bottom right *X*
12	2	Bottom right *X*
14	2	Scale, units per inch
16	4	Unused, must be zero
20	2	Checksum

The header contains the (*X*,*Y*) coordinates of the top left and bottom right corners of a bounding rectangle for the image drawn by the metafile. Scale is the number of units per inch at which the image should be drawn. The *checksum* is the XOR of the rest of the header, taken as ten 16-bit words.

Placeable metafile restrictions

A placeable metafile may not contain any of the following calls: BitBlt, Escape, OffsetClipRgn, SelectClipRgn, SetMapMode, SetViewportExt, SetViewportOrg, SetWindExt, SetWindOrg.

SaveDC and RestoreDC must be properly matched. Avoid pattern brushes because their appearance varies from one device to another.

Example

Table 25-23 contains an example of a single metafile record that draws two lines from (100,101) to (200,201) and then to (300,301).

Sample polyline Table 25-23

Offset	Data	Description
0	10	Doubleword number of words in the record
4	325H	Polyline opcode
6	3	Three pairs follow
8	100	First *X*
10	101	First *Y*
12	200	Second *X*
14	201	Second *Y*
16	300	Third *X*
18	301	Third Y

Note: Data in decimal unless followed by an H for hex.

Finally, Table 25-24 contains a complete metafile dumped in symbolic form. For each function, the arguments are listed as 16-bit words in the order they occur in the file.

Table 25-24 **Sample metafile**

File header

Version = 300, number of objects = 5,

max recordsize = 16

Records

SetWindowOrg(0, 0)

SetWindowExt(480, 640)

CreatePenIndirect(0, 0, 0, 0, 0)

(*Black pen, handle 0*)

SelectObject(0)

CreateBrushIndirect(0, -1, 255, 0)

(*White brush, handle 1*)

SelectObject(1)

Rectangle(440, 600, 40, 40)

CreatePenIndirect(5, 0, 0, -1, 255)

(*White pen, handle 2*)

SelectObject(2)

DeleteObject(0)

CreateBrushIndirect(1, 0, 0, 0)

(*Hollow black brush, handle 0*)

SelectObject(0)

DeleteObject(1)

CreatePenIndirect(0, 0, 0, 0, 0)

(*Black pen, handle 1*)

SelectObject(1)

CreateBrushIndirect(0, -1, 255, 0)

(*White brush, handle 3*)

SelectObject(3)

```
Rectangle( 200, 360, 80, 240)
SelectObject( 2)
DeleteObject( 1)
SelectObject( 0)
DeleteObject( 3)
CreatePenIndirect( 0, 0, 0, 0, 0)
    (Black pen, handle 1)
SelectObject( 1)
CreateBrushIndirect( 0, -1, 255, 0)
    (White brush, handle 3)
SelectObject( 3)
Rectangle( 400, 200, 280, 80)
SelectObject( 2)
DeleteObject( 1)
SelectObject( 0)
DeleteObject( 3)
CreatePenIndirect( 0, 0, 0, 0, 0)
SelectObject( 1)
CreateBrushIndirect( 0, -1, 255, 0)
SelectObject( 3)
Ellipse( 380, 520, 300, 120)
SelectObject( 2)
DeleteObject( 1)
SelectObject( 0)
DeleteObject( 3)
CreatePenIndirect( 0, 0, 0, 0, 0)
SelectObject( 1)
CreateBrushIndirect( 0, -1, 255, 0)
SelectObject( 3)
Ellipse( 400, 560, 280, 440)
SelectObject( 2)
DeleteObject( 1)
```

Table 25-24 **Continued**

Records
SelectObject(0)
DeleteObject(3)
CreatePenIndirect(0, 0, 0, 0, 0)
SelectObject(1)
Polyline(3, 80, 240, 140, 120, 200, 240)
SelectObject(2)
DeleteObject(1)
CreatePenIndirect(0, 0, 0, 0, 0)
SelectObject(1)
Polyline(2, 100, 200, 180, 200)
SelectObject(2)
DeleteObject(1)
CreatePenIndirect(0, 0, 0, 0, 0)
SelectObject(1)
CreateBrushIndirect(0, -1, 255, 0)
SelectObject(3)
Polygon(4, 240, 240, 300, 120, 360, 240, 240, 240)
SelectObject(2)
DeleteObject(1)
SelectObject(0)
DeleteObject(3)
CreateFontIndirect(50, 30, 0, 0, 0, 0, x500, 0, 0, x6548, x766C, 0) (*Helv font*)
SelectObject(1)
TextOut(5, x6548, x6C6C, x6F, x140, xF0) (*string Hello<null>*)
CreateFontIndirect(16, 7, 0, 0, 513, 0, 0, x201, x2202, x7953, x7473, x6D65, 0) (*semibold System font*)

```
SelectObject( 3)
DeleteObject( 1)
CreateFontIndirect( 50, 30, 0, 0, 0, 0,
    x500, 0, 0, x6548, x766C, 0)
    (Helv font)
SelectObject( 1)
TextOut( 4, 25924, 28525, 120, 400)
    (string is Demo)
SelectObject( 3)
DeleteObject( 1)
CreatePenIndirect( 0, 0, 0, 0, 0)
SelectObject( 1)
CreateBrushIndirect( 0, -1, 255, 0)
SelectObject( 4)
Ellipse( 296, 376, 184, 264)
SelectObject( 2)
DeleteObject( 1)
SelectObject( 0)
DeleteObject( 4)
code000( void)
    (zero opcode to end file)
```

Reference

Microsoft Corp. *Microsoft Windows Programmer's Reference*. 1990. Redmond. WA: Microsoft Press.

## CHAPTER 26

PICT

Name	PICT (QuickDraw Picture Format)
Image type	Vector and bitmap; binary page-description language
Intended use	Format for Macintosh QuickDraw pictures
Owner	Apple Computer, Inc.
Last version/ revision/ release date	Color QuickDraw (Version 2)
Platforms	Primarily Macintosh; some support on PCs, UNIX workstations
Supporting applications	Many Macintosh applications; some PC word processing, desktop publishing, and graphics programs; a few PC CAD applications; UNIX graphics-translation programs
Overall assessment	Valuable for simple bitmap or vector data exchange with Macintosh; fair color capability in Color version; compact for storage of monochrome bitmap images

Advantages

PICT is one of the most commonly supported types of graphics data file on the Macintosh. PICT for Color QuickDraw Version 2.0 supports 8-bit (256-color) images drawing upon a 48-bit RGB palette (or *color table* in Macintosh terms). Monochrome bitmap data are usually stored using the fairly efficient PackBits compression scheme (see chapter 5 on MacPaint format for details of PackBits).

Disadvantages

The PICT format could support greater color depth, but is limited by Color QuickDraw, which reads and writes PICT files on the

Macintosh. Compression is available only for monochrome bitmaps in Version 2.0 QuickDraw. No gamma curve or CIE color model is included in the PICT file.

Variants

Principal PICT variations are due only to the release of new versions of QuickDraw.

PICT files for Version 1 of QuickDraw support only monochrome (black-and-white) files of up to 32K in practice (64K in theory) and fixed resolution of 72 dpi. Version 1 uses 1-byte operator codes and byte-aligned opcode data. Bitmaps are only one bit deep.

PICT files for Version 2 of QuickDraw (Color QuickDraw) support the color and larger image size noted previously. Image resolution is variable, and the original image resolution can be stored in the file. Version 2 PICT files use 2-byte operator codes, and their data are aligned on 2-byte word boundaries. In addition to monochrome bitmaps, Version 2 uses *pixel maps*, which supply up to eight bits per pixel.

Overview of file structure

PICT is a graphics-description language in which operators and data are encoded in binary. Because it is a language, not a format, PICT has few structuring requirements.

PICT files begin with a 512-byte header containing application-specific information, which can be ignored. On the Macintosh, only the data fork is used; the resource fork is empty.

After the 512-byte header, all PICT files begin with two data fields: a picture size and a picture *frame*. Then, a version opcode and number are given.

In Version 1, the remainder of the file comprises the opcodes and their associated data that, together, describe the picture. In Version 2, a short secondary header precedes this picture information. In both versions, at the end of the picture data, an end-of-file opcode is given.

Format details

This discussion presents only enough information to allow you to read or write a simple PICT file, with emphasis on bitmap images. This discussion uses mnemonic names when discussing PICT opcodes, but remember, PICT uses binary opcodes. Hexadecimal is used for all opcodes. Version 1 files use 1-byte codes; Version 2 uses 2-byte words for codes, and Version 2 data are aligned on 2-byte word boundaries.

Initial data and opcodes

PICT files begin with a 512-byte header, which can be ignored. Following this header are two data fields: a 2-byte picture size, and an 8-byte picture frame, as given in Table 26-1.

Table 26-1 **PICT initial data and opcodes**

Offset	Size (bytes)	Contents
0	2	Size of file in bytes (16 lsb only if > 64K)
2	2	Frame: top left corner *X* at 72 dpi
4	2	Frame: top left corner *Y*
6	2	Frame: lower right corner *X*
8	2	Frame: lower right corner *Y*
10(9)	2(1)	Version opcode (Version 1 is 1 byte long)
12(10)	2(1)	Version number (Version 1 is 1 byte long)

The size field is fixed at two bytes for compatibility with Version 1, so if the size of a Version 2 file exceeds 2^{16} bytes, the size field contains only the 16 least-significant bits of the size! In other words, the size field is not especially useful for Version 2 files.

The frame is an all-inclusive boundary for the picture. The coordinates are given in "dots" at 72 dots/inch (regardless of the actual resolution of the original image). For example, a 1-inch-wide picture will be recorded as 72 dots wide, regardless of its actual resolution in pixels.

Following the size and frame fields is a version opcode. The version opcode is 11 (hexadecimal) in Version 1, and 0011 in Version 2. Version 1 readers will interpret a 2-byte opcode as a 1-byte no-operation symbol, 00, followed by a 1-byte version opcode of 11.

The version number follows. The number is 01 for Version 1 and 02FF for Version 2. (Early Macintoshes, lacking a 4.1 System patch, will read 02FF as a version number of 02 and an opcode of FF. The latter is the end-of-file opcode, so QuickDraw stops reading at that point and draws nothing.)

Version 2 additional header

In Version 1, picture data follow at this point. In Version 2 files, an additional 26-byte header comes next. At minimum, this header contains a header opcode of 0C00 in the first two bytes, with 24 bytes of zero following. More recent versions might employ a fuller header, as shown in Table 26-2, that contains information on the original resolution of the image.

Table 26-2

PICT Version 2 additional header data

Offset	Size (bytes)	Contents
14	2	Version 2 header opcode, 0C00
16	2	FFFF or FFFE (-1 or -2 decimal for V2)
18	2	0000 (reserved for future use)
20	4	FFEF or original horizontal pixels/inch
24	4	Zero or original vertical pixels/inch
28	8	Zero or picture frame at original resolution
36	4	Reserved for future use

If the word following the header opcode is FFFE (-2 decimal), it indicates that original-image resolution and frame data are present in the header, at offsets 20, 24, and 28. The picture frame field (offset 28) is defined as the lower left and upper right corner (x,y) coordinates, in pixels, at the original image resolution. These data are redundant if the image section of the file contains the hRes, vRes, and bounds opcodes.

Image section

The image is designated by a series of opcodes and their data. There are operators for *text*, *lines*, *arcs*, *polygons*, *patterns*, *colors*, and *bitmap images*. This chapter omits considerations of text- and font-related operators.

Opcodes The opcodes of Version 1 are given in Table 26-3. In Version 2, the Version 1 opcodes are essentially the same, but they occupy two bytes instead of one; the first byte is zero. Version 2 also introduces new opcodes, given in Table 26-4.

Table 26-3

PICT Version 1 Opcodes

Opcode	Function	Type	Data size (bytes)
00	NOP	none	0
01	clip region	region	region
02	backgnd pattern	pattern	8
03	text font	font (word)	2
04	text typeface	face (byte)	1
05	text mode	mode (word)	2
06	extra space	extra (fixed point)	4
07	pen size	pen size (point)	4
08	pen mode	mode (word)	2
09	pen pattern	pattern	8
0A	fill pattern	pattern	8
0B	oval size	(point)	4

0C	origin point	dh, dv (words)	4
0D	text size	size (word)	2
0E	foreground color	color (long)	4
0F	background color	color (long)	4
10	text ratio	numerator (point), denominator (point)	8
11	PICT version	version (byte)	1
20	line	pen location (point), new point (point)	8
21	line from	new point (point)	4
22	short line	pen loc. (point); dh, dv (signed byte)	6
23	short line from	dh, dv (signed byte)	2
28	long text	text loc. (point), count (byte), text	5+text
29	DH text	dh (byte), count (byte), text	2+text
2A	DV text	dv (byte), count (byte), text	2+text
2B	DHDV text	dh, dv (byte), count (byte), text	3+text
30	frame rectangle	rect	8
31	paint rectangle	rect	8
32	erase rectangle	rect	8
33	invert rectangle	rect	8
34	fill rectangle	rect	8
38	frame same rect	rect	0
39	paint same rect	rect	0
3A	erase same rect	rect	0
3B	invert same rect	rect	0
3C	fill same rect	rect	0
40	frame rounded rect	rect (corner width, ht.: see code 0B)	8
41	paint rounded rect	rect	8
42	erase rounded rect	rect	8

Table 26-3 **Continued**

Opcode	Function	Type	Data size (bytes)
43	invert rounded rect	rect	8
44	fill rounded rect	rect	8
48	frame same r.rect	rect	0
49	paint same r.rect	rect	0
4A	erase same r.rect	rect	0
4B	invert same r.rect	rect	0
4C	fill same r. rect	rect	0
50	frame oval	rect	8
51	paint oval	rect	8
52	erase oval	rect	8
53	invert oval	rect	8
54	fill oval	rect	8
58	frame same oval	rect	0
59	paint same oval	rect	0
5A	erase same oval	rect	0
5B	invert same oval	rect	0
5C	fill same oval	rect	0
60	frame arc	rect, start angle, arc angle	12
61	paint arc	rect, start angle, arc angle	12
62	erase arc	rect, start angle, arc angle	12
63	invert arc	rect, start angle, arc angle	12
64	fill arc	rect, start angle, arc angle	12
68	frame same arc	start angle, arc angle	4
69	paint same arc	start angle, arc angle	4
6A	erase same arc	start angle, arc angle	4

6B	invert same arc	start angle, arc angle	4
6C	fill same arc	start angle, arc angle	4
70	frame polygon	poly	poly
71	paint polygon	poly	poly
72	erase polygon	poly	poly
73	invert polygon	poly	poly
74	fill polygon	poly	poly
78	frame same poly.	(not implemented; same as 70, etc.)	0
79	paint same poly.	(not implemented)	0
7A	erase same poly.	(not implemented)	0
7B	invert same poly.	(not implemented)	0
7C	fill same poly.	(not implemented)	0
80	frame region	region	region
81	paint region	region	region
82	erase region	region	region
83	invert region	region	region
84	fill region	region	region
88	frame same region	(not implemented; same as 80, etc.)	0
89	paint same region	(not implemented)	0
8A	erase same region	(not implemented)	0
8B	invert same region	(not implemented)	0
8C	fill same region	(not implemented)	1
90	bits rectangle	rowBytes, bounds, srcRect, dstRect, mode, unpacked bit data	28+unpacked bit data
91	bits region	rowBytes, bounds, srcRect, dstRect, mode, mask region, unpacked bit data	28+rgn+ bit data
98	PackBits rectangle	rowBytes, bounds, srcRect, dstRect,	

Table 26-3 **Continued**

Opcode	Function	Type	Data size (bytes)
		mode, packed bit data for each row	28+packed bit data
99	PackBits region	rowBytes, bounds, srcRect, dstRect, mode, mask region, packed bit data for each row	28+rgn+ packed bit data
A0	short comment	kind(word)	2
A1	long comment	kind(word), size(word), data	4+data
FF	end of picture	none	0

✻ **Data types** The data types used with the PICT opcodes have the byte lengths given below:
byte=1
signed=1 (range −128 to +127)
fixed point=4 (16 bits integer, 16 bits fraction)
integer=2
long integer=4
mode=2
pattern=8
point=4 (units of 1/72")
poly=10 or more. First word gives data size.
rect=8 (top-left, bottom-right corners *x*,*y* words)
region=10 or more. First word gives data size.
rowBytes=2.

✻ **Additional Version 2 graphics opcodes** In Version 2.0, there are some additional opcodes defined, as listed in Table 26-4.

Table 26-4 **PICT Version 2.0 Opcodes**

Opcode (bytes)	Description	Size	Data Size
0012	color background pattern	varies	varies
0013	color pen pattern	varies	varies

0014	color fill pattern	varies	varies
0015	fractional pen position	position (word)	2
0016	extra space for each character	space (word)	2
001A	RGB foreground color	R,G,B (words)	6
001B	RGB background color	R,G,B (words)	6
001C	highlight mode	none	0
001D	highlight color	R,G,B (words)	6
001E	use highlight color default	none	0
001F	RGB opColor for arithmetic modes	R,G,B (words)	6
0090	pixel rectangle ("BitsRect")	see Bitmap graphics	
0091	pixel region ("BitsRgn")	see Bitmap graphics	
0098	packed pixel rectangle ("PackBitsRect")	see Bitmap graphics	
0099	packed pixel region ("PackBitsRgn")	see Bitmap graphics	
0C00	header	see Table 26-2	

Bitmap graphics Bitmap graphics are performed with the codes 90, 91, 98, and 99. The data for these codes differ between Versions 1 and 2; a *pixmap* is substituted for the Version 1 *bitmap*. The codes operate with pixmaps only if the highest bit of the *rowBytes* value in the bitmap/pixmap data structure is set.

Only Version 2.0 operation is detailed here. (Version 1 operation uses a subset of the Version 2 data fields that can be determined by consulting Table 26-3.) The data structure that follows these opcodes is discussed in the order in which data appear: the opcodes are immediately followed by the pixMap data structure shown in Table 26-5, a color table (Table 26-6), a *source* rectangle and a *destination* rectangle (Table 26-7), a *mode*, and finally the pixel data.

A number of features that are unused are provided in Version 2.0, and values are therefore fixed. For example, while separate color planes are provided for in the data structure, they are not used by Color QuickDraw 2.0. Instead, RGB data appear in sequence for each pixel in what is termed *chunky* mode.

Table 26-5 **PICT Version 2.0 "PixMap" data structure**

Offset	Bytes	Content
0	4	base address = 0 (unused)
4	2	rowBytes: bytes/scanline. In V2 top 3 bits = flags.
6	8	bounding rectangle (top left x,y; lower right x,y)
14	2	version = 0 (for Version 2.0)
16	2	packing type = 0
18	4	packed size = 0
22	4	source *x* resolution (fixed point); default = 0048.0000
26	4	source *y* resolution (fixed point); default = 0048.0000
30	2	pixel type = 0 (signifies "chunky": RGBRGB...)
32	2	pixel size (total bits per pixel: 1,2,4,8)
34	2	# planes = 1 (for chunky)
36	2	component size = pixel size (see offset 32) for chunky
38	4	offset to next color plane = 0 (for chunky)
42	4	reserved = 0

Source *X* and *Y* resolution are in dpi, defaulting to 72.00 dpi (48 H). RowBytes is equal to the offset between scan lines in bytes; it must be an even number.

The image is based on a palette, or color table, given in Table 26-6. In this table, the RGB data are given. Pixel values are indices (up to 8-bit) to this table.

Table 26-6 **PICT Version 2.0 color table data structure**

Offset	Bytes	Content
46	4	identification number for color table = 0
50	2	color table flags = 0
52	2	# of entries, c, in color table
54	(c-1)*	2-byte values each for red, green, and blue, in sequence.

Source and destination rectangles following color table Table 26-7

Offset	Bytes	Content
Source rectangle:		
0	2	top left corner *X* at original resolution
2	2	top left corner *Y*
4	2	lower right corner *X*
6	2	lower right corner *Y*
Destination rectangle:		
8	2	top left corner *X* at 72 dpi
10	2	top left corner *Y*
12	2	lower right corner *X*
14	2	lower right corner *Y*

After the source and destination rectangles, a 2-byte *transfer mode* is given whose internal structure is not specified. This field indicates to QuickDraw how new data are to be logically combined with existing data on the output device.

The *region* opcodes 91 and 99 have a mask region of 10 or more data bytes defined at this point, depending on the shape of the region. The first word of the region gives the size of the region field.

Pixel data, the *PixData* field, is the last data field to appear. In Version 2.0 pixel maps, it contains unpacked binary data of one, two, four, or eight bits that are indices to the color table.

For Version 1 data, data are unpacked if rowBytes (bytes per row) is less than eight; otherwise they are packed according to the PackBits algorithm given in chapter 5 on MacPaint. A total of all bytes in the map, *byteCount,* is computed from the product of the rowBytes count and Ymax-Ymin of the bounding rectangle. Double this figure for a RowBytes greater than 250.

All PICT pictures end with a 00FF opcode (FF in Version 1).

There are a number of unassigned opcodes. It is important to know the length of their data fields so they can be skipped when earlier-version readers are interpreting later-version code. Their data lengths are given in Table 26-8.

Table 26-8 **Unassigned opcodes, data lengths**

Opcode group	Data length in bytes
0017–0019	0
0024–0027	2 (specifying data length) + data length
002C–002F	2 (specifying data length) + data length
0035–0037	8
003D–003F	0
0045–0047	8
004D–004F	0
0055–0057	8
005D–005F	0
0065–0067	12
006D–006F	4
0075–0077	previously specified polygon size
007D–007F	0
0085–0087	previously specified region size
008D–008F	0
0092–0097	2 (specifying data length) + data length
009A–009F	2 (specifying data length) + data length
00A2–00AF	2 (specifying data length) + data length
00B0–00CF	0
00D0–00FE	4 (specifying data length) + data length
0100–7FFF	2*nn*, where *nn* is first byte of opcode.

References

Apple Computer, Inc. *Inside Macintosh, Volume IV*. 1988. Reading, MA: Addison-Wesley Publishing Co.

Birse, Cameron, Guillermo Ortiz, and Jon Zap. "Things You Wanted To Know About PackBits," *Macintosh Technical Note #171*. 1987, 1990. Apple Computer Developer Technical Support.

Jernigan, Ginger, and Rick Blair. ""QuickDraw's Internal Picture Definition 1," *Macintosh Technical Note #21*. Apple Computer Developer Technical Support.

Ortiz, Guillermo. "32-Bit QuickDraw: Version 1.2 Features," *Macintosh Technical Note #275*. Apple Computer Developer Technical Support.

CHAPTER 27

CGM

Name	CGM (Computer Graphics Metafile)
Image type	Metafile
Intended use	Storage and interchange of graphics images
Owner	American National Standards Institute, 11 W 42nd St., New York, NY 10036, (212) 642-4900.
Last version/ revision/ release date	ANSI/ISO 8632, 1991
Platforms	PCs and workstations
Supporting applications	Most CAD programs, many drawing programs such as CorelDRAW
Similarities	Windows Metafile
Overall assessment	An official standard for graphics interchange. Large, hard to implement, and implementations are often not interoperable.

Advantages

The only official graphics file standard at this point

Disadvantages

Limited to 2-D images, hard to implement and validate, three incompatible encodings, less widely supported than simpler formats

Variants

There are three different standard encodings: *character*, *binary word*, and *readable text*. Also, implementations can and do add private element types.

Overview of file structure

The Computer Graphics Metafile is intended to be a vendor- and hardware-neutral storage and interchange format for graphics images. It was inspired by the Graphical Kernel System (ISO 7942), a standard set of graphics subroutines, and there is a fairly close correspondence between GKS routines and CGM elements. GKS is a 2-D system, and so is CGM. The newer Programmer's Hierarchical Interactive Graphics System (PHIGS) is a 3-D graphics library, and there will eventually be a 3-D version of CGM corresponding to PHIGS. PHIGS does include a CGM-like archive file format, but there is no standard binary encoding for it yet. PHIGS is in the process of being extended to PHIGS-PLUS and no standard metafile is likely until PHIGS-PLUS is complete.

CGM is a very rich format, providing support for lines, circles, ellipses, polygons, text strings, and bitmaps. A complete description would take several hundred pages, so here we look at the structure of a metafile and the three standard encodings.

A metafile is a sequence of elements, the commands defined in the CGM language. A single metafile might contain several pictures, which can be either separate images or sequential images in an animated sequence. The metafile starts with a BEGIN METAFILE element and the metafile header containing the metafile name and some overall parameters; for example, the number of bits in a color map index. Then comes a BEGIN PICTURE element and the picture header that contains the picture name and parameters for the picture, such as the scaling. Following that is the BEGIN PICTURE BODY element and the picture body, with the elements to draw the picture, and the END PICTURE element. Another picture might follow, starting with another BEGIN PICTURE. Finally, an END METAFILE marks the end of the file.

In many cases, there are multiple ways to specify something. For example, a circular arc can be specified by the center, radius, and rays that cross at the starting and ending points, or by three points through which the arc must pass. There are three different numeric encodings: *integer*, *fixed point real*, and *floating point real*, each of which has several possible sizes. Colors can be specified as explicit RGB triples of arbitrary depth, or as indices into an arbitrarily large color table.

Geometry

All image coordinates are given in terms of *Virtual Device Coordinates* (VDC). VDC can be abstract, to be scaled to the display device, or metric, in millimeters. They can be specified in any of the three numeric formats. The picture header for each picture contains the VDC of the lower left and upper right corners of the image area. By suitable choice of corner coordinates, the origin can be put anywhere inside or outside the image area. *X* coordinates can increase to the left or to the right, and *Y* coordinates can increase upwards or downwards.

Each drawing element takes a set of parameters, most of which are in terms of VDC. For example, the POLYGON element takes a set of pairs of VDC, the (X,Y) coordinates of the vertices of a polygon to be drawn.

Several dozen drawing attributes can be set. For example, when drawing a filled area, one can control whether the edges are drawn, and the width, color, and type (dotted, dashed, etc.) of the edge. Attributes can be set separately by elements, such as EDGE TYPE and EDGE WIDTH, or a group of related attributes can be "bundled" and changed as a group.

Text

The metafile header contains a list of all of the fonts used in the metafile and the character sets. For example, a font might be Swiss Bold 12-point, and a character set might be US ASCII. The set of fonts to be used is not well-standardized, and there is no well-defined fallback when a reader does not have a font that a metafile uses.

Cell arrays

CELL ARRAY elements correspond to bitmap data. Each item in the array is an RGB color or a color-map index. Curiously, the array can cover an arbitrary parallelogram, not just a rectangle, even though there probably has never been a device that can directly display a nonrectangular bitmap.

Escapes

CGM offers two escapes to allow implementations to add implementation-specific extensions. The GENERALIZED DRAWING PRIMITIVE (GDP) operator takes an integer code that says which local extension to use, a list of points in VDC that give the position, size, etc., of the object to be drawn, and a chunk of arbitrary data. The ESCAPE primitive takes an integer code and a chunk of data, and is intended for control of devices and other nondrawing extensions.

The problem with the escapes is that they make CGM files very nonportable because there is no agreement from one implementation to another as to what the escapes mean. Actual implementations have used escapes for things like nonstandard crosshatch styles.

Encodings

The CGM standard defines three separate encodings for a CGM file. The character encoding is the most compact and is intended to be usable in a data stream to a terminal, where it would be introduced by an escape sequence. The binary encoding, by far the most commonly used, is a reasonably compact sequence of bytes and 16-bit words that is intended to be easy for programs to generate and decode. The clear-text format is a verbose text version useful for debugging.

Character encoding

The character encoding is compatible with ISO 2022, the international version of the standard that defines the familiar ANSI escape sequences. Data are encoded into regular printing characters, so that they are not damaged by hardware or software that treats control characters specially. There are two slightly different variants of character encoding, depending on whether the eighth bit of each byte can be used.

A metafile is introduced by ESC % F and followed by ESC % @. Each operator is assigned a 1- or 2-byte opcode; for example, POLYGON is 26 H. Numbers are encoded in a variable length format; for example, 0 through 15 are 40 H through 5F H, 100 (64 H) is 63 44 H, and 2000 (7D0 H) is 63 7D 40 H. Real numbers are encoded in a similar way, with a fraction and an exponent. In elements that take lists of points, such as POLYGON, there is an extremely complex optional incremental mode that encodes sequential points using a fixed, table Huffman code of relative motions. CELL ARRAY data can be encoded in several formats, ranging from a list of RGB triples to run-length-encoded bit streams, all packed five or six bits to a byte with high bits set to make the bytes end up as printable characters. String data are preceded by ESC X and followed by ESC \, or in 8-bit mode preceded by 98 and followed by 9C.

Binary encoding

The binary encoding is the most commonly used, because it is by far the easiest to generate and decode and it is still reasonably compact. A metafile is a sequence of bytes and 16-bit words. Each element is a 16-bit word, high byte first, followed by a set of byte-encoded parameters.

Each element starts with a word in this format, with each letter indicating a bit:

CCCC IIIIII LLLLL

CCCC, the element class, and IIIIII, the element ID, together identify which element this is. For example, POLYGON is class 4, element 7. LLLLL is the number of bytes of parameter data that follow this header word. If there are more than 30 bytes of data, an LLLLL of all ones means that the following word contains the parameter list length. If the high bit of that word is set, another length word and more parameter data follow the data. If the data length is odd, a padding byte follows the data so that the next header is word-aligned.

Integer values, by default, are two bytes, but they can be one, two, three, or four bytes long, depending on elements that set the length of integers used as VDC separately, as color indices, and some other contexts. Reals can be 32-bit fixed point (16 integer, 16 fraction), 64-bit fixed-point (32-bit integer, 32-bit fraction), 32-bit IEEE float, or 64-bit IEEE double, with fixed vs. float, and sizes being set separately for VDC and other real values such as character spacing. VDC can be integer or either type of real.

CELL ARRAY DATA can be from one to 32 bits deep, and can be either a plain pixel list or run-length encoded.

Strings are preceded by a count byte; or, if they are 255 bytes or longer, they are preceded by an FF H byte and a 16-bit length.

Clear text encoding

The clear text encoding is intended to be readable and writable by humans using an ordinary text editor. Elements are identified by their names; for example, POLYGON is POLYGON. Some have abbreviations; COLOUR INDEX PRECISION is COLRINDEXPREC. Integers are written in decimal or with an optional base: 100, 16#64, and 8#144 are the same number. Real numbers are written with a decimal and an optional E-format exponent. Points are a pair of numbers separated by a comma, optionally enclosed in parentheses.

Each element is terminated with a semicolon; thus a complete command might be POLYGON (10,10) (110,110) (200,10). Elements that take lists of points can take absolute or relative point lists, so the same example could be written INCRPOLYGON (10,10) (100,100) (90,-100).

CELL ARRAYS are lists of pixel values, with the values for each row optionally delimited by parentheses.

Strings are delimited by single or double quotes. Comments can be present anywhere in the file a space is allowed, delimited by percent signs.

Device independence & portability

Although CGM files are intended to be portable and device-independent, in practice one CGM implementation often cannot successfully read a file generated by another. Problems include:

- Because the standard is so large, many implementations do not handle every defined element.
- The image model is more general than many devices can handle. For example, a pen plotter has only a small, fixed set of colors and no reasonable way to draw a bitmap.
- The interpretation of some elements is deliberately left ambiguous. For example, if the color map is changed part way through a picture, it is implementation-dependent whether elements already drawn change color. If the output model is a raster-scan CRT, it makes sense for them to change; if the output is a color inkjet printer, they don't.
- There is no practical standardization of font names, and some implementations don't even try to display text in unknown fonts.
- Files that use GDP or ESCAPE elements are not portable.

The message here is not to assume that an application can handle a particular CGM file until you actually try it. Simple files with small numbers of colors, and no text, are relatively safe, but the more complex the file the greater the likelihood of failure.

References

American National Standards Institute/International Organization for Standards. ANSI/ISO 8632-1987.1. *Information Processing Systems—Computer Graphics—Metafile for the Storage and Transfer of Picture Description Information—Part 1*: "Functional Description." 1987. New York: ANSI. (Formerly ANSI X3.122-1986.)

American National Standards Institute/International Organization for Standards. ANSI/ISO 8632-1987.2. *Information Processing Systems—Computer Graphics—Metafile for the Storage and Transfer of Picture Description Information—Part 2*: "Character Encoding". 1987. New York: ANSI. (Formerly ANSI X3.122-1986.)

American National Standards Institute/International Organization for Standards. ANSI/ISO 8632-1987.3. *Information Processing Systems—Computer Graphics—Metafile for the Storage and Transfer of Picture Description Information—Part 3*: "Binary Encoding." 1987. New York: ANSI. (Formerly ANSI X3.122-1986.)

American National Standards Institute/International Organization for Standards. ANSI/ISO 8632-1987.4. *Information Processing Systems—Computer Graphics—Metafile for the Storage and Transfer of Picture Description Information—Part 4*: "Clear Text Encoding." 1987. New York: ANSI. (Formerly ANSI X3.122-1986.)

American National Standards Institute/International Organization for Standards. ANSI/ISO 9592. *Computer Graphics*—"Programmer's Hierarchical Interactive Graphics Systems (PHIGS)." 1989. New York: ANSI. (Formerly ANSI X3.144-1988.)

CHAPTER 28

RIB

Name	RIB (Renderman* Interface Bytestream)
Image type	Scene description (contains vector data for 3-D objects)
Intended use	Convey scene, camera, and lighting information to rendering applications
Owner	Pixar, 3240 Kerner Blvd., San Rafael, CA 94901 (415) 258-8100
Last version/ revision/ release date	Version 3.1, September 1989
Platforms	Platform-independent; found on UNIX workstations, Macintoshes, and PCs.
Supporting applications	Pixar software; Wavefront software; Alias' Open Digital Studio; Digital Arts' RenderManager (all UNIX SGI); Alias' Upfront (PC/Mac); Autodesk's AutoShade (PC); MacroMedia's Macromodel & 3-D (Mac); Point Line Renderman (PC); Pixar's Showplace (Mac); Stone Design's 3-D Reality (NEXTstep); Valis Tookit (Mac); VIDI's Presenter Professional (Mac); others
Similarities	Superficially, PostScript in structure; DXF in conveying 3-D data
Overall assessment	A highly specialized "language" for high-quality rendering; contains and accepts 3-D model data.

Advantages

RIB is one of the most sophisticated systems for conveying information to a rendering application—software that creates realistic two-dimensional images from three-dimensional scene information. It is, arguably, the closest thing to an industry standard for this purpose. It conveys 3-D shapes, surfaces, surface qualities and textures, lighting, camera, spatial transformations, and image quality; it can convey multiple frames for animated sequences. The 3-D model data contained with RIB or RIB Entity files may be of use in non-rendering applications if no other source of the data is available. The RIB specification, while arcane, is easily obtained from Pixar.

Disadvantages

RIB readers are complex applications to write, on the order of PostScript readers or higher. To be Renderman-compliant, the application must be capable of executing all the standard functions defined in the Renderman interface specification. RIB is not designed for other, more limited uses, such as simply storing 3-D models. It does not contain 2-D bitmap or vector images.

Variants

RIB has two principal forms: ASCII, and for compactness, a mixed ASCII/binary form that will not be covered here. Another variant of RIB is the RIB Entity file, which typically contains only a single object such as a 3-D shape, with no scene context.

RIB is itself a variant of *Renderman*. Renderman (or, more accurately, the Renderman Interface) is a specification that has two forms of implementation, or "binding": a C-language form, comprising defined function calls to a scene renderer, and the RIB form, which is a more general, non-language-specific implementation, or metafile. Function call names in the C-language binding are generally identical to the RIB commands, but are prefixed by the letters "Ri."

Overview of file structure

The RIB file consists of a series of command lines (typically ASCII, but possibly binary) using predefined terms, such as Sphere, and associated parameters such as a number representing the diameter of the sphere. The terms define not only the 3-D objects to be imaged, but also a "graphic state" that specifies a camera, lighting, mattes, color variables, opacity, coordinate systems, and other variables that affect the appearance of the image to be created. Many of the special effects that the Renderman interface is capable of specifying come from terms that invoke "shaders" developed by Pixar and others. Shaders affect various parts of the image, ranging from a single surface of an object to the entire scene. The shader ShinyMetal, for instance, gives an object a reflective metallic appearance, while the shader Fog induces an atmospheric effect for the entire scene. When an object appears in the RIB file, it takes on the appearance currently defined by the graphics state: the current color, surface pattern, lighting shaders, surface shaders, etc. Certain elements of the graphics state (such as default object color or surface shaders) may then be changed prior to the next object's definition, and so forth for all objects in the scene.

RIB files are structured hierarchically. Terms that define the camera, the image plane, and other factors in the graphic state relating to the overall scene (called "options") appear within the top level of the hierarchy, which is defined at the beginning of the file. Subordinate to those terms is the "world," which specifies the content of the scene. To make it easier to associate certain appearances (such as lights or surface qualities) with individual objects, "attribute" blocks may be defined within a world. There may also be User Entities within a world that combine various objects and surface qualities into a module, comprising a sort of "clip art" entity. RIB files may optionally be divided into one or more Frames—individual cells that permit rendering of animation sequences.

Format details

The Renderman Interface specification defines more than 100 functions that affect the rendered image. The details of these functions—how they affect the image and how they interrelate—are complex. Many of them involve special geometric and rendering concepts, such as *splines* and *texture mapping*. A full description would be beyond the scope of this book. This chapter will focus upon a minimal subset of RIB terms that might permit obtaining a 2-D image from simple geometric primitives contained in an RIB file, or conveying a very basic scene to a Renderman renderer. It will describe the fundamental terms that convey 3-D geometric data, camera orientation, coordinate systems, and image information, and will provide only a few examples of shaders, lighting, and other terms that control rendering.

Commands & structural hints

RIB files are made up of two fundamental types of terms: *commands* (actually, calls to procedures) and *structural hints*, which are preceded by the characters ##. There are also comment lines, preceded by the single character, #.

RIB commands are followed on a line by arguments. For example, the command Surface is followed by a *name* and an argument that is called a *parameter list* as follows:

Surface *name parameterlist*

For instance: Surface "metal" "Ka" 0.1 "Kd" 0.6 "Ks" 0.4 "roughness" 0.1

The *name* metal describes a surface shader giving a metallic appearance, and the *parameter list* (composed of token-value pairs such as Ka and 0.1) describes how it reflects light. Often, arguments are either integers or floating point numbers with absolute values between 0 and 1.

Structural hints may appear in the RIB header or at the start of a frame, and can generally be ignored. They are not commands to the rendering software, but to a higher-level rendering manager program that chooses appropriate renderer(s) and other resources necessary to create the image. In the header they convey administrative information or specify any additional, non-standard rendering "resources" or "capabilities" used by the RIB file (see following section for definitions of these terms). For example, one structural hint used in the header is ##CreationDate. Structural hints may also appear at the start of a *frame* (a single cell of an animation) and may specify special resources needed by the frame.

Commands may appear just about anywhere within the file. Depending on where they appear in the file hierarchy, their scope will be different. For example, commands appearing in the header will generally relate to all frames in the file; commands appearing within an "attribute" block will relate to a particular object or set of objects in the scene.

Resources

Some commands, like Surface, invoke "resources." Renderman resources consist of software routines called "shaders," "textures," or "capabilities." In the previous example, metal is a shader; another shader, paintedplastic, takes a texture as an argument. *Shaders* are routines written in the C-like Renderman Shading Language, compiled with a special compiler and made available by the software that manages the rendering task.

A shader gives a particular appearance, such as "ShinyMetal" or "Fog," or creates a light source. Their effect varies in scope and may include the whole scene, a set of objects, a single object, or just a piece of an object, depending upon the shader and where in the Renderman hierarchy it is invoked. There are 14 standard shaders that a Renderman-compliant renderer must provide. (Other, optional shaders, if they are used in an RIB file, are listed after a ##Shaders hint in the file header, and then again within the frame where they are used.) Shaders typically affect exterior surfaces, atmosphere (like "Fog"), interior volumes, surface perturbations ("displacements"), and lights. There may be many lighting or atmosphere shaders active at one time, but only a single surface shader. A *texture* may be used by certain shaders to modify the appearance of a surface.

A capability is a rendering activity that is optional to a Renderman-compliant renderer, such as *ray tracing*, a specific form of rendering. If any such capabilities are required by an RIB file, they are called out in the header by a ##CapabilitiesNeeded hint.

Graphics state

An RIB renderer must maintain a "graphics state." This includes such features as: camera specifications; color and opacity for objects; a current transformation that is applied to objects in order to translate their coordinates into world space; the state of the light source(s); and surface and other shading options. When an object is defined, it takes on the appearance dictated by the current graphics state.

The graphics state changes continually as commands are executed. However, certain aspects of the graphics state can be frozen or effectively made local to different levels of the RIB hierarchy. For example, the camera and its relationship to the world is frozen (cannot be altered) upon entering a World Begin-End block; such options (image qualities relating to the entire scene) must be set up before the block begins. Color or lighting can be effectively made local to an object by bracketing the color change command and the object definition within AttributeBegin-AttributeEnd statements. The graphics state is saved when the AttributeBegin statement is executed, and is restored with the AttributeEnd statement.

Perhaps most critical to proper scene interpretation is the *current transformation*. A transformation matrix similar to that of PostScript (but with an additional dimension) is maintained:

```
a b c 0
d e f 0
g h i 0
j k l 1
```

Commonly, the fourth column is as shown above, but may have other values for operations such as perspective transformations. The matrix describes how to transform subsequently appearing coordinates x, y, z into global coordinates X, Y, Z following the linear equations, $X=ax+dy+gz+j$, $Y=bx+ey+hz+k$, $Z=cx+fy+iz+l$. The default orientation is left-handed: if X is to the right, and Y is up, then Z points away from the observer. The fourth column creates the symmetric 4 x 4 matrix necessary to allow ongoing matrix multiplication (concatenation), the process by which the coordinate system may be repeatedly translated, rotated, or scaled.

It is important to observe that, unlike some other rendering schemes, Renderman transformations are given before an object is defined, not after. It is as if the renderer maintained a stack of sequential transformations; to transform object coordinates into world space, it then popped transformations off the stack and executed them in reverse order. For instance, if two transformation commands appear in an RIB file (first a translation, then a rotation followed by the object), the object coordinates would first be rotated, then translated, to convert them to world coordinates. A more accurate way of thinking about transformations is that each subsequent transformation modifies the coordinate system (in effect, adjusting coordinate space to meet the object, rather than the other way around), but this is less intuitive to visualize.

The current transformation can be directly set by use of the Transform command, or directly concatenated by the ConcatTransform command. It may also be implicitly altered by the more convenient Translate, Rotate, and Scale commands. The syntax for these commands is as follows:

(examples show 0, 0, 0, 1 in the last matrix column, which may not always be the case)

- **Transform** ***[16 parameters of 4 x 4 matrix: a b c 0 d e f 0 g h i 0 j k l 1]*** which sets the current transformation matrix to the given matrix:
- **ConcatTransform** ***[a b c 0 d e f 0 g h i 0 j k l 1]*** which concatenates the given matrix onto the current transformation matrix:
- **Translate** ***delta-X delta-Y delta-Z*** where the arguments are floating point numbers:
- **Rotate** ***rotation delta-X delta-Y delta-Z*** where the arguments are floating point numbers; the rotation is an angle in degrees about the vector given by *delta-X delta-Y delta-Z*. Rotation follows a left-hand rule: align your left thumb along the vector and your fingers will point in the positive rotation direction.

Transformations can be kept local to an object by using TransformBegin—TransformEnd blocks. TransformBegin copies the current transformation, pushing it onto a stack, and TransformEnd pops it off, making it the current transformation again. This allows you to make the transformations necessary to properly orient an object in world space without having to sequentially reverse them again after the object is defined. Another set of statements, AttributeBegin and AttributeEnd, save and restore the entire graphics state, including the transformation, so they implicitly do the same thing.

Header

The header contains structural hints and commands pertaining to all frames, such as camera and image specifications. The most common of the hints include the following:

##RenderMan RIB-Structure 1.0	the required first line of an RIB file
##Frames *count*	the number of frames present (integer)
##Shaders *shadername, shadername, ...*	shaders other than the standard 14
##Textures *texturename, texturename, ...*	special surface appearances
##OptionalCapabilities *capability, capability, ...*	capabilities common to multiple frames, other than the standard Renderman capabilities

Other structural hints are administrative, such as ##Scene, ##Creator, ##CreationDate, and ##For, and take arbitrary, user-determined text as arguments.

After hints, commands that control *options* (variables affecting the entire scene) appear.

Frame

Within an RIB file used for animation there may be frames. Each frame contains its own option commands, followed by a single world, or scene. Its organization is typically as follows; the assigned frame number (an integer) is shown in italics:

FrameBegin *n*
structural hints (as in the header)
"option" commands for frame (e.g., camera orientation and projection)
    WorldBegin
    lights, shaders, transformations ("attributes") to be used for the whole scene
        AttributeBegin
        shaders for a particular object (e.g., a surface shader)
        lights for a particular object
        transformations for a particular object
        geometric primitives defining object, or
        object "instance"
        AttributeEnd
        more attribute begin-end blocks
    WorldEnd
FrameEnd

One important structural hint that may appear in a frame or, for that matter, anywhere within the file is the command ##Include *file*, which specifies another RIB file for inclusion.

Options (camera & display)

"Options" are aspects of the graphics state that apply to the entire image or scene. Commands controlling options are principally for the camera and the display (the 2-D plane where the final image is being created). They must be given before entering a WorldBegin-End block. Options are frozen upon entering a World block, and the current transformation matrix becomes the camera-coordinate transformation, defining the orientation of the camera to the world, with the camera pointed along the +*Z* axis. Options may include specifications for image resolution, pixel-aspect ratio, cropping, rendering region, and camera lens, although these are not essential to our purposes here. More important commands for our purposes are Clipping and Projection. The first, if used, will determine what objects are included and excluded according to their *Z*-axis distance from the camera. The second will determine if a perspective or orthographic projection is wanted.

* **Clipping *min max*** The limits *min* and *max* are positive real numbers along the viewing axis in the camera's coordinate system. Objects between these limits will appear in the final image; outside these limits, they will not. In a perspective projection, these will determine the full range of distance depicted.

* **Projection *type parameterlist*** The argument *type* can be either of the two strings perspective or orthographic (quotes should be written). If orthographic, then no parameter list is given. If perspective, then the *parameterlist* is the token fov followed by a real number in degrees, representing the field of view.

There are many commands to specify the image and camera, but for our purposes here, the defaults that apply when these commands are omitted will, in general, suffice. A couple of common commands are listed below:

* **Display *name type mode parameterlist*** This command determines the output of the rendering job. The argument *name* is either a file name or a named frame buffer, depending upon *mode*, which specifies either file or framebuffer. The argument *mode* specifies color space, and other details of the image plane. This command may also include a parameter list with the parameter origin [*xoffset yoffset*] to reposition the image that is output to the display.

* **Format *hres vres pix_aspect_ratio*** This command specifies resolution and aspect ratio; the resolution terms are integers, and the aspect-ratio term is the ratio of pixel width to pixel height, as a floating point number.

World

A *world* contains the series of objects to be used in a single scene, and may also include specific additions or changes to the graphics state intended to affect specific objects or sets of objects. Objects contained in the world may be bracketed in Attribute begin-end blocks, along with any associated change to the graphics state, such as a transformation or color. A WorldBegin command fixes the relationship of the camera and the image to a set of "world" coordinates according to the current transformation, with the camera pointing along the +*Z* axis. Within the world, subsequent transformations and other changes to the graphics state (e.g., *color*) are made for each object. A WorldEnd command denotes the end of all data for a scene.

Attribute

An AttributeBegin—AttributeEnd block allows modifications to the graphics state to be made specific to certain objects. AttributeBegin saves current attributes (such as shaders, color, and the state of light sources), and AttributeEnd restores the original attributes. Lights, shaders, and other changes to the graphics state effected within the Attribute block are local to objects within that block; they do not apply outside it, because the original graphics state is restored at the end of the block. In effect, the attribute block associates particular appearances (changes to the graphics state) with objects when they occur together within the block.

Occasionally an Attribute Begin-End block will define an area light source, composed of light-radiating geometric primitives. This sort of block will contain an AreaLightSource command, followed by the radiating primitives. It should not be confused with an ordinary light source that is simply illuminating subsequent primitives.

Lighting commands

An RIB file may define a list of light sources to be used, generally before the WorldBegin—WorldEnd block if they are used for the entire scene. Once a light source is defined, it is turned on and remains in existence throughout the remainder of the scene. The state of the source is part of the graphics state, however, allowing the source to be switched on or off at any point with the Illuminate command. Any surfaces defined while a source is on will be subject to illumination from that source. Light sources may also be defined anywhere within the world block, and if they immediately precede an object, will share the current transformation for that object. The location of the source is by default at [0,0,0] in the coordinate system of the current transformation. The direction of the light (if it is directional) is by default along the +*Z* axis of that coordinate system. Both location and direction may also be specified explicitly, relative to that coordinate system.

Light sources may use one of four standard shader types—ambientlight, pointlight, distantlight, or spotlight—or may employ user-defined light-source shaders. "Ambient" light is uniform in all directions; "point" light is a point source; "distant" light is parallel rays, and "spot" light is a conical beam. The principal RIB command used to invoke these shaders is LightSource.

LightSource *"shader" ID [parameters]*

The *shader* is any of the four types listed above. The ID is an arbitrary integer. The parameter list may include a variety of parameters, often one or more of the following: intensity, lightcolor, from, to, coneangle, conedeltaangle, beamdistribution. As with all parameter lists, each term is paired with a value; for example, LightSource "ambientlight" 2 "lightcolor" [0.9 0 0.2]. The ambientlight shader takes the first two parameters listed above; distantlight, the first four; pointlight, the first three; and spotlight, all seven. Parameters not specified will default. The intensity parameter takes a floating point number (default 1); lightcolor takes an RGB float triplet in brackets, such as [0.9 0.5 0] (default [1 1 1]); from and to take *XYZ* coordinates (default [0 0 0] and [0 0 1], respectively, in the current coordinate system), and define a direction vector; coneangle takes an angle in radians (default 30), describing the spread of the light cone from a spotlight.

To turn a light source on or off anywhere within the scene, use its ID number in the following command:

Illuminate *ID enable*

where *enable* is 1 for "on" and 0 for "off."

Geometric primitives

RIB often describes objects in terms of various geometric primitives, including polygons, patches, meshes, and conventional shapes like cones, spheres, and toroids, called *quadrics*. RIB may also use a variety of complex shapes such as parametric surfaces, including Bezier and Non-Uniform rational B-splines (NURBs). Only primitives will be discussed here.

Objects are not solid unless they (singly or in combination) describe a closed volume and are enclosed in SolidBegin and SolidEnd blocks. Objects are defined in their own coordinate space, generally with a left-hand orientation: that is, if *X* is to the right, *Y* is up and *Z* is away from you. If it is otherwise, the command ReverseOrientation appears before objects are defined, and the *Z* axis is flipped.

Primitives have certain required arguments, such as radius for a sphere, followed by required or optional *parameter lists* that may specify positions (typically vertices), a normal vector, color, opacity, or texture coordinates. Parameter lists are composed of token-value pairs. A token appears in quotes, (such as P, for "positions"). A single value or an array of values (in brackets) follows each token. For instance, if the primitive is to have a surface color other than the default color given by the graphic state, the token Cs appears, followed by color values. However, color and most other parameters are of a type called *varying*, meaning that the parameter is specified at the limits of the primitive and linearly interpolated across its surface. Accordingly, for Cs in a polygon, an array containing one RGB triplet for each vertex follows.

Other common letters are Pz (for a polygon type primitive only) indicating an elevation map varying only in one direction (with single

Z values following); N or Np indicates an explicit normal (3-D vector); Os indicates the opacity of each of the following primaries; and s, t and st indicate texture coordinates, which we will not discuss here. The parameter list is generally the last argument in the command line. Generally, the normal for planar primitives is not given, being predefined as perpendicular to the plane of the plane. The default color of an object is derived from the graphics state, as established by the Color command. This color may be overridden by the Cs parameter in the parameter list of an object.

Some of the essential commands for describing objects using geometric primitives are as follows:

- **Color *R G B*** where *R*, *G*, and *B* are floating point values for the default three standard primaries (although other color spaces may be used), and together specify a surface color for subsequent objects.

- **Polygon "P" [*x1 y1 z1 x2 y2 z2* ...]** where P is a token indicating that the subsequent data are vertices, and [*x1 y1 z1 x2 y2 z2* ...] is the list of floating point vertices in 3-D space describing a closed, planar polygon with a convex perimeter and no holes. There may be additional token-value pairs (besides "P"-[ ]) in the parameter list.

- **GeneralPolygon [*verticesA verticesB* ...] "P" [*x1A y1A z1A x2A y2A z2A* ... *x1B y1B z1B x2B y2B z2B* ...]** is similar to the Polygon command, but describes a planar polygon, with perimeter concavity and holes permitted; *verticesA* is a count of vertices in polygon A, with vertices 1, 2, ... given by *x1A y1A z1A x2A y2A z2A* ...; the first polygon describes the outer boundary, and subsequent polygons describe holes in that boundary. As with the polygon command, there may be additional parameters in the list.

- **PointsPolygon [*verticesA verticesB* ...] [*indexA indexB* ...] "P" [*x1A y1A z1A x2A y2A z2A* ... *x1B y1B z1B x2B y2B z2B* ...]** is similar to the GeneralPolygon command, but describes a collection of adjoining polygons not necessarily in the same plane. The term [*indexA indexB* ...] is an array of indices into the vertex list (following P); it gives the set of vertices for each polygon.

- **Sphere *radius-plane +plane angle parameter_list*** defines a sphere (or spherical section). As with all quadrics, it is rotationally symmetric about the primitive's *Z* axis, with coordinates being real numbers and angles given in degrees. The arguments–*plane* and +*plane* give real *Z* values that define minimum and maximum clipping planes for the quadric. The argument *angle* defines a sweep about the *Z* axis beginning at the *X* axis (clockwise, when looking at the *XY* plane). Spherical sections are considered open, not closed surfaces. All four arguments must be given for a quadric.

- **Cone *height radius angle parameter_list*** is a quadric command describing an open cone whose apex is along the *Z* axis at the point *height*, and whose base is upon the *XY* plane. The *radius* and *angle* arguments are as for the Sphere command.

- **Cylinder *radius -plane +plane angle parameter_list*** is a quadric command describing an open cylinder or cylindrical section about the *Z* axis, and follows the form of the Sphere command.

- **Hyperboloid *pointAx pointAy pointAz pointBx pointBy pointBz angle parameter_list*** is a quadric command describing a shape created by sweeping a line segment about the *Z* axis. The *point* arguments are endpoints of the line, and *angle* is as for the Sphere command.

- **Paraboloid *maxradius -plane +plane angle parameter_list*** is a quadric command describing a paraboloid about the *Z* axis whose base is upon the *XY* plane, and whose maximum radius is given by *maxradius* (occurring at *Z* = +*plane*). The *plane*, *radius*, and *angle* arguments are as for the Sphere command. The entire paraboloid must be above the *XY* plane.

- **Disk *height radius angle parameter_list*** is a quadric command describing a disk or disk segment of zero thickness, at *height* above the *XY* plane, and otherwise following the form of the Sphere command.

* **Torus *radius thickness -angle +angle angle parameter_list*** is a quadric command describing a toroid (or segment of a toroid) encircling the *Z* axis, with its inner circumference at distance *radius* from the *Z* axis, and outer circumference at distance *radius+thickness*. The toroid may have a cross-section that is a pie slice, rather than circular, specified by *-angle* and *+angle*, which are angles below and above the *XY* plane. The *angle* argument is as it is for the Sphere command.

* **SolidBegin *boolean* and *SolidEnd*** are delimiters that combine a group of enclosed primitives (of the same type) to form a solid. Primitives such as polygons, if defined outside of such delimiters, are considered hollow. The argument *boolean* is one of the following logical operators: primitive, union, difference, and intersection. The *primitive* operator defines one or more primitives that form an enclosed surface as a solid. The *union* operator yields a single merged solid (if primitives intersect); *difference* subtracts the volumes represented by all subsequent primitives from the first primitive; *intersection* yields a single volume composed of the intersecting, or common, volumes of the given primitives.

* **ObjectBegin *ID#* and ObjectEnd** are delimiters that assign an identification number to a collection of enclosed primitives or solids for future reference. The object is only defined, not rendered, when this block is encountered. The object is rendered with the command ObjectInstance *ID#*, using the current graphics state (e.g., transformation and color).

Example

The following example is based on an RIB file obtained via the Internet from a public archive at Purdue University. Note that RIB files are typically generated automatically and, as a result, may have unnecessary statements, excessively deep nesting of blocks, and other inefficiencies.

```
# Multicolor tetrahedron
Display "colortet.tif" "file" "rgba" # Specify image resolution
Format 450 450 1
# Set up camera
```

```
ScreenWindow -1 1 -1 1
Clipping 0.1 100
Projection "perspective" "fov" 40
# View along -Z axis
ConcatTransform [1 0 0 0 0 1 0 0 0 0 -1 0 0 0 0 1]
# Displacement -3 along Z axis
ConcatTransform [1 0 0 0 0 1 0 0 0 0 1 0 0 0 -3 1]
# Set up ambient light for scene
LightSource "ambientlight" 0 "lightcolor" [0.2 0.2 0.2]
# Set up directional lights for scene
LightSource "distantlight" 9 "intensity" 0.6 "lightcolor" [1 1 1] "to"
[0 0 -10]
LightSource "distantlight" 10 "intensity" 0.5 "lightcolor" [1 1 1] "to"
[0 -1 1]
LightSource "distantlight" 11 "intensity" 0.4 "lightcolor" [1 1 1] "to"
[-1 2 1]
WorldBegin
TransformBegin
# Position object
ConcatTransform [0.393919 0 0 0 0 0.393919 0 0 0 0 0.393919 0 0 -
0.185695 -0.262613 1]
AttributeBegin
# Invoke shader for plastic surfaces
Surface "plastic" "Ka" 0.3 "Kd" 1 "Ks" 0.3 "specularcolor" [1 1 1] "roughness" 0.0666667
# Face 1
Color [0.784314 0 0]
Polygon
"P" [1.63299 -0.942809 -0.666667   0 0 2   -1.63299 -0.942809 -0.666667]
"N" [0 -0.942809 0.333333   0 -0.942809 0.333333   0 -0.942809 0.333333]
# Face 2
Color [0 0.784314 0]
Polygon
"P" [0 1.88562 -0.666667   0 0 2   1.63299 -0.942809 -0.666667]
"N" [0.816497 0.471405 0.333333   0.816497 0.471405 0.333333   0.816497 0.471405
0.333333]
#Face 3
Color [0 0 0.784314]
Polygon
"P" [-1.63299 -0.942809 -0.666667   0 0 2   0 1.88562 -0.666667] "N" [-0.816497 0.471405
0.333333   -0.816497 0.471405 0.333333   -
```

```
0.816497 0.471405 0.333333]
#Face 4
Color [0.784314 0 0.784314]
Polygon
"P" [-1.63299 -0.942809 -0.666667   0 1.88562 -0.666667   1.63299 -
0.942809 -0.666667]
"N" [0 0 -1   0 0 -1   0 0 -1]
AttributeEnd
# push appearance
TransformEnd
WorldEnd
```

References

Pixar. *The Renderman Interface, Version 3.1*. September, 1989. San Rafael, CA.

Upstill, Steve. *The Renderman Companion*. 1992. Addison-Wesley Publishing Co.

CHAPTER 29

FLI/FLC

Name	FLI/FLC (AutoDesk "Flick" Formats)
Image type	Bitmap
Intended use	Animation of color bitmap images
Owner	AutoDesk, Inc., 2320 Marin Ship Way, Sausalito, CA (415) 332-2344
Last version/ revision/ release date	Corresponds to AutoDesk Animator, Animator Pro
Platforms	Principally PCs (Intel byte order implicit)
Supporting applications	AutoDesk Animator, Animator Pro; other PC applications for animation such as Macromedia's Action!, Alpa Software's Bravo, Gold Disk's Animation Works Interactive, IBM's Storyboard Live!, Mathematica's Tempra Show
Similarities	Superficially, Apple QuickTime movies using animation compression (RLE)
Overall assessment	Quick and simple open format for animation; older FLI has limited image quality.

Advantages

FLI and FLC are fairly open formats employing frame-to-frame differencing and run-length compression. They are relatively easy to decode and encode, and are suitable for brief animations of computer-generated color graphics. An increasing number of applications allow import/export.

Disadvantages

The older format, FLI, is limited to images of 320 × 200 pixels, a 64-color palette, and 4000 frames per file. There is no provision for audio in either FLI or FLC. The RLE compression scheme is neither designed nor particularly suitable for video or dithered images. The palette of both formats is limited to 256 colors (differing in bits/pixel), and, although the palette can be changed from line to line to give the effect of more colors per frame, FLI/FLC is not effective for images with many colors or fine gradations in color.

Variants

The two variants of Autodesk "flick" files are FLI and FLC; they are the original and second-generation animation formats, respectively, of Autodesk. FLI is associated with Autodesk's Animator, and FLC with Animator Pro.

The principal improvements offered by FLC are: (a) greater size or resolution—up to 2^{16} pixels in width and height vs. FLI's fixed 320 × 200; (b) variable speed in milliseconds/frame vs. FLI's "ticks per frame" at 70 ticks per second; (c) information on the original $X{:}Y$ aspect ratio of the images vs. FLI's implicit 6:5 ratio; (d) ability to include reduced-size thumbnail or "preview" images, presumably to simplify editing; (e) eight bits per primary color vs. six bits in FLI. These improvements are embodied by differences in the header and the addition of new data chunks.

Overview of file structure

The general structure of an FLI or FLC file is a sequence of frames, each frame containing only pixels that differ from the preceding frame. The first frame, however, is encoded as a complete bitmap (compressed). In general, frames may also contain changes in palette or a code to clear the frame to black. Pixel data are almost always run-length encoded (RLE), but may occasionally be uncompressed for images where RLE is not efficient (such as where data are random). FLI files use single-byte RLE (one byte of count and one byte of data); FLC files use 2-byte (word) RLE to accommodate the larger or higher-resolution images of FLC.

In theory, all FLI/FLC animations must loop; in practice, this requirement is often ignored. If an animation does loop, an extra loop frame appears at the end that gives the difference between the last true frame and the initial frame in the file. This loop frame is not counted in the frame count given by the file header.

Format details

The sequence of frames in an FLI or FLC file is preceded by a header, giving the file size, frame count, frame rate, and resolution. Number fields in this and other FLI headers are in little-endian, or Intel byte order, with least-significant bytes appearing first. After the file header, the file is divided into frames. (FLC files may also have a *prefix* between the header and the frames.) Each frame consists of a frame header and one or more data structures called *chunks*. Chunks of video or palette data are further subdivided into *packets*.

File header

The FLI and FLC headers are 128 bytes long, with contents as shown in Tables 29-1 and 29-2.

Table 29-1

FLI file header

Offset	Size	Name	Description
0	4	Size	Integer, byte length of file
4	2	"magic"	Magic number Hex AF11, FLI identifier
6	2	Size	Number of frames in file; 4000 max
8	2	Width	Screen width (320 pixels)

10	2	Height	Screen height (200 pixels)
12	2	none	blank
14	2	Flags	Set to 0
16	2	Speed	Number of video ticks per frame @ 70 ticks/sec
18	4	Next	Set to 0
22	4	Frit	Set to 0
26	102	Expansion	All zeroes—for future expansion

FLC file header Table 29-2

Offset	Size	Name	Description
0	4	Size	Integer, byte length of file
4	2	"magic"	Magic number Hex AF12, FLC identifier
6	2	Size	Number of frames in file; 4000 max
8	2	Width	Screen width (pixels)
10	2	Height	Screen height (pixels)
12	2	Bits/primary	8
14	2	Flags3	Indicating file properly closed
16	4	Speed	Milliseconds delay per frame
20	4	unused	0
22	4	Created	Creation date, MS-DOS format
26	4	Creator	Serial # of Animator Pro program used to create animation
			If not Animator Pro, then ASCII "FLIB" (hex 464C4942)
30	4	Updated	Most recent update date, MS-DOS format
34	4	Updater	Like Creator, but for most recent update
38	2	AspectX	X portion of aspect ratio X:Y
40	2	AspectY	Y portion of aspect ratio X:Y
42	38	reserved	all zeroes
80	4	Offset1	Offset from beginning of file to first frame chunk
84	4	Offset2	Offset to second frame chunk, used for looping
88	40	reserved	All zeroes

FLC files are generally found in the following resolutions: 320 × 200, 640 × 480, 800 × 600, 1280 × 1024.

In FLC files, a prefix chunk may follow. This data structure contains no information useful for playback and may be omitted or skipped. Its presence may be detected and the prefix skipped by reading the 16 bytes following the file header. Normally, these next 16 bytes are a frame header, as shown in Table 29-3. If a prefix is present, the first four bytes give the prefix size in bytes (including the 16 bytes); the next two bytes contain the code Hex F100.

Frames

A frame contains the data for a single screen of pixels, and generally does not exceed 64K bytes in length. AutoDesk Animator does not accept longer frames. A frame begins with a 16-byte frame header, described in Table 29-3, and is followed by chunks of various types of data. Generally, the order of these chunks is 1) a color chunk if the palette has changed, 2) pixel data chunks. The first frame may also begin with a clear-screen-to-black chunk.

Table 29-3 **FLI/FLC frame header**

Offset	Size	Name	Description
0	4	Size	Bytes in frame, including header (< 64K for FLI)
4	2	ID	Hex F1FA, identifying this as a frame
6	2	Chunks	Number of "chunks" in frame; 0 indicates identical frame
8	8	reserved	All zeroes

FLC files may sometimes have an ID code of Hex 00A1 in the header, signifying that the frame does not contain pixel data, but other Animator Pro data. Such a frame may be skipped by using the frame length given by Size, the 4-byte integer preceding the ID code.

Chunks follow the frame header. Each starts with a chunk header. The chunk header is outlined in Table 29-4.

Chunk header

Table 29-4

Offset	Size	Name	Description
0	4	Size	Bytes in chunk, including header
4	2	Type code	Type of chunk

Chunk types are given by Tables 29-5 and 29-6. FLC files will generally use FLI_COLOR_256 instead of FLI_COLOR, and FLI_WORD_LCinstead of FLI_LC.

FLI Chunk codes & interpretation

Table 29-5

Code	Name	Type of chunk indicated by code
11	FLI_COLOR	Compressed data for 64-color palette
12	FLI_LC	Line compressed (RLE pixel data)
13	FLI_BLACK	Set whole screen to color 0 (appears in first frame only)
15	FLI_BRUN	Bytewise run-length compression—first frame only
16	FLI_COPY	Uncompressed data (64K bytes)

FLC Chunk codes & interpretation

Table 29-6

Code	Name	Type of chunk indicated by code
4	FLI_COLOR_256	Data for 8-bit/primary palette
7	FLI_WORD_LC	2-byte RLE compressed pixel data
11	FLI_COLOR	Data for 6-bit/primary palette
12	FLI_LC	Line compressed (not generally used in FLC)
13	FLI_BLACK	Set whole screen to color 0 (appears in first frame only)
15	FLI_BRUN	Bytewise run-length compression—first frame only
16	FLI_COPY	Uncompressed data (64K bytes)
18	FLI_PREVIEW	"Thumbnail" image data

Bear in mind that all chunks are preceded by the chunk header.

FLI_COLOR & FLI_COLOR_256 chunks (codes 11 & 4)

These chunks update the RGB values in the palette. FLI_COLOR (code 11) is used principally in FLI files, and indicates a 6-bit/primary palette. FLI_COLOR_256 (code 4) is used principally in FLC files, and indicates an 8-bit/primary palette. If FLI_COLOR appears in an FLC file, it indicates that a 6-bit/primary palette is intended (primary values will be in the range of 0-63).

These chunks are structured into packets, as shown in Table 29-7. Basically, each packet indexes a pointer to a palette location where something changes, then gives the changes. A padding byte is added, if necessary, to create an even byte count in the RGB data.

Table 29-7 **FLI_COLOR and FLI_COLOR_256 chunk data**

Offset	Size	Name	Description
0	2	Packets	Number of packets in this chunk
		Packet	
2	1	Skip	Number of colors (RGB triplets) to skip in palette
3	1	Count	Number of RGB triplets to change; 0 signifies 256
4 and up	3	RGB value	One byte each of R, G, and B
.			
.		RGB triplets, repeated "Count" times.	
.			
.		1 (padding byte if necessary for even byte count of RGB data)	

Note that the "skip" and "count" values given by each subsequent packet are cumulative; the pointer to the palette is not reset to zero between packets—the pointer is reset to zero only when a new color chunk is encountered.

FLI_LC line compressed chunks (code 12)

These chunks constitute the largest part of an FLI frame. They may also appear in an FLC file if it originated as an FLI file. Each FLI_LC chunk describes a contiguous group of scan lines, in which lines at least one pixel has changed. Like other types of chunks, an FLI_LC chunk basically gives a pointer to a location where something changes, then gives the changes. In this instance, the chunk points to the first scan line where changes begin, then gives the changed pixels for that line and a number of subsequent lines. Each line is encoded separately. There are one or more packets per line, where each packet gives a contiguous group of changed pixels. See Table 29-8. (Like all FLI chunks, FLI_LC chunks are prefixed by the chunk header of Table 29-4.)

FLI_LC chunk data Table 29-8

Offset	Size	Name	Description
0	2	Skip lines	Number of scan lines to skip (keep the same)
2	2	Change lines	Number of (contiguous) scan lines to be changed
			Data for one line
4	1	Packets	Number of packets in this line (0 if line unchanged)
			Packet
5	1	Skip pix	Number of pixels to skip (keep the same)
6	1	Change pix	Number of pixels to change. (Signed; see below.)
7 and up	1	Pixel data	See next paragraph
			Packet
etc.			

The pixel data may be either a series of pixels (1-byte pointers to the palette) or a single pixel to be duplicated "Change pix" times, depending upon the sign of Change pix. Change pix should be treated as a signed integer: if positive, a series of pixels follows; if negative, a single pixel follows and should be duplicated–(Change pix) times. Any counts larger than this 8-bit scheme permits will require multiple packets. Pixel data is padded by one byte to an even byte count.

If the RLE compression used in FLI_LC fails to compress a frame to less than 60K, AutoDesk Animator will use uncompressed FLI_COPY chunks instead.

FLI_WORD_LC chunks (code 7)

FLI_WORD_LC chunks are the principal form of pixel data used in FLC files. Like FLI_LC chunks, these describe a group of scan lines. Unlike FLI_LC chunks, they convey pixel data in words. The Skip and Change values within a packet specify a count of 2-byte words, each word representing two pixels each. Like FLI_LC, the packet data are encoded according to the sign of the Change Pix value, using the same algorithm as FLI_LC. (See Table 29-9.)

Table 29-9 **FLI_LC chunk data**

Offset	Size	Name	Description
0	2	Line Count	Number of lines in this chunk
			Data for one line
2	2	Content	See following paragraph
			(2 possible additional Content words; see next paragraph)
			Packet
	1	Skip	Number of 2-pixel words to skip (keep the same)
	1	Change	Number of 2-pixel words to change. (Signed; see FLI_LC)
	2	Pixel words	Encoded as for FLI_LC, but 2 bytes long
			Packet
etc.			

The Content word may signify three different types of information, determined by the highest-order two bits of the word, as shown in Table 29-10:

FLC content interpretation Table 29-10

Top 2 bits	Significance
11	This word (Content) specifies the negative of a count of lines–(Content), to be skipped. (will be followed by another Content word, of type 11, 00, or 10)
00	This word (Content) contains the Packet count. (always followed immediately by Packets)
10	The low-order byte of this word (Content) is the last byte of the current line. (used for odd-byte-length images; followed by Content word of all zeros)

FLI_BRUN chunks (code 15)

These chunks deliver a fixed set of 200 scan lines, with pixels RLE compressed. They are essentially FLI_LC chunks without the line skipping. Their structure is given by the section of Table 29-8 labeled "Data for one line," composed of a 1-byte packet count and multiple packets. Data will be padded to an even byte count.

FLI_COPY chunks (code 16)

These are extremely simple chunks, used principally when RLE does not achieve sufficient compression to make it worthwhile to execute the decoding algorithm. After the chunk header comes exactly 64,000 bytes of data, making up a 320 × 200 pixel frame.

FLI_BLACK chunks (code 13)

These are simply a code that indicates that the screen should reset to black. There are no data associated with FLI_BLACK chunks.

FLI_PREVIEW chunks (code 18)

These chunks convey a low-resolution version of the first frame in an animation file, which can be used as a "thumbnail sketch" by editing applications to remind the user of the content of the file. Their structure includes a prefix, shown in Table 29-11, followed by RLE or uncompressed pixel data, or just a special color translation table without pixel data.

Table 29-11 **FLI_PREVIEW chunk prefix**

Offset	Size	Name	Description
0	2	Ypixels	Vertical dimension in pixels
2	2	Xpixels	Horizontal dimension in pixels
4	2	Colorspace	Always 1; see following paragraph
6	1	Datatype	Code indicating data:
			15=BRUN; 16=COPY; 18=color table, etc.

Depending upon the code at offset 6, subsequent data could be either pixel data or an abbreviated color table. A code of 15 indicates a BRUN chunk (at the reduced resolution); 15 indicates a COPY chunk (at the reduced resolution); 18 indicates that it is not pixel data that follow, but a special preview-image color table 256 bytes long, to be used with the pixel data of the actual first frame. This latter instance occurs when the frames are already quite small, making a reduced bitmap unnecessary.

Regardless of whether the preview image pixel data comes from the FLI_PREVIEW chunk or from the first actual frame of the file, the FLI_PREVIEW chunk is intended to be used with its own, smaller RGB color space. This space is either a default color space or the special color table whose presence is indicated by a Datatype of 18. In any case, the pattern is $R_0G_0B_0$, $R_0G_0B_1$, ..., $R_0G_1B_0$, $R_0G_1B_1$, ..., $R_5G_5B_5$. If a special color table is not given, the six default values of each primary are 0, 43, 85, 128, 171, 213. If a special color table is given, the values can be anything. Pixel values, normally taken as indices into a 256-entry table of RGB triplets, are taken as indices into this smaller table.

CHAPTER 30

MPEG overview

Name	Moving Picture Experts Group (MPEG)
Image type	Bitmap motion
Intended use	Real-time compression/decompression of video, with synchronized audio, for multimedia/hypermedia. Format allows for a symmetric real-time coding/decoding process with current technology.
Owner	Moving Picture Experts Group–International Organization for Standardization (ISO). Participants in MPEG include AT&T, Bellcore, GCT, C-Cube Microsystems, DEC, France Telecom, Cost 211 Bis, IBM, JVC, Matsushita, Mitsubishi, NEC, NTT, Phillips, Sony, Telenorma, Thomson, David Sarnoff, Columbia University, MIT, British Telecom, and Motorola.
Last version/ revision/ release date	Dec. 6, 1991 (CD 11172) for MPEG-1 and Nov. 17, 1993 (ISO/IEC 13818 Committee Draft) for MPEG-2
Platforms	Platform-independent; usually implemented in special hardware
Supporting applications	Various multimedia option boards; for example, from C-Cube, Optivision, Sigma Designs. Software only code decoders exist for non-real-time display, especially on UNIX workstations.
Similarities	JPEG
Overall assessment	Complex method of compressing/decompressing video and audio in real time, requiring substantial processing power. Employs both frame-to-frame (temporal) compression and intra-frame compression.

Advantages

An industry standard that reduces bandwidth and capacity requirements of video media, making high-quality full-motion video possible on low-cost computers. Handles high-quality video and audio using data rates as low as 1.5 Mbps for SIF MPEG-1, to MPbps and higher for MPEG-2 broadcast quality.

Disadvantages

Highly complex; generally implementable in hardware only for real-time applications

Overview of data stream structure

The MPEG data stream consists of two layers, the compression layer and the system layer, roughly analogous to the data fork and resource fork, respectively, of a QuickTime file. A system decoder splits the data stream into video and audio, to be processed by separate decoders. System clock references (SCRs) of 33 bits are inserted in the data stream every 700 milliseconds (or faster), to ensure synchronization by periodically setting the video and audio clocks to the same value; 33-bit presentation time stamps (PTSs) are inserted at a similar rate and serve to invoke a particular picture or audio sequence.

The topmost layer for MPEG-1, the video sequence layer, can be expressed as:

```
video sequence is {
        next start code
        repeat {
                sequence header
                repeat {
```

group of pictures
} while (next word in stream is group start code)
} while (next word in stream is sequence header code)
sequence end code
}

MPEG-2 adds extensions which makes an MPEG-2 stream not decodable by an MPEG-1 decoder; however, the reverse is possible since MPEG-2 is a superset of MPEG-1.

The video stream comprises a header, a series of frames, and an end-of-sequence code. Because the stream is temporally compressed (most frames build upon previous frames), there are periodic *Intra Pictures*, or I-pictures. These provide full images to be used as periodic references, and so allow reasonably random access to the data stream. Other frames are "predicted," using either a preceding I-picture (which creates *P-pictures*) or a combination of preceding and following I-pictures, which creates *B-pictures*). The encoder decides how I-, B-, and P-pictures are interspersed and ordered. A typical sequence would be I-B-B-P. The order of pictures in the data stream is not the order of display; for example, the previous sequence would be sent as I-P-B-B.

Frames are broken up into slices 16 pixels high, and each slice is broken up into a vector of *macroblocks* 16 × 16 pixels. Each macroblock contains luminance and chrominance components for each of four 8 × 8 pixel blocks. Color decimation can be applied to a macroblock, which yields four 8 × 8 blocks for luminance and two 8 × 8 blocks (Cb and Cr) of chrominance, using one chrominance value for each four luminance values. This is called the 4:2:0 format; two other formats are available (4:2:2 and 4:4:4, two luminance per chrominance and one to one, respectively), which require higher data rates.

For each macroblock, a spatial offset difference between a macroblock in the predicted and the reference frame(s) is given if one exists (a motion vector), along with a luminance and/or chrominance difference value (an error term) if needed. Macroblocks with no differences can be skipped except in Intra frames. Blocks with differences are internally compressed, using a combination of a

Discrete Cosine Transform (DCT) algorithm on pixel blocks (or error blocks) and variable quantization of the resulting frequency coefficients (rounding off values to one of a limited set of values).

The DCT algorithm accepts signed, 9-bit pixel values and produces signed, 12-bit coefficients. The DCT is applied to one block at a time, and works much like it does for JPEG, converting each 8×8 block into an 8×8 matrix of frequency coefficients (see chapter 17 for details of JPEG). The variable quantization process divides each coefficient by a corresponding factor in a matching 8×8 matrix and rounds to an integer.

Quantization results in numerous zero coefficients, particularly for high-frequency terms at the high end of the matrix. Accordingly, amplitudes are recorded in run-length form following a diagonal scan pattern from low frequency to high frequency. MPEG-2 adds, among other features, an alternate scan order which further improves compression. All control data, vectors, and DCT coefficients are further compressed using Huffman-like variable-length encoding.

References

"Coded Representation of picture, audio, and multimedia/hypermedia information," *Draft Standard*, Dec. 6, 1991. *ISO/IEC*.

Le Gall, Didier. "MPEG: A Video Compression Standard for Multimedia Applications," *Communications of the ACM, Vol. 34, No. 4*. April, 1991.

"Coding of moving pictures and associated audio," *Committee Draft of Standard ISO11172: ISO/MPEG 90/176*. Dec. 1990.

CHAPTER 31

QuickTime animation

Name	QuickTime Animation Format (Lossless RLE)
Image type	Bitmap
Intended use	Bitmap-based animation (not video from cameras) on Macintosh computers
Owner	Apple Computer, Inc., 20525 Mariani Avenue, Cupertino, CA 95014 (408) 996-1010
Last version/ revision/ release date	Coincides with releases of Apple Macintosh System 7 (operating system)
Platforms	Principally Macintosh; occasionally PCs and UNIX workstations
Supporting applications	Nearly all Macintosh multimedia or video applications; also, some PC and UNIX multimedia or video applications can convert output to QuickTime animation format. Playback available on PCs using Apple's QuickTime for Windows.
Similarities	Other RLE-based, frame-differencing animation formats such as Autodesk FLI/FLC
Overall assessment	Modestly efficient format for color /monochrome bitmap animation, ubiquitous on Macintosh

Advantages

May be played on all but slowest Macintosh computers, under System 7 with QuickTime extensions (included in the latest releases of System 7). Mature and well-supported by Macintosh applications. Fairly compact due to combined RLE and frame-difference compression.

Disadvantages

Closed format, best written or read by using official Apple interface (System 7 system calls). The lossless RLE format discussed here is not designed or well-suited for video from cameras; QuickTime's RPZA and cdvc compression formats are the ones designed for video.

Variants

The QuickTime animation format (or RLE format) is one of several variants of the QuickTime movie, corresponding to different QuickTime "compressors": animation (RLE), video (RPZA or Road Pizza), photo (JPEG), uncompressed (raw), graphics (smc), or compact video (cdvc). There are two variants of RLE compression: lossy and lossless. The variant discussed here is lossless. Since QuickTime image formats are not documented by Apple, it is not known what subvariants may exist within the lossless RLE format discussed here.

QuickTime movies allow color depths of 1, 2, 4, 8, 16, 24, and 32 bits, or grayscale depths of 2, 4, or 8 bits, and variable image size and resolution. On platforms other than Macintosh, QuickTime movies often appear in a *flattened* or *single fork* format, which combines the two-fork data structure of Macintosh files into a single fork, with image data first, then resource data.

Overview of file structure

It should be noted that since QuickTime image data formats are undocumented and diverse, and since the entire field of computer video is changing at a rapid rate, these formats are subject to changes and variations that may well be missing from any third-party description of the format, including this one. For any serious commercial applications, you are encouraged to use the intended high-level interface provided by system calls in the Macintosh operating system (accessible using C or Pascal), rather than directly reading or writing the format. Documentation is provided by the QuickTime volume of the *Inside Macintosh* document set, available from Apple. For other platforms, developers should contact Apple to inquire about direct support. A Movie Exchange Toolkit is also available from Apple for creating QuickTime movies of various formats from PC, A/UX, Cray, RS/6000, Sequent, SGI, Sun, and VAX computers.

QuickTime movies are potentially complex structures. They may contain both image and sound data, in the form of *tracks*, and there may be more than one video or audio track, constituting *layers* that can be overlaid, combined, transformed, or prioritized in different ways. Image and sound track data may be randomly distributed in a file, and may even be distributed over several files. This chapter will discuss only 8-bit and 16-bit image data created by the animation (RLE) compressor, focusing on a single, *flattened* or single-fork form of file.

QuickTime movies are hierarchical, using a data structure called a *media* and, subordinate to that, *atoms*. The word "media" (confusingly used as a singular noun) refers to an organizing data structure that pulls together diverse video or audio data to implement a track. Within a media are atoms . . . within . . . atoms . . . within atoms. Some of the principal atoms in this hierarchy are shown in Tables 31-7 and 31-8, along with the 4-letter ASCII code names that identify them in a QuickTime file.

There are two principal atoms. The movie *data* atom (the first one encountered in a single-fork file) provides the actual pixel data. The movie *resource* atom (which follows the movie data atom in a single-fork file) contains atoms that allow you to locate, assemble, and properly interpret image data. In Macintosh format, the movie data appear in the data fork and the resource atoms appear in the resource fork. If the exact type of compression is known (e.g., lossless RLE), very few of these atoms are essential to extracting the movie images.

Movie data consists of images and audio in blocks called *chunks*, each chunk containing a number of samples. The samples can vary in size, timing, compressor, media handler, image dimensions, color depth, location (offset in the file), and other factors, which is one reason why all the various atoms are needed. A simple animation, however, will generally use chunks and samples of uniform length and type. The image data for RLE files are, unsurprisingly, run-length encoded within a frame.

Format details

Following are discussions of 8-bit and 16-bit image data (no audio) created by the animation (RLE) compressor in the lossless mode, focusing on a single, flattened or single-fork form of movie file commonly used on non-Macintosh platforms. The descriptions of the movie data do not apply to the format used for any other pixel depth. We will focus first on the movie data atom because it appears first in a single-fork file.

To determine whether you have an RLE or other type of file, and to determine whether it contains 8-bit or 16-bit image data, it is necessary to find and examine the sample description atom (stsd) described later in this chapter. To be absolutely certain of the location, size, and sequence of chunks and samples, it is also necessary to read the chunk offset atom (stco), sample-to-chunk atom (stsc), and sample size atom (stsz). To extract images from a simple animation, however, these last three atoms are often inessential: the data will generally proceed in frame-sequential order, one sample per frame from the start of the file, with each sample giving its own size.

Movie data atom

The image data are contained in a movie data atom (mdat), which, in a single-fork file, begins the file. The atom begins with the structure shown in Table 31-1. Since QuickTime RLE is a Macintosh format, all data are in big-endian order, most significant byte first.

Table 31-1 **Movie data atom**

Offset	Size	Content
0	4	Count of bytes of image data (including header) before other atoms
4	4	The four ASCII characters "mdat" (the atom name)

The data that follow consist of a series of samples, generally one sample per frame, and identified by a code byte of 8 or 0 at an offset of four bytes into the atom. Samples of type 8 contain pixel data. Samples of type 0, shown in Table 31-2, do not contain pixel data; they appear to be placeholders. The structures for these samples are shown in Tables 31-2 and 31-3.

Table 31-2 **Movie sample type 0**

Offset	Size	Content
0	4	Sample size in bytes
4	2	Code byte: 0x0000
6	1	0x00

Table 31-3 **Movie sample type 8**

Offset	Size	Content
0	4	Sample size in bytes; high byte may contain unknown flags
4	2	Code byte: 0x0008, indicating pixel data follow
6	2	Starting line number
8	2	Unknown
10	2	Number of lines in sample
12	2	Unknown

RLE data, line 1		
14	1	Pixels-to-skip +1
15	1	RLE count/code byte; see description below
16	n	Data depend on preceding byte See description below
16+*n*	1	0xff; end of line
RLE data, line 2, etc.		
•••	•••	•••

The data for a scan line depend upon the RLE count/code byte. The interpretation for 8-bit RLE is given in Table 31-4. Note that the count byte is taken as a signed value, and that its sign is significant. In the 8-bit form, the count is for groups of four pixels.

Interpretation of RLE count/code byte for 8-bit data

Table 31-4

Value	**Interpretation**
0x00	Extended skip; subsequent byte gives pixel skip count
0x80 to 0xff	(Signed) count; subsequent four bytes are a set of four pixels to be repeated (–count) times
0x00 to 0x7f	(Signed) count; subsequent bytes are a stream of pixels, a total of count*4 bytes

Note that, for 8-bit images, the RLE compressor looks for duplication in adjacent sets of four pixels. It encodes the pixels either as one group repeated a given number of times, or as a count of unique groups of four. If the width of the image is not a multiple of four, the image is padded out with pixels. Each pixel value is an 8-bit index into a predefined color map. The color map is the default Apple color map for display mode 0 x 40 (hex 40); it is not contained in the animation file.

For 16-bit data, the interpretation of the RLE count/code byte is given in Table 31-5. Note that the count byte is, again, taken as a signed value and its sign is significant.

Table 31-5 **Interpretation of RLE count/code byte for 16-bit data**

Value	Interpretation
0x00	Extended skip; subsequent byte gives pixel skip count
0x80 to 0xff	(Signed) count; subsequent 2-byte word is a single pixel repeated (–count) times
0x00 to 0x7f	(Signed) count; subsequent 2-byte words are pixels, a total of count pixels

For these so-called 16-bit images (actually 15-bit), the RLE compressor packs an RGB value into a 2-byte word, leaving the most-significant bit unused (0). The bit pattern for a pixel is as follows:

0RRRRRGGGGGBBBBB, providing 5 bits per primary.

Movie resource atom (moov)

The movie atom is a *container* atom for all the resource atoms (those not containing actual pixels). Some of these atoms are formally required by QuickTime; those are identified in Table 31-6 with an asterisk. Additional atoms useful for reading images from the type of file discussed here are shown with a double asterisk.

Table 31-6 **Resource atom hierarchy**

*movie resource atom (moov)**
- *movie header atom (mvhd)**
- *track atom (trak)**
  - *track header atom (tkhd)**
  - *edit atom (edts)*
    - *edit list atom (elst)*
  - *media atom (mdia)**
    - *media header atom (mdhd)**
    - *media handler reference atom (hdlr)*
    - *video media information atom (minf)**
      - *video media information header atom (vmhd)**

*data handler reference atom (hdlr)**

data information atom (dinf)

data reference atom (dref)

*sample table atom (stbl)***

*time-to-sample atom (stts) ***

*sample description atom (stsd)***

*sample size atom (stsz)***

*sample-to-chunk atom (stsc)***

*chunk offset atom (stco)***

In a flattened (single-fork) file, the movie resource atom can be found at the offset specified by the very first four bytes of the file (see Table 31-1, offset 0). In a Macintosh file, the movie resource atom is in the movie resource fork. The header beginning the movie resource atom is as shown in Table 31-7.

Table 31-7

Movie resource atom header

Offset	Size	Content
0	4	Size of resource atom in bytes
4	4	Four ASCII characters "moov"
(other atoms follow)		

Subsequent to the header shown in Table 31-7 are the subordinate atoms. The easiest way to find these in a file is by their 4-letter ASCII names. An atom name is always preceded by a 4-byte value giving the size of the atom. Container atoms, listed here in brackets, consist of an atom size field, the ASCII name field, and then the contained atoms which follow immediately. Values are unsigned integers of the given size unless otherwise indicated.

Table 31-8 lists the most important resource atoms and their data. The table gives the size and offset of each datum, with the offset measured in bytes after the last character in the atom name.

Table 31-8 **Locations of various data relative to atom name**

Atom	Offset after name	Size	Description
mvhd	12	4	Time scale of movie (movie time units / sec.)
	16	4	Duration of movie in movie time units
	20	4	Preferred rate of play
[trak]			Track atom (container)
tkhd	20	4	Duration of track in movie time units
	40	36	Track image transformation matrix by row
	76	4	Track image *X* dimension
	80	4	Track image *Y* dimension
[mdia]			Media atom (container)
[minf]			Video media information atom (container)
mdhd	12	4	Time scale of this media (media time units / sec.)
	16	4	Duration of this media (media time units)
[stbl]			Sample table atom (container)
stts	4	4	Number of count-duration pairs following
	8	4	# of samples; 1st group of samples of equal duration
	12	4	Duration per sample in 1st group, in media time
	16	4	# of samples: 2nd group of samples of equal duration
	12	4	Duration per sample in 2nd group, in media time
	...	4+4	Additional count-duration pairs for remainder of media
stsd	4	4	Number of sample descriptions following
	8	4	Desc. 1 begins: size of description (e.g., 86 bytes)
	12	4	Name of codec in ASCII (e.g., "rle ") for desc. 1
	40	2	Width of image in pixels for desc. 1
	42	2	Height of image in pixels for desc. 1

	56	2	How many frames conforming to desc. 1
	58	32	Name of algorithm (e.g., "Animation") for desc. 1
	90	2	Bit depth of image (e.g., 16) for desc. 1
	92	2	ID# of color map; 0xff= map not used; for desc. 1
	•••	86	Next desc., if any, as for desc. 1 above.
stsz	4	4	Size of all samples in media if samples uniform; otherwise 0 with table of sizes following
	8	4	Number of entries in table following
	12	4	Size of first sample
	•••	4	Sizes of subsequent samples
stsc	4	4	Number of entries following (=1 if only 1 stsd desc.)
	8	4	Starting chunk number for consecutive chunks of identical sample desc. and # samples/chunk
	12	4	How many samples/chunk
	16	4	Description # for samples (index into stsd descriptions)
	•••	4	Starting chunk # for consecutive chunks using another description
stco	4	4	Number of chunks in the media
	8	4	Offset to 1st chunk
	12	4	Offset to 2nd chunk
	•••.	4	Offsets to subsequent chunks

Order & timing in a QuickTime movie

In playing a movie, QuickTime must be able to assemble samples of various descriptions, perhaps distributed throughout a file at random locations, and display them properly for the correct duration.

To perform this task it uses time as an index; that index points to a particular sample and a particular sample description that allows proper decoding.

QuickTime maintains a movie clock running at a specified number of ticks per second, and advancing its "value" by 1 with every tick; this is the time scale of the movie (see the mvhd atom). Each track in the movie corresponds to a single media, and that media has its own time scale and duration (see the mdhd atom). The accumulated media time value provides an index that points to the proper sample for that time.

The index that relates the media time value to the corresponding image sample is found in the time-to-sample (stts) atom. It is, however, somewhat indirect. This atom gives the duration of every sample in order of occurrence; by accumulating durations and comparing that value to the media time value, QuickTime knows when to move on to the next sample. Since a sequence is often composed of samples of a common duration, however, the atom just gives the number of the first sample in that sequence, followed by the common duration. If the duration changes at any point, there is a new entry in the stts atom giving the frame number where this new duration begins, and the new duration. This is a form of run-length encoding (RLE), in which sequential samples of common duration are grouped together.

To locate the sample and properly interpret it, QuickTime uses the sample-to-chunk atom (stsc). This lists the chunks in order of execution, along with the number of samples and type of sample contained in that chunk. Since chunks in a sequence often have the same number and type of samples, however, the stsc atom uses an RLE approach similar to that of the stts atom. The stsc atom just gives the number of the first chunk in a sequence of chunks, followed by the number of samples/chunk in that sequence and the description of the samples used in that sequence. If the samples/chunk or sample description changes at any point, there is a new entry in the stsc atom. This entry gives the chunk number where this new sequence of chunks begins, and the new information about the samples used in that sequence.

As QuickTime progresses sequentially through the chunks, it locates the data in the file by using the chunk-offset atom (stco). Within the chunk, it finds the sample by using data from the sample-size atom (stsz). It ensures proper interpretation of the samples by obtaining an index number from the sample-to-chunk (stsc) atom, which points to one of the descriptions in the sample description (stsd) atom.

Example

The following example is a 16-bit RLE animation file of three frames. Each frame contains a duplicate image, moved slightly to the right in each frame. The image is a set of rectangles, red, green, and blue, stacked vertically in that order and separated by white space, as shown in Fig. 31-1. The frames are 160 pixels horizontally by 120 lines vertically. The file does not employ frame-to-frame compression and contains a redundant image of the last frame. There are three chunks; the first contains two samples; the second contains one sample; the third is redundant.

Figure 31-1

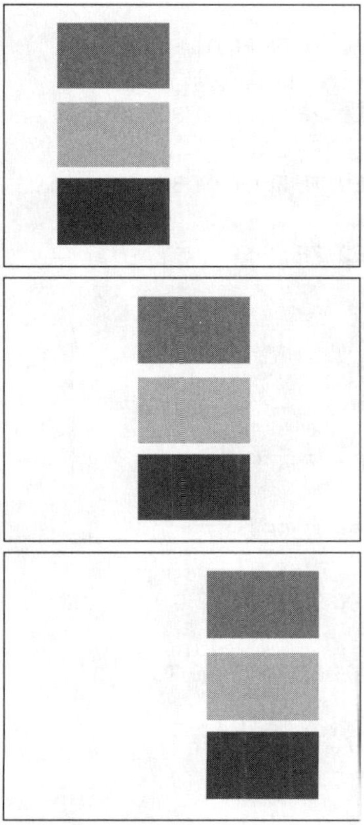

A three-frame animation.

The file listing for this animation follows. The format for each row in the listing is: an offset in hexadecimal, then two sets of eight bytes in hexadecimal, ending in an ASCII translation of those bytes (not to imply that all data are ASCII). Breaks in data are given for clarity. Breaks with ellipses (...) indicate lines have been removed for illustration purposes, and follow a pattern established previously. Such missing lines are indicated by a jump in offset values.

A three-frame animation file, courtesy of Les Bartlett.

```
OFFSET <——————————DATA IN HEX ————————> <-DATA AS ASCII->

       Movie data atom       |——> Chunk 1, sample 1

0000  00 00 13 34 6D 64 61 74-40 00 04 CB 00 08 00 00  ...4mdat@.......

0010  00 00 00 78 00 00 01 80-7F FF E0  7F FF FF 01 80  ...x.............

0020  7F FF E0 7F FF FF 01 80-7F FF E0  7F FF FF 01 80  ................

0030  7F FF E0 7F FF FF 01 80-7F FF E0  7F FF FF 01 80  ................

0040  7F FF E0 7F FF FF 01 80-7F FF E0  7F FF FF

       White

                                                01 80  ................

0050  7F FF E0 7F FF FF 01 80-7F FF E0 7F FF FF 01 E8  ................

0060  7F FF D9 7C 00 9F 7F FF-FF 01 E8 7F FF D9 7C 00  ......|..........|....

0070  9F 7F FF FF 01 E8 7F FF-D9 7C 00 9F 7F FF FF 01  ............|.........

0080  E8 7F FF D9 7C 00 9F 7F-FF FF 01 E8 7F FF D9 7C  .......|............|

0090  00 9F 7F FF  FF 01 E8 7F-FF D9 7C 00 9F 7F FF FF  .........|..........
```

.

. White/Red/White

.

```
0150  01 E8 7F FF D9 7C 00 9F-7F FF FF 01 E8 7F FF D9   .........l...........
0160  7C 00 9F 7F FF FF 01 E8-7F FF D9 7C 00 9F 7F FF   l............l.......
0170  FF 01 E8 7F FF D9 7C 00-9F 7F FF FF 01 E8 7F FF   .........l............
0180  D9 7C 00 9F 7F FF FF 01-E8 7F FF D9 7C 00 9F 7F   .l............l......
0190  FF FF  01 80 7F FF E0 7F-FF FF 01 80  7F FF E0 7F   ....................
01A0  FF FF 01 80 7F FF E0 7F-FF FF
```

White

```
                                          01 80 7F FF E0 7F   .....................
01B0  FF FF 01 80 7F FF E0 7F-FF FF 01 80 7F FF E0 7F   .....................
01C0  FF FF 01 80 7F FF E0 7F-FF FF 01 80 7F FF E0 7F   .....................
01D0  FF FF 01 E8 7F FF D9 03-E0 9F 7F FF FF 01 E8 7F   .....................
01E0  FF D9 03 E0 9F 7F FF FF-01 E8 7F FF D9 03 E0 9F   .....................
01F0  7F FF FF 01 E8 7F FF D9-03 E0 9F 7F FF FF 01 E8   ....................
0200  7F FF D9 03 E0 9F 7F FF-FF
```

.

. White/Green/White

.

```
02F0  01 E8 7F FF D9 03 E0 9F-7F FF FF 01 E8 7F FF D9  ....................
0300  03 E0 9F 7F FF  FF 01 80-7F FF E0 7F FF FF 01 80  ....................
0310  7F FF E0 7F FF  FF 01 80-7F FF E0 7F FF FF 01 80  ....................
0320  7F FF E0 7F FF  FF 01 80-7F FF E0 7F FF FF
      White
                                                 01 80  ....................
0330  7F FF E0 7F FF FF 01 80-7F FF E0 7F FF FF 01 80  ....................
0340  7F FF E0 7F FF FF 01 80-7F FF E0 7F FF FF 01 E8  ....................
0350  7F FF D9 00 1F 9F 7F FF-FF 01 E8 7F FF D9 00 1F  ...................
0360  9F 7F FF FF 01 E8 7F FF-D9 00 1F 9F 7F FF FF 01  ....................
0370  E8 7F FF D9 00 1F 9F 7F-FF FF 01 E8 7F FF D9 00  ...................
0380  1F 9F 7F FF FF 01 E8 7F-FF D9 00 1F 9F 7F FF FF  ...................
.
.    White/Blue/White
.
0440  01 E8 7F FF D9 00 1F 9F-7F FF FF 01 E8 7F FF D9  ..................
0450  00 1F 9F 7F FF FF 01 E8-7F FF D9 00 1F 9F 7F FF  ...................
0460  FF 01 E8 7F FF D9 00 1F-9F 7F FF FF 01 E8 7F FF  ...................
0470  D9 00 1F 9F 7F FF FF 01-E8 7F FF D9 00 1F 9F 7F  ..................
0480  FF FF 01 80 7F FF E0 7F-FF FF
```

White

01 80 7F FF E0 7F ....

04C0 FF FF 01 80 7F FF E0 7F-FF FF 01 80 7F FF E0 7F ....

I——-> Chunk 1, sample 2

04D0 FF FF 00 40 00 04 CB 00-08 00 00 00 00 00 78 00 ...@..........x.

04E0 00 01 80 7F FF E0 7F FF-FF 01 80 7F FF E0 7F FF ....

04F0 FF 01 80 7F FF E0 7F FF-FF 01 80 7F FF E0 7F FF ....

White

0500 FF 01 80 7F FF E0 7F FF-FF 01 80 7F FF E0 7F FF ....

0510 FF 01 80 7F FF E0 7F FF-FF 01 80 7F FF E0 7F FF ....

0520 FF 01 80 7F FF E0 7F FF-FF 01 C5 7F FF D9 7C 00 ....I.....

0530 C2 7F FF FF 01 C5 7F FF-D9 7C 00 C2 7F FF FF

.

. White/Red/White

.

0610 01 C5 7F FF D9 7C 00 C2-7F FF FF 01 C5 7F FF D9 .....I..........

0620 7C 00 C2 7F FF FF 01 C5-7F FF D9 7C 00 C2 7F FF I..........I....

0630 FF 01 C5 7F FF D9 7C 00-C2 7F FF FF 01 C5 7F FF ......I.........

0640 D9 7C 00 C2 7F FF FF 01-C5 7F FF D9 7C 00 C2 7F .I..........I...

0650 FF FF 01 C5 7F FF D9 7C-00 C2 7F FF FF 01 80 7F ......I........

```
0660  FF E0 7F FF FF
.
.    R/G/B as for sample 1, but colors begin 60 pix from left
.
0900  01 C5 7F FF D9 00 1F C2-7F FF FF 01 C5 7F FF D9   ................
0910  00 1F C2 7F FF FF  01 C5-7F FF D9 00 1F C2 7F FF  ................
0920  FF 01 C5 7F FF D9 00 1F-C2 7F FF  FF 01 C5 7F FF  ................
0930  D9 00 1F C2 7F FF FF 01-C5 7F FF D9 00 1F C2 7F   ................
0940  FF FF 01 C5 7F FF  D9 00-1F C2 7F FF FF 01 80 7F  ................
0950  FF E0 7F FF FF  01 80 7F-FF  E0 7F FF FF 01 80 7F ................
0960  FF E0 7F FF FF  01 80 7F-FF  E0 7F FF FF 01 80 7F ................
0970  FF E0 7F FF FF  01 80 7F-FF  E0 7F FF FF 01 80 7F ................
0980  FF E0 7F FF FF  01 80 7F-FF  E0 7F FF FF 01 80 7F ................

                                     |——-> chunk 2, 1 sample

0990  FF E0  7F FF FF 01 80 7F-FF E0 7F FF FF 00 40 00  .............@.
09A0  04 CB 00 08 00 00 00 00-00 78 00 00 01 80 7F FF   .........x......
09B0  E0 7F FF  FF 01 80 7F FF-E0 7F FF FF 01 80 7F FF  ................
09C0  E0 7F FF  FF 01 80 7F FF-E0 7F FF FF 01 80 7F FF  ................
09D0  E0 7F FF  FF 01 80 7F FF-E0 7F FF FF 01 80 7F FF  ................
09E0  E0 7F  FF FF 01 80 7F  FF-E0 7F FF FF 01 80 7F FF ................
```

```
09F0  E0 7F  FF FF 01  A2 7F FF-D9 7C 00 E5 7F FF FF 01   .........l......

0A00  A2 7F FF D9 7C 00 E5 7F-FF FF 01 A2 7F FF D9 7C   ....l..........l

0A10  00 E5 7F FF FF 01  A2 7F-FF D9 7C 00 E5 7F FF FF   ..........l.....

.

.    R/G/B as previously, but colors begin 95 pix from left

.

0DC0  01 A2 7F FF D9 00 1F E5-7F FF FF 01 A2 7F FF D9   ................

0DD0  00 1F E5 7F FF FF 01 A2-7F FF D9 00 1F E5 7F FF   ................

0DE0  FF 01 A2 7F FF D9 00 1F-E5 7F FF FF 01 A2 7F FF   ................

0DF0  D9 00 1F E5 7F FF FF 01-A2 7F FF D9 00 1F E5 7F   ................

0E00  FF FF 01 A2 7F FF D9 00-1F E5 7F FF FF 01 A2 7F   ................

0E10  FF D9 00 1F E5 7F FF FF-01 80 7F FF E0 7F FF FF   ................

0E20  01 80 7F FF E0 7F FF FF-01 80 7F FF E0 7F FF FF   ................

0E30  01 80 7F FF E0 7F FF FF-01 80 7F FF E0 7F FF FF   ................

0E40  01 80 7F FF E0 7F FF FF-01 80 7F FF E0 7F FF FF   ................

0E50  01 80 7F FF E0 7F FF FF-01 80 7F FF E0 7F FF FF   ................

0E60  01 80 7F FF E0 7F FF FF-

                                  l——> Chunk 3, 1 sample (duplicate)

                                  00 40 00 04 CB 00 08 00   .........@.....

0E70  00 00 00 00 78 00 00 01-80 7F FF E0 7F FF FF 01   ....x...........
```

```
0E80  80 7F FF E0 7F FF FF 01-80 7F FF E0 7F FF FF 01   ................

0E90  80 7F FF E0 7F FF FF 01-80 7F FF E0 7F FF FF 01   ................

0EA0  80 7F FF E0 7F FF FF 01-80 7F FF E0 7F FF FF 01   ................

0EB0  80 7F FF E0 7F FF FF 01-80 7F FF E0 7F FF FF 01   ................

0EC0  A2 7F FF D9 7C 00 E5 7F-FF FF 01 A2 7F FF D9 7C  ....l..........l

0ED0  00 E5 7F FF FF 01 A2 7F-FF D9 7C 00 E5 7F FF FF   ..........l.....

.

.    R/G/B as previously

.

12C0  FF FF 01 A2 7F FF D9 00-1F E5 7F FF FF 01 A2 7F   ................

12D0  FF D9 00 1F E5 7F FF FF-01 A2 7F FF D9 00 1F E5   ................

12E0  7F FF FF 01 80 7F FF E0-7F FF FF 01 80 7F FF E0   ................

12F0  7F FF FF 01 80 7F FF E0-7F FF FF 01 80 7F FF E0   ................

1300  7F FF FF 01 80 7F FF E0-7F FF FF 01 80 7F FF E0   ................

1310  7F FF FF 01 80 7F FF E0-7F FF FF 01 80 7F FF E0   ................

1320  7F FF FF 01 80 7F FF E0-7F FF FF 01 80 7F FF E0   ................

1330  7F FF FF 00

                 l—-> Movie resource atom

                 00 00 02 DD-6D 6F 6F 76 00 00 00 6C    ........moov...l

1340  6D 76 68 64 00 00 00 00-A9 31 F8 ED A9 31 F8 EE  mvhd.....1...1..

1350  00 00 02 58 00 00 07 08-00 01 00 00 00 FF 00 00   ...X...........
```

```
1360  00 00 00 00 00 00 00 00-00 01 00 00 00 00 00 00  ................
1370  00 00 00 00 00 00 00 00-00 01 00 00 00 00 00 00  ................
1380  00 00 00 00 00 00 00 00-40 00 00 00 00 00 00 00  ........@.......
1390  00 00 00 00 00 00 00 00-00 00 00 00 00 00 00 00  ................
13A0  00 00 00 00 00 00 00 02-00 00 02 51 74 72 61 6B  ...........Qtrak
13B0  00 00 00 5C 74 6B 68 64-00 00 00 0F A9 31 ED 62  ...\tkhd.....1.b
13C0  A9 31 F8 EE 00 00 00 01-00 00 00 00 00 00 07 08  .1..............
13D0  00 00 00 00 00 00 00 00-00 00 00 00 00 00 00 00  ................
13E0  00 01 00 00 00 00 00 00-00 00 00 00 00 00 00 00  ................
13F0  00 01 00 00 00 00 00 00-00 00 00 00 00 00 00 00  ................
1400  40 00 00 00 00 A0 00 00-00 78 00 00 00 00 00 24  @........x.....$
1410  65 64 74 73 00 00 00 1C-65 6C 73 74 00 00 00 00  edts....elst....
1420  00 00 00 01 00 00 07 08-00 00 00 00 00 01 00 00  ................
1430  00 00 01 C9 6D 64 69 61-00 00 00 20 6D 64 68 64  ....mdia... mdhd
1440  00 00 00 00 A9 31 F8 ED-A9 31 F8 EE 00 00 00 1E  .....1...1......
1450  00 00 00 5A 00 00 00 00-00 00 00 3A 68 64 6C 72  ...Z.......:hdlr
1460  00 00 00 00 6D 68 6C 72-76 69 64 65 61 70 70 6C  ....mhlrvideappl
1470  40 00 00 00 00 01 00 11-19 41 70 70 6C 65 20 56  @........Apple V
1480  69 64 65 6F 20 4D 65 64-69 61 20 48 61 6E 64 6C  ideo Media Handl
1490  65 72 00 00 01 67 6D 69-6E 66 00 00 00 14 76 6D  er...gminf....vm
```

```
14A0  68 64 00 00 00 01 00 40-80 00 80 00 80 00 00 00  hd.....@........
14B0  00 39 68 64 6C 72 00 00-00 00 64 68 6C 72 61 6C  .9hdlr....dhlral
14C0  69 73 61 70 70 6C 40 00-00 00 00 01 00 16 18 41  isappl@........A
14D0  70 70 6C 65 20 41 6C 69-61 73 20 44 61 74 61 20  pple Alias Data
14E0  48 61 6E 64 6C 65 72 00-00 00 24 64 69 6E 66 00  Handler...$dinf.
14F0  00 00 1C 64 72 65 66 00-00 00 00 00 00 00 01 00  ...dref.........
1500  00 00 0C 61 6C 69 73 00-00 00 01 00 00 00 EE 73  ...alis........s
1510  74 62 6C 00 00 00 66 73-74 73 64 00 00 00 00 00  tbl...fstsd.....
1520  00 00 01 00 00 00 56 72-6C 65 20 00 00 00 00 00  ......Vrle .....
1530  00 00 01 00 01 00 01 61-70 70 6C 00 00 00 00 00  .......appl.....
1540  00 02 00 00 A0 00 78 00-48 00 00 00 48 00 00 00  ......x.H...H...
1550  00 00 00 00 01 09 41 6E-69 6D 61 74 69 6F 6E 00  ......Animation.
1560  00 00 00 00 00 00 00 00-00 00 00 00 00 00 00 00  ................
1570  00 00 00 00 00 00 10 FF-FF 00 00 00 28 73 74 74  ............(stt
1580  73 00 00 00 00 00 00 00-03 00 00 00 02 00 00 00  s...............
1590  1E 00 00 00 01 00 00 00-1D 00 00 00 01 00 00 00  ................
15A0  01 00 00 00 28 73 74 73-63 00 00 00 00 00 00 00  ....(stsc.......
15B0  02 00 00 00 01 00 00 00-02 00 00 00 01 00 00 00  ................
15C0  02 00 00 00 01 00 00 00-01 00 00 00 14 73 74 73  ............sts
15D0  7A 00 00 00 00 00 00 04-CB 00 00 00 04 00 00 00  z...............
```

```
15E0  1C 73 74 63 6F 00 00 00-00 00 00 0C 03 00 00 00   .stco...........
15F0  08 00 00 09 9E 00 00 0E-69                         ........i
```

Reference

Apple Computer, Inc. *Inside Macintosh: QuickTime*. March 1993. Reading, MA: Addison-Wesley Publishing Co.

## CHAPTER 32

Other file formats

IN this chapter we briefly discuss several graphics file formats not otherwise covered in this book.

Autodesk Slide

SLD slide files are used as a simple output format for a series of images. They use a simple metafile format with vectors and filled polygons. A variant is a slide library, a file of slides with a directory at the beginning listing the names and file positions of the slides contained in the library.

Epson printer bitmaps

Most Epson dot-matrix printers support the printing of bitmap data at various densities. The image is sent in horizontal bands seven or eight pixels high, each corresponding to one horizontal pass by the print head. Each band starts with an escape sequence, followed by the band of pixel data. Most printers require setup sequences to set the vertical spacing line to line and the horizontal spacing of output pixels. Unfortunately, no two models of Epson printer support quite the same set of escape sequence. Printers within a product line (e.g., MX) are fairly compatible, but even within a product line there are sometimes incompatibilities that affect bitmap printing. Although it is not hard to generate a bitmap file for a particular model, such as the MX-80, which was sold by IBM as their early PC printer, it is not possible to create a bitmap file that prints on all models of Epson printer.

Facesaver

Facesaver is a format defined by Lou Katz of Usenix, and is used in the Unix community for small grayscale images, typically of people's faces digitized at trade fairs. An on-line data base is often used to tag an electronic-mail message with a picture of the author. Files are entirely ASCII, and start with text lines describing the image, followed by pixel data in hex.

Facsimile formats

Group 3 fax machines, the most common kind, use a black-and-white format defined by CCITT recommendation T.4. As computer fax modems have become popular, T.4 images have started to appear on computer systems. Fax images are almost always 1728 pixels wide, and of varying height depending on the size of the paper. Each row is independently run-length encoded using a fixed-table Huffman code. Group 4 fax, recommendation T.6, uses a similar but more complicated 2-D encoding scheme that can transmit just the differences from one line to the next.

TIFF includes both group 3 and group 4 format as compression options.

Grasp GL animations

Grasp (Graphical System for Presentation) is a slide-show format defined by Microtex Industries, Inc., 2091 Business Center Drive, Irvine, CA 92715. The software to create Grasp animations is proprietary, but the animations themselves can be redistributed without restriction. Grasp starts with pictures in PC Paint format and has a complex command language allowing fades, dissolves, wipes, moving subimages, text, etc. Although originally intended for business presentations, Grasp has, without any encouragement from its authors, become the standard tool for creators of amateur blue movies.

HP Paintjet

The HP Paintjet accepts a data stream somewhat similar to PCL. A paintjet image starts with escape sequences that set the rendering mode, image size, and depth, followed by raster lines that can be RLE or PackBits encoded.

IGES & PDES

IGES is the Initial Graphics Exchange Specification, a format for the interchange of graphical (particularly CAD) images. It is maintained by the National Institute of Science and Technology.

PDES, Product Data Exchange using STEP, is intended to be a richer successor to IGES. STEP, the Standard for the Exchange of Product Model Data, is the international equivalent of PDES, being developed for the ISO. It is an enormous standard encompassing geometry, presentation, and other aspects of mechanical design.

Island Graphics TIFF

Island Write, Draw and Paint use a TIFF subset for their image files. Version 3.1 of IWDP supports compressed/uncompressed monochrome and grayscale, plus eight-bit uncompressed palette color.

Major areas to be implemented include photometric RGB (no palette), other image depths, and multiple images per file (subfiles).

The tags used are listed in Table 32-1.

Table 32-1

Island Graphics TIFF tags

Tag description	Tag	Value
Image width	256	
Image length	257	
Bits per sample	258	1 or 8
Compression	259	1, 2 (Read only), 5 (R/W)
Photometric	262	0, 1, 3 (color map)
Strip offsets	273	
Rows per strip	278	
Strip byte counts	279	
Min sample value	280	
Max sample value	281	
x resolution	282	
y resolution	283	
Color map	320	256 color table
Samples per pixel	277	must be 1
Planar config	284	must be 1

Tags ignored on read, but written with following values:

Make	271	"Island Graphics Corp."
Model	272	"Version 2.x"
Software	305	"Island Write, Draw, Paint Version x.x"
Artist	315	logged-in user's name
Hostcomputer	316	"sun4,sun3,hp300,hp700"...
Resolution unit	296	2 (inch)
Thresholding	263	1 (bilevel)
Orientation	274	1 (top left)
Gray response unit	290	2 (hundredths)
Color response unit	300	2 (hundredths)

Kodak ICC

ICC is the format for the Kodak 7700 high-resolution printer. It consists of a header, followed by RGB or grayscale image data, eight or 24 bits per pixel.

Microsoft Windows Icon

Icon files describe a 32 by 32 pixel, 4-bit deep color bitmaps intended for use as an icon. The file is 766 bytes long. The color map is 16 4-byte RGBX entries starting at offset 62. The image itself is packed two pixels per byte, starting at offset 126.

Microsoft Windows Paint

Windows Paint stores monochrome bitmap images. The file format starts with a 32-byte header containing the image size, pixel-aspect ratios, and a checksum, followed by run-length encoded rows of image data.

OFF

OFF is a 3-D CAD file format developed by Digital Equipment Corp. It stores data in either a portable ASCII or compact binary format. Objects are represented as sets of polygons, along with named properties that describe the objects.

PC Paint

PC Paint stores bitmap files up to four bits deep. The format has evolved painfully, in a manner reminiscent of PCX, and has many minor variations.

Pixar PIC

A bitmap format most often found as the output of rendering programs (see Renderman below). Files can be eight or 12 bits per pixel, implicitly referring to an external color map, or 24 or 36 bits per pixel, RGB.

PDS

A bitmap format used for astronomical images, particularly those from the Jet Propulsion Lab in Pasadena, CA. The format is somewhat like FITS, with a text header followed by binary data. Data are typically eight bits per pixel, in either a fixed-length uncompressed format or a variable-length Huffman compressed format.

RIFF

RIFF is a modified version of IFF used by some Microsoft and IBM multimedia products. It uses Intel byte order, the reverse of IFF, and uses a different set of tag names. Otherwise it is similar to IFF.

SGI

Silicon Graphics Inc. has a proprietary bitmap format used by much of their workstation software. Files are either raw grayscale RGB pixels or are RLE compressed.

Sixel

Sixel is a color bitmap format used by some Digital Equipment printers, such as the DEC LJ250 color inkjet. The format is quite sophisticated for a printer and can include a color map. Image data can use simple RLE encoding for multiple pixels. Except for some introductory control characters, Sixel consists mostly of printable ASCII characters; for example, #5!8A for eight pixels in color 5 on the second row of the current group.

Utah RLE

Utah RLE format is a color bitmap format from the University of Utah, designed to support a set of image conversion and manipulation tools. Images are eight bits per color, up to 255 color channels, although images are typically 1-color grayscale, 3-color RGB, or 4-color RGBA where A is an alpha channel. The file starts with a binary header, including the size, number of channels, background color, optional color map, and comment strings. The image data itself is stored by channel by row. Within a row, the data for a channel might be RLE compressed and might be sparse; that is, skipping over areas that remain the background color.

VICAR

VICAR is a bitmap format used for astronomical images, particularly those in CD-ROMs of pictures from the Voyager and Magellan space probes. Data are typically eight bits per pixel, uncompressed, with images often 800 × 800 pixels.

XPM

XPM, for X Pix Map, is an extended version of the XBM bitmap for color bitmaps. Like XBM, the format is readable ASCII and legal C source code. It includes a color map and uses a somewhat more compact pixel representation, storing each pixel as one character rather than as three octal digits.

References

The International Telegraph and Telephone Consultative Committee (CCITT). "*Standardization of Group 3 facsimile apparatus for document transmission*," *Recommendation T.4, Volume VII, Fascicle VII.3, Terminal Equipment and Protocols for Telematic Services*, pp. 16-31. 1985.

The International Telegraph and Telephone Consultative Committee (CCITT). "Standardization of Group 4 facsimile apparatus for document transmission," *Recommendation T.6, Volume VII, Fascicle VII.3, Terminal Equipment and Protocols for Telematic Services*, pp. 40-48. 1985.

Microtex Industries, Inc. GRAphical System for Presentation. Release 1.10. May 1986. Irvine, CA.

Microsoft Corp. *Microsoft Windows 2.0 Software Development Kit Update*. 1988. Part No. 02018. Pp. 90-95.

Rost, Randi J. *OFF—A 3D Object File Format*. Oct 12, 1989. Palo Alto, CA: Digital Equipment Corporation Workstation Systems Engineering.

Thomas, Spencer W. "Design of the Utah RLE Format," *Report 86-15, Alpha_1 Project*. 1986. Salt Lake City, UT: University of Utah, Department of Computer Science.

MIT X Consortium. *X11 Release 4 distribution*, contributed software section.

Index

Illustration numbers are in **boldface**.

C

G

U

V

W

X

About the Authors

David C. Kay is a writer, instructor, and consultant for the computer and electronics industries. The owner of a marketing communications and consulting firm, he holds a degree in electrical engineering from Worcester Polytechnic Institute. John Levine, an independent software consultant and developer, holds a Ph.D. in computer science from Yale University. He is a director of Seque Software, and a frequent contributor to technical forums on electronic networks.